Mathematics
for
3D Game Programming
and
Computer Graphics

MATHEMATICS
FOR
3D GAME PROGRAMMING
AND
COMPUTER GRAPHICS

Eric Lengyel

CHARLES RIVER MEDIA, INC.
Hingham, Massachusetts

Production: Publishers' Design and Production Services, Inc.
Cover Design: The Printed Image

CHARLES RIVER MEDIA, INC.
20 Downer Avenue, Suite 3
Hingham, Massachusetts 02043
781-740-0400
781-740-8816 (FAX)
info@charlesriver.com
www.charlesriver.com

This book is printed on acid-free paper.

Eric Lengyel. *Mathematics for 3D Game Programming and Computer Graphics.*
ISBN 1-58450-037-9

Library of Congress Cataloging-in-Publication Data

Lengyel, Eric.
    Mathematics for 3D game programming and computer graphics / Eric Lengyel.
        p. cm.
        1. Computer games—Programming   2. Three-dimensional display systems—Mathematics.
    3. Computer graphics—Mathematics.   I. Title.
    QA76.76.C672 L47 2001
    794.8′1526—dc21

                                                     2001004578

Printed in the United States of America
01 02 7 6 5 4 3 2 First Edition

CHARLES RIVER MEDIA titles are available for site license or bulk purchase by institutions, user groups, corporations, etc. For additional information, please contact the Special Sales Department at 781-740-0400.

Contents

                   C.1 CYLINDRICAL COORDINATES   358
                   C.2 SPHERICAL COORDINATES   359

APPENDIX D   **TAYLOR SERIES**   **361**
                   D.1 DERIVATION   362
                   D.2 POWER SERIES   363
                   D.3 THE DEMOIVRE FORMULA   365

APPENDIX E   **ANSWERS TO EXERCISES**   **367**
                   CHAPTER 1   368
                   CHAPTER 2   368
                   CHAPTER 3   368
                   CHAPTER 4   368
                   CHAPTER 5   369
                   CHAPTER 6   369
                   CHAPTER 7   369
                   CHAPTER 8   370
                   CHAPTER 9   370
                   CHAPTER 10   370
                   CHAPTER 11   370
                   CHAPTER 12   371

                   BIBLIOGRAPHY   **373**
                   INDEX   **375**

Introduction

This book illustrates mathematical techniques that a software engineer would need to develop a professional-quality 3D graphics engine. Particular attention is paid to the derivation of key results in order to provide a complete exposition of the subject and to encourage a deep understanding of the mechanics behind the mathematical tools used by game programmers.

Most of the material in this book is presented in a manner that is independent of the underlying 3D graphics system used to render images. We assume that the reader is familiar with the basic concepts needed to use a 3D graphics library and understands how models are constructed out of vertices and polygons. On occasion, we refer to implementation details in the context of the OpenGL architecture to demonstrate how a graphics library can be used to achieve certain effects. In Chapter 6, we present various vertex programs that perform specialized lighting calculations. These programs use the vector instruction sets available on modern graphics hardware, and we adhere to the specification of the GL_NV_vertex_program extension to OpenGL.

Each chapter ends with a summary of the important equations and formulas derived in the chapter. The summary is intended to serve as a quick reference tool so that the reader is not required to wade through long discussions of the subject matter to find a single result. There are also several exercises at the end of each chapter. Answers to exercises requiring a calculation are given in Appendix E.

CONTENTS OVERVIEW

Chapter 1: Vectors. We begin with a thorough review of vector quantities and their properties. Vectors are of fundamental importance in the study of 3D computer graphics, and we make extensive use of operations such as the dot product and cross product throughout the book.

Chapter 2: Matrices. An understanding of matrices is another basic necessity of 3D game programming. This chapter discusses elementary concepts, such as matrix representation of linear systems, as well as more advanced topics, including eigenvectors and diagonalization, which are required later in the book.

Chapter 3: Transforms. In Chapter 3, we investigate matrices as a tool for performing transformations such as translations, rotations, and scales. We introduce the concept of four-dimensional homogeneous coordinates, which are widely used in 3D graphics systems to move between different coordinate spaces. We also study the properties of quaternions and their usefulness as a transformation tool.

Chapter 4: 3D Engine Geometry. It is at this point that we begin to see material presented in the first three chapters applied to practical applications in 3D game programming and computer graphics. After analyzing lines and planes in 3D space, we introduce the view frustum and its relationship to the virtual camera. This chapter includes topics such as field of view, perspective-correct interpolation, and projection matrices.

Chapter 5: Ray Tracing. Ray tracing methods are useful in many areas of game programming, including light-map generation, line-of-sight determination, and collision detection. This chapter begins with analytical and numerical root finding techniques, and then presents methods for intersecting rays with common geometrical objects. Finally, calculation of reflection and refraction vectors is discussed.

Chapter 6: Illumination. Chapter 6 discusses a wide range of topics related to illumination and shading methods. We begin with an enumeration of the different types of light sources and then proceed to simple reflection models. Later, we inspect methods for adding detail to rendered surfaces using texture maps, gloss maps, and bump maps. The chapter closes with a detailed explanation of the Cook-Torrance physical illumination model.

Chapter 7: Visibility Determination. The performance of a 3D engine is heavily dependent on its ability to determine what parts of a scene are visible. This chapter presents methods for constructing various types of bounding volumes and subsequently testing their visibility against the view frustum. Large-scale visibility determination enabled through spatial partitioning and the use of portal systems is also examined.

Chapter 8: Collision Detection. Collision detection is necessary for interaction between different objects in a game universe. This chapter presents general methods for determining whether moving objects collide with the static environment and whether they collide with each other.

Chapter 9: Polygonal Techniques. Chapter 9 presents several techniques involving the manipulation of polygonal models. The first topic covered is decal application to arbitrary surfaces and includes a related method for performing vertex depth offset. Other topics include billboarding techniques used for various special effects, shadow generation using the stencil buffer, and a polygon reduction technique.

Chapter 10: Linear Physics. At this point in the book, we begin a two-chapter survey of various topics in classical physics that pertain to the motion that objects are likely to exhibit in a 3D game. Chapter 10 begins with a discussion of position functions as solutions to second-order differential equations. We then investigate projectile motion both through empty space and through a resistive medium and close with a look at frictional forces.

Chapter 11: Rotational Physics. Chapter 11 continues the treatment of physics with a rather advanced exposition of rotation. We first study the forces experienced by an object in a rotating environment. Next, we examine rigid body motion and derive the relationship between angular velocity and angular momentum through the inertia tensor. Also included is a discussion of the oscillatory motion exhibited by springs and pendulums.

Chapter 12: Fluid Simulation. We finish with a physical model for fluid motion that is based on the two-dimensional wave equation. We develop a method for evaluating the positions of the vertices on a regular grid representing the surface of a fluid and discuss the conditions necessary for stability.

Appendix A: Complex Numbers. Although not used extensively, complex numbers do appear in a few places in the text. Appendix A reviews the concept of complex numbers and discusses the properties used elsewhere in the book.

Appendix B: Trigonometry Reference. Appendix B reviews the trigonometric functions and quickly derives many formulas and identities that are used throughout this book.

Appendix C: Coordinate Systems. Appendix C provides a brief overview of cylindrical coordinates and spherical coordinates. These coordinate systems appear in several places throughout the book but are used most extensively in Chapter 11.

Appendix D: Taylor Series. The Taylor series of various functions are employed in a number of places throughout the book. Appendix D derives the Taylor series and reviews power series representations for many common functions.

Appendix E: Answers to Exercises. Appendix E provides answers to all end-of-chapter exercises requiring a calculation.

NOTATIONAL CONVENTIONS

Italic Roman or Greek letters are used to represent scalar quantities, and bold-face letters are used to represent vectors, quaternions, and matrices. This convention and other notational standards used throughout the book are summarized in the following table.

Quantity/Operation	Notation/Examples
Scalars	Italics letters: x, t, A, α, ω
Angles	Italics Greek letters: θ, ϕ, α
Vectors	Boldface letters: $\mathbf{V}$, $\mathbf{P}$, $\mathbf{x}$, $\boldsymbol{\omega}$
Quaternions	Boldface letters: $\mathbf{q}$, $\mathbf{q}_1$, $\mathbf{q}_2$
Matrices	Boldface letters: $\mathbf{M}$, $\mathbf{P}$
Magnitude of a vector	Double bar: $\|\mathbf{P}\|$
Conjugate of a quaternion	Overbar: $\overline{\mathbf{q}}$
Transpose of a matrix	Superscript T: $\mathbf{M}^{\mathsf{T}}$
Determinant of a matrix	det $\mathbf{M}$ or single bars: $|\mathbf{M}|$
Time derivative	Dot notation: $\frac{d}{dx}\mathbf{x}(t) = \dot{\mathbf{x}}$
Set of real numbers	$\mathbb{R}$
Set of complex numbers	$\mathbb{C}$
Set of quaternions	$\mathbb{H}$

CHAPTER

1

Vectors

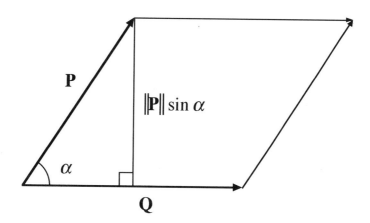

V ectors are of fundamental importance in any 3D game engine. They are used to represent points in space such as the locations of objects in a game or the vertices of a triangle mesh. They are also used to represent spatial directions such as the orientation of the camera or the surface normals of a triangle mesh. Understanding how to manipulate vectors is an essential skill of the successful 3D programmer.

1.1 VECTOR PROPERTIES

We assume that the reader possesses a basic understanding of vectors, but it is beneficial to provide a quick review of properties that are used extensively throughout this book. Although more abstract definitions are possible, we usually restrict ourselves to vectors defined by n-tuples of real numbers, where n is typically 2, 3, or 4. An n-dimensional vector $\mathbf{V}$ can be written as

$$\mathbf{V} = \langle V_1, V_2, \ldots, V_n \rangle \tag{1.1}$$

where the numbers V_i are called the *components* of the vector $\mathbf{V}$. We have used numbered subscripts here, but components are usually labeled with the name of the axis to which they correspond. For instance, the components of a three-dimensional point $\mathbf{P}$ could be written as P_x, P_y, and P_z.

The vector $\mathbf{V}$ in Equation (1.1) may also be represented by a matrix having a single column and n rows:

$$\mathbf{V} = \begin{bmatrix} V_1 \\ V_2 \\ \vdots \\ V_n \end{bmatrix}. \tag{1.2}$$

We treat this column vector as having a meaning identical to that of the comma-separated list of components written in Equation (1.1). Vectors are normally expressed in these forms, but we sometimes need to express vectors as a matrix consisting of a single row and n columns. We write row vectors as the transpose of their corresponding column vectors:

$$\mathbf{V}^{\mathsf{T}} = [V_1 \ \ V_2 \ \cdots \ V_n]. \tag{1.3}$$

A vector may be multiplied by a scalar to produce a new vector whose components retain the same relative proportions. The product of a scalar a and a vector $\mathbf{V}$ is defined as

$$a\mathbf{V} = \mathbf{V}a = \langle aV_1, \ aV_2, \ldots, \ aV_n \rangle. \tag{1.4}$$

In the case that $a = -1$, we use the slightly simplified notation $-\mathbf{V}$ to represent the negation of the vector $\mathbf{V}$.

Vectors add and subtract componentwise. Thus, given two vectors $\mathbf{P}$ and $\mathbf{Q}$, we define the sum $\mathbf{P} + \mathbf{Q}$ as

$$\mathbf{P} + \mathbf{Q} = \langle P_1 + Q_1,\ P_2 + Q_2,\ldots,\ P_n + Q_n\rangle. \tag{1.5}$$

The difference between two vectors, written $\mathbf{P} - \mathbf{Q}$, is really just a notational simplification of the sum $\mathbf{P} + (-\mathbf{Q})$.

With these definitions in hand, we are now ready to examine some fundamental properties of vector arithmetic.

> **Theorem 1.1.** Given any two scalars a and b and any three vectors $\mathbf{P}$, $\mathbf{Q}$, and $\mathbf{R}$, the following properties hold.
>
> (a) $\mathbf{P} + \mathbf{Q} = \mathbf{Q} + \mathbf{P}$
> (b) $(\mathbf{P} + \mathbf{Q}) + \mathbf{R} = \mathbf{P} + (\mathbf{Q} + \mathbf{R})$
> (c) $(ab)\mathbf{P} = a(b\mathbf{P})$
> (d) $a(\mathbf{P} + \mathbf{Q}) = a\mathbf{P} + a\mathbf{Q}$
> (e) $(a + b)\mathbf{P} = a\mathbf{P} + b\mathbf{P}$

Using the associative and commutative properties of the real numbers, these properties are easily verified through direct computation.

The *magnitude* of an n-dimensional vector $\mathbf{V}$ is a scalar denoted by $\|\mathbf{V}\|$ and is given by the formula

$$\|\mathbf{V}\| = \sqrt{\sum_{i=1}^{n} V_i^2}\ . \tag{1.6}$$

The magnitude of a vector is also sometimes called the *norm* or the *length* of a vector. A vector having a magnitude of exactly one is said to have *unit length* or may simply be called a *unit vector*. When $\mathbf{V}$ represents a three-dimensional point or direction, Equation (1.6) can be written as

$$\|\mathbf{V}\| = \sqrt{V_x^2 + V_y^2 + V_z^2}. \tag{1.7}$$

A vector $\mathbf{V}$ having at least one nonzero component can be resized to unit length through multiplication by $1/\|\mathbf{V}\|$. This operation is called *normalization* and is used often in 3D graphics. It should be noted that the word *normalize* is in no way related to the term *normal vector*, which refers to a vector that is perpendicular to a surface at a particular point.

The magnitude function given in Equation (1.6) obeys the following rules.

Theorem 1.2. Given any scalar a and any two vectors $\mathbf{P}$ and $\mathbf{Q}$, the following properties hold.

(a) $\|\mathbf{P}\| \geq 0$

(b) $\|\mathbf{P}\| = 0$ if and only if $\mathbf{P} = \langle 0, 0, \ldots, 0 \rangle$

(c) $\|a\mathbf{P}\| = |a|\, \|\mathbf{P}\|$

(d) $\|\mathbf{P} + \mathbf{Q}\| \leq \|\mathbf{P}\| + \|\mathbf{Q}\|$

Proof.

(a)   This follows from the fact that the radicand in equation (1.6) is a sum of squares, which cannot be less than zero.

(b)   Suppose that $\mathbf{P} = \langle 0, 0, \ldots, 0 \rangle$. Then the radicand in equation (1.6) evaluates to zero, so $\|\mathbf{P}\| = 0$. Conversely, if we assume $\|\mathbf{P}\| = 0$, then each component of $\mathbf{P}$ must be zero since otherwise the sum in equation (1.6) would be a positive number.

(c)   Evaluating Equation (1.6), we have the following.

$$
\begin{aligned}
\|a\mathbf{P}\| &= \sqrt{\sum_{i=1}^{n} a^2 P_i^2} \\
&= \sqrt{a^2 \sum_{i=1}^{n} P_i^2} \\
&= |a| \sqrt{\sum_{i=1}^{n} P_i^2} \\
&= |a|\, \|\mathbf{P}\|
\end{aligned}
\tag{1.8}
$$

(d)   This is known as the *triangle inequality* since a geometric proof can be given if we treat $\mathbf{P}$ and $\mathbf{Q}$ as two sides of a triangle. As shown in Figure 1.1, $\mathbf{P} + \mathbf{Q}$ forms the third side of the triangle, which cannot have a length greater than the sum of the other two sides.

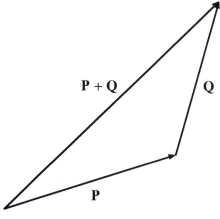

FIGURE **1.1** *The triangle inequality.*

We will be able to give an algebraic proof of the triangle inequality after introducing the dot product in the next section.

1.2 DOT PRODUCTS

The *dot product* of two vectors, also known as the *scalar product* or *inner product*, is one of the most heavily used operations in 3D graphics because it supplies a measure of the difference between the directions in which the two vectors point.

> **Definition 1.3.** The dot product of two *n*-dimensional vectors **P** and **Q**, written as **P** · **Q**, is the scalar quantity given by the formula
>
> $$\mathbf{P} \cdot \mathbf{Q} = \sum_{i=1}^{n} P_i Q_i. \tag{1.9}$$

This definition states that the dot product of two vectors is given by the sum of the products of each component. In three dimensions, we have

$$\mathbf{P} \cdot \mathbf{Q} = P_x Q_x + P_y Q_y + P_z Q_z. \tag{1.10}$$

The dot product **P** · **Q** may also be expressed as the matrix product

$$\mathbf{P}^{\mathsf{T}}\mathbf{Q} = \begin{bmatrix} P_1 & P_2 & \cdots & P_n \end{bmatrix} \begin{bmatrix} Q_1 \\ Q_2 \\ \vdots \\ Q_n \end{bmatrix}, \tag{1.11}$$

which yields a 1×1 matrix (i.e., a scalar) whose single entry is equal to the sum in Equation (1.9).

Now for an important theorem that reveals the ubiquitous utility of the dot product.

Theorem 1.4. Given two n-dimensional vectors $\mathbf{P}$ and $\mathbf{Q}$, the dot product $\mathbf{P} \cdot \mathbf{Q}$ satisfies the equation

$$\mathbf{P} \cdot \mathbf{Q} = \|\mathbf{P}\| \|\mathbf{Q}\| \cos \alpha, \tag{1.12}$$

where α is the planar angle between the lines connecting the origin to the points represented by $\mathbf{P}$ and $\mathbf{Q}$.

Proof. Let α be the angle between the line segments $\overline{OP}$ and $\overline{OQ}$, as shown in Figure 1.2. By the law of cosines (see appendix B, section B.6), we know

$$\|\mathbf{P} - \mathbf{Q}\|^2 = \|\mathbf{P}\|^2 + \|\mathbf{Q}\|^2 - 2\|\mathbf{P}\| \|\mathbf{Q}\| \cos \alpha. \tag{1.13}$$

This expands to

$$\sum_{i=1}^{n} \left(P_i - Q_i \right)^2 = \sum_{i=1}^{n} P_i^2 + \sum_{i=1}^{n} Q_i^2 - 2\|\mathbf{P}\| \|\mathbf{Q}\| \cos \alpha. \tag{1.14}$$

All of the P_i^2 and Q_i^2 terms cancel and we are left with

$$\sum_{i=1}^{n} -2P_i Q_i = -2\|\mathbf{P}\| \|\mathbf{Q}\| \cos \alpha. \tag{1.15}$$

Dividing both sides by -2 gives us the desired result.

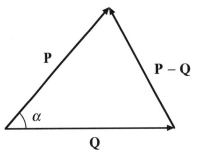

FIGURE *The dot product is related to the angle between two vectors.*
1.2

A couple of important facts follow immediately from theorem 1.4. The first is that two vectors **P** and **Q** are perpendicular if and only if **P** · **Q** = 0. This follows from the fact that the cosine function is zero at an angle of 90 degrees. Vectors whose dot product yields zero are called *orthogonal*. We define that zero vector, **0** = ⟨0, 0,..., 0⟩, to be orthogonal to every vector **P** since **0** · **P** always equals zero.

The second fact is that the sign of the dot product tells us how close two vectors are to pointing in the same direction. Referring to figure 1.3, we can consider the plane passing through the origin and perpendicular to a vector **P**. Any vector lying on the same side of the plane as **P** yields a positive dot product with **P**, and any vector lying on the opposite side of the plane from **P** yields a negative dot product with **P**.

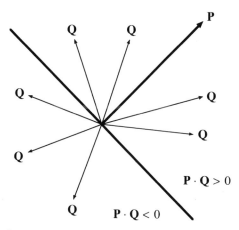

FIGURE *The sign of the dot product tells us whether two vectors lie on the same side or on*
1.3 *opposite sides of a plane.*

Several additional properties of the dot product are presented by the following theorem.

Theorem 1.5. Given any scalar a and any three vectors **P**, **Q**, and **R**, the following properties hold.

(a) **P** · **Q** = **Q** · **P**
(b) $(a\textbf{P})$ · **Q** = $a(\textbf{P}$ · **Q**$)$
(c) **P** · (**Q** + **R**) = **P** · **Q** + **P** · **R**
(d) **P** · **P** = $\|\textbf{P}\|^2$
(e) $|\textbf{P}$ · **Q**$| \leq \|\textbf{P}\|\,\|\textbf{Q}\|$

Proof. Parts (a), (b), and (c) are easily verified using the associative and commutative properties of the real numbers. Part (d) follows directly from the definition of $\|\textbf{P}\|$ given in Equation (1.6) and the definition of the dot product given in Equation (1.9). Part (e) is implied by Theorem 1.4 since $|\cos \alpha| \leq 1$.

We use the notation $\mathbf{P}^2$ when we take the dot product of a vector $\mathbf{P}$ with itself. Thus by part (d) of Theorem 1.5, we can say that $\mathbf{P} \cdot \mathbf{P}$, $\mathbf{P}^2$, and $\|\mathbf{P}\|^2$ all have identical meanings.

Part (e) of Theorem 1.5, known as the *Cauchy-Schwarz inequality*, gives us a tool that we can use to provide the following algebraic proof of the triangle inequality.

Proof of Theorem 1.2(d) (Triangle Inequality). Beginning with $\|\mathbf{P} + \mathbf{Q}\|^2$, we can calculate

$$
\begin{aligned}
\|\mathbf{P}\| + \mathbf{Q}\|^2 &= (\mathbf{P} + \mathbf{Q}) \cdot (\mathbf{P} + \mathbf{Q}) \\
&= \mathbf{P}^2 + \mathbf{Q}^2 + 2\mathbf{P} \cdot \mathbf{Q} \\
&\leq \mathbf{P}^2 + \mathbf{Q}^2 + 2\|\mathbf{P}\| \|\mathbf{Q}\| \\
&= (\|\mathbf{P}\| + \|\mathbf{Q}\|)^2,
\end{aligned} \tag{1.16}
$$

where Theorem 1.5(e) has been used to attain the inequality. Taking square roots, we arrive at the desired result.

The situation often arises in which we need to decompose a vector $\mathbf{P}$ into components that are parallel and perpendicular to another vector $\mathbf{Q}$. As shown in Figure 1.4, if we think of the vector $\mathbf{P}$ as the hypotenuse of a right triangle, then the perpendicular projection of $\mathbf{P}$ onto the vector $\mathbf{Q}$ produces the side adjacent to the angle α between $\mathbf{P}$ and $\mathbf{Q}$.

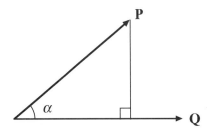

FIGURE *Calculating the projection of one vector onto another.*
1.4

Basic trigonometry tells us that the length of the side adjacent to α is given by $\|\mathbf{P}\| \cos \alpha$. Theorem 1.4 gives us a way to calculate the same quantity without knowing the angle α:

$$
\|\mathbf{P}\| \cos \alpha = \frac{\mathbf{P} \cdot \mathbf{Q}}{\|\mathbf{Q}\|}. \tag{1.17}
$$

To obtain a vector that has this length and is parallel to $\mathbf{Q}$, we simply multiply by the unit vector $\mathbf{Q}/\|\mathbf{Q}\|$. We now have the following formula for the projection of $\mathbf{P}$ onto $\mathbf{Q}$, which we denote by $\text{proj}_{\mathbf{Q}}\,\mathbf{P}$.

$$\text{proj}_{\mathbf{Q}}\,\mathbf{P} = \frac{\mathbf{P}\cdot\mathbf{Q}}{\|\mathbf{Q}\|^2}\,\mathbf{Q} \tag{1.18}$$

The perpendicular component of $\mathbf{P}$ with respect to $\mathbf{Q}$, denoted by $\text{perp}_{\mathbf{Q}}\,\mathbf{P}$, is simply the vector left over when we subtract the parallel component given by Equation (1.18) from the original vector $\mathbf{P}$:

$$\text{perp}_{\mathbf{Q}}\,\mathbf{P} = \mathbf{P} - \text{proj}_{\mathbf{Q}}\,\mathbf{P}$$

$$= \mathbf{P} - \frac{\mathbf{P}\cdot\mathbf{Q}}{\|\mathbf{Q}\|^2}\,\mathbf{Q}. \tag{1.19}$$

The projection of $\mathbf{P}$ onto $\mathbf{Q}$ is a linear transformation of $\mathbf{P}$ and can thus be expressed as a matrix-vector product. In three dimensions, $\text{proj}_{\mathbf{Q}}\,\mathbf{P}$ can be computed using the alternative formula

$$\text{proj}_{\mathbf{Q}}\,\mathbf{P} = \frac{1}{\|\mathbf{Q}\|^2}\begin{bmatrix} Q_x^2 & Q_xQ_y & Q_xQ_z \\ Q_xQ_y & Q_y^2 & Q_yQ_z \\ Q_xQ_z & Q_yQ_z & Q_z^2 \end{bmatrix}\begin{bmatrix} P_x \\ P_y \\ P_z \end{bmatrix}. \tag{1.20}$$

1.3 CROSS PRODUCTS

The *cross product* of two three-dimensional vectors, also known as the *vector product*, returns a new vector that is perpendicular to the two vectors multiplied together. This property has many uses in computer graphics, one of which is a method for calculating a surface normal at a particular point given two distinct tangent vectors.

> **Definition 1.6.** The cross product of two 3D vectors $\mathbf{P}$ and $\mathbf{Q}$, written as $\mathbf{P} \times \mathbf{Q}$, is a vector quantity given by the formula
>
> $$\mathbf{P} \times \mathbf{Q} = \langle P_yQ_z - P_zQ_y,\ P_zQ_x - P_xQ_z,\ P_xQ_y - P_yQ_x\rangle. \tag{1.21}$$

A commonly used tool for remembering this formula is to calculate cross products by evaluating the pseudodeterminant

$$\mathbf{P} \times \mathbf{Q} = \begin{vmatrix} \mathbf{i} & \mathbf{j} & \mathbf{k} \\ P_x & P_y & P_z \\ Q_x & Q_y & Q_z \end{vmatrix},$$

(1.22)

where $\mathbf{i}$, $\mathbf{j}$, and $\mathbf{k}$ are unit vectors parallel to the x-, y-, and z-axes:

$\mathbf{i} = \langle 1, 0, 0 \rangle$

$\mathbf{j} = \langle 0, 1, 0 \rangle$

$\mathbf{k} = \langle 0, 0, 1 \rangle$.

(1.23)

We call the right side of Equation (1.22) a pseudodeterminant because the top row of the matrix consists of vectors, whereas the remaining entries are scalars. Nevertheless, the usual method for evaluating a determinant does produce the correct value for the cross product, as shown below.

$$\begin{vmatrix} \mathbf{i} & \mathbf{j} & \mathbf{k} \\ P_x & P_y & P_z \\ Q_x & Q_y & Q_z \end{vmatrix} = \mathbf{i}(P_y Q_z - P_z Q_y) - \mathbf{j}(P_x Q_z - P_z Q_x) + \mathbf{k}(P_x Q_y - P_y Q_x)$$

(1.24)

The cross product $\mathbf{P} \times \mathbf{Q}$ can also be expressed as a linear transformation derived from $\mathbf{P}$ that operates on $\mathbf{Q}$, as follows.

$$\mathbf{P} \times \mathbf{Q} = \begin{bmatrix} 0 & -P_z & P_y \\ P_z & 0 & -P_x \\ -P_y & P_x & 0 \end{bmatrix} \begin{bmatrix} Q_x \\ Q_y \\ Q_z \end{bmatrix}$$

(1.25)

As mentioned previously, the cross product $\mathbf{P} \times \mathbf{Q}$ produces a vector that is perpendicular to both of the vectors $\mathbf{P}$ and $\mathbf{Q}$. This fact is summarized by the following theorem.

Theorem 1.7. Let $\mathbf{P}$ and $\mathbf{Q}$ be any two 3D vectors. Then $(\mathbf{P} \times \mathbf{Q}) \cdot \mathbf{P} = 0$ and $(\mathbf{P} \times \mathbf{Q}) \cdot \mathbf{Q} = 0$.

Proof. Applying the definitions of the cross product and the dot product, we have the following for $(\mathbf{P} \times \mathbf{Q}) \cdot \mathbf{P}$.

$$\begin{aligned}(\mathbf{P} \times \mathbf{Q}) \cdot \mathbf{P} &= \langle P_y Q_z - P_z Q_y, P_z Q_x - P_x Q_z, P_x Q_y - P_y Q_x \rangle \cdot \mathbf{P} \\ &= P_x P_y Q_z - P_x P_z Q_y + P_y P_z Q_x - P_x P_y Q_z + P_x P_z Q_y - P_y P_z Q_x \\ &= 0 \end{aligned}$$

(1.26)

The fact that $(\mathbf{P} \times \mathbf{Q}) \cdot \mathbf{Q} = 0$ is proven in a similar manner.

The same result arises when we consider the fact that given any three 3D vectors **P**, **Q**, and **R**, the expression $(\mathbf{P} \times \mathbf{Q}) \cdot \mathbf{R}$ may be evaluated by calculating the determinant

$$(\mathbf{P} \times \mathbf{Q}) \cdot \mathbf{R} = \begin{vmatrix} P_x & P_y & P_z \\ Q_x & Q_y & Q_z \\ R_x & R_y & R_z \end{vmatrix}. \tag{1.27}$$

If any one of the vectors **P**, **Q**, or **R** can be expressed as a linear combination of the other two vectors, then this determinant evaluates to zero. This includes the cases in which $\mathbf{R} = \mathbf{P}$ or $\mathbf{R} = \mathbf{Q}$.

Like the dot product, the cross product has trigonometric significance.

Theorem 1.8. Given two 3D vectors **P** and **Q**, the cross product $\mathbf{P} \times \mathbf{Q}$ satisfies the equation

$$\|\mathbf{P} \times \mathbf{Q}\| = \|\mathbf{P}\| \, \|\mathbf{Q}\| \sin \alpha, \tag{1.28}$$

where α is the planar angle between the lines connecting the origin to the points represented by **P** and **Q**.

Proof. Squaring $\|\mathbf{P} \times \mathbf{Q}\|$, we have

$$\|\mathbf{P} \times \mathbf{Q}\|^2 = \left\| \left\langle P_y Q_z - P_z Q_y, P_z Q_x - P_x Q_z, P_x Q_y - P_y Q_x \right\rangle \right\|^2$$

$$= \left(P_y Q_z - P_z Q_y \right)^2 + \left(P_z Q_x - P_x Q_z \right)^2 + \left(P_x Q_y - P_y Q_x \right)^2$$

$$= \left(P_y^2 + P_z^2 \right) Q_x^2 + \left(P_x^2 + P_z^2 \right) Q_y^2 + \left(P_x^2 + P_y^2 \right) Q_z^2 \tag{1.29}$$

$$- 2 P_x Q_x P_y Q_y - 2 P_x Q_x P_z Q_z - 2 P_y Q_y P_z Q_z.$$

By adding and subtracting $P_x^2 Q_x^2 + P_y^2 Q_y^2 + P_z^2 Q_z^2$ on the right side of this equation, we can write

$$\|\mathbf{P} \times \mathbf{Q}\|^2 = \left(P_x^2 + P_y^2 + P_z^2 \right) \left(Q_x^2 + Q_y^2 + Q_z^2 \right)$$

$$- \left(P_x Q_x + P_y Q_y + P_z Q_z \right)^2$$

$$= \|\mathbf{P}\|^2 \|\mathbf{Q}\|^2 - (\mathbf{P} \cdot \mathbf{Q})^2. \tag{1.30}$$

Replacing the dot product with the right side of Equation (1.12), we have

$$\|\mathbf{P} \times \mathbf{Q}\|^2 = \|\mathbf{P}\|^2\|\mathbf{Q}\|^2 - \|\mathbf{P}\|^2\|\mathbf{Q}\|^2 \cos^2 \alpha$$
$$= \|\mathbf{P}\|^2\|\mathbf{Q}\|^2(1 - \cos^2 \alpha)$$
$$= \|\mathbf{P}\|^2\|\mathbf{Q}\|^2 \sin^2 \alpha. \qquad (1.31)$$

Taking square roots proves the theorem.

As shown in Figure 1.5, Theorem 1.8 demonstrates that the magnitude of the cross product $\mathbf{P} \times \mathbf{Q}$ is equal to the area of the parallelogram whose sides are formed by the vectors $\mathbf{P}$ and $\mathbf{Q}$. As a consequence, the area A of an arbitrary triangle whose vertices are given by the points $\mathbf{V}_1$, $\mathbf{V}_2$, and $\mathbf{V}_3$ can be calculated using the formula

$$A = \frac{1}{2}\left\|(\mathbf{V}_2 - \mathbf{V}_1) \times (\mathbf{V}_3 - \mathbf{V}_1)\right\|. \qquad (1.32)$$

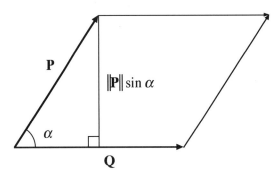

FIGURE **1.5** *The magnitude of the cross product of two vectors is equal to the area of the parallelogram whose sides are formed by the two vectors.*

We know that any nonzero result of the cross product must be perpendicular to the two vectors being multiplied together, but there are two possible directions that satisfy this requirement. It turns out that the cross product follows a pattern called the *right hand rule*. As shown in Figure 1.6, if the fingers of the right hand are aligned with a vector $\mathbf{P}$, and the palm is Facing in the direction of a vector $\mathbf{Q}$, then the thumb points along the direction of the cross product $\mathbf{P} \times \mathbf{Q}$.

The unit vectors $\mathbf{i}$, $\mathbf{j}$, and $\mathbf{k}$, which point in the directions of the positive x-, y-, and z-axes respectively, behave as follows. If we order the axes in a circular fashion so that $\mathbf{i}$ precedes $\mathbf{j}$, $\mathbf{j}$ precedes $\mathbf{k}$, and $\mathbf{k}$ precedes $\mathbf{i}$, then the cross product of two of these vectors *in order* yields the third vector, as follows.

$$\mathbf{i} \times \mathbf{j} = \mathbf{k}$$

$$\mathbf{j} \times \mathbf{k} = \mathbf{i}$$

$$\mathbf{k} \times \mathbf{i} = \mathbf{j} \qquad (1.33)$$

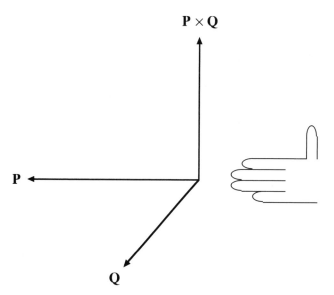

FIGURE *The right hand rule provides a way for determining in which direction the cross*
1.6 *product points.*

The cross product of two of the vectors in *reverse order* yields the negation of
the third vector, as follows.

$$\mathbf{j} \times \mathbf{i} = -\mathbf{k}$$

$$\mathbf{k} \times \mathbf{j} = -\mathbf{i}$$

$$\mathbf{i} \times \mathbf{k} = -\mathbf{j} \tag{1.34}$$

Several additional properties of the cross product are presented by the following theorem.

Theorem 1.9. Given any two scalars a and b and any three 3D vectors $\mathbf{P}$, $\mathbf{Q}$,
and $\mathbf{R}$, the following properties hold.

(a) $\mathbf{Q} \times \mathbf{P} = -(\mathbf{P} \times \mathbf{Q})$

(b) $(a\mathbf{P}) \times \mathbf{Q} = a(\mathbf{P} \times \mathbf{Q})$

(c) $\mathbf{P} \times (\mathbf{Q} + \mathbf{R}) = \mathbf{P} \times \mathbf{Q} + \mathbf{P} \times \mathbf{R}$

(d) $\mathbf{P} \times \mathbf{P} = \mathbf{0} = \langle 0, 0, 0 \rangle$

(e) $(\mathbf{P} \times \mathbf{Q}) \cdot \mathbf{R} = (\mathbf{R} \times \mathbf{P}) \cdot \mathbf{Q} = (\mathbf{Q} \times \mathbf{R}) \cdot \mathbf{P}$

(f) $\mathbf{P} \times (\mathbf{Q} \times \mathbf{P}) = \mathbf{P} \times \mathbf{Q} \times \mathbf{P} = P^2\mathbf{Q} - (\mathbf{P} \cdot \mathbf{Q})\mathbf{P}$

Proof. Parts (a) through (d) follow immediately from the definition of the
cross product and the associative and commutative properties of the real

numbers. Part (e) can be directly verified using equation (1.27). For part (f), we first observe that

$$\mathbf{P} \times (\mathbf{Q} \times \mathbf{P}) = \mathbf{P} \times -(\mathbf{P} \times \mathbf{Q})$$
$$= -[-(\mathbf{P} \times \mathbf{Q}) \times \mathbf{P}]$$
$$= \mathbf{P} \times \mathbf{Q} \times \mathbf{P}. \tag{1.35}$$

Direct computation of the x-component gives us

$$\left(\mathbf{P} \times \mathbf{Q} \times \mathbf{P}\right)_x = \left(\left\langle P_y Q_z - P_z Q_y, P_z Q_x - P_x Q_z, P_x Q_y - P_y Q_x \right\rangle \times \mathbf{P}\right)$$
$$= \left(P_z Q_x - P_x Q_z\right)P_z - \left(P_x Q_y - P_y Q_x\right)P_y$$
$$= \left(P_y^2 + P_z^2\right)Q_x - \left(P_y Q_y + P_z Q_z\right)P_x, \tag{1.36}$$

which isn't quite what we need, but we can add and subtract a $P_x^2 Q_x$ term to achieve the following desired result.

$$\left(P_y^2 + P_z^2\right)Q_x - \left(P_y Q_y + P_z Q_z\right)P_x$$
$$= \left(P_y^2 + P_z^2\right)Q_x + P_x^2 Q_x - \left(P_y Q_y + P_z Q_z\right)P_x - P_x^2 Q.$$
$$= \left(P_x^2 + P_y^2 + P_z^2\right)Q_x - \left(P_x Q_x + P_y Q_y + P_z Q_z\right)P_x$$
$$= P^2 Q_x - \left(\mathbf{P} \cdot \mathbf{Q}\right)P_x \tag{1.37}$$

The y- and z-components can be checked in a similar manner.

By part (a) of Theorem 1.9, the cross product is not a commutative operation. Because reversing the order of the vectors has the effect of negating the product, the cross product is labeled *anticommutative*. Additionally, it is worth noting that the cross product is not an associative operation. That is, given any three 3D vectors $\mathbf{P}$, $\mathbf{Q}$, and $\mathbf{R}$, it may be true that $(\mathbf{P} \times \mathbf{Q}) \times \mathbf{R} \neq \mathbf{P} \times (\mathbf{Q} \times \mathbf{R})$. As an example, let $\mathbf{P} = \langle 1, 1, 0 \rangle$, $\mathbf{Q} = \langle 0, 1, 1 \rangle$, and $\mathbf{R} = \langle 1, 0, 1 \rangle$. First calculating $(\mathbf{P} \times \mathbf{Q}) \times \mathbf{R}$, we have

$$\mathbf{P} \times \mathbf{Q} = \begin{vmatrix} \mathbf{i} & \mathbf{j} & \mathbf{k} \\ 1 & 1 & 0 \\ 0 & 1 & 1 \end{vmatrix} = \langle 1, -1, 1 \rangle$$

$$\left(\mathbf{P} \times \mathbf{Q}\right) \times \mathbf{R} = \begin{vmatrix} \mathbf{i} & \mathbf{j} & \mathbf{k} \\ 1 & -1 & 1 \\ 1 & 0 & 1 \end{vmatrix} = \langle -1, 0, 1 \rangle. \tag{1.38}$$

Now calculating $\mathbf{P} \times (\mathbf{Q} \times \mathbf{R})$, we have

$$\mathbf{Q} \times \mathbf{R} = \begin{vmatrix} \mathbf{i} & \mathbf{j} & \mathbf{k} \\ 0 & 1 & 1 \\ 1 & 0 & 1 \end{vmatrix} = \langle 1, 1, -1 \rangle$$

$$\mathbf{P} \times (\mathbf{Q} \times \mathbf{R}) = \begin{vmatrix} \mathbf{i} & \mathbf{j} & \mathbf{k} \\ 1 & 1 & 0 \\ 1 & 1 & -1 \end{vmatrix} = \langle -1, 1, 0 \rangle, \tag{1.39}$$

which yields a different result.

1.4 VECTOR SPACES

The vectors we have dealt with so far belong to sets called *vector spaces*. An examination of vector spaces allows us to introduce concepts that are important for our study of matrices in the next chapter.

Definition 1.10. A vector space is a set V, whose elements are called vectors, for which addition and scalar multiplication are defined and the following properties hold.

(a) V is closed under addition. That is, for any elements $\mathbf{P}$ and $\mathbf{Q}$ in V, the sum $\mathbf{P} + \mathbf{Q}$ is an element of V.

(b) V is closed under scalar multiplication. That is, for any real number a and any element $\mathbf{P}$ in V, the product $a\mathbf{P}$ is an element of V.

(c)   There exists an element in V called $\mathbf{0}$ such that for any element $\mathbf{P}$ in V, $\mathbf{P} + \mathbf{0} = \mathbf{0} + \mathbf{P} = \mathbf{P}$.

(d)   For every element $\mathbf{P}$ in V, there exists an element $\mathbf{Q}$ in V such that $\mathbf{P} + \mathbf{Q} = \mathbf{0}$.

(e)   Addition is associative. That is, for any elements $\mathbf{P}$, $\mathbf{Q}$, and $\mathbf{R}$ in V, $(\mathbf{P} + \mathbf{Q}) + \mathbf{R} = \mathbf{P} + (\mathbf{Q} + \mathbf{R})$.

(f)   Scalar multiplication is associative. That is, for any real numbers a and b and any element $\mathbf{P}$ in V, $(ab)\mathbf{P} = a(b\mathbf{P})$.

(g)   Scalar multiplication distributes over vector addition. That is, for any real number a and any elements $\mathbf{P}$ and $\mathbf{Q}$ in V, $a(\mathbf{P} + \mathbf{Q}) = a\mathbf{P} + a\mathbf{Q}$.

(h)   Addition of scalars distributes over scalar multiplication. That is, for any real numbers a and b and any element $\mathbf{P}$ in V, $(a + b)\mathbf{P} = a\mathbf{P} + b\mathbf{P}$.

Many of the properties required of vector spaces are mentioned in section 1.1 and are easily shown to be satisfied for vectors having the form of n-tuples of real numbers. We denote the vector space consisting of all such n-tuples by $\mathbb{R}^n$. For instance, the vector space consisting of all 3D vectors is denoted by $\mathbb{R}^3$.

Every vector space can be generated by linear combinations of a subset of vectors called a basis for the vector space. Before we can say exactly what a basis is, we need to know what it means for a set of vectors to be linearly independent.

> **Definition 1.11.** A set of n vectors $\{\mathbf{e}_1, \mathbf{e}_2, \ldots, \mathbf{e}_n\}$ is *linearly independent* if there do not exist real numbers $a_1, a_2, \ldots, a_n$, where at least one of the a_i is not zero, such that
>
> $$a_1\mathbf{e}_1 + a_2\mathbf{e}_2 + \ldots + a_n\mathbf{e}_n = \mathbf{0}. \tag{1.40}$$
>
> Otherwise, the set $\{\mathbf{e}_1, \mathbf{e}_2, \ldots, \mathbf{e}_n\}$ is called *linearly dependent*.

An n-dimensional vector space is one that can be generated by a set of n linearly independent vectors. Such a generating set is called a basis, whose formal definition follows.

> **Definition 1.12.** A basis $\mathcal{B}$ for a vector space V is a set of n linearly independent vectors $\mathcal{B} = \{\mathbf{e}_1, \mathbf{e}_2, \ldots, \mathbf{e}_n\}$ for which, given any element $\mathbf{P}$ in V, there exist real numbers $a_1, a_2, \ldots, a_n$ such that
>
> $$\mathbf{P} = a_1\mathbf{e}_1 + a_2\mathbf{e}_2 + \ldots + a_n\mathbf{e}_n. \tag{1.41}$$

Every basis of an n-dimensional vector space has exactly n vectors in it. For instance, it is impossible to find a set of four linearly independent vectors in $\mathbb{R}^3$, and a set of two linearly independent vectors is insufficient to generate the entire vector space.

There are infinitely many choices for a basis of any of the vector spaces $\mathbb{R}^n$. We assign special terms to bases that have certain properties.

> **Definition 1.13.** A basis $\mathcal{B} = \{\mathbf{e}_1, \mathbf{e}_2, \ldots, \mathbf{e}_n\}$ for a vector space is called *orthogonal* if for every pair (i, j) with $i \neq j$, we have $\mathbf{e}_i \cdot \mathbf{e}_j = 0$.

The fact that the dot product between two vectors is zero actually implies that the vectors are linearly independent, as the following theorem demonstrates.

> **Theorem 1.14.** Given two nonzero vectors $\mathbf{e}_1$ and $\mathbf{e}_2$, if $\mathbf{e}_1 \cdot \mathbf{e}_2 = 0$, then $\mathbf{e}_1$ and $\mathbf{e}_2$ are linearly independent.

Proof. We suppose that $\mathbf{e}_1$ and $\mathbf{e}_2$ are not linearly independent and arrive at a contradiction. If $\mathbf{e}_1$ and $\mathbf{e}_2$ are linearly dependent, then there exist scalars a_1 and a_2 such that $a_1\mathbf{e}_1 + a_2\mathbf{e}_2 = \mathbf{0}$. Note that a_2 cannot be zero since it would require that a_1 is also zero. Thus, we can write $\mathbf{e}_2 = -\frac{a_1}{a_2}\mathbf{e}_1$. Then, however, $\mathbf{e}_1 \cdot \mathbf{e}_2 = -\frac{a_1}{a_2}\mathbf{e}_1^2 \neq \mathbf{0}$, a contradiction.

This theorem shows that if we can find any n orthogonal vectors in a vector space V, then they form a basis for V.

A more specific term is given to a basis whose elements all have unit length. For convenience, we introduce the *Kronecker delta* symbol δ_{ij}, which is defined as

$$\delta_{ij} = \begin{cases} 1, & \text{if } i = j; \\ 0, & \text{if } i \neq j. \end{cases} \tag{1.42}$$

Definition 1.15. A basis $\mathcal{B} = \{\mathbf{e}_1, \mathbf{e}_2,..., \mathbf{e}_n\}$ for a vector space is called *orthonormal* if for every pair (i, j), we have $\mathbf{e}_i \cdot \mathbf{e}_j = \delta_{ij}$.

The set $\{\mathbf{i}, \mathbf{j}, \mathbf{k}\}$ is obviously an orthonormal basis for $\mathbb{R}^3$. A slightly less trivial example of an orthonormal basis for $\mathbb{R}^3$ is given by the three vectors $\left\langle \frac{\sqrt{2}}{2}, \frac{\sqrt{2}}{2}, 0 \right\rangle$, $\left\langle -\frac{\sqrt{2}}{2}, \frac{\sqrt{2}}{2}, 0 \right\rangle$ and $\langle 0, 0, 1 \rangle$.

There is a simple method by which a linearly independent set of n vectors can be transformed into an orthogonal basis for $\mathbb{R}^n$. The basic idea is to subtract the projection of each vector onto the vectors preceding it in the set. Whatever vector is left over must then be orthogonal to its predecessors. The exact procedure is as follows.

Algorithm 1.16. Gram-Schmidt Orthogonalization. Given a set of n linearly independent vectors $\mathcal{B} = \{\mathbf{e}_1, \mathbf{e}_2,..., \mathbf{e}_n\}$, this algorithm produces a set $\mathcal{B}' = \{\mathbf{e}_1', \mathbf{e}_2',..., \mathbf{e}_n'\}$ such that $\mathbf{e}_i' \cdot \mathbf{e}_j' = 0$ whenever $i \neq j$.

A   Set $\mathbf{e}_1' = \mathbf{e}_1$.

B   Begin with the index $i = 2$.

C   Subtract the projection of $\mathbf{e}_i$ onto the vectors $\mathbf{e}_1', \mathbf{e}_2',..., \mathbf{e}_{i-1}'$ from $\mathbf{e}_i$ and store the result in $\mathbf{e}_i'$. That is,

$$\mathbf{e}_i' = \mathbf{e}_i - \sum_{k=1}^{i-1} \frac{\mathbf{e}_i \cdot \mathbf{e}_k}{\mathbf{e}_k^2}\mathbf{e}_k. \tag{1.43}$$

D   If $i < n$, increment i and loop to step C.

CHAPTER 1 SUMMARY

DOT PRODUCTS

The dot product between two n-dimensional vectors $\mathbf{P}$ and $\mathbf{Q}$ is a scalar defined by

$$\mathbf{P} \cdot \mathbf{Q} = \sum_{i=1}^{n} P_i Q_i = P_1 Q_1 + P_2 Q_2 + \cdots + P_n Q_n.$$

The dot product is related to the angle θ between the vectors $\mathbf{P}$ and $\mathbf{Q}$ by the formula

$$\mathbf{P} \cdot \mathbf{Q} = \|\mathbf{P}\| \, \|\mathbf{Q}\| \cos \theta.$$

VECTOR PROJECTIONS

The projection of a vector $\mathbf{P}$ onto a vector $\mathbf{Q}$ is given by

$$\text{proj}_{\mathbf{Q}} \, \mathbf{P} = \frac{\mathbf{P} \cdot \mathbf{Q}}{\|\mathbf{Q}\|^2} \mathbf{Q},$$

and the component of $\mathbf{P}$ that is perpendicular to $\mathbf{Q}$ is given by

$$\text{perp}_{\mathbf{Q}} \, \mathbf{P} = \mathbf{P} - \text{proj}_{\mathbf{Q}} \, \mathbf{P}$$

$$= \mathbf{P} - \frac{\mathbf{P} \cdot \mathbf{Q}}{\|\mathbf{Q}\|^2} \mathbf{Q}.$$

CROSS PRODUCTS

The cross product between two 3D vectors $\mathbf{P}$ and $\mathbf{Q}$ is a 3D vector defined by

$$\mathbf{P} \times \mathbf{Q} = \langle P_y Q_z - P_z Q_y, \; P_z Q_x - P_x Q_z, \; P_x Q_y - P_y Q_x \rangle.$$

This can also be written as the matrix-vector product

$$\mathbf{P} \times \mathbf{Q} = \begin{bmatrix} 0 & -P_z & P_y \\ P_z & 0 & -P_x \\ -P_y & P_x & 0 \end{bmatrix} \begin{bmatrix} Q_x \\ Q_y \\ Q_z \end{bmatrix}.$$

The magnitude of the cross product is related to the angle θ between the vectors $\mathbf{P}$ and $\mathbf{Q}$ by the formula

$$\|\mathbf{P} \times \mathbf{Q}\| = \|\mathbf{P}\| \, \|\mathbf{Q}\| \sin \alpha.$$

Gram-Schmidt Orthogonalization

A basis $\mathcal{B} = \{\mathbf{e}_1, \mathbf{e}_2, \ldots, \mathbf{e}_n\}$ for an n-dimensional vector space can be orthogonalized by constructing a new set of vectors $\mathcal{B}' = \{\mathbf{e}_1', \mathbf{e}_2', \ldots, \mathbf{e}_n'\}$ using the formula

$$\mathbf{e}_i' = \mathbf{e}_i - \sum_{k=1}^{i-1} \frac{\mathbf{e}_i \cdot \mathbf{e}_k}{\mathbf{e}_k^2} \mathbf{e}_k.$$

Exercises for Chapter 1

1. Let $\mathbf{P} = \langle 2, 2, 1 \rangle$ and $\mathbf{Q} = \langle 1, -2, 0 \rangle$. Calculate the following.

    (a) $\mathbf{P} \cdot \mathbf{Q}$

    (b) $\mathbf{P} \times \mathbf{Q}$

    (c) $\text{proj}_{\mathbf{Q}} \, \mathbf{P}$

2. Orthogonalize the following set of vectors.

$$\mathbf{e}_1 = \left\langle \frac{\sqrt{2}}{2}, \frac{\sqrt{2}}{2}, 0 \right\rangle$$

$$\mathbf{e}_2 = \langle -1, 1, -1 \rangle$$

$$\mathbf{e}_3 = \langle 0, -2, -2 \rangle$$

3. Prove that, for any three 3D vectors $\mathbf{P}$, $\mathbf{Q}$, and $\mathbf{R}$,

$$\mathbf{P} \times \mathbf{Q} \times \mathbf{R} = (\mathbf{P} \cdot \mathbf{R})\mathbf{Q} - (\mathbf{Q} \cdot \mathbf{R})\mathbf{P}.$$

4. Implement a C++ class that encapsulates a 3D vector. The class should possess floating-point data members for the vector's x-, y-, and z-components. In addition to a default constructor, which should not perform any initialization, the class should have a constructor that takes three floating-point numbers as arguments and initializes the vector's components to those values. The class should also include overloaded operators for addition, subtraction, multiplication, and division by scalars, the dot product, and the cross product. Finally, write a function that calculates the magnitude of a 3D vector object.

CHAPTER

2

Matrices

$$\mathbf{F} + \mathbf{G} = \begin{bmatrix} F_{11} + G_{11} & F_{12} + G_{12} & \cdots & F_{1m} + G_{1m} \\ F_{21} + G_{21} & F_{22} + G_{22} & \cdots & F_{2m} + G_{2m} \\ \vdots & \vdots & \ddots & \vdots \\ F_{n1} + G_{n1} & F_{n2} + G_{n2} & \cdots & F_{nm} + G_{nm} \end{bmatrix}$$

We have casually referred to matrices several times in chapter 1. A more formal treatment of matrix properties is needed before proceeding to the applications in 3D graphics programming that require their use.

2.1 MATRIX PROPERTIES

An $n \times m$ matrix $\mathbf{M}$ is an array of numbers having n rows and m columns. If $n = m$, then we say that the matrix $\mathbf{M}$ is *square*. We write M_{ij} to refer to the entry of $\mathbf{M}$ that resides at the i-th row of the j-th column. As an example, suppose that $\mathbf{F}$ is a 3×4 matrix. Then we could write

$$\mathbf{F} = \begin{bmatrix} F_{11} & F_{12} & F_{13} & F_{14} \\ F_{21} & F_{22} & F_{23} & F_{24} \\ F_{31} & F_{32} & F_{33} & F_{34} \end{bmatrix}. \tag{2.1}$$

The entries for which $i = j$ are called the *main diagonal* entries of the matrix. A square matrix whose only nonzero entries appear on the main diagonal is called a *diagonal* matrix.

The *transpose* of an $n \times m$ matrix $\mathbf{M}$, which we denote by $\mathbf{M}^{\mathrm{T}}$, is an $m \times n$ matrix for which the (i, j) entry is equal to M_{ji} (i.e., $M_{ij}^{\mathrm{T}} = M_{ji}$). The transpose of the matrix $\mathbf{F}$ in Equation (2.1) is

$$\mathbf{F}^{\mathrm{T}} = \begin{bmatrix} F_{11} & F_{21} & F_{31} \\ F_{12} & F_{22} & F_{32} \\ F_{13} & F_{23} & F_{33} \\ F_{14} & F_{24} & F_{34} \end{bmatrix}. \tag{2.2}$$

As with vectors (which are really $n \times 1$ matrices), scalar multiplication is defined for matrices. Given a scalar a and an $n \times m$ matrix $\mathbf{M}$, the product $a\mathbf{M}$ is given by

$$a\mathbf{M} = \mathbf{M}a = \begin{bmatrix} aM_{11} & aM_{12} & \cdots & aM_{1m} \\ aM_{21} & aM_{22} & \cdots & aM_{2m} \\ \vdots & \vdots & \ddots & \vdots \\ aM_{n1} & aM_{n2} & \cdots & aM_{nm} \end{bmatrix}. \tag{2.3}$$

Also in a manner similar to vectors, matrices add entrywise. Given two $n \times m$ matrices $\mathbf{F}$ and $\mathbf{G}$, the sum $\mathbf{F} + \mathbf{G}$ is given by

$$\mathbf{F} + \mathbf{G} = \begin{bmatrix} F_{11} + G_{11} & F_{12} + G_{12} & \cdots & F_{1m} + G_{1m} \\ F_{21} + G_{21} & F_{22} + G_{22} & \cdots & F_{2m} + G_{2m} \\ \vdots & \vdots & \ddots & \vdots \\ F_{n1} + G_{n1} & F_{n2} + G_{n2} & \cdots & F_{nm} + G_{nm} \end{bmatrix} \tag{2.4}$$

Two matrices $\mathbf{F}$ and $\mathbf{G}$ can be multiplied together provided that the number of columns in $\mathbf{F}$ is equal to the number of rows in $\mathbf{G}$. If $\mathbf{F}$ is an $n \times m$ matrix and $\mathbf{G}$ is an $m \times p$ matrix, then the product $\mathbf{FG}$ is an $n \times p$ matrix whose (i, j) entry is given by

$$\left(\mathbf{FG}\right)_{ij} = \sum_{k=1}^{m} F_{ik} G_{kj}. \tag{2.5}$$

Another way of looking at this is that the (i, j) entry of $\mathbf{FG}$ is equal to the dot product of the i-th row of $\mathbf{F}$ and the j-th column of $\mathbf{G}$.

There is an $n \times n$ matrix called the *identity* matrix, denoted by $\mathbf{I}_n$, for which $\mathbf{MI}_n = \mathbf{I}_n\mathbf{M} = \mathbf{M}$ for any $n \times n$ matrix $\mathbf{M}$. The identity matrix has the form

$$\mathbf{I}_n = \begin{bmatrix} 1 & 0 & \cdots & 0 \\ 0 & 1 & \cdots & 0 \\ \vdots & \vdots & \ddots & \vdots \\ 0 & 0 & \cdots & 1 \end{bmatrix}. \tag{2.6}$$

We usually drop the subscript n and denote the identity matrix simply by $\mathbf{I}$ because the size of the matrix can be inferred from the context.

Several additional properties of matrices are given by the two theorems that follow.

> **Theorem 2.1.** Given any two scalars a and b and any three $n \times m$ matrices $\mathbf{F}$, $\mathbf{G}$, and $\mathbf{H}$, the following properties hold.
>
> (a) $\mathbf{F} + \mathbf{G} = \mathbf{G} + \mathbf{F}$
>
> (b) $(\mathbf{F} + \mathbf{G}) + \mathbf{H} = \mathbf{F} + (\mathbf{G} + \mathbf{H})$
>
> (c) $a(b\mathbf{F}) = (ab)\mathbf{F}$
>
> (d) $a(\mathbf{F} + \mathbf{G}) = a\mathbf{F} + a\mathbf{G}$
>
> (e) $(a + b)\mathbf{F} = a\mathbf{F} + b\mathbf{F}$

As with vectors, these properties are easily verified through direct computation using the associative and commutative properties of the real numbers.

Theorem 2.2. Given any scalar a, an $n \times m$ matrix $\mathbf{F}$, an $m \times p$ matrix $\mathbf{G}$, and a $p \times q$ matrix $\mathbf{H}$, the following properties hold.

(a) $(a\mathbf{F})\mathbf{G} = a(\mathbf{FG})$

(b) $(\mathbf{FG})\mathbf{H} = \mathbf{F}(\mathbf{GH})$

(c) $(\mathbf{FG})^{\mathsf{T}} = \mathbf{G}^{\mathsf{T}}\mathbf{F}^{\mathsf{T}}$

Proof.

(a)   Using the definition for matrix multiplication given by Equation (2.5), the (i, j) entry of $(a\mathbf{F})\mathbf{G}$ is

$$\left[(a\mathbf{F})\mathbf{G}\right]_{ij} = \sum_{k=1}^{m} (a\mathbf{F})_{ik} G_{kj}$$

$$= \sum_{k=1}^{m} a\left(F_{ik}G_{kj}\right)$$

$$= a\sum_{k=1}^{m} F_{ik}G_{kj}$$

$$= a\left(\mathbf{FG}\right)_{ij}. \tag{2.7}$$

(b)   Again using Equation (2.5), the (i, j) entry of $(\mathbf{FG})\mathbf{H}$ is

$$\left[(\mathbf{FG})\mathbf{H}\right]_{ij} = \sum_{k=1}^{p} (\mathbf{FG})_{ik} H_{kj}$$

$$= \sum_{k=1}^{p} \left(\sum_{l=1}^{m} F_{il}G_{lk}\right) H_{kj}$$

$$= \sum_{l=1}^{m} F_{il} \left(\sum_{k=1}^{p} G_{lk}H_{kj}\right)$$

$$= \sum_{l=1}^{m} F_{il}\left(\mathbf{GH}\right)_{lj}$$

$$= \left[\mathbf{F}(\mathbf{GH})\right]_{ij}. \tag{2.8}$$

(c)   Applying Equation (2.5), and reversing the indexes whenever a transpose operation is added or removed, we have for the (i, j) entry of $(\mathbf{FG})^{\mathsf{T}}$

$$\left(\mathbf{FG}\right)^{\mathsf{T}}_{ij} = \left(\mathbf{FG}\right)_{ji}$$

$$= \sum_{k=1}^{m} F_{jk} G_{ki}$$

$$= \sum_{k=1}^{m} F^{\mathsf{T}}_{kj} G^{\mathsf{T}}_{ik}$$

$$= \left(\mathbf{G}^{\mathsf{T}} \mathbf{F}^{\mathsf{T}}\right)_{ij}. \tag{2.9}$$

2.2 LINEAR SYSTEMS

Matrices provide a compact and convenient way to represent systems of linear equations. For instance, the linear system given by the equations

$$3x + 2y - 3z = 5$$
$$4x - 3y + 6z = 1$$
$$x - z = 3 \tag{2.10}$$

can be represented in matrix form as

$$\begin{bmatrix} 3 & 2 & -3 \\ 4 & -3 & 6 \\ 1 & 0 & -1 \end{bmatrix} \begin{bmatrix} x \\ y \\ z \end{bmatrix} = \begin{bmatrix} 5 \\ 1 \\ 3 \end{bmatrix}. \tag{2.11}$$

The matrix preceding the vector $\langle x, y, z \rangle$ of unknowns is called the *coefficient matrix*, and the column vector on the right side of the equals sign is called the *constant vector*. Linear systems for which the constant vector is nonzero (like the example above) are called *nonhomogeneous*. Linear systems for which every entry of the constant vector is zero are called *homogeneous*.

Finding solutions to a system of linear equations can be achieved by performing *elementary row operations* on the matrix formed by concatenating the coefficient matrix and the constant vector.

Definition 2.3. An *elementary row operation* is one of the following three operations that can be performed on a matrix.

(a)   Exchange two rows.
(b)   Multiply a row by a nonzero scalar.
(c)   Add a multiple of one row to another row.

For the example given by Equation (2.11), the augmented matrix formed by concatenating the coefficient matrix and constant vector is

$$\begin{bmatrix} 3 & 2 & -3 & | & 5 \\ 4 & -3 & 6 & | & 1 \\ 1 & 0 & -1 & | & 3 \end{bmatrix}. \tag{2.12}$$

Elementary row operations modify the augmented matrix representation of a linear system in such a way that the solution to the system is not affected, but it becomes much easier to calculate. When solving a linear system using elementary row operations, our goal is to transform the coefficient matrix into its *reduced form*, defined as follows.

> **Definition 2.4.** A matrix is in *reduced* form if and only if it satisfies the following conditions.
>
> (a) For every nonzero row, the leftmost nonzero entry, called the *leading entry*, is one.
> (b) Every nonzero row precedes every row of zeros. That is, all rows of zeros reside at the bottom of the matrix.
> (c) If a row's leading entry resides in column j, then no other row has a nonzero entry in column j.
> (d) For every pair of nonzero rows i_1 and i_2 such that $i_2 > i_1$, the columns j_1 and j_2 containing those rows' leading entries must satisfy $j_2 > j_1$.

This definition tells us that the leading entries of a matrix in reduced form move to the right as we move downward through its rows. Furthermore, any column containing a leading entry of a row has a one at that location and zeros everywhere else.

> **Example 2.5.** The following matrix is in reduced form.
>
> $$\begin{bmatrix} 1 & 0 & -3 & 0 \\ 0 & 1 & 2 & 0 \\ 0 & 0 & 0 & 1 \\ 0 & 0 & 0 & 0 \end{bmatrix} \tag{2.13}$$
>
> However, the matrix

$$\begin{bmatrix} 1 & 0 & 0 & 3 \\ 0 & 0 & 1 & 0 \\ 0 & 2 & 0 & 0 \\ 0 & 0 & 0 & 1 \end{bmatrix} \tag{2.14}$$

is *not* in reduced form because the leading entry of the third row does not fall to the right of the leading entry of the second row. Furthermore, the fourth column, which contains the leading entry of the fourth row, is not zero everywhere else.

Algorithm 2.6 describes which elementary row operations to apply to the augmented matrix representation of a linear system in order to transform its coefficient matrix into its reduced form.

Algorithm 2.6. This algorithm transforms an $n \times (n + 1)$ augmented matrix **M**, representing a linear system, into its reduced form. At each step, **M** refers to the *current* state of the matrix, not the original state.

A   Set the row i equal to 1.
B   Set the column j equal to 1. We will loop through columns 1 to n.
C   Find the first row k with $k \geq i$ such that $M_{kj} \neq 0$. If no such row exists, then skip to step H.
D   If $k \neq i$, then exchange rows k and i using elementary row operation (a) under definition 2.3.
E   Multiply row i by $1/M_{ij}$. This sets (i, j) entry of **M** to one using elementary row operation (b).
F   For each row r, where $1 \leq r \leq n$ and $r \neq i$, add $-M_{rj}$ times row i to row r. This step clears each entry above and below row i in column j to zero using elementary row operation (c).
G   Increment i.
H   If $j < n$, increment j and loop to step C.

The following example demonstrates the application of Algorithm 2.6 to the nonhomogeneous linear system given by Equation (2.11). After the augmented coefficient matrix is reduced, the solution to the system becomes obvious.

Example 2.7. Solve the nonhomogeneous linear system

$$\begin{bmatrix} 3 & 2 & -3 \\ 4 & -3 & 6 \\ 1 & 0 & -1 \end{bmatrix} \begin{bmatrix} x \\ y \\ z \end{bmatrix} = \begin{bmatrix} 5 \\ 1 \\ 3 \end{bmatrix}. \tag{2.15}$$

Solution. We first form the augmented matrix

$$\left[\begin{array}{ccc|c} 3 & 2 & -3 & 5 \\ 4 & -3 & 6 & 1 \\ 1 & 0 & -1 & 3 \end{array}\right]. \tag{2.16}$$

Multiplying the first row by $\frac{1}{3}$ produces a leading entry of one, as follows.

$$\xrightarrow{\text{Multiply row 1 by } \frac{1}{3}} \left[\begin{array}{ccc|c} 1 & \frac{2}{3} & -1 & \frac{5}{3} \\ 4 & -3 & 6 & 1 \\ 1 & 0 & -1 & 3 \end{array}\right] \tag{2.17}$$

Applying step G of Algorithm 2.6, we now eliminate the other nonzero entries in the first column.

$$\begin{array}{c} \xrightarrow[\text{Add } -1 \text{ times row 1 to row 3}]{\text{Add } -4 \text{ times row 1 to row 2}} \end{array} \left[\begin{array}{ccc|c} 1 & \frac{2}{3} & -1 & \frac{5}{3} \\ 0 & -\frac{17}{3} & 10 & -\frac{17}{3} \\ 0 & -\frac{2}{3} & 0 & \frac{4}{3} \end{array}\right] \tag{2.18}$$

Moving to the second row, we multiply by $-\frac{3}{17}$ to obtain a leading entry of one.

$$\xrightarrow{\text{Multiply row 2 by } -\frac{3}{17}} \left[\begin{array}{ccc|c} 1 & \frac{2}{3} & -1 & \frac{5}{3} \\ 0 & 1 & -\frac{30}{17} & 1 \\ 0 & -\frac{2}{3} & 0 & \frac{4}{3} \end{array}\right] \tag{2.19}$$

Again applying step G, we eliminate the other nonzero entries in the second column.

$$\begin{array}{c} \xrightarrow[\text{Add } \frac{2}{3} \text{ times row 2 to row 3}]{\text{Add } -\frac{2}{3} \text{ times row 2 to row 1}} \end{array} \left[\begin{array}{ccc|c} 1 & 0 & \frac{3}{17} & 1 \\ 0 & 1 & -\frac{30}{17} & 1 \\ 0 & 0 & -\frac{20}{17} & 2 \end{array}\right] \tag{2.20}$$

Finally, we apply the same steps to the third row, as follows.

$$\xrightarrow{\text{Multiply row 3 by } -\frac{17}{20}} \left[\begin{array}{ccc|c} 1 & 0 & \frac{3}{17} & 1 \\ 0 & 1 & -\frac{30}{17} & 1 \\ 0 & 0 & 1 & -\frac{17}{10} \end{array}\right]$$

$$\begin{array}{c} \xrightarrow[\text{Add } \frac{30}{17} \text{ times row 3 to row 2}]{\text{Add } -\frac{3}{17} \text{ times row 3 to row 1}} \end{array} \left[\begin{array}{ccc|c} 1 & 0 & 0 & \frac{13}{10} \\ 0 & 1 & 0 & -2 \\ 0 & 0 & 1 & -\frac{17}{10} \end{array}\right] \tag{2.21}$$

The coefficient matrix has now been completely transformed into its reduced form. The reduced augmented matrix represents the equation

$$
\begin{bmatrix} 1 & 0 & 0 \\ 0 & 1 & 0 \\ 0 & 0 & 1 \end{bmatrix} \begin{bmatrix} x \\ y \\ z \end{bmatrix} = \begin{bmatrix} \frac{13}{10} \\ -2 \\ -\frac{17}{10} \end{bmatrix}, \tag{2.22}
$$

from which the solution to the original system is immediate:

$$ x = \tfrac{13}{10} $$

$$ y = -2 $$

$$ z = -\tfrac{17}{10}. \tag{2.23} $$

In the previous example, we found that the reduced form of the coefficient matrix was equal to the identity matrix. In such a case, the corresponding linear system has exactly one solution. When the reduced coefficient matrix has one or more rows of zeros, however, the corresponding system may have no solution at all or may have infinitely many solutions. If the entry in the constant vector corresponding to a row of zeros in the coefficient matrix is *not* zero, then the system has no solution because that row equates zero to a nonzero number. In the remaining case, in which the entry in the constant vector is zero, there are infinitely many solutions to the linear system that must be expressed in terms of arbitrary constants. The number of arbitrary constants is equal to the number of rows of zeros, and arbitrary constants are assigned to variables corresponding to columns of the reduced coefficient matrix that do not contain a leading entry.

Example 2.8. Solve the following homogeneous linear system.

$$ 2x + y + 3z = 0 $$

$$ y - z = 0 $$

$$ x + 3y - z = 0 \tag{2.24} $$

Solution. The augmented matrix representation of this system is given by

$$
\left[\begin{array}{ccc|c} 2 & 1 & 3 & 0 \\ 0 & 1 & -1 & 0 \\ 1 & 3 & -1 & 0 \end{array} \right]. \tag{2.25}
$$

Using Algorithm 2.6 to calculate the reduced form gives us the matrix

$$\begin{bmatrix} 1 & 0 & 2 & | & 0 \\ 0 & 1 & -1 & | & 0 \\ 0 & 0 & 0 & | & 0 \end{bmatrix}. \tag{2.26}$$

Since this matrix has a row of zeros, we can assign an arbitrary value to the variable corresponding to the third column since it does not contain a leading entry; in this case we set $z = a$. The first two rows then represent the equations

$$x + 2a = 0$$
$$y - a = 0, \tag{2.27}$$

so the solution to the system can be written as

$$\begin{bmatrix} x \\ y \\ z \end{bmatrix} = a \begin{bmatrix} -2 \\ 1 \\ 1 \end{bmatrix}. \tag{2.28}$$

Homogeneous linear systems always have at least one solution—the zero vector. Nontrivial solutions exist only when the reduced form of the coefficient matrix possesses at least one row of zeros.

2.3 MATRIX INVERSES

An $n \times n$ matrix $\mathbf{M}$ is *invertible* if there exists a matrix, which we denote by $\mathbf{M}^{-1}$, such that $\mathbf{MM}^{-1} = \mathbf{M}^{-1}\mathbf{M} = \mathbf{I}$. The matrix $\mathbf{M}^{-1}$ is called the *inverse* of $\mathbf{M}$. Not every matrix has an inverse, and those that do not are called *singular*. An example of a singular matrix is any one that has a row or column consisting of all zeros.

Theorem 2.9. A matrix possessing a row or column consisting entirely of zeros is not invertible.

Proof. Suppose every entry in row r of an $n \times n$ matrix $\mathbf{F}$ is zero. For any $n \times n$ matrix $\mathbf{G}$, the (r, r) entry of the product $\mathbf{FG}$ is given by $\sum_{k=1}^{n} F_{rk}G_{kr}$. Since each of the F_{rk} is zero, the (r, r) entry of $\mathbf{FG}$ is zero. Since the inverse of $\mathbf{F}$ would need to produce a one in the (r, r) entry, $\mathbf{F}$ cannot have an inverse. A similar argument proves the theorem for a matrix possessing a column of zeros.

Using this theorem, we will be able to show later in this section that any matrix possessing a row that is a linear combination of the other rows of the matrix is singular. The same is true for the columns of a matrix due to the following fact.

Theorem 2.10. A matrix $\mathbf{M}$ is invertible if and only if $\mathbf{M}^{\mathrm{T}}$ is invertible.

Proof. Assume $\mathbf{M}$ is invertible. Then $\mathbf{M}^{-1}$ exists, so we can write

$$\mathbf{M}^{\mathrm{T}}\left(\mathbf{M}^{-1}\right)^{\mathrm{T}} = \left(\mathbf{M}^{-1}\mathbf{M}\right)^{\mathrm{T}} = \mathbf{I}^{\mathrm{T}} = \mathbf{I} \tag{2.29}$$

and

$$\left(\mathbf{M}^{-1}\right)^{\mathrm{T}}\mathbf{M}^{\mathrm{T}} = \left(\mathbf{M}\mathbf{M}^{-1}\right)^{\mathrm{T}} = \mathbf{I}^{\mathrm{T}} = \mathbf{I}. \tag{2.30}$$

Therefore, $(\mathbf{M}^{-1})^{\mathrm{T}}$ is the inverse of $\mathbf{M}^{\mathrm{T}}$. Similarly, if we assume that $\mathbf{M}^{\mathrm{T}}$ is invertible, then $(\mathbf{M}^{\mathrm{T}})^{-1}$ exists, so we can write

$$\mathbf{M}\left[\left(\mathbf{M}^{\mathrm{T}}\right)^{-1}\right]^{\mathrm{T}} = \left[\left(\mathbf{M}^{\mathrm{T}}\right)^{-1}\mathbf{M}^{\mathrm{T}}\right]^{\mathrm{T}} = \mathbf{I}^{\mathrm{T}} = \mathbf{I} \tag{2.31}$$

and

$$\left[\left(\mathbf{M}^{\mathrm{T}}\right)^{-1}\right]^{\mathrm{T}}\mathbf{M} = \left[\mathbf{M}^{\mathrm{T}}\left(\mathbf{M}^{\mathrm{T}}\right)^{-1}\right]^{\mathrm{T}} = \mathbf{I}^{\mathrm{T}} = \mathbf{I}. \tag{2.32}$$

Therefore, $[(\mathbf{M}^{\mathrm{T}})^{-1}]^{\mathrm{T}}$ is the inverse of $\mathbf{M}$.

Before proceeding to a method for calculating inverses, we make one more observation.

Theorem 2.11. If $\mathbf{F}$ and $\mathbf{G}$ are $n \times n$ invertible matrices, then the product $\mathbf{FG}$ is invertible and $(\mathbf{FG})^{-1} = \mathbf{G}^{-1}\mathbf{F}^{-1}$.

Proof. We can verify this theorem through direct computation using the fact that matrix multiplication is associative:

$$\mathbf{G}^{-1}\mathbf{F}^{-1}(\mathbf{FG}) = \mathbf{G}^{-1}(\mathbf{F}^{-1}\mathbf{F})\mathbf{G} = \mathbf{G}^{-1}\mathbf{G} = \mathbf{I}. \tag{2.33}$$

A method similar to that used to transform a matrix into its reduced form (see Algorithm 2.6) can also be used to calculate the inverse of a matrix. To find the inverse of an $n \times n$ matrix $\mathbf{M}$, we first construct an $n \times 2n$ matrix $\tilde{\mathbf{M}}$ by concatenating the identity matrix to the right of $\mathbf{M}$, as shown below.

$$\tilde{\mathbf{M}} = \begin{bmatrix} M_{11} & M_{12} & \cdots & M_{1n} & 1 & 0 & \cdots & 0 \\ M_{21} & M_{22} & \cdots & M_{2n} & 0 & 1 & \cdots & 0 \\ \vdots & \vdots & \ddots & \vdots & \vdots & \vdots & \ddots & \vdots \\ M_{n1} & M_{n2} & \cdots & M_{nn} & 0 & 0 & \cdots & 1 \end{bmatrix} \tag{2.34}$$

Performing elementary row operations on the entire matrix $\tilde{\mathbf{M}}$ until the left side $n \times n$ matrix becomes the identity matrix $\mathbf{I}_n$ yields the inverse of $\mathbf{M}$ in the right side $n \times n$ matrix. This process is illustrated in Algorithm 2.12.

Algorithm 2.12. This algorithm calculates the inverse of an $n \times n$ matrix $\mathbf{M}$.

A Construct the augmented matrix $\tilde{\mathbf{M}}$ given in Equation (2.34). Throughout this algorithm, $\tilde{\mathbf{M}}$ refers to the *current* state of the augmented matrix, not the original state.

B Set the column j equal to 1. We will loop through columns 1 to n.

C Find the first row i with $i \geq j$ such that $\tilde{M}_{ij} \neq 0$. If no such row exists, then $\mathbf{M}$ is not invertible.

D If $i \neq j$, then exchange rows i and j using elementary row operation (a) under Definition 2.3.

E Multiply row j by $1/\tilde{M}_{jj}$. This sets (j, j) entry of $\tilde{\mathbf{M}}$ to 1 using elementary row operation (b).

F For each row r where $1 \leq r \leq n$ and $r \neq j$, add $-\tilde{M}_{rj}$ times row j to row r. This step clears each entry above and below row j in column j to 0 using elementary row operation (c).

G If $j < n$, increment j and loop to step C.

The implementation of Algorithm 2.12 is straightforward and has the benefit that it can determine whether a matrix is invertible. The following example demonstrates the inner workings of the algorithm.

Example 2.13. Calculate the inverse of the 3×3 matrix $\mathbf{M}$ given by

$$\mathbf{M} = \begin{bmatrix} 2 & 3 & 8 \\ 6 & 0 & -3 \\ -1 & 3 & 2 \end{bmatrix}. \tag{2.35}$$

Solution. Concatenating the identity matrix to $\mathbf{M}$, we have

$$\tilde{\mathbf{M}} = \begin{bmatrix} 2 & 3 & 8 & 1 & 0 & 0 \\ 6 & 0 & -3 & 0 & 1 & 0 \\ -1 & 3 & 2 & 0 & 0 & 1 \end{bmatrix}. \tag{2.36}$$

We now apply steps C through F of the algorithm for $j = 1$.

$$\xrightarrow{\text{Multiply row 1 by } \frac{1}{2}} \left[\begin{array}{ccc|ccc} 1 & \frac{3}{2} & 4 & \frac{1}{2} & 0 & 0 \\ 6 & 0 & -3 & 0 & 1 & 0 \\ -1 & 3 & 2 & 0 & 0 & 1 \end{array}\right]$$

$$\xrightarrow[\text{Add row 1 to row 3}]{\text{Add } -6 \text{ times row 1 to row 2}} \left[\begin{array}{ccc|ccc} 1 & \frac{3}{2} & 4 & \frac{1}{2} & 0 & 0 \\ 0 & -9 & -27 & -3 & 1 & 0 \\ 0 & \frac{9}{2} & 6 & \frac{1}{2} & 0 & 1 \end{array}\right] \tag{2.37}$$

Applying the same steps for $j = 2$ gives us the following.

$$\xrightarrow{\text{Multiply row 2 by } -\frac{1}{9}} \left[\begin{array}{ccc|ccc} 1 & \frac{3}{2} & 4 & \frac{1}{2} & 0 & 0 \\ 0 & 1 & 3 & \frac{1}{3} & -\frac{1}{9} & 0 \\ 0 & \frac{9}{2} & 6 & \frac{1}{2} & 0 & 1 \end{array}\right]$$

$$\xrightarrow[\text{Add } -\frac{9}{2} \text{ times row 2 to row 3}]{\text{Add } -\frac{3}{2} \text{ times row 2 to row 1}} \left[\begin{array}{ccc|ccc} 1 & 0 & -\frac{1}{2} & 0 & \frac{1}{6} & 0 \\ 0 & 1 & 3 & \frac{1}{3} & -\frac{1}{9} & 0 \\ 0 & 0 & -\frac{15}{2} & -1 & \frac{1}{2} & 1 \end{array}\right] \tag{2.38}$$

Finally, we apply the algorithm for $j = 3$.

$$\xrightarrow{\text{Multiply row 3 by } -\frac{2}{15}} \left[\begin{array}{ccc|ccc} 1 & 0 & -\frac{1}{2} & 0 & \frac{1}{6} & 0 \\ 0 & 1 & 3 & \frac{1}{3} & -\frac{1}{9} & 0 \\ 0 & 0 & 1 & \frac{2}{15} & -\frac{1}{15} & -\frac{2}{15} \end{array}\right]$$

$$\xrightarrow[\text{Add } -3 \text{ times row 3 to row 2}]{\text{Add } \frac{1}{2} \text{ times row 3 to row 1}} \left[\begin{array}{ccc|ccc} 1 & 0 & 0 & \frac{1}{15} & \frac{2}{15} & -\frac{1}{15} \\ 0 & 1 & 0 & -\frac{1}{15} & \frac{4}{45} & \frac{2}{5} \\ 0 & 0 & 1 & \frac{2}{15} & -\frac{1}{15} & -\frac{2}{15} \end{array}\right] \tag{2.39}$$

The right side 3×3 matrix is now equal to the inverse of $\mathbf{M}$:

$$\mathbf{M}^{-1} = \frac{1}{45}\left[\begin{array}{ccc} 3 & 6 & -3 \\ -3 & 4 & 18 \\ 6 & -3 & -6 \end{array}\right]. \tag{2.40}$$

To understand why Algorithm 2.12 supplies the inverse of a matrix, we need the following theorem.

Theorem 2.14. Let $\mathbf{M}'$ be the $n \times n$ matrix resulting from the performance of an elementary row operation on the $n \times n$ matrix $\mathbf{M}$. Then $\mathbf{M}' = \mathbf{EM}$ where $\mathbf{E}$ is the $n \times n$ matrix resulting from the same elementary row operation performed on the identity matrix.

Proof. We shall give separate proofs for each of the three elementary row operations listed in Definition 2.3.

(a) Let $\mathbf{E}$ be equal to the identity matrix after rows r and s have been exchanged. Then the entries of $\mathbf{E}$ are given by

$$E_{ij} = \begin{cases} \delta_{ij}, & \text{if } i \neq r \text{ and } i \neq s; \\ \delta_{sj}, & \text{if } i = r; \\ \delta_{rj}, & \text{if } i = s, \end{cases} \tag{2.41}$$

where δ_{ij} is the Kronecker delta symbol defined by Equation (1.42). The entries of the product $\mathbf{EM}$ are then given by

$$(\mathbf{EM})_{ij} = \sum_{k=1}^{n} E_{ik} M_{kj} = \begin{cases} M_{ij}, & \text{if } i \neq r \text{ and } i \neq j; \\ M_{sj}, & \text{if } i = r; \\ M_{rj}, & \text{if } i = s. \end{cases} \tag{2.42}$$

Thus, rows r and s of the matrix $\mathbf{M}$ have been exchanged.

(b) Let $\mathbf{E}$ be equal to the identity matrix after row r has been multiplied by a scalar a. Then the entries of $\mathbf{E}$ are given by

$$E_{ij} = \begin{cases} \delta_{ij}, & \text{if } i \neq r; \\ a\delta_{ij}, & \text{if } i = r. \end{cases} \tag{2.43}$$

The entries of the product $\mathbf{EM}$ are then given by

$$(\mathbf{EM})_{ij} = \sum_{k=1}^{n} E_{ik} M_{kj} = \begin{cases} M_{ij}, & \text{if } i \neq r; \\ a M_{ij}, & \text{if } i = r. \end{cases} \tag{2.44}$$

Thus, row r of the matrix $\mathbf{M}$ has been multiplied by a.

(c) Let $\mathbf{E}$ be equal to the identity matrix after row r has been multiplied by a scalar a and added to row s. Then the entries of $\mathbf{E}$ are given by

$$E_{ij} = \begin{cases} \delta_{ij}, & \text{if } i \neq s; \\ \delta_{ij} + a\delta_{rj}, & \text{if } i = s. \end{cases} \tag{2.45}$$

The entries of the product **EM** are then given by

$$\left(\mathbf{EM}\right)_{ij} = \sum_{k=1}^{n} E_{ik}M_{kj} = \begin{cases} M_{ij}, & \text{if } i \neq s; \\ M_{ij} + aM_{rj}, & \text{if } i = s. \end{cases} \qquad (2.46)$$

Thus, row r of the matrix **M** has been multiplied by a and added to row s.

The matrix **E**, which represents the result of an elementary row operation performed on the identity matrix, is called an *elementary* matrix. If we have to apply k elementary row operations to transform a matrix **M** into the identity matrix, then

$$\mathbf{I} = \mathbf{E}_k \mathbf{E}_{k-1} \cdots \mathbf{E}_1 \mathbf{M}, \qquad (2.47)$$

where the matrices $\mathbf{E}_1, \mathbf{E}_2, \ldots, \mathbf{E}_k$ are the elementary matrices corresponding to the same k row operations applied to the identity matrix. This actually shows that the product $\mathbf{E}_k \mathbf{E}_{k-1} \cdots \mathbf{E}_1$ is equal to the inverse of **M**, and it is exactly what we get when we apply the k row operations to the identity matrix concatenated to the matrix **M** in Equation (2.34).

If a matrix **M** is singular, then finding elementary matrices $\mathbf{E}_1, \mathbf{E}_2, \ldots, \mathbf{E}_k$ that satisfy Equation (2.47) is impossible. This is true because singular matrices are exactly those whose rows form a linearly dependent set, as the following theorem states.

Theorem 2.15. An $n \times n$ matrix **M** is invertible if and only if the rows of **M** form a linearly independent set of vectors.

Proof. Let the rows of **M** be denoted by $\mathbf{R}_1^\mathsf{T}, \mathbf{R}_2^\mathsf{T}, \ldots, \mathbf{R}_n^\mathsf{T}$. We prove this theorem in two parts.

(a) We prove that if **M** is invertible, then the rows of **M** form a linearly independent set of vectors by proving the contrapositive, which states that if the rows of **M** form a linearly dependent set of vectors, then **M** must be singular. So assume that the rows of **M** are linearly dependent. Then there exists a row r that can be written as a linear combination of k other rows of the matrix, as follows.

$$\mathbf{R}_r^\mathsf{T} = a_1 \mathbf{R}_{s_1}^\mathsf{T} + a_2 \mathbf{R}_{s_2}^\mathsf{T} + \cdots + a_k \mathbf{R}_{s_k}^\mathsf{T} \qquad (2.48)$$

The a_i's are scalars, and the s_i's index k rows in the matrix **M** other than row r. Let the $n \times n$ matrix $\mathbf{E}_i$ be equal to the elementary matrix representing the addition of a_i times row s_i to row r. Then we can write

$$\mathbf{M} = \mathbf{E}_k \mathbf{E}_{k-1} \cdots \mathbf{E}_1 \mathbf{M}', \tag{2.49}$$

where $\mathbf{M}'$ is equal to $\mathbf{M}$ except that row r has been replaced by all zeros. By Theorem 2.9, the matrix $\mathbf{M}'$ is singular, and thus $\mathbf{M}$ is singular.

(b)   Now assume that the rows of $\mathbf{M}$ form a linearly independent set of vectors. We first observe that performing elementary row operations on a matrix does not alter the property of linear independence within the rows. Running through Algorithm 2.12, if step C fails, then rows j through n of the matrix at that point form a linearly dependent set since the number of columns for which the rows $\mathbf{R}_j^{\mathrm{T}}$ through $\mathbf{R}_n^{\mathrm{T}}$ have at least one nonzero entry is less than the number of rows itself. This is a contradiction, so step C of the algorithm cannot fail, and $\mathbf{M}$ must be invertible.

This theorem tells us that *every* singular matrix can be written as a product of elementary matrices and a matrix that has a row of zeros. With the introduction of determinants in the next section, this fact allows us to devise a test for singularity.

2.4 DETERMINANTS

The determinant of a square matrix is a scalar quantity derived from the entries of the matrix. The determinant of a matrix $\mathbf{M}$ is denoted by det $\mathbf{M}$. When displaying the entries of a matrix, we replace the brackets on the left and right of the matrix with vertical bars to indicate that we are evaluating the determinant. For example, the determinant of a 3×3 matrix $\mathbf{M}$ is written as

$$\det \mathbf{M} = \begin{vmatrix} M_{11} & M_{12} & M_{13} \\ M_{21} & M_{22} & M_{23} \\ M_{31} & M_{32} & M_{33} \end{vmatrix}. \tag{2.50}$$

The value of the determinant of an $n \times n$ matrix is given by a recursive formula. For notational convenience, let the symbol $\mathbf{M}^{\{i,j\}}$ denote the $(n-1) \times (n-1)$ matrix whose entries consist of the original entries of $\mathbf{M}$ after deleting the i-th row and the j-th column. For example, suppose that $\mathbf{M}$ is the following 3×3 matrix.

$$\mathbf{M} = \begin{bmatrix} 1 & 2 & 3 \\ 4 & 5 & 6 \\ 7 & 8 & 9 \end{bmatrix} \tag{2.51}$$

Then $\mathbf{M}^{\{2,3\}}$ is the following 2×2 matrix.

$$\mathbf{M}^{\{2,3\}} = \begin{bmatrix} 1 & 2 \\ 7 & 8 \end{bmatrix} \tag{2.52}$$

Using this notation, a method for calculating the determinant of an $n \times n$ matrix can be expressed as follows. First, define the determinant of a 1×1 matrix to be the entry of the matrix itself. Then the determinant of an $n \times n$ matrix $\mathbf{M}$ is given by both the formula

$$\det \mathbf{M} = \sum_{i=1}^{n} (-1)^{i+k} M_{ik} \det \mathbf{M}^{\{i,k\}} \tag{2.53}$$

and the formula

$$\det \mathbf{M} = \sum_{j=1}^{n} (-1)^{k+j} M_{kj} \det \mathbf{M}^{\{k,j\}}, \tag{2.54}$$

where k is an arbitrarily chosen constant such that $1 \le k \le n$. Remarkably, both formulas give the same value for the determinant regardless of the choice of k.

An explicit formula for the determinant of a 2×2 matrix is easy to extract from Equations (2.53) and (2.54):

$$\begin{vmatrix} a & b \\ c & d \end{vmatrix} = ad - bc. \tag{2.55}$$

We also give an explicit formula for the determinant of a 3×3 matrix. The following is written as one would evaluate Equation (2.54) with $k = 1$.

$$\begin{vmatrix} a_{11} & a_{12} & a_{13} \\ a_{21} & a_{22} & a_{23} \\ a_{31} & a_{32} & a_{33} \end{vmatrix} = a_{11} \begin{vmatrix} a_{22} & a_{23} \\ a_{32} & a_{33} \end{vmatrix} - a_{12} \begin{vmatrix} a_{21} & a_{23} \\ a_{31} & a_{33} \end{vmatrix} + a_{13} \begin{vmatrix} a_{21} & a_{22} \\ a_{31} & a_{32} \end{vmatrix}$$

$$= a_{11}\left(a_{22}a_{33} - a_{23}a_{32}\right) - a_{12}\left(a_{21}a_{33} - a_{23}a_{31}\right) \tag{2.56}$$

$$+ a_{13}\left(a_{21}a_{32} - a_{22}a_{31}\right)$$

Clearly, the determinant of the identity matrix $\mathbf{I}_n$ is one for any n because we can evaluate it using Equation (2.54) with $k = 1$ at each stage of the recursive formula.

We can derive some useful information from studying how elementary row operations (see Definition 2.3) affect the determinant of a matrix. This provides a way of evaluating determinants that is usually more efficient than direct application of Equations (2.53) and (2.54).

Theorem 2.16. Performing elementary row operations on a matrix has the following effects on the determinant of that matrix.

(a) Exchanging two rows negates the determinant.

(b) Multiplying a row by a scalar a multiplies the determinant by a.

(c) Adding a multiple of one row to another row has no effect on the determinant.

Proof.

(a) We prove this by induction. The operation does not apply to 1×1 matrices, but for a 2×2 matrix, we can observe the result through direct computation.

$$\begin{vmatrix} c & d \\ a & b \end{vmatrix} = cb - ad = -(ad - cb) = \begin{vmatrix} a & b \\ c & d \end{vmatrix} \qquad (2.57)$$

Now, for an $n \times n$ matrix, we can assume that the result is true for all matrices up to size $(n - 1) \times (n - 1)$. Let $\mathbf{G}$ represent the result of exchanging rows r and s of a matrix $\mathbf{F}$. Choosing another row k such that $k \neq r$ and $k \neq s$, evaluation of Equation (2.54) gives us

$$\det \mathbf{G} = \sum_{j=1}^{n} (-1)^{k+j} G_{kj} \det \mathbf{G}^{\{k, j\}}. \qquad (2.58)$$

Since $\mathbf{G}^{\{j, k\}}$ is an $(n - 1) \times (n - 1)$ matrix, we know by induction that $\det \mathbf{G}^{\{j, k\}} = -\det \mathbf{F}^{\{j, k\}}$ for each j. Thus, $\det \mathbf{G} = -\det \mathbf{F}$.

(b) Let $\mathbf{G}$ represent the result of multiplying row k of a matrix $\mathbf{F}$ by the scalar a. Then evaluation of Equation (2.54) gives us

$$\det \mathbf{G} = \sum_{j=1}^{n} (-1)^{k+j} G_{kj} \det \mathbf{G}^{\{k, j\}}$$

$$= \sum_{j=1}^{n} (-1)^{k+j} a F_{kj} \det \mathbf{F}^{\{k, j\}}. \qquad (2.59)$$

Thus, $\mathbf{G} = a \det \mathbf{F}$.

Before we can prove part (c), we need the following corollary to part (a).

Corollary 2.17. The determinant of a matrix having two identical rows is zero.

Proof. Suppose the matrix **M** has two identical rows. If we exchange these rows, then no change has been made to the matrix, but the determinant has been negated. So det **M** = −det **M**, and we must therefore have det **M** = 0.

Proof of Theorem 2.16(c). Let **G** represent the result of adding the scalar a times row r of a matrix **F** to row k of **F**. Then evaluation of Equation (2.54) gives us

$$\det \mathbf{G} = \sum_{j=1}^{n} (-1)^{k+j} G_{kj} \det \mathbf{G}^{\{k,j\}}$$

$$= \sum_{j=1}^{n} (-1)^{k+j} \left(F_{kj} + aF_{rj} \right) \det \mathbf{F}^{\{k,j\}}$$

$$= \det \mathbf{F} + a \sum_{j=1}^{n} (-1)^{k+j} F_{rj} \det \mathbf{F}^{\{k,j\}}. \tag{2.60}$$

The sum $\sum_{j=1}^{n}(-1)^{k+j} F_{rj} \det \mathbf{F}^{\{k,j\}}$ is equivalent to the determinant of the matrix **F** with the entries in row k replaced by the entries from row r. Since this matrix has two identical rows, its determinant is zero, by Corollary 2.17. Therefore, det **G** = det **F**.

Since elementary matrices are representative of elementary row operations performed on the identity matrix, we can deduce their determinants from Theorem 2.16. An elementary matrix that represents an exchange of rows has a determinant of −1, an elementary matrix that represents a row multiplied by a scalar a has a determinant of a, and an elementary matrix that represents a multiple of one row added to another row has a determinant of 1. These are the exact numbers by which the determinant of any matrix is multiplied when the corresponding elementary row operations are performed on them. We can therefore conclude that if **E** is an $n \times n$ elementary matrix, then det **EM** = det **E** det **M** for any $n \times n$ matrix **M** since multiplication by **E** performs the elementary row operation on **M**. This result leads us to the following two important theorems.

Theorem 2.18. An $n \times n$ matrix **M** is invertible if and only if det **M** ≠ 0.

Proof. Suppose that **M** is invertible. Then **M** can be written as a product of elementary matrices, each having a nonzero determinant. Since the determinant of a product of elementary matrices is equal to the product of the determinants of those matrices, the determinant of **M** cannot be zero. Now suppose that **M** is singular. Then **M** can be written as a product of elementary matrices and a matrix having a row of zeros because the rows of $\mathbf{M}$ must be linearly dependent. Since the determinant of a matrix possessing a row of zeros is zero, the determinant of the product is also zero.

Theorem 2.19. For any two $n \times n$ matrices $\mathbf{F}$ and $\mathbf{G}$, det $\mathbf{FG}$ = det $\mathbf{F}$ det $\mathbf{G}$.

Proof. If either $\mathbf{F}$ or $\mathbf{G}$ is singular, then $\mathbf{FG}$ is singular and the Equation holds since both sides are zero. Otherwise, both $\mathbf{F}$ and $\mathbf{G}$ can be factored completely into elementary matrices. Since the determinant of a product of elementary matrices is the product of the determinants, the Equation holds.

Theorem 2.18 gives us a test for singularity. Once we know that the determinant of an $n \times n$ matrix $\mathbf{M}$ is not zero, we can use the following formula to calculate the entries of $\mathbf{M}^{-1}$.

Theorem 2.20. Let $\mathbf{F}$ be an $n \times n$ matrix and define the entries of an $n \times n$ matrix $\mathbf{G}$ using the formula

$$\mathbf{G}_{ij} = (-1)^{i+j} \frac{\det \mathbf{F}^{\{j,i\}}}{\det \mathbf{F}}. \tag{2.61}$$

Then $\mathbf{G} = \mathbf{F}^{-1}$.

Proof. Using the multiplication formula for $\mathbf{FG}$, we have

$$(\mathbf{FG})_{ij} = \sum_{k=1}^{n} F_{ik} G_{kj} = \sum_{k=1}^{n} F_{ik} (-1)^{k+j} \frac{\det \mathbf{F}^{\{j,k\}}}{\det \mathbf{F}}$$

$$= \frac{1}{\det \mathbf{F}} \sum_{k=1}^{n} (-1)^{k+j} F_{ik} \det \mathbf{F}^{\{j,k\}}. \tag{2.62}$$

If $i = j$, then the summation gives the determinant of $\mathbf{F}$ equivalently to Equation (2.53), so multiplying by $1/\det \mathbf{F}$ gives us $(\mathbf{FG})_{ij} = 1$. If $i \neq j$, then the summation gives the determinant of a matrix equal to $\mathbf{F}$ except that row j has been replaced by the entries in row i. Since the matrix has two identical rows, its determinant is zero, and thus $(\mathbf{FG})_{ij} = 0$. Since the main diagonal entries of $\mathbf{FG}$ are one and all the remaining entries are zero, $\mathbf{FG}$ is the identity matrix. A similar argument proves that $\mathbf{GF}$ is the identity matrix, so $\mathbf{G} = \mathbf{F}^{-1}$.

Using Equation (2.61), we can derive explicit formulas for the inverses of matrices having sizes that are commonly used in computer graphics. The inverse of a 2×2 matrix $\mathbf{A}$ is given by

$$\mathbf{A}^{-1} = \frac{1}{\det \mathbf{A}} \begin{bmatrix} A_{22} & -A_{12} \\ -A_{21} & A_{11} \end{bmatrix}. \tag{2.63}$$

The inverse of a 3×3 matrix $\mathbf{B}$ is given by

$$\mathbf{B}^{-1} = \frac{1}{\det \mathbf{B}} \begin{bmatrix} B_{22}B_{33} - B_{23}B_{32} & B_{13}B_{32} - B_{12}B_{33} & B_{12}B_{23} - B_{13}B_{22} \\ B_{23}B_{31} - B_{21}B_{33} & B_{11}B_{33} - B_{13}B_{31} & B_{13}B_{21} - B_{11}B_{23} \\ B_{21}B_{32} - B_{22}B_{31} & B_{12}B_{31} - B_{11}B_{32} & B_{11}B_{22} - B_{12}B_{21} \end{bmatrix}. \tag{2.64}$$

2.5 EIGENVALUES AND EIGENVECTORS

For every invertible square matrix, there exist vectors that, when multiplied by the matrix, are changed only in magnitude and not in direction. That is, for an $n \times n$ matrix $\mathbf{M}$, there exist nonzero n-dimensional vectors $\mathbf{V}_1, \mathbf{V}_2, \ldots, \mathbf{V}_n$ such that

$$\mathbf{MV}_i = \lambda_i \mathbf{V}_i. \tag{2.65}$$

The scalars λ_i are called the *eigenvalues* of the matrix $\mathbf{M}$ and the vectors $\mathbf{V}_i$ are called the *eigenvectors* that correspond to those eigenvalues.

The eigenvalues of a matrix can be determined by first rearranging Equation (2.65) to read

$$(\mathbf{M} - \lambda_i \mathbf{I})\mathbf{V}_i = \mathbf{0}, \tag{2.66}$$

where $\mathbf{I}$ is the $n \times n$ identity matrix. For this equation to be true for nonzero vectors $\mathbf{V}_i$, the matrix $\mathbf{M} - \lambda_i \mathbf{I}$ must be singular. This is necessary because otherwise, we could invert $\mathbf{M} - \lambda_i \mathbf{I}$ and write

$$\mathbf{V}_i = (\mathbf{M} - \lambda_i \mathbf{I})^{-1}\mathbf{0} = \mathbf{0}, \tag{2.67}$$

contradicting the assumption that $\mathbf{V}_i \neq \mathbf{0}$. Since $\mathbf{M} - \lambda_i \mathbf{I}$ is singular, its determinant must be zero, so we can calculate the eigenvalues λ_i by solving the equation

$$\det(\mathbf{M} - \lambda \mathbf{I}) = 0. \tag{2.68}$$

The degree n polynomial in λ given by Equation (2.68) is called the *characteristic polynomial* of the matrix $\mathbf{M}$. The roots of this polynomial yield the eigenvalues of the matrix $\mathbf{M}$.

Example 2.21. Calculate the eigenvalues of the matrix

$$\mathbf{M} = \begin{bmatrix} 1 & 1 \\ 3 & -1 \end{bmatrix}. \tag{2.69}$$

Solution. The matrix $\mathbf{M} - \lambda\mathbf{I}$ is given by

$$\mathbf{M} - \lambda\mathbf{I} = \begin{bmatrix} 1-\lambda & 1 \\ 3 & -1-\lambda \end{bmatrix}.$$

Evaluating the determinant of $\mathbf{M} - \lambda\mathbf{I}$ produces the characteristic polynomial

$$(1-\lambda)(-1-\lambda) - 3. \tag{2.70}$$

Simplifying this polynomial and setting it equal to zero gives

$$\lambda^2 - 4 = 0, \tag{2.71}$$

from which it follows that the eigenvalues of $\mathbf{M}$ are $\lambda_1 = 2$ and $\lambda_2 = -2$.

Once the eigenvalues have been determined, the corresponding eigenvectors are calculated by solving the homogeneous system given by Equation (2.66). Since the matrix $\mathbf{M} - \lambda_i\mathbf{I}$ is singular, its reduced form has at least one row of zeros, so there are infinitely many solutions. An obvious property of Equation (2.65) is that if $\mathbf{V}_i$ is an eigenvector corresponding to the eigenvalue λ_i, then any scalar multiple $a\mathbf{V}_i$ is also an eigenvector. Thus, eigenvectors are always written in terms of an arbitrary constant, which if desired, may be chosen so that the eigenvector has unit length.

Example 2.22. Calculate the eigenvectors of the matrix

$$\mathbf{M} = \begin{bmatrix} 1 & 1 \\ 3 & -1 \end{bmatrix}. \tag{2.72}$$

Solution. In example 2.21, we found that the matrix $\mathbf{M}$ has the eigenvalues $\lambda_1 = 2$ and $\lambda_2 = -2$. Corresponding eigenvectors are found by solving the linear system $(\mathbf{M} - \lambda_i\mathbf{I})\mathbf{V}_i = \mathbf{0}$. For the eigenvalue $\lambda_1 = 2$ we have

$$\begin{bmatrix} -1 & 1 \\ 3 & -3 \end{bmatrix}\mathbf{V}_1 = \begin{bmatrix} 0 \\ 0 \end{bmatrix}, \tag{2.73}$$

and for the eigenvalue $\lambda_2 = -2$ we have

$$\begin{bmatrix} 3 & 1 \\ 3 & 1 \end{bmatrix}\mathbf{V}_2 = \begin{bmatrix} 0 \\ 0 \end{bmatrix}. \tag{2.74}$$

These systems yield the solutions

$$\mathbf{V}_1 = a\begin{bmatrix} 1 \\ 1 \end{bmatrix}$$

$$\mathbf{V}_2 = b\begin{bmatrix} 1 \\ -3 \end{bmatrix}, \tag{2.75}$$

where the scalars a and b are arbitrary nonzero constants.

In general, the eigenvalues of a matrix, given by the roots of its characteristic polynomial, are complex numbers. This means that the corresponding eigenvectors can also have complex entries. A type of matrix that is guaranteed to have real eigenvalues and therefore real eigenvectors, however, is the symmetric matrix.

Definition 2.23. An $n \times n$ matrix $\mathbf{M}$ is *symmetric* if and only if $M_{ij} = M_{ji}$ for all i and j. That is, a matrix whose entries are symmetric about the main diagonal is called symmetric.

The eigenvalues and eigenvectors of symmetric matrices possess the properties given by the following two theorems.

Theorem 2.24. The eigenvalues of a symmetric matrix $\mathbf{M}$ having real entries are real numbers.

Proof. Let λ be an eigenvalue of the matrix $\mathbf{M}$, and let $\mathbf{V}$ be a corresponding eigenvector such that $\mathbf{MV} = \lambda \mathbf{V}$. Multiplying both sides of this equation on the left by the row vector $\overline{\mathbf{V}}^{\mathrm{T}}$ gives us

$$\overline{\mathbf{V}}^{\mathrm{T}}\mathbf{MV} = \overline{\mathbf{V}}^{\mathrm{T}}\lambda\mathbf{V} = \lambda\overline{\mathbf{V}}^{\mathrm{T}}\mathbf{V}, \tag{2.76}$$

where the overbar denotes complex conjugation, which for vectors and matrices is performed componentwise. Since the product of a complex number $a + bi$ and its conjugate $a - bi$ is equal to the real number $a^2 + b^2$, the product $\overline{\mathbf{V}}^{\mathrm{T}}\mathbf{V}$ is a real number. By showing that the product $\overline{\mathbf{V}}^{\mathrm{T}}\mathbf{MV}$ is also a real number, we can conclude that λ is real. We can examine the conjugate of $\overline{\mathbf{V}}^{\mathrm{T}}\mathbf{MV}$ to get

$$\overline{\overline{\mathbf{V}}^{\mathrm{T}}\mathbf{MV}} = \mathbf{V}^{\mathrm{T}}\mathbf{M}\overline{\mathbf{V}}, \tag{2.77}$$

where we have used the fact that $\overline{\mathbf{M}} = \mathbf{M}$ because the matrix $\mathbf{M}$ has real entries. Since the quantity $\overline{\mathbf{V}}^{\mathrm{T}}\mathbf{MV}$ is a 1×1 matrix, it is equal to its own transpose. We may thus write

$$\mathbf{V}^T\mathbf{M}\overline{\mathbf{V}} = \left(\mathbf{V}^T\mathbf{M}\overline{\mathbf{V}}\right)^T = \overline{\mathbf{V}}^T\mathbf{M}^T\mathbf{V}. \tag{2.78}$$

Because the matrix $\mathbf{M}$ is symmetric, $\mathbf{M}^T = \mathbf{M}$, so we now have

$$\overline{\mathbf{V}^T\mathbf{M}\mathbf{V}} = \overline{\mathbf{V}}^T\mathbf{M}\mathbf{V}, \tag{2.79}$$

showing that the quantity $\overline{\mathbf{V}}^T\mathbf{M}\mathbf{V}$ is equal to its own conjugate and is therefore a real number. This proves that the eigenvalue λ must be a real number.

Theorem 2.25. Any two eigenvectors associated with distinct eigenvalues of a symmetric matrix $\mathbf{M}$ are orthogonal.

Proof. Let λ_1 and λ_2 be distinct eigenvalues of the matrix $\mathbf{M}$, and let $\mathbf{V}_1$ and $\mathbf{V}_2$ be the associated eigenvectors. Then we have the equations $\mathbf{M}\mathbf{V}_1 = \lambda_1\mathbf{V}_1$ and $\mathbf{M}\mathbf{V}_2 = \lambda_2\mathbf{V}_2$. We can show that $\lambda_1\mathbf{V}_1^T\mathbf{V}_2 = \lambda_2\mathbf{V}_1^T\mathbf{V}_2$ by writing

$$\begin{aligned}
\lambda_1\mathbf{V}_1^T\mathbf{V}_2 &= \left(\lambda_1\mathbf{V}_1\right)^T\mathbf{V}_2 \\
&= \left(\mathbf{M}\mathbf{V}_1\right)^T\mathbf{V}_2 \\
&= \mathbf{V}_1^T\mathbf{M}\mathbf{V}_2 \\
&= \lambda_2\mathbf{V}_1^T\mathbf{V}_2,
\end{aligned} \tag{2.80}$$

where we have used the fact that $\mathbf{M}^T = \mathbf{M}$. This tells us that

$$\left(\lambda_1 - \lambda_2\right)\mathbf{V}_1^T\mathbf{V}_2 = 0, \tag{2.81}$$

but the eigenvalues λ_1 and λ_2 are distinct, so we must have $\mathbf{V}_1^T\mathbf{V}_2 = 0$. Since this quantity is simply the dot product $\mathbf{V}_1 \cdot \mathbf{V}_2$, the eigenvectors are orthogonal.

2.6 DIAGONALIZATION

Recall that a diagonal matrix has nonzero entries only along the main diagonal. That is, an $n \times n$ matrix $\mathbf{M}$ is a diagonal matrix if $M_{ij} = 0$ whenever $i \neq j$. Given a square matrix $\mathbf{M}$, if we can find a matrix $\mathbf{A}$ such that $\mathbf{A}^{-1}\mathbf{M}\mathbf{A}$ is a diagonal matrix, then we say that $\mathbf{A}$ *diagonalizes* $\mathbf{M}$. Although not true in general, the following theorem states that any $n \times n$ matrix for which we can find n linearly independent eigenvectors can be diagonalized.

Theorem 2.26. Let $\mathbf{M}$ be an $n \times n$ matrix having eigenvalues $\lambda_1, \lambda_2,..., \lambda_n$, and suppose that there exist corresponding eigenvectors $\mathbf{V}_1, \mathbf{V}_2,..., \mathbf{V}_n$ that form a linearly independent set. Then the matrix $\mathbf{A}$ given by

$$\mathbf{A} = [\mathbf{V}_1 \ \mathbf{V}_2 \ \cdots \ \mathbf{V}_n] \tag{2.82}$$

(i.e., the columns of the matrix $\mathbf{A}$ are the eigenvectors $\mathbf{V}_1, \mathbf{V}_2, \ldots, \mathbf{V}_n$) diagonalizes $\mathbf{M}$ and the main diagonal entries of the product $\mathbf{A}^{-1}\mathbf{M}\mathbf{A}$ are the eigenvalues of $\mathbf{M}$:

$$\mathbf{A}^{-1}\mathbf{M}\mathbf{A} = \begin{bmatrix} \lambda_1 & 0 & \cdots & 0 \\ 0 & \lambda_2 & \cdots & 0 \\ \vdots & \vdots & \ddots & \vdots \\ 0 & 0 & \cdots & \lambda_n \end{bmatrix}. \tag{2.83}$$

Conversely, if there exists an invertible matrix $\mathbf{A}$ such that $\mathbf{A}^{-1}\mathbf{M}\mathbf{A}$ is a diagonal matrix, then the columns of $\mathbf{A}$ must be eigenvectors of $\mathbf{M}$ and the main diagonal entries of $\mathbf{A}^{-1}\mathbf{M}\mathbf{A}$ are the corresponding eigenvalues of $\mathbf{M}$.

Proof. We first examine the product $\mathbf{M}\mathbf{A}$. Since the j-th column of $\mathbf{A}$ is the eigenvector $\mathbf{V}_j$, the j-th column of $\mathbf{M}\mathbf{A}$ is equal to $\mathbf{M}\mathbf{V}_j$. Since $\mathbf{V}_j$ is an eigenvector, we have $\mathbf{M}\mathbf{V}_j = \lambda_j\mathbf{V}_j$, so the product $\mathbf{M}\mathbf{A}$ can be written as

$$\mathbf{M}\mathbf{A} = \begin{bmatrix} \lambda_1\mathbf{V}_1 & \lambda_2\mathbf{V}_2 & \cdots & \lambda_n\mathbf{V}_n \end{bmatrix}$$

$$= \begin{bmatrix} \mathbf{V}_1 & \mathbf{V}_2 & \cdots & \mathbf{V}_n \end{bmatrix} \begin{bmatrix} \lambda_1 & 0 & \cdots & 0 \\ 0 & \lambda_2 & \cdots & 0 \\ \vdots & \vdots & \ddots & \vdots \\ 0 & 0 & \cdots & \lambda_n \end{bmatrix}$$

$$= \mathbf{A} \begin{bmatrix} \lambda_1 & 0 & \cdots & 0 \\ 0 & \lambda_2 & \cdots & 0 \\ \vdots & \vdots & \ddots & \vdots \\ 0 & 0 & \cdots & \lambda_n \end{bmatrix}. \tag{2.84}$$

Since the eigenvectors $\mathbf{V}_j$ are linearly independent, the matrix $\mathbf{A}$ is invertible and the product $\mathbf{A}^{-1}\mathbf{M}\mathbf{A}$ can be written as

$$\mathbf{A}^{-1}\mathbf{M}\mathbf{A} = \mathbf{A}^{-1}\mathbf{A}\begin{bmatrix} \lambda_1 & 0 & \cdots & 0 \\ 0 & \lambda_2 & \cdots & 0 \\ \vdots & \vdots & \ddots & \vdots \\ 0 & 0 & \cdots & \lambda_n \end{bmatrix}$$

$$= \begin{bmatrix} \lambda_1 & 0 & \cdots & 0 \\ 0 & \lambda_2 & \cdots & 0 \\ \vdots & \vdots & \ddots & \vdots \\ 0 & 0 & \cdots & \lambda_n \end{bmatrix}. \tag{2.85}$$

Now we prove the converse assertion that any invertible matrix $\mathbf{A}$ that diagonalizes $\mathbf{M}$ must be composed of the eigenvectors of $\mathbf{M}$. Suppose that $\mathbf{D}$ is an $n \times n$ diagonal matrix such that $\mathbf{D} = \mathbf{A}^{-1}\mathbf{M}\mathbf{A}$ for some $n \times n$ matrix $\mathbf{A}$. Then we may write

$$\mathbf{A}\mathbf{D} = \mathbf{M}\mathbf{A}. \tag{2.86}$$

Let $\mathbf{V}_j$ denote the j-th column of $\mathbf{A}$, and let $d_1, d_2, \ldots, d_n$ be the main diagonal entries of $\mathbf{D}$. The product $\mathbf{A}\mathbf{D}$ is given by

$$\mathbf{A}\mathbf{D} = \begin{bmatrix} \mathbf{V}_1 & \mathbf{V}_2 & \cdots & \mathbf{V}_n \end{bmatrix}\begin{bmatrix} d_1 & 0 & \cdots & 0 \\ 0 & d_2 & \cdots & 0 \\ \vdots & \vdots & \ddots & \vdots \\ 0 & 0 & \cdots & d_n \end{bmatrix}$$

$$= \begin{bmatrix} d_1\mathbf{V}_1 & d_2\mathbf{V}_2 & \cdots & d_n\mathbf{V}_n \end{bmatrix}, \tag{2.87}$$

and the product $\mathbf{M}\mathbf{A}$ is given by

$$\mathbf{M}\mathbf{A} = [\mathbf{M}\mathbf{V}_1 \; \mathbf{M}\mathbf{V}_2 \; \ldots \; \mathbf{M}\mathbf{V}_n]. \tag{2.88}$$

Equating the j-th column of $\mathbf{A}\mathbf{D}$ with the j-th column of $\mathbf{M}\mathbf{A}$ demonstrates that $\mathbf{M}\mathbf{V}_j = d_j\mathbf{V}_j$, and thus each $\mathbf{V}_j$ is an eigenvector of $\mathbf{M}$ corresponding to the eigenvalue d_j.

Since the eigenvectors of a symmetric matrix $\mathbf{M}$ are orthogonal, the matrix $\mathbf{A}$ whose columns are composed of unit-length eigenvectors of $\mathbf{M}$ is an orthogonal matrix and therefore satisfies $\mathbf{A}^{-1} = \mathbf{A}^{\mathrm{T}}$. The diagonal matrix $\mathbf{D}$, consisting of the eigenvalues of a symmetric matrix $\mathbf{M}$, can thus be expressed as

$$\mathbf{D} = \mathbf{A}^{\mathrm{T}}\mathbf{M}\mathbf{A}. \tag{2.89}$$

Example 2.27. Find a matrix that diagonalizes the matrix

$$\mathbf{M} = \begin{bmatrix} 2 & 1 & 0 \\ 1 & 1 & 0 \\ 0 & 0 & -1 \end{bmatrix}. \tag{2.90}$$

Solution. The characteristic polynomial for $\mathbf{M}$ is

$$\det(\mathbf{M} - \lambda\mathbf{I}) = -\lambda^3 + 2\lambda^2 + 2\lambda - 1$$

$$= -(\lambda + 1)(\lambda^2 - 3\lambda + 1). \tag{2.91}$$

The roots of this polynomial give us the eigenvalues

$$\lambda_1 = -1$$

$$\lambda_2 = \frac{3 + \sqrt{5}}{2}$$

$$\lambda_3 = \frac{3 - \sqrt{5}}{2}. \tag{2.92}$$

The eigenvector $\mathbf{V}_1$ corresponding to the eigenvalue λ_1 is given by the solution to the homogeneous linear system

$$\begin{bmatrix} 3 & 1 & 0 \\ 1 & 2 & 0 \\ 0 & 0 & 0 \end{bmatrix} \mathbf{V}_1 = \begin{bmatrix} 0 \\ 0 \\ 0 \end{bmatrix}. \tag{2.93}$$

Reducing the coefficient matrix gives us

$$\begin{bmatrix} 1 & 0 & 0 \\ 0 & 1 & 0 \\ 0 & 0 & 0 \end{bmatrix} \mathbf{V}_1 = \begin{bmatrix} 0 \\ 0 \\ 0 \end{bmatrix}, \tag{2.94}$$

and the solution is thus given by

$$\mathbf{V}_1 = a \begin{bmatrix} 0 \\ 0 \\ 1 \end{bmatrix}. \tag{2.95}$$

For the eigenvalue λ_2, we need to solve the system

$$\begin{bmatrix} \dfrac{1-\sqrt{5}}{2} & 1 & 0 \\ 1 & \dfrac{-1-\sqrt{5}}{2} & 0 \\ 0 & 0 & \dfrac{-5-\sqrt{5}}{2} \end{bmatrix} \mathbf{V}_2 = \begin{bmatrix} 0 \\ 0 \\ 0 \end{bmatrix}. \tag{2.96}$$

This reduces to

$$\begin{bmatrix} 1 & \dfrac{-1-\sqrt{5}}{2} & 0 \\ 0 & 0 & 1 \\ 0 & 0 & 0 \end{bmatrix} \mathbf{V}_2 = \begin{bmatrix} 0 \\ 0 \\ 0 \end{bmatrix}, \tag{2.97}$$

and our second eigenvector is given by

$$\mathbf{V}_2 = b \begin{bmatrix} \dfrac{1+\sqrt{5}}{2} \\ 1 \\ 0 \end{bmatrix}. \tag{2.98}$$

Similarly, the eigenvector $\mathbf{V}_3$ is equal to

$$\mathbf{V}_3 = c \begin{bmatrix} \dfrac{1-\sqrt{5}}{2} \\ 1 \\ 0 \end{bmatrix}. \tag{2.99}$$

We choose the constants a, b, and c so that the eigenvectors have unit length. A quick test verifies that the eigenvectors are orthogonal, as expected, since the matrix $\mathbf{M}$ is symmetric. Define the matrix $\mathbf{A}$ as

$$\mathbf{A} = \begin{bmatrix} \dfrac{\mathbf{V}_1}{\|\mathbf{V}_1\|} & \dfrac{\mathbf{V}_2}{\|\mathbf{V}_2\|} & \dfrac{\mathbf{V}_3}{\|\mathbf{V}_3\|} \end{bmatrix}$$

$$\approx \begin{bmatrix} 0 & 0.851 & -0.526 \\ 0 & 0.526 & 0.851 \\ 1 & 0 & 0 \end{bmatrix}. \tag{2.100}$$

A is an orthogonal matrix that diagonalizes **M**:

$$\mathbf{A}^{-1}\mathbf{MA} = \mathbf{A}^{\mathsf{T}}\mathbf{MA} = \begin{bmatrix} -1 & 0 & 0 \\ 0 & \dfrac{3 + \sqrt{5}}{2} & 0 \\ 0 & 0 & \dfrac{3 - \sqrt{5}}{2} \end{bmatrix}. \tag{2.101}$$

CHAPTER 2 SUMMARY

Matrix Products

If **F** is an $n \times m$ matrix and **G** is an $m \times p$ matrix, then the product **FG** is an $n \times p$ matrix whose (i, j) entry is given by

$$\left(\mathbf{FG} \right)_{ij} = \sum_{k=1}^{m} F_{ik} G_{kj}.$$

Determinants

The determinant of an $n \times n$ matrix **M** is given by the formulas

$$\det \mathbf{M} = \sum_{i=1}^{n} (-1)^{i+k} M_{ik} \det \mathbf{M}^{\{i,k\}}$$

and

$$\det \mathbf{M} = \sum_{j=1}^{n} (-1)^{k+j} M_{kj} \det \mathbf{M}^{\{k,j\}}.$$

The determinant of a matrix is given by

$$\begin{vmatrix} a & b \\ c & d \end{vmatrix} = ad - bc.$$

and the determinant of a 3×3 matrix is given by

$$\begin{vmatrix} a_{11} & a_{12} & a_{13} \\ a_{21} & a_{22} & a_{23} \\ a_{31} & a_{32} & a_{33} \end{vmatrix} = a_{11}\left(a_{22}a_{33} - a_{23}a_{32}\right) - a_{12}\left(a_{21}a_{33} - a_{23}a_{31}\right) + a_{13}\left(a_{21}a_{32} - a_{22}a_{31}\right).$$

Matrix Inverses

An $n \times n$ matrix $\mathbf{M}$ is invertible if and only if the columns of $\mathbf{M}$ form a linearly independent set. Equivalently, $\mathbf{M}$ is invertible if and only if det $\mathbf{M} \neq 0$.

The entries of the inverse $\mathbf{G}$ of an $n \times n$ matrix $\mathbf{F}$ can be calculated by using the explicit formula

$$\mathbf{G}_{ij} = \left(-1\right)^{i+j} \frac{\det \mathbf{F}^{\{j,i\}}}{\det \mathbf{F}}.$$

Using this formula, the inverse of a 2×2 matrix $\mathbf{A}$ is given by

$$\mathbf{A}^{-1} = \frac{1}{\det \mathbf{A}} \begin{bmatrix} A_{22} & -A_{12} \\ -A_{21} & A_{11} \end{bmatrix}$$

and the inverse of a 3×3 matrix $\mathbf{B}$ is given by

$$\mathbf{B}^{-1} = \frac{1}{\det \mathbf{B}} \begin{bmatrix} B_{22}B_{33} - B_{23}B_{32} & B_{13}B_{32} - B_{12}B_{33} & B_{12}B_{23} - B_{13}B_{22} \\ B_{23}B_{31} - B_{21}B_{33} & B_{11}B_{33} - B_{13}B_{31} & B_{13}B_{21} - B_{11}B_{23} \\ B_{21}B_{32} - B_{22}B_{31} & B_{12}B_{31} - B_{11}B_{32} & B_{11}B_{22} - B_{12}B_{21} \end{bmatrix}.$$

Eigenvalues and Eigenvectors

The eigenvalues of an $n \times n$ matrix $\mathbf{M}$ are equal to the roots of the characteristic polynomial given by

$$\det(\mathbf{M} - \lambda \mathbf{I}).$$

An eigenvector $\mathbf{V}$ associated with the eigenvalue λ of the matrix $\mathbf{M}$ is given by the solution to the homogeneous linear system

$$(\mathbf{M} - \lambda \mathbf{I})\mathbf{V} = \mathbf{0}.$$

The eigenvalues of a real symmetric matrix are real, and the eigenvectors corresponding to distinct eigenvalues of a real symmetric matrix are orthogonal.

Diagonalization

If $\mathbf{V}_1, \mathbf{V}_2, \ldots, \mathbf{V}_n$ are linearly independent eigenvectors of an $n \times n$ matrix $\mathbf{M}$, then the matrix $\mathbf{A}$ given by

$$\mathbf{A} = [\mathbf{V}_1 \ \mathbf{V}_2 \ \cdots \ \mathbf{V}_n]$$

diagonalizes $\mathbf{M}$, meaning that

$$\mathbf{A}^{-1}\mathbf{M}\mathbf{A} = \begin{bmatrix} \lambda_1 & 0 & \cdots & 0 \\ 0 & \lambda_2 & \cdots & 0 \\ \vdots & \vdots & \ddots & \vdots \\ 0 & 0 & \cdots & \lambda_3 \end{bmatrix},$$

where $\lambda_1, \lambda_2,..., \lambda_n$ are the eigenvalues of $\mathbf{M}$.

EXERCISES FOR CHAPTER 2

1. Calculate the determinants of the following matrices.

(a) $\begin{bmatrix} 2 & 7 \\ -3 & \frac{1}{2} \end{bmatrix}$

(b) $\begin{bmatrix} 0 & 0 & 1 \\ 0 & 1 & 0 \\ 1 & 0 & 0 \end{bmatrix}$

(c) $\begin{bmatrix} \frac{1}{2} & \frac{\sqrt{3}}{2} & 0 \\ -\frac{\sqrt{3}}{2} & \frac{1}{2} & 0 \\ 0 & 0 & 1 \end{bmatrix}$

(d) $\begin{bmatrix} 5 & 7 & 1 \\ 17 & 2 & 64 \\ 10 & 14 & 2 \end{bmatrix}$

2. Calculate the inverses of the following matrices.

(a) $\begin{bmatrix} 2 & 0 & 0 \\ 0 & 3 & 0 \\ 0 & 0 & 4 \end{bmatrix}$

(b) $\begin{bmatrix} 1 & 0 & 0 \\ 0 & 2 & 2 \\ 3 & 0 & 8 \end{bmatrix}$

(c) $\begin{bmatrix} \cos\theta & 0 & -\sin\theta \\ 0 & 1 & 0 \\ \sin\theta & 0 & \cos\theta \end{bmatrix}$

(d) $\begin{bmatrix} 1 & 0 & 0 & 4 \\ 0 & 1 & 0 & 3 \\ 0 & 0 & 1 & 7 \\ 0 & 0 & 0 & 1 \end{bmatrix}$

3. Solve the following homogeneous linear system.

$$4x + 3y + 2z = 0$$

$$x - y - 3z = 0$$

$$2x + 3y + 4z = 0$$

4. Calculate the eigenvalues of the following matrix.

$$\begin{bmatrix} 2 & 0 & 0 \\ 5 & 2 & 3 \\ -4 & 3 & 2 \end{bmatrix}$$

5. Let $\mathbf{M}$ be an $n \times n$ matrix whose rows are given by the vectors $\mathbf{R}_1^T, \mathbf{R}_2^T, \ldots, \mathbf{R}_n^T$. Prove that if the rows of $\mathbf{M}$ form a linearly independent set, then the rows of the matrix $\mathbf{EM}$, where $\mathbf{E}$ is an elementary matrix, also form a linearly independent set.

6. An *upper triangular* matrix $\mathbf{M}$ is one for which $M_{ij} = 0$ whenever $i > j$. That is, all entries below the main diagonal are zero. Prove that the determinant of an upper triangular matrix is equal to the product of the entries on the main diagonal.

7. Let $\mathbf{D}$ be an $n \times n$ diagonal matrix whose main diagonal entries are $d_1, d_2, \ldots, d_n$:

$$\mathbf{D} = \begin{bmatrix} d_1 & 0 & \cdots & 0 \\ 0 & d_2 & \cdots & 0 \\ \vdots & \vdots & \ddots & \vdots \\ 0 & 0 & \cdots & d_n \end{bmatrix}.$$

Show that the inverse of $\mathbf{D}$ is also a diagonal matrix and that its main diagonal entries are given by $1/d_1, 1/d_2, \ldots, 1/d_n$.

8. Implement a C++ class that encapsulates a 3×3 matrix. The class should possess storage for the nine entries of the matrix. In addition to the default constructor, which should not perform any initialization, the class should have a constructor that takes nine floating-point numbers as arguments and initializes the matrix's entries to those values. The class should also include overloaded operators for addition, subtraction, multiplication, and division by scalars; multiplication by another 3×3 matrix; and multiplication by a 3D vector object (see Chapter 1, Exercise 4). Provide a function that initializes a matrix to the identity. Finally, write functions that calculate the determinant of a 3×3 matrix and calculate the inverse of a 3×3 matrix.

3 Transforms

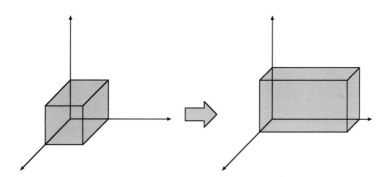

Throughout 3D game development, it is often necessary to transform a set of vectors in some way. Common transformations include translations, scales, and rotations. The translation of a set of points is performed by simply adding an offset vector to each point. Uniform scales (i.e., scales that affect all coordinates of a vector equally) can be accomplished through scalar multiplication. Nonuniform scales, rotations, and more complex transforms require the use of matrix multiplication.

3.1 GENERAL TRANSFORMS

An invertible $n \times n$ matrix $\mathbf{M}$ can be generally regarded as a transformation from one coordinate system to another. The columns of $\mathbf{M}$ give the images to which the principal axes of the original system are mapped in the new system. For instance, suppose that $\mathbf{M}$ is an invertible 3×3 matrix. When $\mathbf{M}$ operates on the vectors $\langle 1, 0, 0 \rangle$, $\langle 0, 1, 0 \rangle$, and $\langle 0, 0, 1 \rangle$, we have

$$\begin{bmatrix} M_{11} & M_{12} & M_{13} \\ M_{21} & M_{22} & M_{23} \\ M_{31} & M_{32} & M_{33} \end{bmatrix} \begin{bmatrix} 1 \\ 0 \\ 0 \end{bmatrix} = \begin{bmatrix} M_{11} \\ M_{21} \\ M_{31} \end{bmatrix}$$

$$\begin{bmatrix} M_{11} & M_{12} & M_{13} \\ M_{21} & M_{22} & M_{23} \\ M_{31} & M_{32} & M_{33} \end{bmatrix} \begin{bmatrix} 0 \\ 1 \\ 0 \end{bmatrix} = \begin{bmatrix} M_{12} \\ M_{22} \\ M_{32} \end{bmatrix}$$

$$\begin{bmatrix} M_{11} & M_{12} & M_{13} \\ M_{21} & M_{22} & M_{23} \\ M_{31} & M_{32} & M_{33} \end{bmatrix} \begin{bmatrix} 0 \\ 0 \\ 1 \end{bmatrix} = \begin{bmatrix} M_{13} \\ M_{23} \\ M_{33} \end{bmatrix}. \tag{3.1}$$

Similarly, the columns of $\mathbf{M}^{-1}$ give the images to which the principal axes of the new system are mapped in the original system. Thus, given any arbitrary linearly independent vectors $\mathbf{U}$, $\mathbf{V}$, and $\mathbf{W}$, we can construct a transformation matrix that maps these vectors to the vectors $\langle 1, 0, 0 \rangle$, $\langle 0, 1, 0 \rangle$, and $\langle 0, 0, 1 \rangle$. As shown below, the inverse of the matrix whose columns are given by $\mathbf{U}$, $\mathbf{V}$, and $\mathbf{W}$ has this property.

$$\begin{bmatrix} U_x & V_x & W_x \\ U_y & V_y & W_y \\ U_z & V_z & W_z \end{bmatrix}^{-1} \begin{bmatrix} U_x \\ U_y \\ U_z \end{bmatrix} = \begin{bmatrix} 1 \\ 0 \\ 0 \end{bmatrix}$$

$$\begin{bmatrix} U_x & V_x & W_x \\ U_y & V_y & W_y \\ U_z & V_z & W_z \end{bmatrix}^{-1} \begin{bmatrix} V_x \\ V_y \\ V_z \end{bmatrix} = \begin{bmatrix} 0 \\ 1 \\ 0 \end{bmatrix}$$

$$\begin{bmatrix} U_x & V_x & W_x \\ U_y & V_y & W_y \\ U_z & V_z & W_z \end{bmatrix}^{-1} \begin{bmatrix} W_x \\ W_y \\ W_z \end{bmatrix} = \begin{bmatrix} 0 \\ 0 \\ 1 \end{bmatrix}. \tag{3.2}$$

Multiple transforms can be concatenated and represented by a single matrix by multiplying the matrices together. Suppose that we wish to transform an object first using a matrix $\mathbf{M}$ and then using a second matrix $\mathbf{G}$. Because matrix multiplication is associative, $\mathbf{G}(\mathbf{MP}) = (\mathbf{GM})\mathbf{P}$ for any vector $\mathbf{P}$, so we can simply store the product $\mathbf{GM}$ as the object's transform. This allows us to apply an unlimited number of transformations to a vertex list without incurring any additional storage or computational overhead.

3.1.1 ORTHOGONAL MATRICES

An orthogonal matrix is one whose inverse is equal to its transpose.

Definition 3.1. An invertible $n \times n$ matrix $\mathbf{M}$ is called *orthogonal* if and only if $\mathbf{M}^{-1} = \mathbf{M}^{\mathsf{T}}$.

As the following theorem demonstrates, any matrix whose columns form an orthonormal set of vectors is orthogonal.

Theorem 3.2. If the vectors $\mathbf{V}_1, \mathbf{V}_2, \ldots, \mathbf{V}_n$ form an orthonormal set, then the $n \times n$ matrix constructed by setting the j-th column equal to $\mathbf{V}_j$ for all $1 \le j \le n$ is orthogonal.

Proof. Suppose that the vectors $\mathbf{V}_1, \mathbf{V}_2, \ldots, \mathbf{V}_n$ form an orthonormal set. Let $\mathbf{M}$ be the $n \times n$ matrix whose columns are given by the $\mathbf{V}_j$'s. Since the $\mathbf{V}_j$'s are orthonormal, $\mathbf{V}_i \cdot \mathbf{V}_j = \delta_{ij}$, where δ_{ij} is the Kronecker delta symbol. Since the (i, j) entry of the matrix product $\mathbf{M}^{\mathsf{T}}\mathbf{M}$ is equal to the dot product $\mathbf{V}_i \cdot \mathbf{V}_j$ we have $\mathbf{M}^{\mathsf{T}}\mathbf{M} = \mathbf{I}$. Therefore, $\mathbf{M}^{\mathsf{T}} = \mathbf{M}^{-1}$.

Orthogonal matrices also possess the property in which they preserve lengths and angles when they are used to transform vectors. A matrix $\mathbf{M}$ preserves length if for any vector $\mathbf{P}$ we have

$$\|\mathbf{MP}\| = \|\mathbf{P}\|. \tag{3.3}$$

A matrix that preserves lengths also preserves angles if for any two vectors $\mathbf{P}_1$ and $\mathbf{P}_2$ we have

$$(\mathbf{MP}_1) \cdot (\mathbf{MP}_2) = \mathbf{P}_1 \cdot \mathbf{P}_2. \tag{3.4}$$

The following theorem proves that an orthogonal matrix satisfies Equations (3.3) and (3.4).

Theorem 3.3. If the $n \times n$ matrix $\mathbf{M}$ is orthogonal, then $\mathbf{M}$ preserves lengths and angles.

Proof. Let $\mathbf{M}$ be orthogonal. We will first show that the dot product between two vectors $\mathbf{P}_1$ and $\mathbf{P}_2$ is preserved by a transformation by $\mathbf{M}$ and then use that result to show that $\mathbf{M}$ preserves lengths. Examining the dot product between the transformed vectors gives us

$$(\mathbf{MP}_1) \cdot (\mathbf{MP}_2) = (\mathbf{MP}_1)^{\mathrm{T}} \mathbf{MP}_2 = \mathbf{P}_1^{\mathrm{T}} \mathbf{M}^{\mathrm{T}} \mathbf{MP}_2. \tag{3.5}$$

Since $\mathbf{M}$ is orthogonal, $\mathbf{M}^{-1} = \mathbf{M}^{\mathrm{T}}$, so

$$\mathbf{P}_1^{\mathrm{T}} \mathbf{M}^{\mathrm{T}} \mathbf{MP}_2 = \mathbf{P}_1^{\mathrm{T}} \mathbf{P}_2 = \mathbf{P}_1 \cdot \mathbf{P}_2. \tag{3.6}$$

This also implies that the length of a vector $\mathbf{P}$ is preserved when transformed by the matrix $\mathbf{M}$ since $\|\mathbf{P}\|^2 = \mathbf{P} \cdot \mathbf{P}$.

Since orthogonal matrices preserve lengths and angles, they preserve the overall structure of a coordinate system. Orthogonal matrices can thus represent only combinations of rotations and reflections. Rotations are discussed in detail in Section 3.3. *Reflection* refers to the operation performed when points are mirrored in a certain direction. For example, the matrix

$$\begin{bmatrix} 1 & 0 & 0 \\ 0 & 1 & 0 \\ 0 & 0 & -1 \end{bmatrix} \tag{3.7}$$

reflects the z-coordinate of a point across the x-y plane.

3.1.2 HANDEDNESS

In three dimensions, a basis $\mathcal{B}$ for a coordinate system given by the 3D vectors $\mathbf{V}_1$, $\mathbf{V}_2$, and $\mathbf{V}_3$ possesses a property called *handedness*. A right-handed basis is one for which $(\mathbf{V}_1 \times \mathbf{V}_2) \cdot \mathbf{V}_3 > 0$. That is, in a right-handed coordinate system, the direction in which the cross product between $\mathbf{V}_1$ and $\mathbf{V}_2$ points (which follows the right hand rule) forms an acute angle with the direction in which $\mathbf{V}_3$ points. If $\mathcal{B}$ is an orthonormal right-handed basis, we have $\mathbf{V}_1 \times \mathbf{V}_2 = \mathbf{V}_3$. If $(\mathbf{V}_1 \times \mathbf{V}_2) \cdot \mathbf{V}_3 < 0$, then the basis $\mathcal{B}$ is left-handed.

Performing an odd number of reflections reverses handedness. An even number of reflections is always equivalent to a rotation, so any series of reflections can always be regarded as a single rotation followed by at most one reflection. The existence of a reflection within a 3×3 matrix can be detected by examining the determinant. If the determinant of a 3×3 matrix $\mathbf{M}$ is negative, then a reflection is present, and $\mathbf{M}$ reverses the handedness of any set of basis vectors transformed by it. If the determinant is positive, then $\mathbf{M}$ preserves handedness.

An orthogonal matrix $\mathbf{M}$ can only have a determinant of 1 or -1. If $\det \mathbf{M} = 1$, the matrix $\mathbf{M}$ represents a pure rotation. If $\det \mathbf{M} = -1$, then the matrix $\mathbf{M}$ represents a rotation followed by a reflection.

3.2 SCALING TRANSFORMS

To scale a vector $\mathbf{P}$ by a factor of a, we simply calculate $\mathbf{P}' = a\mathbf{P}$. In three dimensions, this operation can also be expressed as the matrix product

$$\mathbf{P}' = \begin{bmatrix} a & 0 & 0 \\ 0 & a & 0 \\ 0 & 0 & a \end{bmatrix} \begin{bmatrix} P_x \\ P_y \\ P_z \end{bmatrix}. \tag{3.8}$$

This is called a *uniform* scale. If we wish to scale a vector by different amounts along the x-, y-, and z-axes, as shown in Figure 3.1, then we can use a matrix that is similar to the uniform scale matrix but whose diagonal entries are not necessarily all equal. This is called a *nonuniform* scale and can be expressed as the matrix product

$$\mathbf{P}' = \begin{bmatrix} a & 0 & 0 \\ 0 & b & 0 \\ 0 & 0 & c \end{bmatrix} \begin{bmatrix} P_x \\ P_y \\ P_z \end{bmatrix}. \tag{3.9}$$

A slightly more complex scaling operation that one may wish to perform is a nonuniform scale that is applied along three arbitrary axes. Suppose that we want to scale by a factor a along the axis $\mathbf{U}$, by a factor b along the axis $\mathbf{V}$, and

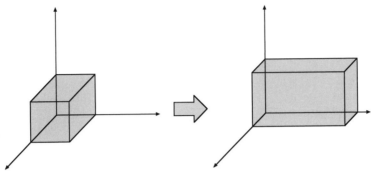

FIGURE *Nonuniform scaling.*
3.1

by a factor c along the axis **W**. Then we can transform from the (**U**, **V**, **W**) coordinate system to the (**i**, **j**, **k**) coordinate system, apply the scaling operation in this system using Equation (3.9), and then transform back into the (**U**, **V**, **W**) coordinate system. This gives us the following matrix product.

$$\mathbf{P}' = \begin{bmatrix} U_x & V_x & W_x \\ U_y & V_y & W_y \\ U_z & V_z & W_z \end{bmatrix} \begin{bmatrix} a & 0 & 0 \\ 0 & b & 0 \\ 0 & 0 & c \end{bmatrix} \begin{bmatrix} U_x & V_x & W_x \\ U_y & V_y & W_y \\ U_z & V_z & W_z \end{bmatrix}^{-1} \begin{bmatrix} P_x \\ P_y \\ P_z \end{bmatrix} \tag{3.10}$$

3.3 ROTATION TRANSFORMS

We can find 3×3 matrices that rotate a coordinate system through an angle θ about the x-, y-, or z-axis without much difficulty. We consider a rotation by a positive angle about the axis **A** to be that which performs a counterclockwise rotation when the axis **A** is pointing toward us.

First, we will find a general formula for rotations in two dimensions. As shown in Figure 3.2, we can perform a 90-degree counterclockwise rotation of a two-dimensional (2D) vector **P** in the x-y plane by exchanging the x- and y-coordinates and negating the new x-coordinate. Calling the rotated vector **Q**, we have $\mathbf{Q} = \langle -P_y, P_x \rangle$. The vectors **P** and **Q** form an orthogonal basis for the x-y plane. We can therefore express any vector in the x-y plane as a linear combination of these two vectors. In particular, as shown in figure 3.3, any 2D vector **P'** that results from the rotation of the vector **P** through an angle θ can be expressed in terms of its components that are parallel to **P** and **Q**. Basic trigonometry lets us write

$$\mathbf{P}' = \mathbf{P} \cos \theta + \mathbf{Q} \sin \theta. \tag{3.11}$$

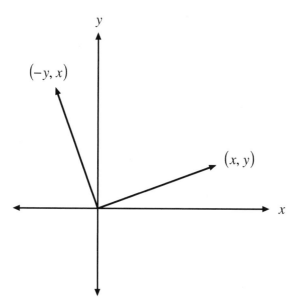

FIGURE   *Rotation by 90 degrees in the x-y plane.*
3.2

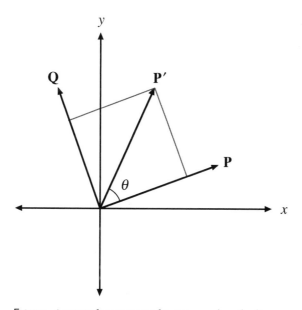

FIGURE   *A rotated vector can be expressed as the linear combination of the original vector*
3.3   *and the 90-degree counterclockwise rotation of the original vector.*

This gives us the following expressions for the components of $\mathbf{P}'$.

$$P'_x = P_x \cos\theta - P_y \sin\theta$$

$$P'_y = P_y \cos\theta + P_x \sin\theta \qquad (3.12)$$

We can rewrite this in matrix form as follows.

$$\mathbf{P}' = \begin{bmatrix} \cos\theta & -\sin\theta \\ \sin\theta & \cos\theta \end{bmatrix} \mathbf{P} \qquad (3.13)$$

The 2D rotation matrix in Equation (3.13) can be extended to a rotation about the z-axis in three dimensions by taking the third row and column from the identity matrix. This ensures that the z-coordinate of a vector remains fixed during a rotation about the z-axis, as we would expect. Thus, the matrix $\mathbf{R}_z(\theta)$, which performs a rotation through the angle θ about the z-axis, is given by

$$\mathbf{R}_z(\theta) = \begin{bmatrix} \cos\theta & -\sin\theta & 0 \\ \sin\theta & \cos\theta & 0 \\ 0 & 0 & 1 \end{bmatrix}. \qquad (3.14)$$

Similarly, we can derive the following 3×3 matrices $\mathbf{R}_x(\theta)$ and $\mathbf{R}_y(\theta)$, which perform rotations through an angle θ about the x- and y-axes, respectively.

$$\mathbf{R}_x(\theta) = \begin{bmatrix} 1 & 0 & 0 \\ 0 & \cos\theta & -\sin\theta \\ 0 & \sin\theta & \cos\theta \end{bmatrix}$$

$$\mathbf{R}_y(\theta) = \begin{bmatrix} \cos\theta & 0 & \sin\theta \\ 0 & 1 & 0 \\ -\sin\theta & 0 & \cos\theta \end{bmatrix} \qquad (3.15)$$

3.3.1 ROTATION ABOUT AN ARBITRARY AXIS

Suppose that we wish to rotate a vector $\mathbf{P}$ through an angle θ about an arbitrary axis whose direction is represented by a unit vector $\mathbf{A}$. We can decompose the vector $\mathbf{P}$ into components that are parallel to $\mathbf{A}$ and perpendicular to $\mathbf{A}$, as shown in Figure 3.4. Since the parallel component (the projection of $\mathbf{P}$ onto $\mathbf{A}$) remains unchanged during the rotation, we can reduce the problem to that of rotating the perpendicular component of $\mathbf{P}$ about $\mathbf{A}$.

Since $\mathbf{A}$ is a unit vector, we have the following simplified formula for the projection of $\mathbf{P}$ onto $\mathbf{A}$.

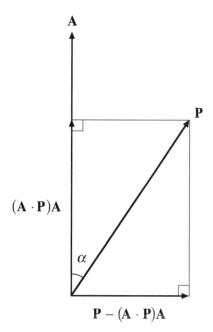

$(\mathbf{A} \cdot \mathbf{P})\mathbf{A}$

α

$\mathbf{P} - (\mathbf{A} \cdot \mathbf{P})\mathbf{A}$

FIGURE *Rotation about an arbitrary axis.*
3.4

$$\operatorname{proj}_{\mathbf{A}} \mathbf{P} = (\mathbf{A} \cdot \mathbf{P})\mathbf{A} \tag{3.16}$$

The component of **P** that is perpendicular to **A** is then given by

$$\operatorname{perp}_{\mathbf{A}} \mathbf{P} = \mathbf{P} - (\mathbf{A} \cdot \mathbf{P})\mathbf{A}. \tag{3.17}$$

Once we rotate this perpendicular component about **A**, we will add the constant parallel component given by Equation (3.16) to arrive at our final answer.

The rotation of the perpendicular component takes place in the plane perpendicular to the axis **A**. As before, we express the rotated vector as a linear combination of $\operatorname{perp}_{\mathbf{A}} \mathbf{P}$ and the vector that results from a 90-degree counterclockwise rotation of $\operatorname{perp}_{\mathbf{A}} \mathbf{P}$ about **A**. Fortunately, such an expression is easy to find. Let α be the angle between the original vector **P** and the axis **A**. Note that the length of $\operatorname{perp}_{\mathbf{A}} \mathbf{P}$ is equal to $\|\mathbf{P}\| \sin \alpha$ because it forms the side opposite the angle α shown in Figure 3.4. A vector of the same length that points in the direction that we want is given by $\mathbf{A} \times \mathbf{P}$.

We can now express the rotation of $\operatorname{perp}_{\mathbf{A}} \mathbf{P}$ through an angle θ as

$$\left[\mathbf{P} - (\mathbf{A} \cdot \mathbf{P})\mathbf{A} \right] \cos \theta + (\mathbf{A} \times \mathbf{P}) \sin \theta. \tag{3.18}$$

Adding $\text{proj}_\mathbf{A} \, \mathbf{P}$ to this gives us the following expression for the rotation of the original vector $\mathbf{P}$ about the axis $\mathbf{A}$.

$$\mathbf{P}' = \mathbf{P}\cos\theta + (\mathbf{A} \times \mathbf{P})\sin\theta + \mathbf{A}(\mathbf{A} \cdot \mathbf{P})(1 - \cos\theta) \tag{3.19}$$

Replacing $\mathbf{A} \times \mathbf{P}$ and $\mathbf{A}(\mathbf{A} \cdot \mathbf{P})$ in Equation (3.19) with their matrix equivalents given by Equations (1.25) and (1.20), respectively, we have

$$\mathbf{P}' = \begin{bmatrix} 1 & 0 & 0 \\ 0 & 1 & 0 \\ 0 & 0 & 1 \end{bmatrix} \mathbf{P}\cos\theta + \begin{bmatrix} 0 & -A_z & A_y \\ A_z & 0 & -A_x \\ -A_y & A_x & 0 \end{bmatrix} \mathbf{P}\sin\theta$$

$$+ \begin{bmatrix} A_x^2 & A_xA_y & A_xA_z \\ A_xA_y & A_y^2 & A_yA_z \\ A_xA_z & A_yA_z & A_z^2 \end{bmatrix} \mathbf{P}(1 - \cos\theta). \tag{3.20}$$

Combining these terms and setting $C = \cos\theta$ and $S = \sin\theta$ gives us the following formula for the matrix $\mathbf{R}_\mathbf{A}(\theta)$, which rotates a vector through an angle θ about the axis $\mathbf{A}$.

$$\mathbf{R}_\mathbf{A}(\theta) = \begin{bmatrix} C + A_x^2(1 - C) & A_xA_y(1 - C) - A_zS & A_xA_z(1 - C) + A_yS \\ A_xA_y(1 - C) + A_zS & C + A_y^2(1 - C) & A_yA_z(1 - C) - A_xS \\ A_xA_z(1 - C) - A_yS & A_yA_z(1 - C) + A_xS & C + A_z^2(1 - C) \end{bmatrix} \tag{3.21}$$

3.4 HOMOGENEOUS COORDINATES

Up to this point, we have dealt only with transforms which can be expressed as the operation of a 3×3 matrix on a three-dimensional vector. A series of such transforms could be represented by a single 3×3 matrix equal to the product of the matrices corresponding to the individual transforms. An important transform that has been left out is the translation operation. A coordinate system is translated in space without otherwise affecting the orientation or scale of the axes by simply adding an offset vector. This operation cannot be expressed in terms of a 3×3 matrix. Thus, to transform a point $\mathbf{P}$ from one coordinate system to another, we usually find ourselves performing the operation

$$\mathbf{P}' = \mathbf{M}\mathbf{P} + \mathbf{T}, \tag{3.22}$$

where $\mathbf{M}$ is some invertible 3×3 matrix and $\mathbf{T}$ is a 3D translation vector. Performing two operations of the type shown in Equation (3.22) results in the rather messy equation

$$\mathbf{P}' = \mathbf{M}_2\big(\mathbf{M}_1\mathbf{P} + \mathbf{T}_1\big) + \mathbf{T}_2$$

$$= \big(\mathbf{M}_2\mathbf{M}_1\big)\mathbf{P} + \mathbf{M}_2\mathbf{T}_1 + \mathbf{T}_2, \tag{3.23}$$

requiring that we keep track of the matrix component $\mathbf{M}_n\mathbf{M}_{n-1}$ as well as the translation component $\mathbf{M}_n\mathbf{T}_{n-1} + \mathbf{T}_n$ at each stage when concatenating n transforms.

3.4.1 FOUR-DIMENSIONAL TRANSFORMS

Fortunately, there is a compact and elegant way to represent these transforms within a single mathematical entity. We can do this by extending our vectors to four dimensions and using 4×4 matrices to transform them. A 3D point $\mathbf{P}$ is extended to four dimensions by setting its fourth coordinate, which we call the w-coordinate, equal to one. We construct a 4×4 transformation matrix $\mathbf{F}$ corresponding to the 3×3 matrix $\mathbf{M}$ and the 3D translation $\mathbf{T}$, as follows.

$$\mathbf{F} = \left[\begin{array}{c|c} \mathbf{M} & \mathbf{T} \\ \hline \mathbf{0} & 1 \end{array}\right] = \left[\begin{array}{ccc|c} M_{11} & M_{12} & M_{13} & T_x \\ M_{21} & M_{22} & M_{23} & T_y \\ M_{31} & M_{32} & M_{33} & T_z \\ \hline 0 & 0 & 0 & 1 \end{array}\right] \tag{3.24}$$

Multiplying this matrix by the vector $\langle P_x, P_y, P_z, 1 \rangle$ transforms the x-, y-, and z-coordinates of the vector in exactly the same way as Equation (3.22) and leaves a one in the w-coordinate. Furthermore, multiplying two transformation matrices of the form shown in Equation (3.24) yields another matrix of the same form that is equivalent to the pair of transforms performed in Equation (3.23).

If we solve Equation (3.22) for $\mathbf{P}$, we have

$$\mathbf{P} = \mathbf{M}^{-1}\mathbf{P}' - \mathbf{M}^{-1}\mathbf{T}. \tag{3.25}$$

We would therefore expect the inverse of the 4×4 matrix $\mathbf{F}$ from Equation (3.24) to be

$$\mathbf{F}^{-1} = \left[\begin{array}{c|c} \mathbf{M}^{-1} & -\mathbf{M}^{-1}\mathbf{T} \\ \hline \mathbf{0} & 1 \end{array}\right] = \left[\begin{array}{ccc|c} M_{11}^{-1} & M_{12}^{-1} & M_{13}^{-1} & -\big(\mathbf{M}^{-1}\mathbf{T}\big)_x \\ M_{21}^{-1} & M_{22}^{-1} & M_{23}^{-1} & -\big(\mathbf{M}^{-1}\mathbf{T}\big)_y \\ M_{31}^{-1} & M_{32}^{-1} & M_{33}^{-1} & -\big(\mathbf{M}^{-1}\mathbf{T}\big)_z \\ \hline 0 & 0 & 0 & 1 \end{array}\right], \tag{3.26}$$

and the following computation verifies that this is true.

$$FF^{-1} = \begin{bmatrix} \mathbf{M} & \mathbf{T} \\ \mathbf{0} & 1 \end{bmatrix} \begin{bmatrix} \mathbf{M}^{-1} & -\mathbf{M}^{-1}\mathbf{T} \\ \mathbf{0} & 1 \end{bmatrix}$$

$$= \begin{bmatrix} \mathbf{M}\mathbf{M}^{-1} & \mathbf{M}(-\mathbf{M}^{-1}\mathbf{T}) + \mathbf{T} \\ \mathbf{0} & 1 \end{bmatrix}$$

$$= \begin{bmatrix} \mathbf{I}_3 & \mathbf{0} \\ \mathbf{0} & 1 \end{bmatrix} = \mathbf{I}_4 \tag{3.27}$$

3.4.2 POINTS AND DIRECTIONS

We have now come to a point where it is necessary to make a distinction between vectors that represent points in three-dimensional space and vectors that represent directions in three-dimensional space. Unlike points, direction vectors should remain invariant under translation. For example, shifting a coordinate system, as shown in Figure 3.5, should not affect the direction in which a vector representing the tangent to a curve points.

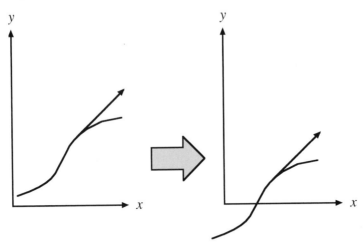

FIGURE *Translating a coordinate system does not alter the direction in which a tangent*
3.5 *vector points.*

To transform direction vectors using the same 4 × 4 transformation matrices that we use to transform points, we extend direction vectors to four dimensions by setting the w-coordinate to zero. This nullifies the fourth column of the matrix **F** in Equation (3.24), leaving only the upper left 3 × 3 portion of the matrix to affect the direction vector.

The difference between two points **P** and **Q** having a w-coordinate of one results in a direction vector **Q** – **P** having a w-coordinate of zero. This makes sense because $\mathbf{Q} - \mathbf{P}$ represents the direction pointing from $\mathbf{P}$ to $\mathbf{Q}$, which we would expect not to be affected by a translation.

3.4.3 GEOMETRICAL INTERPRETATION OF THE W-COORDINATE

The w-coordinates of the four-dimensional (4D) vectors with which we have been working so far have a meaning that goes beyond their utility during transformations using 4×4 matrices. Before, we extended a three-dimensional point to four-dimensional space by adding a one in the w-coordinate position. Now, we define a mapping that works in the reverse direction. Suppose we have a 4D point $\mathbf{P} = \langle x, y, z, w \rangle$ whose w-coordinate is not zero. Then we define the image of $\mathbf{P}$ in 3D space, which we denote by $\tilde{\mathbf{P}}$ as the projection of $\mathbf{P}$ into the three-dimensional space in which $w = 1$ using the formula

$$\tilde{\mathbf{P}} = \left\langle \frac{x}{w}, \frac{y}{w}, \frac{z}{w} \right\rangle. \tag{3.28}$$

As shown in Figure 3.6 (but without the z-axis to make visualization easier), the 3D point $\tilde{\mathbf{P}}$ corresponds to the point where the line connecting the point $\mathbf{P}$ to the origin intersects the space where $w = 1$. Thus, any scalar multiple of the 4D vector $\mathbf{P}$ represents the same point in three-dimensional space. The importance of this projection in 3D graphics is discussed in detail in Section 4.5.

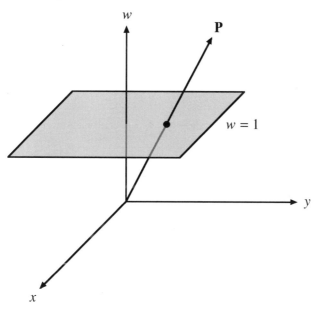

FIGURE *A 4D point* **P** *is projected into three-dimensional space by calculating the point where*
3.6 *the line connecting the point to the origin intersects the space where* w = 1.

3.5 TRANSFORMING NORMAL VECTORS

In addition to its position in space, a vertex belonging to a polygonal model usually carries additional information about how it fits into the surrounding surface. In particular, a vertex may have a tangent vector and a normal vector associated with it. When we transform a model, we need to transform the vertex positions as well as the associated vectors.

Tangent vectors can often be calculated by taking the difference between one vertex and another, and thus we would expect that a transformed tangent vector could be expressed as the difference between two transformed points. If **M** is a 3×3 matrix with which we transform a vertex position, then the same matrix **M** can be used to correctly transform the tangent vector at that vertex. (We limit ourselves to 3×3 matrices in this section since tangent and normal directions are unaffected by translations.) Some care must be taken when transforming normal vectors, however. Figure 3.7 shows what can happen when a nonorthogonal matrix **M** is used to transform a normal vector **N**. The transformed normal can often end up pointing in a direction that is not perpendicular to the transformed surface.

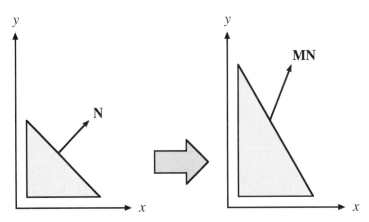

FIGURE *Transforming a normal vector **N** with a nonorthogonal matrix **M**.*
3.7

Since tangents and normals are perpendicular, the tangent vector **T** and the normal vector **N** associated with a vertex must satisfy the equation $\mathbf{N} \cdot \mathbf{T} = 0$. We must also require that this equation be satisfied by the transformed tangent vector **T**′ and the transformed normal vector **N**′. Given a transformation matrix **M**, we know that **T**′ = **MT**. We would like to find the transformation matrix **G** with which the vector **N** should be transformed so that

$$\mathbf{N}' \cdot \mathbf{T}' = (\mathbf{GN}) \cdot (\mathbf{MT}) = 0. \qquad (3.29)$$

A little algebraic manipulation gives us

$$(\mathbf{GN}) \cdot (\mathbf{MT}) = (\mathbf{GN})^{\mathsf{T}} (\mathbf{MT})$$

$$= \mathbf{N}^{\mathsf{T}} \mathbf{G}^{\mathsf{T}} \mathbf{MT}. \qquad (3.30)$$

Since $\mathbf{N}^{\mathsf{T}} \mathbf{T} = 0$ the equation $\mathbf{N}^{\mathsf{T}} \mathbf{G}^{\mathsf{T}} \mathbf{MT} = 0$ is satisfied if $\mathbf{G}^{\mathsf{T}} \mathbf{M} = \mathbf{I}$. We therefore conclude that $\mathbf{G} = (\mathbf{M}^{-1})^{\mathsf{T}}$. This tells us that a normal vector is correctly transformed using the *inverse transpose* of the matrix used to transform points. Vectors that must be transformed in this way are called *covariant*, and vectors that are transformed in the ordinary fashion using the matrix $\mathbf{M}$ (such as points and tangent vectors) are called *contravariant*.

If the matrix $\mathbf{M}$ is orthogonal, then $\mathbf{M}^{-1} = \mathbf{M}^{\mathsf{T}}$, and thus $(\mathbf{M}^{-1})^{\mathsf{T}} = \mathbf{M}$. Therefore, the inverse transpose operation required to transform normal vectors can be avoided when $\mathbf{M}$ is known to be orthogonal, as is the case when $\mathbf{M}$ is equal to one of the rotation matrices $\mathbf{R}_x$, $\mathbf{R}_y$, $\mathbf{R}_z$, or $\mathbf{R}_A$ presented earlier in this chapter.

3.6 QUATERNIONS

A *quaternion* is an alternative mathematical entity that 3D graphics programmers use to represent rotations. The use of quaternions has advantages over the use of rotation matrices in many situations because quaternions require less storage space, concatenation of quaternions requires fewer arithmetic operations, and quaternions are more easily interpolated for producing smooth animation.

3.6.1 QUATERNION MATHEMATICS

The set of quaternions, known by mathematicians as the ring of Hamiltonian quaternions and denoted by $\mathbb{H}$, can be thought of as a four-dimensional vector space for which an element $\mathbf{q}$ has the form

$$\mathbf{q} = \langle w, x, y, z \rangle = w + xi + yj + zk. \qquad (3.31)$$

A quaternion is often written as $\mathbf{q} = s + \mathbf{v}$, where s represents the scalar part corresponding to the w-component of $\mathbf{q}$, and $\mathbf{v}$ represents the vector part corresponding to the x-, y-, and z-components of $\mathbf{q}$.

The set of quaternions is a natural extension of the set of complex numbers. Multiplication of quaternions is defined using the ordinary distributive law and adhering to the following rules when multiplying the "imaginary" components i, j, and k.

$$i^2 = j^2 = k^2 = -1$$

$$ij = -ji = k$$

$$jk = -kj = i$$

$$ki = -ik = j \qquad (3.32)$$

Multiplication of quaternions is not commutative, therefore we must be careful to multiply terms in the correct order. For two quaternions $\mathbf{q}_1 = w_1 + x_1 i + y_1 j + z_1 k$ and $\mathbf{q}_2 = w_2 + x_2 i + y_2 j + z_2 k$, the product $\mathbf{q}_1\mathbf{q}_2$ is given by

$$
\begin{aligned}
\mathbf{q}_1\mathbf{q}_2 = & \left(w_1 w_2 - x_1 x_2 - y_1 y_2 - z_1 z_2\right) \\
& + \left(w_1 x_2 + x_1 w_2 + y_1 z_2 - z_1 y_1\right)i \\
& + \left(w_1 y_2 - x_1 z_2 + y_1 w_2 + z_1 x_2\right)j \\
& + \left(w_1 z_2 + x_1 y_2 - y_1 x_2 + z_1 w_2\right)k.
\end{aligned}
\qquad (3.33)
$$

When written in scalar-vector form, the product of two quaternions $\mathbf{q}_1 = s_1 + \mathbf{v}_1$ and $\mathbf{q}_2 = s_2 + \mathbf{v}_2$ can be written as

$$\mathbf{q}_1\mathbf{q}_2 = s_1 s_2 - \mathbf{v}_1 \cdot \mathbf{v}_2 + s_1\mathbf{v}_2 + s_2\mathbf{v}_1 + \mathbf{v}_1 \times \mathbf{v}_2. \qquad (3.34)$$

Like complex numbers (see appendix A), quaternions have conjugates.

Definition 3.4. The *conjugate* of a quaternion $\mathbf{q} = s + \mathbf{v}$, denoted by $\bar{\mathbf{q}}$, is given by $\bar{\mathbf{q}} = s - \mathbf{v}$.

A short calculation reveals that the product of a quaternion $\mathbf{q}$ and its conjugate $\bar{\mathbf{q}}$ is equal to the dot product of $\mathbf{q}$ with itself, which is also equal to the square of the magnitude of $\mathbf{q}$. That is,

$$\mathbf{q}\bar{\mathbf{q}} = \bar{\mathbf{q}}\mathbf{q} = \mathbf{q} \cdot \mathbf{q} = \|\mathbf{q}\|^2 = q^2. \qquad (3.35)$$

This leads us to a formula for the multiplicative inverse of a quaternion.

Theorem 3.5. The *inverse* of a nonzero quaternion $\mathbf{q}$, denoted by $\mathbf{q}^{-1}$, is given by

$$\mathbf{q}^{-1} = \frac{\bar{\mathbf{q}}}{q^2}. \qquad (3.36)$$

Proof. Applying Equation (3.35), we have

$$\mathbf{q}\mathbf{q}^{-1} = \frac{\mathbf{q}\bar{\mathbf{q}}}{q^2} = \frac{q^2}{q^2} = 1 \tag{3.37}$$

and

$$\mathbf{q}^{-1}\mathbf{q} = \frac{\bar{\mathbf{q}}\mathbf{q}}{q^2} = \frac{q^2}{q^2} = 1, \tag{3.38}$$

thus proving the theorem.

3.6.2 ROTATIONS WITH QUATERNIONS

A rotation in three dimensions can be thought of as a function φ that maps $\mathbb{R}^3$ onto itself. For φ to represent a rotation, it must preserve lengths, angles, and handedness. Length preservation is satisfied if

$$\|\varphi(\mathbf{P})\| = \|\mathbf{P}\|. \tag{3.39}$$

The angle between the line segments connecting the origin to any two points $\mathbf{P}_1$ and $\mathbf{P}_2$ is preserved if

$$\varphi(\mathbf{P}_1) \cdot \varphi(\mathbf{P}_2) = \mathbf{P}_1 \cdot \mathbf{P}_2. \tag{3.40}$$

Finally, handedness is preserved if

$$\varphi(\mathbf{P}_1) \times \varphi(\mathbf{P}_2) = \varphi(\mathbf{P}_1 \times \mathbf{P}_2). \tag{3.41}$$

Extending the function φ to a mapping from $\mathbb{H}$ onto itself by requiring that $\varphi(s + v) = s + \varphi(\mathbf{v})$ allows us to rewrite Equation (3.40) as

$$\varphi(\mathbf{P}_1) \cdot \varphi(\mathbf{P}_2) = \varphi(\mathbf{P}_1 \cdot \mathbf{P}_2). \tag{3.42}$$

Treating $\mathbf{P}_1$ and $\mathbf{P}_2$ as quaternions with zero scalar part enables us to combine Equations (3.41) and (3.42) since $\mathbf{P}_1\mathbf{P}_2 = -\mathbf{P}_1 \cdot \mathbf{P}_2 + \mathbf{P}_1 \times \mathbf{P}_2$. We can therefore write the angle preservation and handedness preservation requirements as the single equation

$$\varphi(\mathbf{P}_1)\varphi(\mathbf{P}_2) = \varphi(\mathbf{P}_1\mathbf{P}_2). \tag{3.43}$$

A function φ that satisfies this equation is called a *homomorphism*.

The class of functions given by

$$\varphi_{\mathbf{q}}(\mathbf{P}) = \mathbf{q}\mathbf{P}\mathbf{q}^{-1}, \tag{3.44}$$

where $\mathbf{q}$ is a nonzero quaternion, satisfies the requirements stated in Equations (3.39) and (3.43), and thus represents a set of rotations. This fact can be proven by first observing that the function $\varphi_{\mathbf{q}}$ preserves lengths because

$$\left\|\varphi_{\mathbf{q}}(\mathbf{P})\right\| = \left\|\mathbf{q}\mathbf{P}\mathbf{q}^{-1}\right\| = \left\|\mathbf{q}\right\|\left\|\mathbf{P}\right\|\left\|\mathbf{q}^{-1}\right\| = \left\|\mathbf{P}\right\|\frac{\left\|\mathbf{q}\right\|\left\|\overline{\mathbf{q}}\right\|}{q^2} = \left\|\mathbf{P}\right\|. \tag{3.45}$$

Furthermore, $\varphi_{\mathbf{q}}$ is a homomorphism since

$$\varphi_{\mathbf{q}}(\mathbf{P}_1)\varphi_{\mathbf{q}}(\mathbf{P}_2) = \mathbf{q}\mathbf{P}_1\mathbf{q}^{-1}\mathbf{q}\mathbf{P}_2\mathbf{q}^{-1} = \mathbf{q}\mathbf{P}_1\mathbf{P}_2\mathbf{q}^{-1} = \varphi_{\mathbf{q}}(\mathbf{P}_1\mathbf{P}_2). \tag{3.46}$$

We now need to find a formula for the quaternion $\mathbf{q}$ corresponding to a rotation through the angle θ about the axis $\mathbf{A}$. A quick calculation shows that $\varphi_{a\mathbf{q}} = \varphi_{\mathbf{q}}$ for any nonzero scalar a, so to keep things as simple as possible, we will concern ourselves only with unit quaternions.

Let $\mathbf{q} = s + \mathbf{v}$ be a unit quaternion. Then $\mathbf{q}^{-1} = s - \mathbf{v}$, and given a point $\mathbf{P}$ we have

$$\begin{aligned}
\mathbf{q}\mathbf{P}\mathbf{q}^{-1} &= (s + \mathbf{v})\mathbf{P}(s - \mathbf{v}) \\
&= (-\mathbf{v} \cdot \mathbf{P} + s\mathbf{P} + \mathbf{v} \times \mathbf{P})(s - \mathbf{v}) \\
&= -s\mathbf{v} \cdot \mathbf{P} + s^2\mathbf{P} + s\mathbf{v} \times \mathbf{P} + (\mathbf{v} \cdot \mathbf{P})\mathbf{v} - s\mathbf{P}\mathbf{v} - (\mathbf{v} \times \mathbf{P})\mathbf{v} \\
&= s^2\mathbf{P} + 2s\mathbf{v} \times \mathbf{P} + (\mathbf{v} \cdot \mathbf{P})\mathbf{v} - \mathbf{v} \times \mathbf{P} \times \mathbf{v}.
\end{aligned} \tag{3.47}$$

After applying Theorem 1.9(f) to the cross product $\mathbf{v} \times \mathbf{P} \times \mathbf{v}$, this becomes

$$\mathbf{q}\mathbf{P}\mathbf{q}^{-1} = (s^2 - \mathbf{v}^2)\mathbf{P} + 2s\mathbf{v} \times \mathbf{P} + 2(\mathbf{v} \cdot \mathbf{P})\mathbf{v}. \tag{3.48}$$

Setting $\mathbf{v} = t\mathbf{A}$, where $\mathbf{A}$ is a unit vector, lets us rewrite this equation as

$$\mathbf{q}\mathbf{P}\mathbf{q}^{-1} = (s^2 - t^2)\mathbf{P} + 2st\mathbf{A} \times \mathbf{P} + 2t^2(\mathbf{A} \cdot \mathbf{P})\mathbf{A}. \tag{3.49}$$

When we compare this to the formula for rotation about an arbitrary axis given in Equation (3.19), we can infer the following equalities.

$$\begin{aligned}
s^2 - t^2 &= \cos\theta \\
2st &= \sin\theta \\
2t^2 &= 1 - \cos\theta
\end{aligned} \tag{3.50}$$

The third equality gives us

$$t = \sqrt{\frac{1 - \cos\theta}{2}} = \sin\frac{\theta}{2}. \tag{3.51}$$

The first and third equalities together tell us that $s^2 + t^2 = 1$, so we must have $s = \cos\frac{\theta}{2}$. (The fact that $\sin 2\theta = 2 \sin\theta \cos\theta$ verifies that the second equality is satisfied by these values for s and t.)

We have now determined that the unit quaternion $\mathbf{q}$ corresponding to a rotation through the angle θ about the axis $\mathbf{A}$ is given by

$$\mathbf{q} = \cos\frac{\theta}{2} + \mathbf{A}\sin\frac{\theta}{2}. \tag{3.52}$$

It should be noted that any scalar multiple of the quaternion $\mathbf{q}$ (in particular, $-\mathbf{q}$) also represents the same rotation since

$$(a\mathbf{q})\mathbf{P}(a\mathbf{q})^{-1} = a\mathbf{q}\mathbf{P}\frac{\mathbf{q}^{-1}}{a} = \mathbf{q}\mathbf{P}\mathbf{q}^{-1}. \tag{3.53}$$

The product of two quaternions $\mathbf{q}_1$ and $\mathbf{q}_2$ also represents a rotation. Specifically, the product $\mathbf{q}_1\mathbf{q}_2$ represents the rotation resulting from first rotating by $\mathbf{q}_2$ and then by $\mathbf{q}_1$. Since

$$\mathbf{q}_1\left(\mathbf{q}_2\mathbf{P}\mathbf{q}_2^{-1}\right)\mathbf{q}_1^{-1} = (\mathbf{q}_1\mathbf{q}_2)\mathbf{P}(\mathbf{q}_1\mathbf{q}_2)^{-1}, \tag{3.54}$$

we can concatenate as many quaternions as we want to produce a single quaternion representing the entire series of rotations. Multiplying two quaternions together requires 16 multiply-add operations, whereas multiplying two 3×3 matrices together requires 27 such operations. Thus, some computational efficiency can be gained by using quaternions in situations in which many rotations may be applied to an object.

It is often necessary to convert a quaternion into the equivalent 3×3 rotation matrix, for instance, to pass the transform for an object to a 3D graphics library. We can determine the formula for the matrix corresponding to the quaternion $\mathbf{q} = s + t\mathbf{A}$ by using Equations (1.25) and (1.20) to write Equation (3.49) in matrix form. (This is nearly identical to the technique used in Section 3.3.1.) This gives us

$$\mathbf{q}\mathbf{P}\mathbf{q}^{-1} = \begin{bmatrix} s^2 - t^2 & 0 & 0 \\ 0 & s^2 - t^2 & 0 \\ 0 & 0 & s^2 - t^2 \end{bmatrix}\mathbf{P} + \begin{bmatrix} 0 & -2stA_z & 2stA_y \\ 2stA_z & 0 & -2stA_x \\ -2stA_y & 2stA_x & 0 \end{bmatrix}\mathbf{P}$$

$$+ \begin{bmatrix} 2t^2A_x^2 & 2t^2A_xA_y & 2t^2A_xA_z \\ 2t^2A_xA_y & 2t^2A_y^2 & 2t^2A_yA_z \\ 2t^2A_xA_z & 2t^2A_yA_z & 2t^2A_z^2 \end{bmatrix}\mathbf{P}. \tag{3.55}$$

Writing the quaternion $\mathbf{q}$ as the four-dimensional vector $\mathbf{q} = \langle w, x, y, z \rangle$, we have $w = s$, $x = tA_x$, $y = tA_y$, and $z = tA_z$. Since $\mathbf{A}$ is a unit vector, $x^2 + y^2 + z^2 = t^2 A^2 = t^2$. Rewriting Equation (3.55) in terms of the components w, x, y, and z gives us

$$\mathbf{qPq}^{-1} = \begin{bmatrix} w^2 - x^2 - y^2 - z^2 & 0 & 0 \\ 0 & w^2 - x^2 - y^2 - z^2 & 0 \\ 0 & 0 & w^2 - x^2 - y^2 - z^2 \end{bmatrix} \mathbf{P}$$

$$+ \begin{bmatrix} 0 & -2wz & 2wy \\ 2wz & 0 & -2wx \\ -2wy & 2wx & 0 \end{bmatrix} \mathbf{P} + \begin{bmatrix} 2x^2 & 2xy & 2xz \\ 2xy & 2y^2 & 2yz \\ 2xz & 2yz & 2z^2 \end{bmatrix} \mathbf{P}. \tag{3.56}$$

Since $\mathbf{q}$ is a unit quaternion, we know that $w^2 + x^2 + y^2 + z^2 = 1$, so we can write

$$w^2 - x^2 - y^2 - z^2 = 1 - 2x^2 - 2y^2 - 2z^2. \tag{3.57}$$

Using this equation and combining the three matrices gives us the following formula for the matrix $\mathbf{R_q}$, the rotation matrix corresponding to the quaternion $\mathbf{q}$.

$$\mathbf{R_q} = \begin{bmatrix} 1 - 2y^2 - 2z^2 & 2xy - 2wz & 2xz + 2wy \\ 2xy + 2wz & 1 - 2x^2 - 2z^2 & 2yz - 2wx \\ 2xz - 2wy & 2yz + 2wx & 1 - 2x^2 - 2y^2 \end{bmatrix} \tag{3.58}$$

3.6.3 SPHERICAL LINEAR INTERPOLATION

Because quaternions are represented by vectors, they are well suited for interpolation. When an object is being animated, interpolation is useful for generating intermediate orientations that fall between precalculated key frames.

The simplest type of interpolation is *linear interpolation*. For two unit quaternions $\mathbf{q}_1$ and $\mathbf{q}_2$, the linearly interpolated quaternion $\mathbf{q}(t)$ is given by

$$\mathbf{q}(t) = (1 - t)\mathbf{q}_1 + t\mathbf{q}_2. \tag{3.59}$$

The function $\mathbf{q}(t)$ changes smoothly along the line segment connecting $\mathbf{q}_1$ and $\mathbf{q}_2$ as t varies from zero to one. As shown in Figure 3.8, $\mathbf{q}(t)$ does not maintain the unit length of $\mathbf{q}_1$ and $\mathbf{q}_2$, but we can renormalize at each point by instead using the function

$$\mathbf{q}(t) = \frac{(1 - t)\mathbf{q}_1 + t\mathbf{q}_2}{\|(1 - t)\mathbf{q}_1 + t\mathbf{q}_2\|}. \tag{3.60}$$

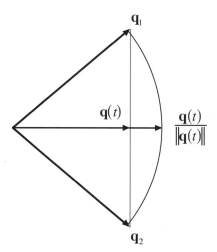

FIGURE Linear interpolation of quaternions.
3.8

Now we have a function that traces out the arc between $\mathbf{q}_1$ and $\mathbf{q}_2$, shown in Figure 3.8 as a two-dimensional cross-section of what is actually occurring on the surface of the four-dimensional unit hypersphere.

Although linear interpolation is efficient, it has the drawback that the function $\mathbf{q}(t)$ given by Equation (3.60) does not trace out the arc between $\mathbf{q}_1$ and $\mathbf{q}_2$ at a constant rate. The graph of $\cos^{-1}(\mathbf{q}(t) \cdot \mathbf{q}_1)$ shown in Figure 3.9 demonstrates that the rate at which the angle between $\mathbf{q}(t)$ and $\mathbf{q}_1$ changes is relatively slow at the endpoints where $t = 0$ and $t = 1$ and is the fastest where $t = \frac{1}{2}$.

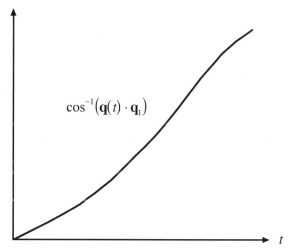

FIGURE Graph of $\cos^{-1}(\mathbf{q}(t) \cdot \mathbf{q}_1)$, where $\mathbf{q}(t)$ is the normalized linear interpolation function
3.9 given by Equation (3.60).

We would like to find a function $\mathbf{q}(t)$ that interpolates the quaternions $\mathbf{q}_1$ and $\mathbf{q}_2$, preserves unit length, and sweeps through the angle between $\mathbf{q}_1$ and $\mathbf{q}_2$ at a constant rate. If $\mathbf{q}_1$ and $\mathbf{q}_2$ are separated by an angle θ, then such a function would generate quaternions forming the angle θt between $\mathbf{q}(t)$ and $\mathbf{q}_1$ as t varies from zero to one.

Figure 3.10 shows the quaternion $\mathbf{q}(t)$ lying on the arc connecting $\mathbf{q}_1$ and $\mathbf{q}_2$, forming the angle θt with $\mathbf{q}_1$, and forming the angle $\theta(1 - t)$ with $\mathbf{q}_2$. We can write $\mathbf{q}(t)$ as

$$\mathbf{q}(t) = a(t)\mathbf{q}_1 + b(t)\mathbf{q}_2 \qquad (3.61)$$

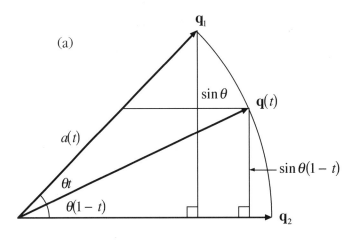

(a)

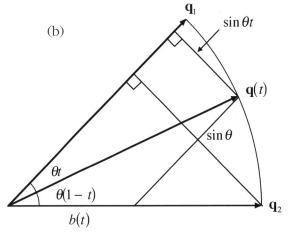

(b)

FIGURE *Similar triangles can be used to determine the length of (a) the component of $\boldsymbol{q}(t)$*
3.10 *that lies along the direction of $\boldsymbol{q}_1$ and (b) the component of $\boldsymbol{q}(t)$ that lies along the direction of $\boldsymbol{q}_2$.*

by letting $a(t)$ and $b(t)$ represent the lengths of the components of $\mathbf{q}(t)$ that lie along the directions $\mathbf{q}_1$ and $\mathbf{q}_2$. As shown in Figure 3.10(a), we can determine the length $a(t)$ by constructing similar triangles. The perpendicular distance from $\mathbf{q}_1$ to the line segment connecting the origin to $\mathbf{q}_2$ is equal to $\|\mathbf{q}_1\| \sin \theta$. The perpendicular distance from $\mathbf{q}(t)$ to this line segment is equal to $\|\mathbf{q}(t)\| \sin \theta(1 - t)$. Using similar triangles, we have the relation

$$\frac{a(t)}{\|\mathbf{q}_1\|} = \frac{\|\mathbf{q}(t)\| \sin \theta(1 - t)}{\|\mathbf{q}_1\| \sin \theta}. \tag{3.62}$$

Since $\|\mathbf{q}_1\| = 1$ and $\|\mathbf{q}(t)\| = 1$, we can simplify this to

$$a(t) = \frac{\sin \theta(1 - t)}{\sin \theta}. \tag{3.63}$$

Figure 3.10(b) shows the same procedure used to find the length $b(t)$, which is given by

$$b(t) = \frac{\sin \theta t}{\sin \theta}. \tag{3.64}$$

We can now define the spherical linear interpolation function $\mathbf{q}(t)$ as follows.

$$\mathbf{q}(t) = \frac{\sin \theta(1 - t)}{\sin \theta} \mathbf{q}_1 + \frac{\sin \theta t}{\sin \theta} \mathbf{q}_2 \tag{3.65}$$

The angle θ is given by

$$\theta = \cos^{-1}(\mathbf{q}_1 \cdot \mathbf{q}_2). \tag{3.66}$$

and thus $\sin \theta$ can be replaced by

$$\sin \theta = \sqrt{1 - (\mathbf{q}_1 \cdot \mathbf{q}_2)^2}, \tag{3.67}$$

if desired. Since the quaternions $\mathbf{q}$ and $-\mathbf{q}$ represent the same rotation, the signs of the quaternions $\mathbf{q}_1$ and $\mathbf{q}_2$ are usually chosen such that $\mathbf{q}_1 \cdot \mathbf{q}_2 \geq 0$. This also ensures that the interpolation takes place over the shortest path.

Chapter 3 Summary

Orthogonal Matrices

An invertible $n \times n$ matrix $\mathbf{M}$ is called *orthogonal* if and only if $\mathbf{M}^{-1} = \mathbf{M}^{\mathsf{T}}$. A matrix whose columns form a linearly independent set of vectors is orthogonal.

Orthogonal matrices preserve lengths and angles and thus perform only rotations and reflections.

Scaling Transforms

A scaling operation in three dimensions is performed using the transformation matrix

$$\begin{bmatrix} a & 0 & 0 \\ 0 & b & 0 \\ 0 & 0 & c \end{bmatrix}.$$

If $a = b = c$, then this matrix represents a uniform scale, which can also be performed using scalar multiplication.

Rotation Transforms

Rotations through an angle θ about the x-, y-, and z-axes are performed using the following transformation matrices.

$$\mathbf{R}_x(\theta) = \begin{bmatrix} 1 & 0 & 0 \\ 0 & \cos\theta & -\sin\theta \\ 0 & \sin\theta & \cos\theta \end{bmatrix}$$

$$\mathbf{R}_y(\theta) = \begin{bmatrix} \cos\theta & 0 & \sin\theta \\ 0 & 1 & 0 \\ -\sin\theta & 0 & \cos\theta \end{bmatrix}$$

$$\mathbf{R}_z(\theta) = \begin{bmatrix} \cos\theta & -\sin\theta & 0 \\ \sin\theta & \cos\theta & 0 \\ 0 & 0 & 1 \end{bmatrix}$$

A rotation through an angle θ about an arbitrary axis $\mathbf{A}$ is performed using the transformation matrix

$$\mathbf{R}_\mathbf{A}(\theta) = \begin{bmatrix} C + A_x^2(1-C) & A_x A_y(1-C) - A_z S & A_x A_z(1-C) + A_y S \\ A_x A_y(1-C) + A_z S & C + A_y^2(1-C) & A_y A_z(1-C) - A_x S \\ A_x A_z(1-C) - A_y S & A_y A_z(1-C) + A_x S & C + A_z^2(1-C) \end{bmatrix},$$

where $C = \cos\theta$ and $S = \sin\theta$.

Homogeneous Coordinates

A vector **P** representing a three-dimensional-point is extended to four-dimensional homogeneous coordinates by setting the w-coordinate to one. A vector **D** representing a three-dimensional-direction is extended to homogeneous coordinates by setting the w-coordinate to zero.

A 3×3 transformation matrix **M** and a 3D translation vector **T** can be combined using the 4×4 transformation matrix

$$\mathbf{F} = \begin{bmatrix} M_{11} & M_{12} & M_{13} & T_x \\ M_{21} & M_{22} & M_{23} & T_y \\ M_{31} & M_{32} & M_{33} & T_z \\ 0 & 0 & 0 & 1 \end{bmatrix}.$$

Normal vectors must be transformed using the inverse transpose of the matrix used to transform points.

Quaternions

The unit quaternion corresponding to a rotation through an angle θ about the unit axis **A** is given by

$$\mathbf{q} = \cos\frac{\theta}{2} + \mathbf{A}\sin\frac{\theta}{2}.$$

A quaternion **q** applies a rotation transformation to a point **P** using the homomorphism $\mathbf{P}' = \mathbf{q}\mathbf{P}\mathbf{q}^{-1}$. The transformation performed by the quaternion $\mathbf{q} = \langle w, x, y, z \rangle$ is equivalent to the transformation performed by the 3×3 matrix

$$\mathbf{R_q} = \begin{bmatrix} 1 - 2y^2 - 2z^2 & 2xy - 2wz & 2xz + 2wy \\ 2xy + 2wz & 1 - 2x^2 - 2z^2 & 2yz - 2wx \\ 2xz - 2wy & 2yz + 2wx & 1 - 2x^2 - 2y^2 \end{bmatrix}.$$

Spherical Linear Interpolation

Two quaternions $\mathbf{q}_1$ and $\mathbf{q}_2$ are spherically interpolated using the formula

$$\mathbf{q}(t) = \frac{\sin\theta(1-t)}{\sin\theta}\mathbf{q}_1 + \frac{\sin\theta t}{\sin\theta}\mathbf{q}_2,$$

where $0 \leq t \leq 1$.

EXERCISES FOR CHAPTER 3

1. Calculate the 3×3 rotation matrices that perform a rotation of 30 degrees about the x-, y-, and z-axes.
2. Exhibit a unit quaternion that performs a rotation of 60 degrees about the axis $\langle 0, 3, 4 \rangle$.
3. Prove Equation (3.34).
4. Let $\mathbf{N}$ be the normal vector to a surface at a point $\mathbf{P}$, and let $\mathbf{S}$ and $\mathbf{T}$ be tangent vectors at the point $\mathbf{P}$ such that $\mathbf{S} \times \mathbf{T} = \mathbf{N}$. Given an invertible 3×3 matrix $\mathbf{M}$, show that $(\mathbf{MS}) \times (\mathbf{MT}) = (\det \mathbf{M})(\mathbf{M}^{-1})^{\mathrm{T}}(\mathbf{S} \times \mathbf{T})$, supporting the fact that normals are correctly transformed by the inverse transpose of the matrix $\mathbf{M}$. [*Hint.* Use Equation (1.25) to write the cross product $(\mathbf{MS}) \times (\mathbf{MT})$ as

$$
(\mathbf{MS}) \times (\mathbf{MT}) = \begin{bmatrix} 0 & -(\mathbf{MS})_z & (\mathbf{MS})_y \\ (\mathbf{MS})_z & 0 & -(\mathbf{MS})_x \\ -(\mathbf{MS})_y & (\mathbf{MS})_x & 0 \end{bmatrix} \mathbf{MT}.
$$

Then find a matrix $\mathbf{G}$ such that

$$
\mathbf{G} \begin{bmatrix} 0 & -S_z & S_y \\ S_z & 0 & -S_x \\ -S_y & S_x & 0 \end{bmatrix} = \begin{bmatrix} 0 & -(\mathbf{MS})_z & (\mathbf{MS})_y \\ (\mathbf{MS})_z & 0 & -(\mathbf{MS})_x \\ -(\mathbf{MS})_y & (\mathbf{MS})_x & 0 \end{bmatrix} \mathbf{M},
$$

and finally use Equation (2.64) to show that $\mathbf{G} = (\det \mathbf{M})(\mathbf{M}^{-1})^{\mathrm{T}}$.]
5. Implement a C++ class that encapsulates a quaternion. The class should possess data members for the quaternion's w-, x-, y-, and z-components. In addition to a default constructor, which should not perform any initialization, the class should have a constructor that takes four floating-point numbers as arguments and initializes the quaternion's components to those values. The class should also include overloaded operators for addition, subtraction, multiplication, and division by scalars, and the quaternion product defined by Equation (3.33). Include a function that takes an angle θ and an axis $\mathbf{A}$ as parameters and returns the unit quaternion that represents the rotation through the angle θ about the axis $\mathbf{A}$. Also include a function that converts a quaternion into a 3×3 rotation matrix using Equation (3.58). Finally, write functions that calculate the magnitude of a quaternion and the inverse of a quaternion.

4

3D Engine Geometry

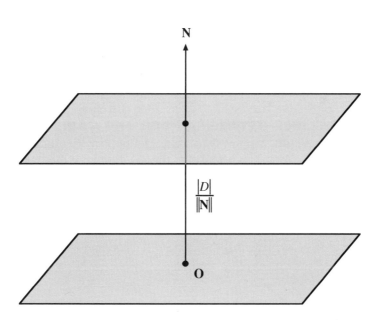

In this chapter, we begin our study of the practical applications of the material presented in the first three chapters to the art and science of 3D game programming. After a treatment of the nature of lines and planes in three-dimensional space, we introduce the view frustum and examine some of the important mathematics governing the virtual camera through which we see our game universe.

4.1 LINES IN 3D SPACE

Given two 3D points $\mathbf{P}_1$ and $\mathbf{P}_2$, we can define the line that passes through these points parametrically as

$$\mathbf{P}(t) = (1 - t)\mathbf{P}_1 + t\mathbf{P}_2, \tag{4.1}$$

where the parameter t ranges over all real numbers. The line segment connecting $\mathbf{P}_1$ and $\mathbf{P}_2$ corresponds to values of t between zero and one.

A *ray* is a line having a single endpoint $\mathbf{P}_0$ and extending to infinity in a given direction $\mathbf{V}$. Rays are typically expressed by the parametric equation

$$\mathbf{P}(t) = \mathbf{P}_0 + t\mathbf{V}, \tag{4.2}$$

where t is allowed to be greater than or equal to zero. This equation is often used to represent lines as well. Note that this equation is equivalent to Equation (4.1) if we let $\mathbf{P}_0 = \mathbf{P}_1$ and $\mathbf{V} = \mathbf{P}_2 - \mathbf{P}_1$.

4.1.1 DISTANCE BETWEEN A POINT AND A LINE

The distance d from a point $\mathbf{Q}$ to a line defined by the endpoint $\mathbf{P}_0$ and the direction $\mathbf{V}$ can be found by calculating the magnitude of the component of $\mathbf{Q} - \mathbf{P}_0$ that is perpendicular to the line, as shown in Figure 4.1.

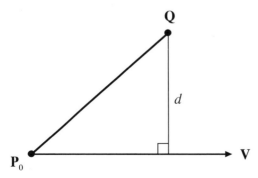

FIGURE *Calculating the distance from a point to a line.*
4.1

Using the Pythagorean theorem, the squared distance between the point $\mathbf{Q}$ and the line can be obtained by subtracting the square of the projection of $\mathbf{Q} - \mathbf{P}_0$ onto the direction $\mathbf{V}$ from the square of $\mathbf{Q} - \mathbf{P}_0$. This gives us

$$d^2 = \left(\mathbf{Q} - \mathbf{P}_0\right)^2 - \left[\text{proj}_{\mathbf{D}}\left(\mathbf{Q} - \mathbf{P}_0\right)\right]^2$$

$$= \left(\mathbf{Q} - \mathbf{P}_0\right)^2 - \left[\frac{\left(\mathbf{Q} - \mathbf{P}_0\right) \cdot \mathbf{V}}{V^2}\mathbf{V}\right]^2$$

$$= \left(\mathbf{Q} - \mathbf{P}_0\right)^2 - \frac{\left[\left(\mathbf{Q} - \mathbf{P}_0\right) \cdot \mathbf{V}\right]^2}{V^2}. \tag{4.3}$$

Taking the square root gives us the distance d that we desire.

4.1.2 DISTANCE BETWEEN TWO LINES

In two dimensions, two lines are either parallel or they intersect at a single point. In three dimensions, this is not true. Two lines that are not parallel and do not intersect are called *skew*. A formula giving the minimum distance between points on skew lines can be found by using a little calculus.

Suppose that we have two lines, as shown in Figure 4.2, defined by the parametric functions

$$\mathbf{P}(s) = \mathbf{P}_0 + s\mathbf{V}_P$$

$$\mathbf{Q}(t) = \mathbf{Q}_0 + t\mathbf{V}_Q, \tag{4.4}$$

where s and t range over all real numbers. Then the squared distance between a point on the line $\mathbf{P}(s)$ and a point on the line $\mathbf{Q}(t)$ can be written as the following function of the parameters s and t.

$$f(s, t) = \|\mathbf{P}(s) - \mathbf{Q}(t)\|^2 \tag{4.5}$$

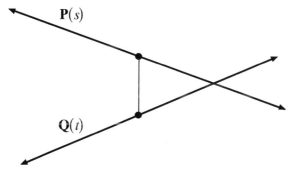

FIGURE   *Measuring the distance between skew lines.*
4.2

Expanding the square and substituting the definitions of the functions $\mathbf{P}(s)$ and $\mathbf{Q}(t)$ gives us

$$
\begin{aligned}
f(s,t) &= \mathbf{P}(s)^2 + \mathbf{Q}(t)^2 - 2\mathbf{P}(s) \cdot \mathbf{Q}(t) \\
&= \left(\mathbf{P}_0 + s\mathbf{V}_P\right)^2 + \left(\mathbf{Q}_0 + t\mathbf{V}_Q\right)^2 \\
&\quad - 2\mathbf{P}_0 \cdot \mathbf{Q}_0 - 2s\mathbf{V}_P \cdot \mathbf{Q}_0 - 2t\mathbf{V}_Q \cdot \mathbf{P}_0 - 2st\mathbf{V}_P \cdot \mathbf{V}_Q \\
&= P_0^2 + s^2 V_P^2 + 2s\mathbf{P}_0 \cdot \mathbf{V}_P + Q_0^2 + t^2 V_Q^2 + 2t\mathbf{Q}_0 \cdot \mathbf{V}_Q \\
&\quad - 2\mathbf{P}_0 \cdot \mathbf{Q}_0 - 2s\mathbf{V}_P \cdot \mathbf{Q}_0 - 2t\mathbf{V}_Q \cdot \mathbf{P}_0 - 2st\mathbf{V}_P \cdot \mathbf{V}_Q.
\end{aligned}
\tag{4.6}
$$

The minimum value attained by the function f can be found by setting partial derivatives with respect to s and t equal to zero. This provides us with the equations

$$
\frac{\partial f}{\partial s} = 2s V_P^2 + 2\mathbf{P}_0 \cdot \mathbf{V}_P - 2\mathbf{V}_P \cdot \mathbf{Q}_0 - 2t\mathbf{V}_P \cdot \mathbf{V}_Q = 0
\tag{4.7}
$$

and

$$
\frac{\partial f}{\partial t} = 2t V_Q^2 + 2\mathbf{Q}_0 \cdot \mathbf{V}_Q - 2\mathbf{V}_Q \cdot \mathbf{P}_0 - 2s\mathbf{V}_P \cdot \mathbf{V}_Q = 0.
\tag{4.8}
$$

After removing a factor of 2, we can write these equations in matrix form, as follows.

$$
\begin{bmatrix} V_P^2 & -\mathbf{V}_P \cdot \mathbf{V}_Q \\ -\mathbf{V}_P \cdot \mathbf{V}_Q & V_Q^2 \end{bmatrix} \begin{bmatrix} s \\ t \end{bmatrix} = \begin{bmatrix} (\mathbf{Q}_0 - \mathbf{P}_0) \cdot \mathbf{V}_P \\ (\mathbf{P}_0 - \mathbf{Q}_0) \cdot \mathbf{V}_Q \end{bmatrix}
\tag{4.9}
$$

Solving this equation for s and t gives us

$$
\begin{aligned}
\begin{bmatrix} s \\ t \end{bmatrix} &= \begin{bmatrix} V_P^2 & -\mathbf{V}_P \cdot \mathbf{V}_Q \\ -\mathbf{V}_P \cdot \mathbf{V}_Q & V_Q^2 \end{bmatrix}^{-1} \begin{bmatrix} (\mathbf{Q}_0 - \mathbf{P}_0) \cdot \mathbf{V}_P \\ (\mathbf{P}_0 - \mathbf{Q}_0) \cdot \mathbf{V}_Q \end{bmatrix} \\
&= \frac{1}{V_P^2 V_Q^2 - (\mathbf{V}_P \cdot \mathbf{V}_Q)^2} \begin{bmatrix} V_Q^2 & \mathbf{V}_P \cdot \mathbf{V}_Q \\ \mathbf{V}_P \cdot \mathbf{V}_Q & V_P^2 \end{bmatrix} \begin{bmatrix} (\mathbf{Q}_0 - \mathbf{P}_0) \cdot \mathbf{V}_P \\ (\mathbf{P}_0 - \mathbf{Q}_0) \cdot \mathbf{V}_Q \end{bmatrix}.
\end{aligned}
\tag{4.10}
$$

Plugging these values of s and t back into the function f gives us the minimum squared distance between the two lines. Taking a square root gives us the actual distance we want. If the direction vectors $\mathbf{V}_P$ and $\mathbf{V}_Q$ have unit length, then Equation (4.10) simplifies a bit since $V_P^2 = 1$ and $V_Q^2 = 1$.

If the quantity $V_P^2 V_Q^2 - \left(\mathbf{V}_P \cdot \mathbf{V}_Q\right)^2$ is zero, then the lines are parallel, in which case the distance between the two lines is equal to the distance between any point on one of the lines and the other line. This is illustrated in Figure 4.3. In particular, we can use Equation (4.3) to measure the distance from the point $\mathbf{P}_0$ to the line $\mathbf{Q}(t)$ or the distance from the point $\mathbf{Q}_0$ to the line $\mathbf{P}(s)$.

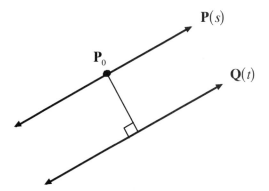

FIGURE **4.3** *Measuring the distance between parallel lines.*

4.2 PLANES IN 3D SPACE

Given a 3D point $\mathbf{P}_0$ and a normal vector $\mathbf{N}$, the plane passing through the point $\mathbf{P}_0$ and perpendicular to the direction $\mathbf{N}$ can be defined as the set of points $\mathbf{P}$ such that $\mathbf{N} \cdot (\mathbf{P} - \mathbf{P}_0) = 0$. As shown in Figure 4.4, this is the set of points whose difference with $\mathbf{P}_0$ is perpendicular to the normal direction $\mathbf{N}$.

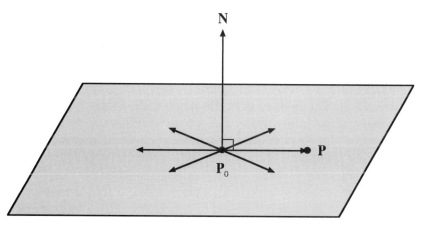

FIGURE **4.4** *A plane is defined by the set of points **P** whose difference with a point **P**$_0$ known to lie in the plane is perpendicular to the normal direction **N**.*

The equation for a plane is commonly written as

$$Ax + By + Cz + D = 0, \tag{4.11}$$

where A, B, and C are the x-, y-, and z-components of the normal vector $\mathbf{N}$, and $D = -\mathbf{N} \cdot \mathbf{P}_0$. As shown in Figure 4.5, the value $|D|/\|\mathbf{N}\|$ is the distance by which the plane is offset from a parallel plane that passes through the origin.

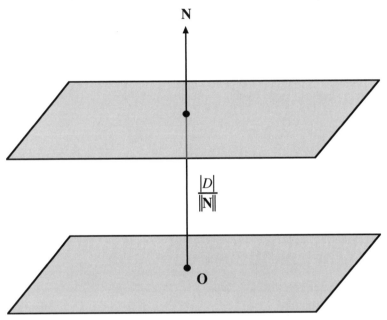

FIGURE *The value of* D *in Equation (4.11) is proportional to the perpendicular distance from*
4.5 *the origin to the plane.*

The normal vector $\mathbf{N}$ is often normalized to unit length because in that case the equation

$$d = \mathbf{N} \cdot \mathbf{Q} + D \tag{4.12}$$

gives the signed distance from the plane to an arbitrary point $\mathbf{Q}$. If $d = 0$, then the point $\mathbf{Q}$ lies in the plane. If $d > 0$, we say that the point $\mathbf{Q}$ lies on the positive side of the plane because $\mathbf{Q}$ would be on the side in which the normal vector points. Otherwise, if $d < 0$, we say that the point $\mathbf{Q}$ lies on the negative side of the plane.

It is convenient to represent a plane using a four-dimensional vector. The shorthand notation $\langle \mathbf{N}, D \rangle$ is used to denote the plane consisting of points $\mathbf{Q}$ satisfying $\mathbf{N} \cdot \mathbf{Q} + D = 0$. If we treat our three-dimensional points instead as four-dimensional homogeneous points having a w-coordinate of one, then equation

(4.12) can be rewritten as $d = \mathbf{L} \cdot \mathbf{Q}$, where $\mathbf{L} = \langle \mathbf{N}, D \rangle$. A point $\mathbf{Q}$ lies in the plane if $\mathbf{L} \cdot \mathbf{Q} = 0$.

4.2.1 INTERSECTION OF A LINE AND A PLANE

Finding the point where a line intersects a plane is a common calculation performed by 3D engines. In particular, it is used extensively during polygon clipping, which is discussed in detail in Sections 7.4.1 and 9.2.2.

Let $\mathbf{P}(t) = \mathbf{Q} + t\mathbf{V}$ represent a line containing the point $\mathbf{Q}$ and running parallel to the direction $\mathbf{V}$. For a plane defined by the normal direction $\mathbf{N}$ and the signed distance D from the origin, we can find the point where the line intersects the plane by solving the equation

$$\mathbf{N} \cdot \mathbf{P}(t) + D = 0 \tag{4.13}$$

for t. Substituting $\mathbf{Q} + t\mathbf{V}$ for $\mathbf{P}(t)$ gives us

$$\mathbf{N} \cdot \mathbf{Q} + (\mathbf{N} \cdot \mathbf{V})t + D = 0, \tag{4.14}$$

and after solving this for t, we arrive at

$$t = \frac{-(\mathbf{N} \cdot \mathbf{Q} + D)}{\mathbf{N} \cdot \mathbf{V}}. \tag{4.15}$$

Plugging this value of t back into the line equation $\mathbf{P}(t) = \mathbf{Q} + t\mathbf{V}$ produces the point of intersection. If $\mathbf{N} \cdot \mathbf{V}$ is zero, then the line is parallel to the plane (the plane normal $\mathbf{N}$ is perpendicular to the line direction $\mathbf{V}$). In this case, the line lies in the plane itself if $\mathbf{N} \cdot \mathbf{Q} + D = 0$; otherwise, there is no intersection.

We may also express the value of t given in Equation (4.15) in terms of the four-dimensional representation of a plane. Given a plane $\mathbf{L} = \langle \mathbf{N}, D \rangle$, we have

$$t = -\frac{\mathbf{L} \cdot \mathbf{Q}}{\mathbf{L} \cdot \mathbf{V}}. \tag{4.16}$$

Since $\mathbf{Q}$ is a point, its w-coordinate is one. However, since $\mathbf{V}$ is a direction vector, its extension to homogeneous coordinates requires that we assign it a w-coordinate of zero (as discussed in Section 3.4.2). This confirms that Equation (4.16) is equivalent to Equation (4.15).

4.2.2 INTERSECTION OF THREE PLANES

Regions of space are often defined by a list of planes that form the boundary of a convex polyhedron. The edges and vertices belonging to this polyhedron can be found by performing a series of calculations that determine the points at which sets of three planes intersect.

Let $\mathbf{L}_1 = \langle \mathbf{N}_1, D_1 \rangle$, $\mathbf{L}_2 = \langle \mathbf{N}_2, D_2 \rangle$, and $\mathbf{L}_3 = \langle \mathbf{N}_3, D_3 \rangle$ be three arbitrary planes. We can find a point $\mathbf{Q}$ that lies in all three planes by solving the following system:

$$\mathbf{L}_1 \cdot \mathbf{Q} = 0$$

$$\mathbf{L}_2 \cdot \mathbf{Q} = 0$$

$$\mathbf{L}_3 \cdot \mathbf{Q} = 0. \tag{4.17}$$

This can be written in matrix form as

$$\mathbf{MQ} = \begin{bmatrix} -D_1 \\ -D_2 \\ -D_3 \end{bmatrix}, \tag{4.18}$$

where the matrix $\mathbf{M}$ is given by

$$\mathbf{M} = \begin{bmatrix} (\mathbf{N}_1)_x & (\mathbf{N}_1)_y & (\mathbf{N}_1)_z \\ (\mathbf{N}_2)_x & (\mathbf{N}_2)_y & (\mathbf{N}_2)_z \\ (\mathbf{N}_3)_x & (\mathbf{N}_3)_z & (\mathbf{N}_3)_z \end{bmatrix}. \tag{4.19}$$

Assuming that the matrix $\mathbf{M}$ is invertible, solving for the point $\mathbf{Q}$, as follows, produces the unique point where the three planes intersect.

$$\mathbf{Q} = \mathbf{M}^{-1} \begin{bmatrix} -D_1 \\ -D_2 \\ -D_3 \end{bmatrix}. \tag{4.20}$$

If $\mathbf{M}$ is singular (i.e., det $\mathbf{M} = 0$), then the three planes do not intersect at a point. This happens when the three normal vectors all lie in the same plane, an example of which is shown in Figure 4.6.

When two nonparallel planes $\mathbf{L}_1 = \langle \mathbf{N}_1, D_1 \rangle$ and $\mathbf{L}_2 = \langle \mathbf{N}_2, D_2 \rangle$ intersect, they do so at a line. As shown in Figure 4.7, the direction $\mathbf{V}$, in which the line of intersection runs, is perpendicular to the normals of both planes and can thus be expressed by $\mathbf{V} = \mathbf{N}_1 \times \mathbf{N}_2$.

To form a complete description of a line, we also need to provide a point that lies on the line. This can be accomplished by constructing a third plane $\mathbf{L}_3 = \langle \mathbf{V}, 0 \rangle$, which passes through the origin and whose normal direction is $\mathbf{V}$. As shown in Figure 4.8, we can then solve for the point where all three planes intersect, which is guaranteed to exist in this situation. Using Equation (4.20), we can compute a point $\mathbf{Q}$ that lies on the line of intersection as follows.

$$\mathbf{Q} = \begin{bmatrix} (\mathbf{N}_1)_x & (\mathbf{N}_1)_y & (\mathbf{N}_1)_z \\ (\mathbf{N}_2)_x & (\mathbf{N}_2)_y & (\mathbf{N}_2)_z \\ V_x & V_y & V_z \end{bmatrix}^{-1} \begin{bmatrix} -D_1 \\ -D_2 \\ 0 \end{bmatrix} \tag{4.21}$$

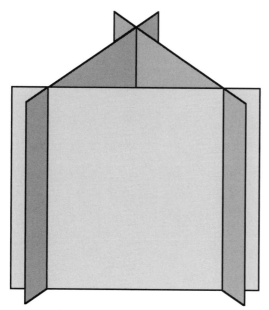

FIGURE   *Three planes do not necessarily intersect at a point.*
4.6

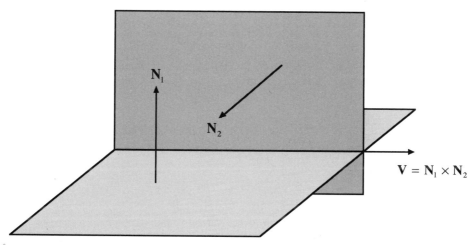

FIGURE   *Two nonparallel planes intersect at a line whose direction runs perpendicular to the*
4.7   *normals of both planes.*

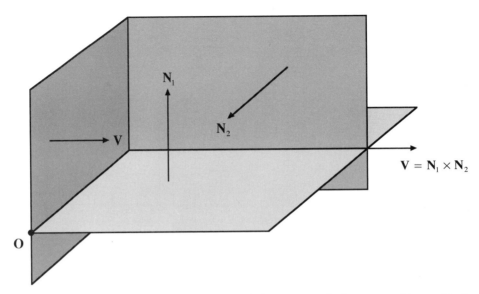

FIGURE *Adding a third plane that passes through the origin and whose normal is equal to the*
4.8   *direction in which the line runs allows us to find a point lying on the line where the*
first two planes intersect.

The line where the two planes $\mathbf{L}_1$ and $\mathbf{L}_2$ intersect is given by $\mathbf{P}(t) = \mathbf{Q} + t\mathbf{V}$.

4.2.3 TRANSFORMING PLANES

Suppose that we wish to transform a plane using a 3×3 matrix $\mathbf{M}$ and a 3D translation vector $\mathbf{T}$. We know that we can transform the normal direction $\mathbf{N}$ using the inverse transpose of $\mathbf{M}$, but we also have the signed distance from the origin D to worry about. If we know that a point $\mathbf{P}_0$ lies in the original plane, then we can calculate the signed distance D' from the transformed plane to the origin using the equation

$$D' = -\left(\left(\mathbf{M}^{-1}\right)^{\mathsf{T}}\mathbf{N}\right) \cdot \left(\mathbf{M}\mathbf{P}_0 + \mathbf{T}\right)$$

$$= -\left(\left(\mathbf{M}^{-1}\right)^{\mathsf{T}}\mathbf{N}\right)^{\mathsf{T}}\mathbf{M}\mathbf{P}_0 - \left(\left(\mathbf{M}^{-1}\right)^{\mathsf{T}}\mathbf{N}\right)^{\mathsf{T}}\mathbf{T}$$

$$= -\mathbf{N}^{\mathsf{T}}\mathbf{M}^{-1}\mathbf{M}\mathbf{P}_0 - \mathbf{N}^{\mathsf{T}}\mathbf{M}^{-1}\mathbf{T}$$

$$= D - \mathbf{N} \cdot \mathbf{M}^{-1}\mathbf{T}. \tag{4.22}$$

Recall from Equation (3.26) that the inverse of the 4×4 matrix $\mathbf{F}$ constructed from the 3×3 matrix $\mathbf{M}$ and the 3D translation vector $\mathbf{T}$ is given by

$$\mathbf{F}^{-1} = \left[\begin{array}{c|c} \mathbf{M}^{-1} & -\mathbf{M}^{-1}\mathbf{T} \\ \hline \mathbf{0} & 1 \end{array} \right]. \qquad (4.23)$$

We therefore have for the transpose of $\mathbf{F}^{-1}$

$$\left(\mathbf{F}^{-1}\right)^{\mathrm{T}} = \left[\begin{array}{c|c} \left(\mathbf{M}^{-1}\right)^{\mathrm{T}} & \mathbf{0} \\ \hline -\mathbf{M}^{-1}\mathbf{T} & 1 \end{array} \right]. \qquad (4.24)$$

The quantity $D - \mathbf{N} \cdot \mathbf{M}^{-1}\mathbf{T}$ is exactly the dot product between the fourth row of $(\mathbf{F}^{-1})^{\mathrm{T}}$ and the 4D vector $\langle \mathbf{N}_x, \mathbf{N}_y, \mathbf{N}_z, D \rangle$. This shows that we may treat planes as four-dimensional vectors that transform in the same manner as three-dimensional normal vectors, except that we use the inverse transpose of the 4×4 transformation matrix. Thus, the plane $\mathbf{L} = \langle \mathbf{N}, D \rangle$ transforms using the 4×4 matrix $\mathbf{F}$ as

$$\mathbf{L}' = (\mathbf{F}^{-1})^{\mathrm{T}}\mathbf{L}. \qquad (4.25)$$

4.3 THE VIEW FRUSTUM

Figure 4.9 shows the *view frustum*, the volume of space containing everything that is visible in a three-dimensional scene. The view frustum is shaped like a

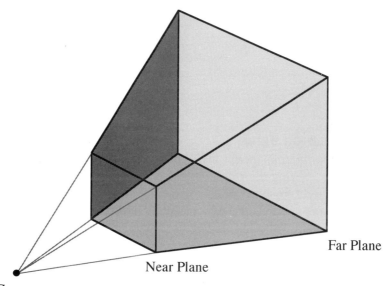

Far Plane

Near Plane

Camera

FIGURE   *The view frustum.*
4.9

pyramid whose apex lies at the camera position. It has this shape because it represents the exact volume that would be visible to a camera that is looking through a rectangular window—the computer screen. The view frustum is bounded by six planes, four of which correspond to the edges of the screen and are called the *left*, *right*, *bottom*, and *top* frustum planes. The remaining two planes are called the *near* and *far* frustum planes and define the minimum and maximum distances at which objects in a scene are visible to the camera.

The view frustum is aligned to *camera space*. Camera space, also called *eye space*, is the coordinate system in which the camera lies at the origin, the x-axis points to the right, and the y-axis points upward. The direction in which the z-axis points depends on the 3D graphics library being used. Under OpenGL, the z-axis points in the direction opposite that in which the camera points. This forms a right-handed coordinate system and is shown in Figure 4.10. Under Direct3D, the z-axis points in the same direction that the camera points and forms a left-handed coordinate system.

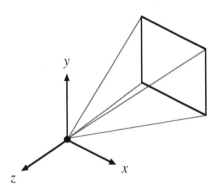

FIGURE *Camera space in OpenGL.*
4.10

4.3.1 FIELD OF VIEW

The projection plane, shown in Figure 4.11, is a plane that is perpendicular to the camera's viewing direction and lies at the distance e from the camera where the left and right frustum planes intersect it at $x = -1$ and $x = 1$. The distance e, which is sometimes called the *focal length* of the camera, depends on the angle α formed between the left and right frustum plane. The angle α is called the *horizontal field of view* angle.

For a desired horizontal field of view α, the distance e to the projection plane is given by the trigonometric relation

$$e = \frac{1}{\tan(\alpha/2)}. \tag{4.26}$$

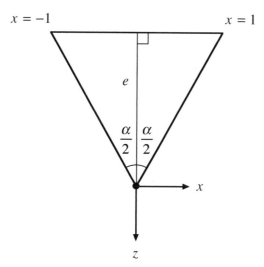

$x = -1$ $x = 1$

e

$\dfrac{\alpha}{2}$ $\dfrac{\alpha}{2}$

x

z

FIGURE *The distance from the camera to the projection plane depends on the horizontal field*
4.11 *of view angle* α.

Larger fields of view are equivalent to shorter focal lengths. A camera can be made to "zoom in" by diminishing the field of view angle, thus causing a longer focal length.

The *aspect ratio* of a display screen is equal to its height divided by its width. For example, a 640×480 pixel display has an aspect ratio of 0.75. Since most displays are not square, but rectangular, the *vertical* field of view is not equal to the horizontal field of view. The bottom and top frustum planes intersect the projection plane at $y = \pm a$, where a is the aspect ratio of the display. This forms the triangle shown in Figure 4.12, and thus the vertical field of view angle β is given by

$$\beta = 2 \tan^{-1}(a/e). \tag{4.27}$$

The four side planes of the view frustum carve a rectangle out of the projection plane at a distance e from the camera whose edges lie at $x = \pm 1$ and $y = \pm a$. The OpenGL function `glFrustum()` requires that we specify a rectangle at the distance n from the camera, where n is the near plane distance. Scaling our rectangle by a factor of n/e, we place the left edge at $x = -n/e$, the right edge at $x = n/e$, the bottom edge at $y = -an/e$, and the top edge at $y = an/e$.

4.3.2 FRUSTUM PLANES

The camera-space normal directions for the six view frustum planes are shown in Figure 4.13. The inward-pointing normal directions for the four side planes are found by rotating the directions along which the sides point 90 degrees toward the center of the frustum. The four side planes each pass through the ori-

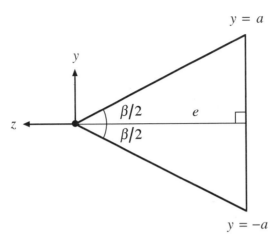

FIGURE   *The vertical field of view angle β depends on the aspect ratio a.*
4.12

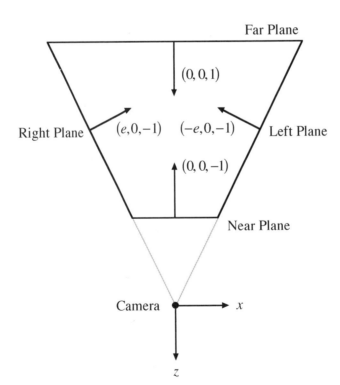

FIGURE   *View frustum plane normal directions in OpenGL camera space.*
4.13

gin, so they each have $D = 0$. The near plane lies at a distance n from the origin in the same direction in which its normal points, so it has $D = -n$. The far plane lies at a distance f from the origin in the opposite direction in which its normal points, so it has $D = f$. The four-dimensional plane vectors corresponding to the six sides of the view frustum are summarized in Table 4.1. In this table, the normal directions for the four side planes have been normalized to unit length.

Table 4.1 View frustum plane vectors in OpenGL camera space in terms of the focal length e, the aspect ratio a, the near plane distance n, and the far plane distance f.

Plane	$\langle \mathbf{N}, D \rangle$
Near	$\langle 0, 0, -1, -n \rangle$
Far	$\langle 0, 0, 1, f \rangle$
Left	$\left\langle \dfrac{e}{\sqrt{e^2 + 1}}, 0, -\dfrac{1}{\sqrt{e^2 + 1}}, 0 \right\rangle$
Right	$\left\langle -\dfrac{e}{\sqrt{e^2 + 1}}, 0, -\dfrac{1}{\sqrt{e^2 + 1}}, 0 \right\rangle$
Bottom	$\left\langle 0, \dfrac{e}{\sqrt{e^2 + a^2}}, -\dfrac{a}{\sqrt{e^2 + a^2}}, 0 \right\rangle$
Top	$\left\langle 0, -\dfrac{e}{\sqrt{e^2 + a^2}}, -\dfrac{a}{\sqrt{e^2 + a^2}}, 0 \right\rangle$

4.4 PERSPECTIVE-CORRECT INTERPOLATION

When a 3D graphics processor renders a triangle on the screen, it rasterizes it one scanline at a time. The vertices of a triangle, in addition to their positions in camera space, carry information such as lighting colors and texture mapping coordinates which must be interpolated across the face of the triangle. When a single scanline of a triangle is drawn, the information at each pixel is an interpolated value derived from the values known at the left and right endpoints.

As shown in Figure 4.14, correct interpolation across the face of a triangle is not linear since equally spaced steps taken on the projection plane correspond

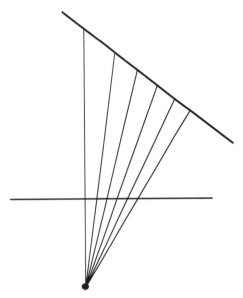

FIGURE   *Equally spaced steps taken on the projection plane correspond to larger steps taken on*
4.14   *the face of a triangle as the distance from the camera increases. Thus, correct*
           interpolation across the face of a triangle is not linear.

to larger steps taken on the face of a triangle as the distance from the camera increases. Graphics processors must use a nonlinear method of interpolation for texture mapping coordinates to avoid distortion of the texture map. Although modern hardware now interpolates other types of information associated with a vertex, such as lighting colors, older graphics cards simply use linear interpolation since the difference is not as noticeable as it is with texture maps.

4.4.1 DEPTH INTERPOLATION

It is important to note that the z-coordinates (representing the depth) of points on the face of a triangle are interpolated linearly by 3D graphics hardware, contrary to the perspective-correct method presented in this section. An explanation for this follows in Section 4.5.1, which discusses the perspective projection matrix.

Figure 4.15 shows a line segment lying in the x-z plane that corresponds to a single scanline of a triangle. During rasterization, points on this line segment are sampled by casting rays through equally spaced points on the projection plane, which represent pixels on the display screen. Assuming that the segment does not belong to a line that passes through the origin (in which case the triangle would be viewed edge-on and would thus not be visible), we can describe the line with the equation

$$ax + bz = c, \tag{4.28}$$

where $c \neq 0$.

Given a point (x, z) that lies on the line, we can cast a ray from the origin (the camera position) to the point (x, z) and determine where it intersects the projection plane. The z-coordinate at the projection plane is always equal to $-e$. We can find the x-coordinate p on the projection plane corresponding to the point (x, z) by using the following relationship derived from the similar triangles shown in Figure 4.15.

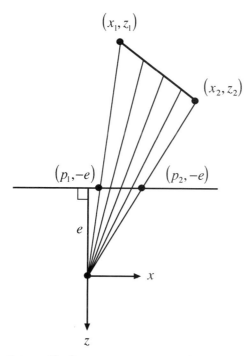

FIGURE 4.15 The line segment corresponding to a single scanline of a triangle is sampled by casting rays through equally spaced points on the projection plane.

$$\frac{p}{x} = \frac{-e}{z} \tag{4.29}$$

Solving this for x and plugging back into Equation (4.28) lets us rewrite our line equation as follows.

$$\left(-\frac{ap}{e} + b\right)z = c \tag{4.30}$$

It is convenient for us to manipulate this equation further by writing it in such a way that $1/z$ appears on one side:

$$\frac{1}{z} = -\frac{ap}{ce} + \frac{b}{c}. \tag{4.31}$$

Let us call the endpoints of the line segment (x_1, z_1) and (x_2, z_2) and their images on the projection plane $(p_1, -e)$ and $(p_2, -e)$. Let $p_3 = (1 - t)p_1 + tp_2$, for some t satisfying $0 \le t \le 1$, be the x-coordinate of an interpolated point on the projection plane. We would like to find the z-coordinate of the point (x_3, z_3) where the ray cast through the point $(p_3, -e)$ intersects the face of the triangle. Plugging $p_3 = (1 - t)p_1 + tp_2$ and z_3 into Equation (4.31) gives us

$$\frac{1}{z_3} = -\frac{ap_3}{ce} + \frac{b}{c}$$

$$= -\frac{ap_1}{ce}\left(1 - t\right) - \frac{ap_2}{ce}t + \frac{b}{c}$$

$$= \left(-\frac{ap_1}{ce} + \frac{b}{c}\right)(1 - t) + \left(-\frac{ap_2}{ce} + \frac{b}{c}\right)t$$

$$= \frac{1}{z_1}\left(1 - t\right) + \frac{1}{z_2}t. \tag{4.32}$$

This result demonstrates that the *reciprocal* of the z-coordinate is correctly interpolated in a linear manner across the face of a triangle.

4.4.2 VERTEX ATTRIBUTE INTERPOLATION

Vertices carry information, such as lighting colors and texture mapping coordinates, that from here on are collectively referred to as vertex attributes. Each vertex attribute must be interpolated across the face of a triangle when it is rasterized. Suppose that the endpoints of a scanline have depth values of z_1 and z_2 and possess scalar attributes b_1 and b_2, respectively. We would expect the interpolated attribute value b_3 to form the same proportion with the total difference along the line segment as does the interpolated depth value z_3. That is, the equation

$$\frac{b_3 - b_1}{b_2 - b_1} = \frac{z_3 - z_1}{z_2 - z_1} \tag{4.33}$$

should be satisfied. Substituting the value

$$z_3 = \frac{1}{\dfrac{1}{z_1}(1-t) + \dfrac{1}{z_2}t} \tag{4.34}$$

given by Equation (4.32) and solving for b_3 gives us

$$b_3 = \frac{b_1 z_2 (1-t) + b_2 z_1 t}{z_2 (1-t) + z_1 t}. \tag{4.35}$$

Multiplying the numerator and denominator by $1/z_1 z_2$ allows us to extract a factor of z_3 from the right-hand side of the equation, as follows.

$$b_3 = \frac{\dfrac{b_1}{z_1}(1-t) + \dfrac{b_2}{z_2}t}{\dfrac{1}{z_1}(1-t) + \dfrac{1}{z_2}t} \tag{4.36}$$

This demonstrates that the value b/z can be linearly interpolated across the face of a triangle. Graphics processors first calculate the linearly interpolated value of $1/z$ when rasterizing a scanline. The reciprocal is then calculated and multiplied by the linearly interpolated value of b/z to obtain the perspective-correct interpolated value of any vertex attribute b.

4.5 PROJECTIONS

To render a three-dimensional scene on a two-dimensional display screen, we need to determine where on the screen each vertex in the scene should be drawn. As we have already seen, we can determine where a vertex located at a position **P** falls on the projection plane by calculating where the ray cast from the origin toward the point **P** intersects it. The x- and y-coordinates of the projected point are given by the formulas

$$x = -\frac{e}{P_z}P_x \text{ and } y = -\frac{e}{P_z}P_y. \tag{4.37}$$

(Remember that the value of P_z is negative since the camera points in the negative z direction.)

Applying the above formula to the z-coordinate would always result in a projected depth of $-e$. Useful depth information is needed, however, to perform hidden surface removal, so 3D graphics systems instead use homogeneous coordinates to project vertices in four-dimensional space.

4.5.1 PERSPECTIVE PROJECTIONS

A perspective projection that maps x- and y-coordinates to the correct place on the projection plane while maintaining depth information is achieved by mapping the view frustum to a cube, as shown in Figure 4.16. This cube, called *homogeneous clip space*, is centered at the origin in OpenGL and extends from negative one to positive one on each of the x-, y-, and z-axes.

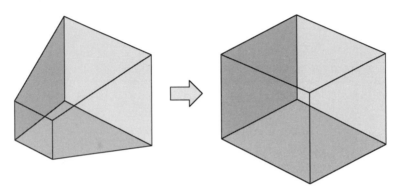

FIGURE *The perspective projection maps the view frustum to the cube called homogeneous clip*
4.16 *space.*

The mapping to homogeneous clip space is performed using a 4×4 projection matrix that, among other actions, places the negative z-coordinate of a camera-space point into the w-coordinate of the transformed point. Subsequent division by the w-coordinate produces a three-dimensional point that lies in clip space.

Let $\mathbf{P} = \langle P_x, P_y, P_z, 1 \rangle$ be a homogeneous point in camera space that lies inside the view frustum. The OpenGL function `glFrustum()` takes as parameters the left edge $x = 1$, the right edge $x = r$, the bottom edge $y = b$, and the top edge $y = t$ of the rectangle carved out of the near plane by the four side planes of the view frustum. The near plane lies at $z = -n$, so we can calculate the projected x- and y-coordinates of the point $\mathbf{P}$ on the near plane using the equations

$$x = -\frac{n}{P_z} P_x \text{ and } y = -\frac{n}{P_z} P_y. \tag{4.38}$$

Any point in lying in the view frustum satisfies $l \le x \le r$ and $b \le y \le t$ on the near plane. We want to map these ranges to the $[-1, 1]$ range needed to fit the view frustum into homogeneous clip space. This can be accomplished using the simple linear functions

$$x' = (x - l)\frac{2}{r - l} - 1 \tag{4.39}$$

and

$$y' = (y - b)\frac{2}{t - b} - 1. \tag{4.40}$$

Substituting the values of x and y given in Equation (4.38) and simplifying yields

$$x' = \frac{2n}{r - l}\left(-\frac{P_x}{P_z}\right) - \frac{r + l}{r - l} \tag{4.41}$$

and

$$y' = \frac{2n}{t - b}\left(-\frac{P_y}{P_z}\right) - \frac{t + b}{t - b}. \tag{4.42}$$

Mapping the projected z-coordinate to the range $[-1, 1]$ involves somewhat more complex computation. Since the point $\mathbf{P}$ lies inside the view frustum, its z-coordinate must satisfy $-f \leq P_z \leq -n$, where n and f are the distances from the camera to the near and far planes, respectively. We wish to find a function that maps $-n \rightarrow -1$ and $-f \rightarrow 1$. (Note that such a mapping reflects the z-axis; therefore, homogeneous clip space is left-handed.) Since z-coordinates must have their reciprocals interpolated during rasterization, we construct this mapping function so that it is a function of $1/z$, consequently allowing projected depth values to be interpolated linearly. Our mapping function thus has the form

$$z' = \frac{A}{z} + B. \tag{4.43}$$

We can solve for the unknowns A and B by plugging in the known mappings $-n \rightarrow -1$ and $-f \rightarrow 1$ to get

$$-1 = \frac{A}{-n} + B \text{ and } 1 = \frac{A}{-f} + B. \tag{4.44}$$

A little algebra yields the following values for A and B:

$$A = \frac{2nf}{f - n} \text{ and } B = \frac{f + n}{f - n}. \tag{4.45}$$

The z-coordinate is thus mapped to the range $[-1,1]$ by the function

$$z' = -\frac{2nf}{f - n}\left(-\frac{1}{P_z}\right) + \frac{f + n}{f - n}. \tag{4.46}$$

Equations (4.41), (4.42), and (4.46) each contain a division by $-P_z$. The 3D point $\tilde{\mathbf{P}}' = \langle x', y', z' \rangle$ is equivalent to the 4D homogeneous point $\mathbf{P}' = \langle -x'P_z, -y'P_z, -z'P_z, -P_z \rangle$ after division by the w-coordinate. Since the values of $-x'P_z$, $-y'P_z$, and $-z'P_z$ given by the equations

$$-x'P_z = \frac{2n}{r - l} P_x + \frac{r + l}{r - l} P_z, \tag{4.47}$$

$$-y'P_z = \frac{2n}{t - b} P_y + \frac{t + b}{t - b} P_z, \tag{4.48}$$

and

$$-z'P_z = -\frac{f + n}{f - n} P_z - \frac{2nf}{f - n} \tag{4.49}$$

are linear functions of the coordinates of the point **P**, we can use a 4×4 matrix to calculate the point **P**′ as follows.

$$\mathbf{P}' = \begin{bmatrix} \dfrac{2n}{r - l} & 0 & \dfrac{r + l}{r - l} & 0 \\ 0 & \dfrac{2n}{t - b} & \dfrac{t + b}{t - b} & 0 \\ 0 & 0 & -\dfrac{f + n}{f - n} & -\dfrac{2nf}{f - n} \\ 0 & 0 & -1 & 0 \end{bmatrix} \mathbf{P} \tag{4.50}$$

The matrix in Equation (4.50) is the OpenGL perspective projection matrix generated by the `glFrustum()` function. Camera-space points are transformed by this matrix into homogeneous clip coordinates in such a way that the w-coordinate holds the negation of the original camera-space z-coordinate. When interpolating vertex attributes (see Section 4.4.2), it is actually this w-coordinate whose reciprocal is interpolated, serving as the value of z in Equation (4.36).

4.5.2 ORTHOGRAPHIC PROJECTIONS

An orthographic projection, also known as a parallel projection, is one in which no perspective distortion occurs. As shown in Figure 4.17, camera-space points are always mapped to the projection plane by casting rays that are parallel to the camera's viewing direction.

The view volume for an orthographic projection is defined by a rectangle lying in the x-y plane and near and far plane distances. Since there is no perspective distortion, depth values for a triangle in an orthographic projection can be interpolated linearly. Thus, our mapping to homogeneous clip space can be performed linearly on all three axes. The functions mapping the x- and y-coordinates from the ranges $[l, r]$ and $[b, t]$ to the range $[-1, 1]$ are given by

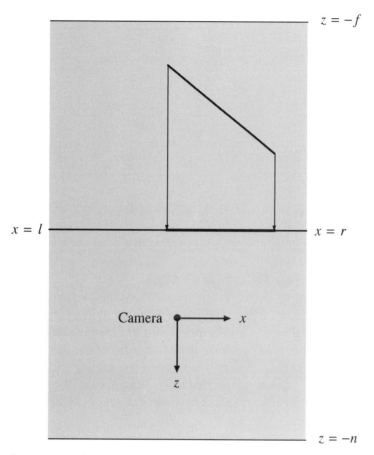

$z = -f$

$x = l$

$x = r$

Camera x

z

$z = -n$

FIGURE *An orthographic projection.*
4.17

$$x' = \frac{2}{r - l}\, x - \frac{r + l}{r - l} \tag{4.51}$$

and

$$y' = \frac{2}{t - b}\, y - \frac{t + b}{t - b}. \tag{4.52}$$

In a similar manner, but negating z so that $-n \to -1$ and $-f \to 1$, we can map the z-coordinate from the range $[-f, -n]$ to the range $[-1, 1]$ using the function

$$z' = \frac{-2}{f - n}\, z - \frac{f + n}{f - n}. \tag{4.53}$$

Writing these three functions in matrix form gives us

$$\mathbf{P}' = \begin{bmatrix} \dfrac{2}{r-l} & 0 & 0 & \dfrac{r+l}{r-l} \\ 0 & \dfrac{2}{t-b} & 0 & \dfrac{t+b}{t-b} \\ 0 & 0 & \dfrac{-2}{f-n} & \dfrac{f+n}{f-n} \\ 0 & 0 & 0 & 1 \end{bmatrix} \mathbf{P}. \tag{4.54}$$

The matrix in Equation (4.54) is the OpenGL orthographic projection matrix generated by the `glOrtho()` function. Note that the w-coordinate remains one after the transformation, and thus no perspective projection takes place.

4.5.3 EXTRACTING FRUSTUM PLANES

It is remarkably simple to extract the four-dimensional vectors corresponding to the six camera-space view frustum planes from an arbitrary projection matrix $\mathbf{M}$. The technique presented here derives from the fact that the planes are always the same in clip space. They are actually rather trivial since, as shown in Figure 4.18, each plane's normal is parallel to one of the principal axes.

Let $\mathbf{L}'$ be one of the six planes that bound clip space. The inverse of the matrix $\mathbf{M}$ transforms from clip space into camera space. Since planes are trans-

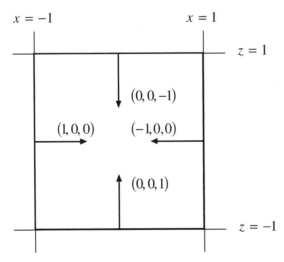

FIGURE *The four-dimensional plane vectors bounding the cube-shaped homogeneous*
4.18 *clip space.*

formed by the inverse transpose of a matrix, the camera-space plane $\mathbf{L}$ corresponding to the clip-space plane $\mathbf{L}'$ is given by

$$\mathbf{L} = \left(\left(\mathbf{M}^{-1} \right)^{-1} \right)^{\mathsf{T}} \mathbf{L}' = \mathbf{M}^{\mathsf{T}} \mathbf{L}'. \tag{4.55}$$

The clip-space plane vectors are listed in Table 4.2. Since each plane vector contains two nonzero entries, and these entries are all ±1, we can write each camera-space view frustum plane as a sum or difference of two columns of the matrix $\mathbf{M}^{\mathsf{T}}$, which is equivalent to the sum or difference of two rows of the matrix $\mathbf{M}$.

Table 4.2 Clip-space plane vectors.

Plane	$\langle \mathbf{N}, D \rangle$
Near	$\langle 0, 0, 1, 1 \rangle$
Far	$\langle 0, 0, -1, 1 \rangle$
Left	$\langle 1, 0, 0, 1 \rangle$
Right	$\langle -1, 0, 0, 1 \rangle$
Bottom	$\langle 0, 1, 0, 1 \rangle$
Top	$\langle 0, -1, 0, 1 \rangle$

Using the notation $\mathbf{M}_i$ to represent row i of the matrix $\mathbf{M}$, we have the following formulas for the camera-space view frustum planes. These do not produce plane vectors having unit normals, so they need to be rescaled.

$$
\begin{aligned}
near &= \mathbf{M}_4 + \mathbf{M}_3 \\
far &= \mathbf{M}_4 - \mathbf{M}_3 \\
left &= \mathbf{M}_4 + \mathbf{M}_1 \\
right &= \mathbf{M}_4 - \mathbf{M}_1 \\
bottom &= \mathbf{M}_4 + \mathbf{M}_2 \\
top &= \mathbf{M}_4 - \mathbf{M}_2
\end{aligned}
\tag{4.56}
$$

These equations are valid for *any* projection matrix. It should be noted, however, that if the focal length and aspect ratio are known for a particular view frustum, then the formulas in Table 4.1 provide a significantly more efficient way of calculating the frustum planes.

CHAPTER 4 SUMMARY

Lines

A line passing through the point $\mathbf{P}_0$ and running parallel to the direction $\mathbf{V}$ is expressed as

$$\mathbf{P}(t) = \mathbf{P}_0 + t\mathbf{V}.$$

The distance from a point $\mathbf{Q}$ to the line $\mathbf{P}(t)$ is given by

$$d = \sqrt{\left(\mathbf{Q} - \mathbf{P}_0\right)^2 - \frac{\left[\left(\mathbf{Q} - \mathbf{P}_0\right) \cdot \mathbf{V}\right]^2}{V^2}}.$$

Planes

A plane having normal direction $\mathbf{N}$ and containing the point $\mathbf{P}_0$ is expressed as

$$\mathbf{N} \cdot \mathbf{P} + D = 0,$$

where $D = -\mathbf{N} \cdot \mathbf{P}_0$. This can also be expressed as $\mathbf{L} \cdot \mathbf{P} = 0$, where $\mathbf{L}$ is the 4D vector $\langle \mathbf{N}, D \rangle$ and $\mathbf{P}$ is a homogeneous point with a w-coordinate of one. The distance from a point $\mathbf{Q}$ to a plane $\mathbf{L}$ is simply $\mathbf{L} \cdot \mathbf{Q}$.

Planes must be transformed using the inverse transpose of a matrix used to transform points.

Intersection of a Line and a Plane

The parameter t where a line $\mathbf{P}(t) = \mathbf{Q} + t\mathbf{V}$ intersects a plane $\mathbf{L}$ is given by

$$t = -\frac{\mathbf{L} \cdot \mathbf{Q}}{\mathbf{L} \cdot \mathbf{V}}.$$

The View Frustum

The focal length e of a view frustum having a horizontal field of view angle α is given by

$$e = \frac{1}{\tan\left(\alpha/2\right)}.$$

For a display having an aspect ratio a, the rectangle carved out of the near plane at a distance n from the camera is bounded by $x = \pm n/e$ and $y = \pm an/e$.

Perspective-Correct Interpolation

In a perspective projection, depth values z_1 and z_2 are correctly interpolated by linearly interpolating their reciprocals:

$$\frac{1}{z_3} = \frac{1}{z_1}(1 - t) + \frac{1}{z_2}t.$$

Perspective-correct vertex attribute interpolation uses the similar formula

$$\frac{b_3}{z_3} = \left[\frac{b_1}{z_1}(1 - t) + \frac{b_2}{z_2}t\right],$$

where b_1 and b_2 are vertex attribute values.

Perspective Projections

The perspective projection matrix that transforms points from camera space into clip space is given by

$$\begin{bmatrix} \dfrac{2n}{r - l} & 0 & \dfrac{r + l}{r - l} & 0 \\ 0 & \dfrac{2n}{t - b} & \dfrac{t + b}{t - b} & 0 \\ 0 & 0 & -\dfrac{f + n}{f - n} & -\dfrac{2nf}{f - n} \\ 0 & 0 & -1 & 0 \end{bmatrix},$$

where n and f are the distances from the camera to the near and far planes, and l, r, b, and t are the left, right, bottom, and top edges of the viewing rectangle carved out of the near plane.

EXERCISES FOR CHAPTER 4

1. Determine a 4D vector $\langle \mathbf{N}, D \rangle$ corresponding to the plane that passes through the three points $\langle 1, 2, 0 \rangle$, $\langle 2, 0, -1 \rangle$, and $\langle 3, -2, 1 \rangle$.
2. The horizontal field of view angle for a particular view frustum is 75 degrees. Calculate the corresponding vertical field of view angle for a 1280 × 1024 pixel display.
3. Calculate the left, right, bottom, and top planes for a view frustum having a horizontal field of view of 90 degrees and an aspect ratio of 0.75.
4. Suppose that z-coordinates in homogeneous clip space occupied the range $[0, 1]$ instead of $[-1, 1]$. In a manner similar to that used to derive the matrix in Equation (4.50), derive a perspective projection matrix that maps $-n \rightarrow 0$ and $-f \rightarrow 1$.

5 Ray Tracing

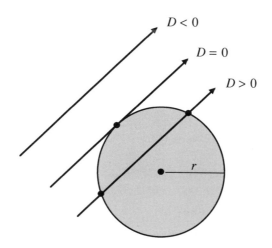

The term *ray tracing* refers to any algorithm that follows beams of light to determine which objects they interact with. Applications include light-map generation, visibility determination, collision detection, and line-of-sight testing. This chapter describes how the points of intersection formed by a ray striking an object can be found and how to alter the path of a ray when it strikes a reflective or refractive surface.

5.1 ROOT FINDING

The problem of finding the points at which a line defined by the equation

$$\mathbf{P}(t) = \mathbf{Q} + t\mathbf{V} \tag{5.1}$$

intersects a surface generally requires finding the roots of a degree n polynomial in t. For planar surfaces, the degree of the polynomial is one, and a solution is easily found. For quadric surfaces, such as a sphere or cylinder, the degree of the polynomial is two, and a solution can be found using the quadratic equation. For more complex surfaces, such as splines and tori, the degree of the polynomial is 3 or 4, in which case we can still find solutions analytically, but at much greater computational expense.

Analytic solutions to polynomials of degrees 2, 3, and 4 are presented in this section. Complete derivations of the solutions to cubic and quartic equations are beyond the scope of this book, however. We also examine a numerical root-finding technique known as the Newton-Raphson iteration method.

5.1.1 QUADRATIC POLYNOMIALS

The roots of a quadratic polynomial in t can be found by using a little algebraic manipulation to solve the equation

$$at^2 + bt + c = 0. \tag{5.2}$$

Subtracting c from both sides and then dividing by a yields

$$t^2 + \frac{b}{a}t = -\frac{c}{a}. \tag{5.3}$$

We can complete the square on the left side of the equation by adding $b^2/4a^2$ to both sides, as follows.

$$t^2 + \frac{b}{a}t + \frac{b^2}{4a^2} = -\frac{c}{a} + \frac{b^2}{4a^2} \tag{5.4}$$

Writing the left side of the equation as a square and using a common denominator on the right side yields

$$\left(t + \frac{b}{2a}\right)^2 = \frac{b^2 - 4ac}{4a^2}. \tag{5.5}$$

Taking square roots and then adding $b/2a$ to both sides yields

$$t = \frac{-b \pm \sqrt{b^2 - 4ac}}{2a}. \tag{5.6}$$

This is the well-known quadratic equation. The quantity $D = b^2 - 4ac$ is called the *discriminant* of the polynomial and reveals how many real roots it has. If $D > 0$, then there are two real roots. If $D = 0$, then there is one real root, and it is given by $t = -b/2a$. For the remaining case, in which $D < 0$, there are no real roots. Evaluating the discriminant allows us to determine whether a ray intersects an object without actually calculating the points of intersection.

5.1.2 CUBIC POLYNOMIALS

A cubic equation having the form

$$t^3 + at^2 + bt + c = 0 \tag{5.7}$$

(where we have performed any necessary division to produce a leading coefficient of one) can be shifted to eliminate the quadratic term by making the substitution

$$t = x - \frac{a}{3}. \tag{5.8}$$

This gives us the equation

$$x^3 + px + q = 0, \tag{5.9}$$

where

$$p = -\frac{1}{3}a^2 + b$$

$$q = \frac{2}{27}a^3 - \frac{1}{3}ab + c. \tag{5.10}$$

Once a solution x to Equation (5.9) is found, we subtract $a/3$ to obtain the solution t to Equation (5.7).

The discriminant D of a cubic polynomial is given by

$$D = -4p^3 - 27q^2. \tag{5.11}$$

By setting

$$r = \sqrt[3]{-\frac{1}{2}q + \sqrt{-\frac{1}{108}D}}$$

$$s = \sqrt[3]{-\frac{1}{2}q - \sqrt{-\frac{1}{108}D}},$$
(5.12)

we can express the three complex roots of Equation (5.9) as

$$x_1 = r + s$$
$$x_2 = \rho r + \rho^2 s$$
$$x_3 = \rho^2 r + \rho s$$
(5.13)

where ρ is the primitive cube root of unity given by $\rho = -\frac{1}{2} + i\frac{\sqrt{3}}{2}$. (Note that $\rho^2 = -\frac{1}{2} - i\frac{\sqrt{3}}{2}$.)

We can simplify our arithmetic significantly by making the substitutions

$$p' = \frac{p}{3} = -\frac{1}{9}a^2 + \frac{1}{3}b$$

$$q' = \frac{q}{2} = \frac{1}{27}a^3 - \frac{1}{6}ab + \frac{1}{2}c.$$
(5.14)

The discriminant is then given by

$$D = -108(p'^3 + q'^2).$$
(5.15)

Setting

$$D' = -\frac{D}{108} = p'^3 + q'^2$$
(5.16)

lets us express r and s as

$$r = \sqrt[3]{-q' + \sqrt{D'}}$$

$$s = \sqrt[3]{-q' - \sqrt{D'}}.$$
(5.17)

As with quadratic equations, the discriminant gives us information about how many real roots exist. If $D < 0$, which corresponds to $D' > 0$, the value of x_1 given in Equation (5.13) represents the only real solution of Equation (5.9).

If $D = D' = 0$, we have $r = s$, so there are two real solutions, one of which is a double root:

$$x_1 = 2r$$
$$x_2, x_3 = (\rho + \rho^2)r = -r.$$
(5.18)

In the remaining case (i.e., $D > 0$ or $D' < 0$), Equation (5.13) yields three distinct real solutions. Unfortunately, we still have to use complex numbers to calculate these solutions. An alternative method can be applied in this case that does not require complex arithmetic. The method relies on the trigonometric identity

$$4 \cos^3 \theta - 3 \cos \theta = \cos 3\theta, \tag{5.19}$$

which can be verified using the DeMoivre theorem (see Exercise 1 at the end of this chapter). Making the substitution $x = 2m \cos \theta$ in Equation (5.9), with $m = \sqrt{-p/3}$, yields

$$8m^3 \cos^3 \theta + 2pm \cos \theta + q = 0. \tag{5.20}$$

(Note that p must be negative in order for D to be positive.) Replacing p with $-3m^2$ and factoring $2m^3$ out of the first two terms yields

$$2m^3(4 \cos^3 \theta - 3 \cos \theta) + q = 0. \tag{5.21}$$

Applying Equation (5.19) and solving for $\cos 3\theta$ yields

$$\cos 3\theta = \frac{-q}{2m^3} = \frac{-q/2}{\sqrt{-p^3/27}} = \frac{-q'}{\sqrt{-p'^3}}. \tag{5.22}$$

Since $D' < 0$, Equation (5.16) implies that $q'^2 < -p'^3$, thereby guaranteeing that the right side of Equation (5.22) is always less than one in absolute value. The inverse cosine is thus defined, and we can solve for θ to arrive at

$$\theta = \frac{1}{3} \cos^{-1}\left(\frac{-q'}{\sqrt{-p'^3}}\right). \tag{5.23}$$

Therefore, one solution to Equation (5.9) is given by

$$x_1 = 2m \cos \theta = 2\sqrt{-p'} \cos \theta. \tag{5.24}$$

Since $\cos(3\theta + 2\pi k) = \cos(3\theta)$ for any integer k, we can write

$$\theta_k = \frac{1}{3} \cos^{-1}\left(\frac{-q'}{\sqrt{-p'^3}}\right) - \frac{2\pi}{3} k. \tag{5.25}$$

Distinct values of $\cos \theta_k$ are generated by choosing three values for k that are congruent to 0, 1, and 2 modulo 3. Using $k = \pm 1$, we can express the remaining two solutions to Equation (5.9) as

$$x_2 = 2\sqrt{-p'}\cos\left(\theta + \frac{2\pi}{3}\right)$$

$$x_3 = 2\sqrt{-p'}\cos\left(\theta - \frac{2\pi}{3}\right). \tag{5.26}$$

5.1.3 QUARTIC POLYNOMIALS

A quartic equation having the form

$$t^4 + at^3 + bt^2 + ct + d = 0 \tag{5.27}$$

(where again we have performed any necessary division to produce a leading coefficient of one) can be shifted to eliminate the cubic term by making the substitution

$$t = x - \frac{a}{4}. \tag{5.28}$$

This yields the equation

$$x^4 + px^2 + qx + r = 0, \tag{5.29}$$

where

$$p = -\frac{3}{8}a^2 + b$$

$$q = \frac{1}{8}a^3 - \frac{1}{2}ab + c$$

$$r = -\frac{3}{256}a^4 + \frac{1}{16}a^2b - \frac{1}{4}ac + d. \tag{5.30}$$

Once a solution x to Equation (5.29) is found, we subtract $a/4$ to obtain the solution t to Equation (5.27).

The roots of the quartic equation are found by first finding a solution to the cubic equation

$$y^3 - \frac{p}{2}y^2 - ry + \frac{4rp - q^2}{8} = 0. \tag{5.31}$$

Let y be any real solution to this equation. If $q \geq 0$, then the solutions to the quartic equation are equal to the solutions to the two quadratic equations

$$x^2 + x\sqrt{2y - p} + y - \sqrt{y^2 - r} = 0$$

$$x^2 - x\sqrt{2y - p} + y + \sqrt{y^2 - r} = 0. \tag{5.32}$$

If $q < 0$, then the solutions to the quartic equation are equal to the solutions to the two quadratic equations

$$x^2 + x\sqrt{2y - p} + y + \sqrt{y^2 - r} = 0$$

$$x^2 - x\sqrt{2y - p} + y - \sqrt{y^2 - r} = 0. \qquad (5.33)$$

5.1.4 NEWTON-RAPHSON ITERATION

The Newton-Raphson iteration method, sometimes just called Newton's method, is a numerical technique that can find roots of an arbitrary continuous function by iterating a formula that depends on the function and its derivative.

Suppose that we wish to find the root of the function f graphed in Figure 5.1. For now, let us assume that we have an initial guess x_0 for the root of the function—more is said about how to choose this value shortly. The slope of the tangent line to the curve at the point $(x, f(x))$ is given by the derivative of f. We can write the equation for this tangent line as follows.

$$y - f(x) = f'(x)(x - x_0) \qquad (5.34)$$

Notice that this line intersects the x-axis at a point that is much closer to the actual root of f than our initial guess x_0. Solving Equation (5.34) for x when $y = 0$ gives us the refinement formula

$$x_{i+1} = x_i - \frac{f(x_i)}{f'(x_i)}, \qquad (5.35)$$

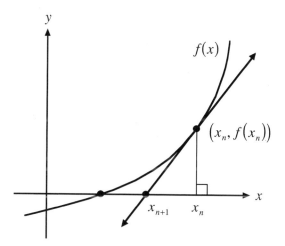

FIGURE *The tangent to a function tends to intersect the x-axis closer to a root of the function.*
5.1

where we have relabeled x with x_{i+1} and x_0 with x_i. Applying this formula multiple times produces a sequence $x_0, x_1, x_2,...$ whose values, under the right conditions, approach the root of f.

Newton's method converges extremely quickly and thus requires very few iterations to exceed any desired precision. We can in fact show that Newton's method converges quadratically, which means that with each iteration the number of significant digits in an approximated root roughly doubles. We prove this claim by first setting

$$g(x) = \frac{f(x)}{f'(x)}. \tag{5.36}$$

Let r be the actual root of the function f to which we are converging. We define ε_i to be the error between the i-th approximation x_i and the root r:

$$\varepsilon_i = x_i - r. \tag{5.37}$$

Using this in Equation (5.35) allows us to write

$$\varepsilon_{i+1} = \varepsilon_i - g(x_i). \tag{5.38}$$

We can approximate the function $g(x_i)$ with the first three terms of its Taylor series (see Appendix D) as follows.

$$g(x_i) = g(r + \varepsilon_i) \approx g(r) + \varepsilon_i g'(r) + \frac{\varepsilon_i^2}{2} g''(r) \tag{5.39}$$

The first and second derivatives of $g(x)$ are given by

$$g'(x) = 1 - \frac{f(x)f''(x)}{[f'(x)]^2}$$

$$g''(x) = \frac{2f(x)f'(x)[f''(x)]^2 - [f'(x)]^2[f(x)f'''(x) + f'(x)f''(x)]}{[f'(x)]^4}. \tag{5.40}$$

Since $f(r) = 0$, these expressions simplify greatly when evaluated at r. The function g and its first two derivatives produce the following values at r.

$$g(r) = 0$$

$$g'(r) = 1$$

$$g''(r) = -\frac{f''(r)}{f'(r)} \tag{5.41}$$

Plugging these into Equation (5.39) gives us

$$g(x_i) \approx \varepsilon_i - \frac{\varepsilon_i^2}{2} \frac{f''(r)}{f'(r)},$$ (5.42)

and finally, substituting this into Equation (5.38) yields

$$\varepsilon_{i+1} \approx \frac{\varepsilon_i^2}{2} \frac{f''(r)}{f'(r)}.$$ (5.43)

Newton's method is not guaranteed to converge to a solution. In particular, if the initial guess is chosen at a point where the derivative of the function is zero, then the tangent line is horizontal and does not intersect the x-axis, thus preventing us from proceeding any further. The initial guess has to be somewhat close to the actual root to guarantee a convergence. When searching for the intersection of a ray with a complex object, we can usually find a good initial guess by first intersecting the ray with the surface of a relatively simple bounding volume. For example, to find where a ray defined by $\mathbf{P}(t) = \mathbf{Q} + t\mathbf{V}$ intersects a torus, we can first find a value of t where the ray intersects a box bounding the torus, and then use this value of t as our initial guess for the torus intersection.

5.1.5 REFINEMENT OF RECIPROCALS AND SQUARE ROOTS

Most modern graphics hardware can approximate the reciprocal of a number, as well as the reciprocal square root of a number, to at least a few bits of precision. For instance, the GL_vertex_program_NV extension to OpenGL exposes the vertex program instructions RCP and RSQ on the GeForce 3 and later graphics processors from Nvidia. These instructions produce an approximation to a reciprocal or reciprocal square root that can be refined to greater precision using Newton's method.

The reciprocal of a number r can be found by calculating the root of the function

$$f(x) = x^{-1} - r$$ (5.44)

since $f(1/r) = 0$. Plugging this function into Equation (5.35) gives us

$$x_{n+1} = x_n - \frac{x_n^{-1} - r}{-x_n^{-2}}$$

$$= x_n(2 - rx_n).$$ (5.45)

This formula can be iterated to produce a high-precision reciprocal of the number r, provided that each $x_i > 0$. This is due to the fact that the function $f(x)$ attains a singularity at $x = 0$. Enforcing this condition on the first refinement x_1

allows us to determine the interval inside which our initial approximation x_0 must fall. Since x_1 must be greater than zero, we have

$$x_0(2 - rx_0) > 0, \tag{5.46}$$

which yields the following restriction on x_0.

$$0 < x_0 < \frac{2}{r} \tag{5.47}$$

Thus, the initial approximation cannot be worse than double the reciprocal of r.

The reciprocal of the square root of a number r can be found by calculating the positive root of the function

$$f(x) = x^{-2} - r. \tag{5.48}$$

Plugging this function into Equation (5.35) gives us

$$x_{n+1} = x_n - \frac{x_n^{-2} - r}{-2x_n^{-3}}$$

$$= \frac{1}{2} x_n \left(3 - rx_n^2\right). \tag{5.49}$$

This sequence converges as long as each $x_i > 0$, so our initial approximation x_0 must satisfy

$$0 < x_0 < \sqrt{\frac{3}{r}}. \tag{5.50}$$

Once the reciprocal square root has been calculated to acceptable precision, the square root of r can be calculated using a single multiplication because

$$\sqrt{r} = r \cdot \left(1/\sqrt{r}\right).$$

5.2 SURFACE INTERSECTIONS

Computing the point at which a ray intersects a surface is central to ray tracing. This section presents specific solutions for the intersection of a ray defined by the equation

$$\mathbf{P}(t) = \mathbf{Q} + t\mathbf{V} \tag{5.51}$$

with a few common types of objects (additional objects are left as exercises). With the exception of the triangle, intersections are computed in *object space*, the space in which the natural center of an object coincides with the origin and the object's natural axes are aligned to the coordinate axes. Intersections with arbitrarily oriented objects are performed by first transforming the ray into object space. Once an intersection is detected, information such as the point of intersection and the normal vector at that point can be transformed back into world space.

5.2.1 INTERSECTION OF A RAY AND A TRIANGLE

A triangle is described by the position in space of its three vertices $\mathbf{P}_0$, $\mathbf{P}_1$, and $\mathbf{P}_2$. We determine the plane in which the triangle lies by first calculating the normal vector $\mathbf{N}$, as follows.

$$\mathbf{N} = (\mathbf{P}_1 - \mathbf{P}_0) \times (\mathbf{P}_2 - \mathbf{P}_0) \qquad (5.52)$$

The signed distance D to the origin is given by the negative dot product of $\mathbf{N}$ with any point in the plane, so we choose the vertex $\mathbf{P}_0$ to construct the 4D plane vector $\mathbf{L} = \langle \mathbf{N}, -\mathbf{N}\cdot\mathbf{P}_0 \rangle$. As discussed in Section 4.2.1, the value of t corresponding to the point where the ray in Equation (5.51) intersects the plane $\mathbf{L}$ is given by

$$t = -\frac{\mathbf{L} \cdot \mathbf{Q}}{\mathbf{L} \cdot \mathbf{V}}. \qquad (5.53)$$

If $\mathbf{L} \cdot \mathbf{V} = 0$, then no intersection occurs. Otherwise, plugging this value of t back into Equation (5.51) produces the point $\mathbf{P}$ where the ray intersects the plane of the triangle.

We now have the problem of determining whether the point $\mathbf{P}$ lies inside the triangle's edges. We reduce the problem to two dimensions by discarding the coordinate for which the corresponding component of $\mathbf{N}$ is the greatest in absolute value. As shown in Figure 5.2, this has the effect of projecting the triangle onto the x-y, x-z, or y-z plane. We continue assuming that the z-coordinate has been discarded—in the other two cases, the axes can be relabeled x and y.

For each edge i of the triangle, where $0 \leq i \leq 2$, we compute the two-dimensional differences

$$\mathbf{E} = \mathbf{P}_{(i+1) \bmod 3} - \mathbf{P}_i$$

$$\mathbf{F} = \mathbf{P}_{(i+2) \bmod 3} - \mathbf{P}_i$$

$$\mathbf{G} = \mathbf{P} - \mathbf{P}_i, \qquad (5.54)$$

essentially shifting our coordinate system so that vertex i lies at the origin. The edge represented by the vector $\mathbf{E}$ has an interior side and an exterior side. By rotating the vector 90 degrees (which direction is not important), we can create a two-dimensional normal vector to the edge, as shown in Figure 5.3. Let $\mathbf{N}_E = \langle -E_y, E_x \rangle$ be this normal vector. Since the point $\mathbf{F}$ must lie on the interior side of the edge, the sign of the dot product $\mathbf{N}_E \cdot \mathbf{F}$ represents the sign of the dot

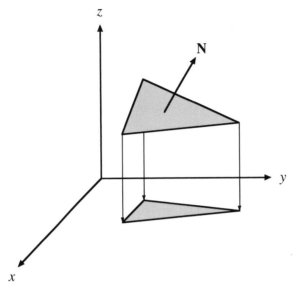

FIGURE *To determine whether a point lies inside a triangle's edges, the triangle is projected*
5.2 *onto the x-y, x-z, or y-z plane.*

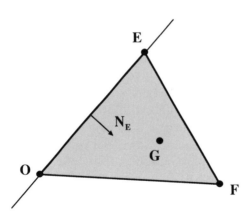

FIGURE *A point lies on the interior side of an edge if its dot product with the edge's normal*
5.3 *has the same sign as the dot product of the third vertex with the edge's normal.*

product of *any* interior point with $\mathbf{N}_E$. Thus, the point $\mathbf{P}$ lies on the interior side
of the edge only if

$$(\mathbf{N}_E \cdot \mathbf{F})(\mathbf{N}_E \cdot \mathbf{G}) \geq 0. \tag{5.55}$$

Any point lying on the interior side of all three edges lies inside the triangle.

5.2.2 INTERSECTION OF A RAY AND A BOX

A box is described by the six plane equations

$$x = 0 \qquad x = r_x$$
$$y = 0 \qquad y = r_y$$
$$z = 0 \qquad z = r_z, \tag{5.56}$$

where r_x, r_y, and r_z represent the dimensions of the box. At most three of these planes need to be considered for intersection by the ray since at least three planes must face away from the ray's direction $\mathbf{V}$. We can determine which planes need to be tested by examining the components of $\mathbf{V}$ one at a time. For instance, if $V_x = 0$, then we know that the ray cannot intersect either of the planes $x = 0$ or $x = r_x$ because $\mathbf{V}$ is parallel to them. If $V_x > 0$, then we do not need to test for an intersection with the plane $x = r_x$ since it represents a back side of the box from the ray's perspective. Similarly, if $V_x < 0$, then we do not need to test for an intersection with the plane $x = 0$. The same principle applies to the y- and z-components of $\mathbf{V}$.

Once we have found the point where a ray intersects a plane, we must check that the point falls within the face of the box by examining the two coordinates corresponding to the directions parallel to the plane. For instance, the value of t corresponding to the point where the ray given by Equation (5.51) intersects the plane $x = r_x$ is given by

$$t = \frac{r_x - Q_x}{V_x}. \tag{5.57}$$

To lie within the corresponding face of the box, the y- and z-coordinates of the point $\mathbf{P}(t)$ must satisfy

$$0 \leq [\mathbf{P}(t)]_y \leq r_y$$
$$0 \leq [\mathbf{P}(t)]_z \leq r_z. \tag{5.58}$$

If either of these conditions fails, then no intersection takes place within the face. If both conditions pass, then an intersection has been found, in which case there is no need to test any other planes since no closer intersection can occur.

5.2.3 INTERSECTION OF A RAY AND A SPHERE

A sphere of radius r centered at the origin is described by the equation

$$x^2 + y^2 + z^2 = r^2. \tag{5.59}$$

Substituting the components of the ray in Equation (5.51) for x, y, and z gives us

$$(Q_x + tV_x)^2 + (Q_y + tV_y)^2 + (Q_z + tV_z)^2 = r^2. \tag{5.60}$$

Expanding the squares and collecting on t yields the following quadratic equation.

$$\left(V_x^2 + V_y^2 + V_z^2\right)t^2 + 2\left(Q_x V_x + Q_y V_y + Q_z V_z\right)t + Q_x^2 + Q_y^2 + Q_z^2 - r^2 = 0 \tag{5.61}$$

The coefficients a, b, and c used in Equation (5.2) can be expressed in terms of the vectors $\mathbf{Q}$ and $\mathbf{V}$ as follows.

$$
\begin{aligned}
a &= V^2 \\
b &= 2(\mathbf{Q} \cdot \mathbf{V}) \\
c &= Q^2 - r^2
\end{aligned} \tag{5.62}
$$

Calculating the discriminant $D = b^2 - 4ac$ tells us whether the ray intersects the sphere. As illustrated in Figure 5.4, if $D < 0$, then no intersection occurs; if $D = 0$, then the ray is tangent to the sphere; and if $D > 0$, then there are two distinct points of intersection. If the ray intersects the sphere at two points, then the point closer to the ray's origin $\mathbf{Q}$, which corresponds to the smaller value of t, is always given by

$$t = \frac{-b - \sqrt{D}}{2a} \tag{5.63}$$

because a is guaranteed to be positive.

The intersection of a ray and an ellipsoid can be determined by replacing Equation (5.59) with the equation

$$x^2 + m^2 y^2 + n^2 z^2 = r^2, \tag{5.64}$$

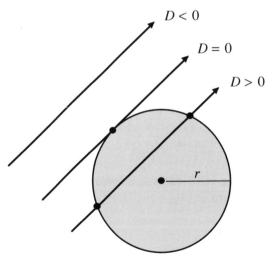

FIGURE **5.4** *The discriminant D indicates whether a ray intersects a sphere.*

where m is the ratio of the y semi-axis length to the x semi-axis length and n is the ratio of the z semi-axis length to the x semi-axis length. Plugging the components of the ray into this equation yields another quadratic polynomial, whose coefficients are given by

$$a = V_x^2 + m^2 V_y^2 + n^2 V_z^2$$

$$b = 2\left(Q_x V_x + m^2 Q_y V_y + n^2 Q_z V_z\right)$$

$$c = Q_x^2 + m^2 Q_y^2 + n^2 Q_z^2 - r^2. \qquad (5.65)$$

Again, the discriminant indicates whether an intersection occurs. If so, the intersection parameter t is given by Equation (5.63).

5.2.4 INTERSECTION OF A RAY AND A CYLINDER

The lateral surface of an elliptical cylinder whose radius on the x-axis is r, whose radius on the y-axis is s, whose height is h, and whose base is centered on the origin of the x-y plane (see Figure 5.5) is described by the equation

$$x^2 + m^2 y^2 = r^2$$

$$0 \leq z \leq h, \qquad (5.66)$$

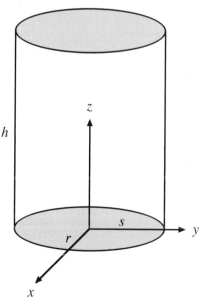

FIGURE   *Object space for an elliptical cylinder.*
5.5

where $m = r/s$. If $r = s$, then the cylinder is circular and $m = 1$. Substituting the components of the ray in Equation (5.51) for x and y gives us

$$(Q_x + tV_x)^2 + m^2(Q_y + tV_y)^2 = r^2. \tag{5.67}$$

Expanding the squares and collecting on t yields the following quadratic equation.

$$\left(V_x^2 + m^2V_y^2\right)t^2 + 2\left(Q_xV_x + m^2Q_yV_y\right)t + Q_x^2 + m^2Q_y^2 - r^2 = 0 \tag{5.68}$$

As with the sphere, the discriminant indicates whether an intersection occurs. Solutions to this equation give the values of t where the ray intersects the infinite cylinder centered on the z-axis. The z-coordinates of the points of intersection must be tested so that they satisfy $0 \le z \le h$.

5.2.5 INTERSECTION OF A RAY AND A TORUS

A cross section of the surface of a circular torus having primary radius r_1 and secondary radius r_2 is shown in Figure 5.6.

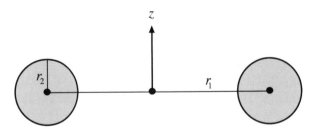

FIGURE *Cross section of a torus.*
5.6

   The circle of radius r_1 lying in the x-y plane represents the center of another circle of radius r_2 perpendicular to the first, which is revolved about the z-axis. The equation describing the revolved circle is

$$s^2 + z^2 = r_2^2, \tag{5.69}$$

where the value of s is the distance to the primary circle in the x-y plane:

$$s = \sqrt{x^2 + y^2} - r_1. \tag{5.70}$$

Substituting this into Equation (5.69) and expanding the square gives us

$$x^2 + y^2 + z^2 + r_1^2 - r_2^2 - 2r_1\sqrt{x^2 + y^2} = 0. \tag{5.71}$$

Isolating the radical and squaring again yields the following equation for a torus.

$$\left(x^2 + y^2 + z^2 + r_1^2 - r_2^2\right)^2 = 4r_1^2\left(x^2 + y^2\right) \tag{5.72}$$

Substituting the components of the ray in Equation (5.51) for x, y, and z gives us

$$\left[\left(Q_x + tV_x\right)^2 + \left(Q_y + tV_y\right)^2 + \left(Q_z + tV_z\right)^2 + r_1^2 - r_2^2\right]^2$$
$$= 4r_1^2\left[\left(Q_x + tV_x\right)^2 + \left(Q_y + tV_y\right)^2\right]. \tag{5.73}$$

After considerable algebraic simplification, this can be expressed as the quartic equation

$$at^4 + bt^3 + ct^2 + dt + e = 0, \tag{5.74}$$

where

$$a = V^4$$

$$b = 4V^2(\mathbf{Q} \cdot \mathbf{V})$$

$$c = 2V^2\left(Q^2 + r_1^2 - r_2^2\right) - 4r_1^2\left(V_x^2 + V_y^2\right) + 4(\mathbf{Q} \cdot \mathbf{V})^2$$

$$d = 8r_1^2 Q_z V_z + 4(\mathbf{Q} \cdot \mathbf{V})\left(Q^2 - r_1^2 - r_2^2\right)$$

$$e = Q_x^4 + Q_y^4 + Q_z^4 + \left(r_1^2 - r_2^2\right)^2$$
$$+ 2\left[Q_x^2 Q_y^2 + Q_z^2\left(r_1^2 - r_2^2\right) + \left(Q_x^2 + Q_y^2\right)\left(Q_z^2 - r_1^2 - r_2^2\right)\right]. \tag{5.75}$$

After dividing by a to obtain a leading coefficient of one, this equation can be solved using the method presented in Section 5.1.3.

5.3 NORMAL VECTOR CALCULATION

It is sometimes convenient to represent a surface using an implicit function $f(x, y, z)$ whose value is zero at any point $\langle x, y, z \rangle$ on the surface and whose value is nonzero elsewhere. An example of such a function is that of an ellipsoid:

$$f(x, y, z) = \frac{x^2}{a^2} + \frac{y^2}{b^2} + \frac{z^2}{c^2} - 1. \tag{5.76}$$

Using the implicit function representation, it is possible for us to derive a general formula for the normal direction at any point on a surface.

Suppose that $f(x, y, z)$ represents a surface S, so that $f(x, y, z) = 0$ for any point on S. Let C be a curve defined by differentiable parametric functions $x(t)$, $y(t)$, and $z(t)$ that lies on the surface S. Then the tangent vector $\mathbf{T}$ to the curve C at the point $\langle x(t), y(t), z(t) \rangle$, is given by

$$\mathbf{T} = \left\langle \frac{d}{dt} x(t), \frac{d}{dt} y(t), \frac{d}{dt} z(t) \right\rangle. \tag{5.77}$$

Since the curve C lies on the surface S, $\mathbf{T}$ is also tangent to the surface S. Also, since $f(x(t), y(t), z(t)) = 0$ for any value of t, we know that $df/dt = 0$ everywhere on the curve C. Using the chain rule, we can write

$$0 = \frac{df}{dt} = \frac{\partial f}{\partial x}\frac{dx}{dt} + \frac{\partial f}{\partial y}\frac{dy}{dt} + \frac{\partial f}{\partial z}\frac{dz}{dt} = \left\langle \frac{\partial f}{\partial x}, \frac{\partial f}{\partial y}, \frac{\partial f}{\partial z} \right\rangle \cdot \mathbf{T}. \tag{5.78}$$

Because its dot product with $\mathbf{T}$ is always zero, the vector $\langle \partial f/\partial x, \partial f/\partial y, \partial f/\partial z \rangle$ must be normal to the surface S. This vector is called the *gradient* of f at the point $\langle x, y, z \rangle$ and is usually written $\nabla f(x, y, z)$, where the symbol ∇ is the *del* operator defined by

$$\nabla = \mathbf{i}\frac{\partial}{\partial x} + \mathbf{j}\frac{\partial}{\partial y} + \mathbf{k}\frac{\partial}{\partial z}. \tag{5.79}$$

We can now express the formula for the normal vector $\mathbf{N}$ to a surface defined by the equation $f(x, y, z) = 0$ as

$$\mathbf{N} = \nabla f(x, y, z). \tag{5.80}$$

Continuing the example given in Equation (5.76), we have the following expression for the normal to the surface of an ellipsoid.

$$\mathbf{N} = \left\langle \frac{2x}{a^2}, \frac{2y}{b^2}, \frac{2z}{c^2} \right\rangle \tag{5.81}$$

5.4 REFLECTION AND REFRACTION VECTORS

When a beam of light strikes the surface of an object, part of its energy is absorbed by the surface, part of its energy is reflected away from the surface, and part of its energy may be transmitted through the object itself. Chapter 6 discusses this interaction in detail. This section explains how the direction of reflection and refraction can be calculated for a ray that intersects a shiny or transparent surface.

5.4.1 REFLECTION VECTOR CALCULATION

The direction of the reflection of light on a shiny surface (such as a mirror) follows the simple rule that the angle of incidence is equal to the angle of reflection. As shown in Figure 5.7, this is the same as saying that the angle between

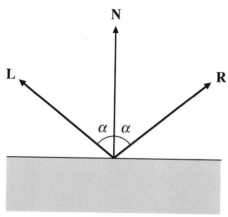

FIGURE   *The direction of reflection **R** forms the same angle with the normal vector **N** as the*
5.7   *direction **L** pointing toward the incoming light.*

the normal vector **N** and the direction **L** pointing toward the incoming light is equal to the angle between the normal vector and the direction **R** of the reflected light.

We assume that the vectors **N** and **L** have been normalized to unit length. To derive a formula that gives us the reflection direction **R** in terms of the light direction **L** and the normal vector **N**, we first calculate the component of **L** that is perpendicular to the normal direction:

$$\text{perp}_\mathbf{N}\, \mathbf{L} = \mathbf{L} - (\mathbf{N} \cdot \mathbf{L})\mathbf{N} \tag{5.82}$$

As shown in Figure 5.8, the vector **R** lies at twice the distance from **L** as does its projection onto the normal vector **N**. We can thus express **R** as

$$\mathbf{R} = \mathbf{L} - 2\,\text{perp}_\mathbf{N}\, \mathbf{L}$$
$$= \mathbf{L} - 2[\mathbf{L} - (\mathbf{N} \cdot \mathbf{L})\mathbf{N}]$$
$$= 2(\mathbf{N} \cdot \mathbf{L})\mathbf{N} - \mathbf{L}. \tag{5.83}$$

5.4.2 REFRACTION VECTOR CALCULATION

Transparent surfaces possess a property called the index of refraction. According to Snell's law, the angle of incidence $\theta_\mathbf{L}$ and the angle of transmission $\theta_\mathbf{T}$ (shown in Figure 5.9) are related by the equation

$$\eta_\mathbf{L} \sin \theta_\mathbf{L} = \eta_\mathbf{T} \sin \theta_\mathbf{T}, \tag{5.84}$$

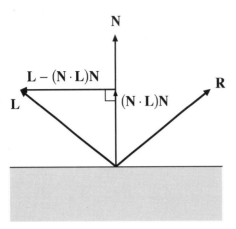

FIGURE **5.8** *The reflection vector **R** is found by subtracting twice the component of **L**, that is perpendicular to **N** from **L** itself.*

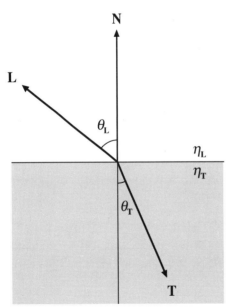

FIGURE **5.9** *The angle of incidence θ_L and the angle of transmission θ_T are related by Snell's law, given in Equation (5.84).*

where η_L is the index of refraction of the material that the light is leaving and η_T is the index of refraction of the material that the light is entering. The index of refraction of air is usually taken to be one. Higher indexes of refraction create a greater bending effect at the interface between two materials.

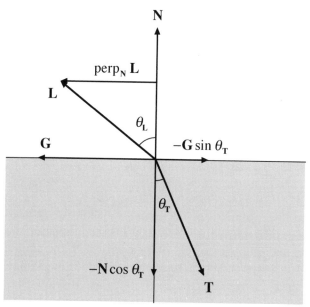

FIGURE
5.10 *The refraction vector **T** is expressed in terms of its components parallel and perpendicular to the normal vector **N**.*

We assume that the normal vector **N** and the direction toward the incoming light **L** have been normalized to unit length. We express the direction **T** in which the transmitted light travels in terms of its components parallel and perpendicular to the normal vector. As shown in Figure 5.10, the component of **T** parallel to the normal vector is simply given by $-\mathbf{N} \cos \theta_T$. The component of **T** perpendicular to the normal vector can be expressed as $-\mathbf{G} \sin \theta_T$, where the vector **G** is the unit-length vector parallel to $\text{perp}_\mathbf{N} \mathbf{L}$. Since **L** has unit length, $\|\text{perp}_\mathbf{N} \mathbf{L}\| = \sin \theta_L$, so

$$\mathbf{G} = \frac{\text{perp}_\mathbf{N} \mathbf{L}}{\sin \theta_L} = \frac{\mathbf{L} - (\mathbf{N} \cdot \mathbf{L})\mathbf{N}}{\sin \theta_L}. \tag{5.85}$$

We can now express the refraction vector **T** as

$$\mathbf{T} = -\mathbf{N} \cos \theta_T - \mathbf{G} \sin \theta_T$$

$$= -\mathbf{N} \cos \theta_T - \frac{\sin \theta_T}{\sin \theta_L}\left[\mathbf{L} - (\mathbf{N} \cdot \mathbf{L})\mathbf{N}\right]. \tag{5.86}$$

Using Equation (5.84), we can replace the quotient of sines with η_L/η_T:

$$\mathbf{T} = -\mathbf{N} \cos \theta_T - \frac{\eta_L}{\eta_T}\left[\mathbf{L} - (\mathbf{N} \cdot \mathbf{L})\mathbf{N}\right]. \tag{5.87}$$

Replacing $\cos\theta_T$ with $\sqrt{1-\sin^2\theta_T}$ and then using Equation (5.84) again to replace $\sin\theta_T$ with $(\eta_L/\eta_T)\sin\theta_L$ yields

$$\mathbf{T} = -\mathbf{N}\sqrt{1-\frac{\eta_L^2}{\eta_T^2}\sin^2\theta_L} - \frac{\eta_L}{\eta_T}\left[\mathbf{L}-(\mathbf{N}\cdot\mathbf{L})\mathbf{N}\right]. \qquad (5.88)$$

Replacing $\sin^2\theta_L$ with $1-\cos^2\theta_L-(\mathbf{N}\cdot\mathbf{L})^2$ finally yields

$$\mathbf{T} = \left(\frac{\eta_L}{\eta_T}\mathbf{N}\cdot\mathbf{L} - \sqrt{1-\frac{\eta_L^2}{\eta_T^2}\left[1-(\mathbf{N}\cdot\mathbf{L})^2\right]}\right)\mathbf{N} - \frac{\eta_L}{\eta_T}\mathbf{L}. \qquad (5.89)$$

If $\eta_L > \eta_T$, then it is possible for the quantity inside the radical in Equation (5.89) to be negative. This happens when light inside a medium having a higher index of refraction makes a wide angle of incidence with the surface, leading to a medium having a lower index of refraction. Specifically, Equation (5.89) is only valid when $\sin\theta_L \le \eta_T/\eta_L$. If the quantity inside the radical is negative, a phenomenon known as *total internal reflection* occurs. This means that light is not refracted but is actually reflected inside the medium using Equation (5.83).

CHAPTER 5 SUMMARY

Analytic Root Finding
Solutions to the quadratic equation $at^2 + bt + c = 0$ are given by the quadratic equation:

$$t = \frac{-b \pm \sqrt{b^2 - 4ac}}{2a}.$$

Cubic and quartic equations can also be solved analytically.

Numerical Root Finding
Roots of a function $f(x)$ can be found numerically using Newton's method, which refines an approximate solution x_n using the formula

$$x_{n+1} = x_n - \frac{f(x_n)}{f'(x_n)}.$$

The refinement formula for the reciprocal x_n of a number r is

$$x_{n+1} = x_n(2 - rx_n),$$

and the refinement formula for the reciprocal square root x_n of a number r is

$$x_{n+1} = \frac{1}{2} x_n \left(3 - r x_n^2\right).$$

Intersection of a Ray and a Sphere

The points where a ray $\mathbf{P}(t) = \mathbf{Q} + t\mathbf{V}$ intersect a sphere of radius r are given by the solutions of the quadratic equation

$$V^2 t^2 + 2(\mathbf{Q} \cdot \mathbf{V})t + Q^2 - r^2 = 0.$$

Normal Vector Calculation

The normal vector at a point $\langle x, y, z \rangle$ on a surface defined by the function $f(x, y, z) = 0$ is given by $\mathbf{N} = \nabla f(x, y, z)$.

Reflection Vector Calculation

The reflection $\mathbf{R}$ of a vector $\mathbf{L}$ across the normal vector $\mathbf{N}$ is given by

$$\mathbf{R} = 2(\mathbf{N} \cdot \mathbf{L})\mathbf{N} - \mathbf{L}.$$

Transmission Vector Calculation

The direction $\mathbf{T}$, in which light is transmitted when leaving a medium having index of refraction η_L and entering a medium having index of refraction η_T, is given by

$$\mathbf{T} = \left(\frac{\eta_L}{\eta_T} \mathbf{N} \cdot \mathbf{L} - \sqrt{1 - \frac{\eta_L^2}{\eta_T^2}\left[1 - \left(\mathbf{N} \cdot \mathbf{L}\right)^2\right]} \right)\mathbf{N} - \frac{\eta_L}{\eta_T} \mathbf{L},$$

where $\mathbf{L}$ is the direction pointing toward the incident light and $\mathbf{N}$ is the surface normal.

EXERCISES FOR CHAPTER 5

1. Use the DeMoivre theorem (which states that $e^{\alpha i} = \cos \alpha + i \sin \alpha$) to verify the trigonometric identity

   $$4 \cos^3 \theta - 3 \cos \theta = \cos(3\theta).$$

   [*Hint.* Equate the real components of the equation $(e^{\theta i})^3 = e^{(3\theta)i}$.]

2. Use the Newton-Raphson iteration method to approximate the root of the function $f(x) = \ln x + x - 7$.

3. Find a general formula that can be used to refine an approximation x_n of the p-th root of a number r using the Newton-Raphson iteration method.

4. Derive the polynomial whose roots give the values of t at which the line $\mathbf{P}(t) = \mathbf{Q} + t\mathbf{V}$ intersects a cone whose radius (at the base) is r, whose

height is h, and whose base is centered on the origin of the x-y plane as shown in Figure 5.11.

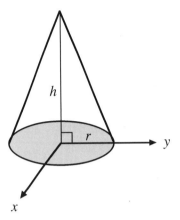

FIGURE *The cone used in Exercise 4.*
5.11

5. Calculate the unit-length surface normal to the paraboloid defined by $f(x, y, z) = 2x^2 + 3y^2 - z = 0$ at the point $\langle -1, 2, 14 \rangle$.

6. Suppose that a coordinate transformation is defined by

$$\begin{bmatrix} x' \\ y' \\ z' \end{bmatrix} = \mathbf{M} \begin{bmatrix} x \\ y \\ z \end{bmatrix},$$

where $\mathbf{M}$ is an invertible 3×3 matrix. The del operator ∇' in the primed coordinate system is defined as

$$\nabla' = \left\langle \frac{\partial}{\partial x'}, \frac{\partial}{\partial y'}, \frac{\partial}{\partial z'} \right\rangle.$$

Show that $\nabla' = (\mathbf{M}^{-1})^{\mathrm{T}} \nabla$. [*Hint.* Treat each unprimed coordinate as a function of all three primed coordinates by writing

$$x = x(x', y', z')$$

$$y = y(x', y', z')$$

$$z = z(x', y', z')$$

and apply the chain rule for partial differentiation, which for the x-coordinate gives us

$$\frac{\partial}{\partial x'} = \frac{\partial x}{\partial x'} \frac{\partial}{\partial x} + \frac{\partial y}{\partial x'} \frac{\partial}{\partial y} + \frac{\partial z}{\partial x'} \frac{\partial}{\partial z} .]$$

7. The *critical angle* at the interface between two media is the smallest angle of incidence at which total internal reflection occurs. Determine the critical angle for a beam of light traveling upward through water toward the surface, where it meets the air. The index of refraction of water is 1.33, and the index of refraction of air is 1.00.

CHAPTER

6

Illumination

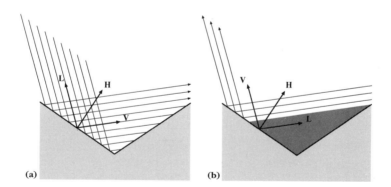

(a)

(b)

T his chapter describes the mathematics used to illuminate a surface. The illumination process, commonly called *shading*, requires that we determine for each pixel representing a surface the color of the light reflected toward the viewer. This color depends on the properties of the light sources illuminating the surface as well as the reflective characteristics of the surface itself.

The interaction between light and a surface is a complex physical process. Photons can be absorbed, reflected, or transmitted when they strike the surface of a material. To model this interaction using the whole of today's knowledge of physics would be far too computationally time consuming. Instead, we must settle for models that approximate the expected appearance of a surface. We begin with simple models that are widely used because they are computationally efficient and produce acceptable results but that really are not physically accurate. Later, we examine more costly techniques that more closely model the true physical interaction of light with a surface.

6.1 RGB COLOR

A precise model describing the reflection of light by a surface would account for every wavelength of light in the visible spectrum. Most computer monitors, however, display color information using a combination of only three wavelengths of light: red, green, and blue. This system is commonly referred to as *RGB color*. Intermediate wavelengths are simulated by blending these three primary colors together in appropriate ratios. For instance, yellow is produced by blending equal parts red and green. Colors that are made up of more than one wavelength of light, such as brown, can also be simulated using RGB color.

The lighting models presented in this chapter adhere to the RGB color system. The reflection of light at a point on a surface is calculated for red, green, and blue wavelengths simultaneously. Since the same operations are performed for each of these components, we express our mathematical formulas using a three-component entity that we simply call a *color*.

Colors are expressed as triplets of red, green, and blue components whose values range from zero to one. These colors represent both the spectral composition of light, which determines what color the eye perceives, as well as the intensity of light. We denote a component of a color $\mathbf{C}$ using a subscript r, g, or b (hence, we can write $\mathbf{C} = \langle C_r, C_g, C_b \rangle$).

A color $\mathbf{C}$ can be multiplied by a scalar s to produce a new color:

$$s\mathbf{C} = \langle sC_r, sC_g, sC_b \rangle. \tag{6.1}$$

Addition and multiplication of colors are performed componentwise. That is, for two colors $\mathbf{C}$ and $\mathbf{D}$, we have

$$\mathbf{C} + \mathbf{D} = \langle C_r + D_r, C_g + D_g, C_b + D_b \rangle$$

$$\mathbf{CD} = \langle C_r D_r, C_g D_g, C_b D_b \rangle. \tag{6.2}$$

Color multiplication, either by another color or by a scalar, is also called *modulation*. The color of a pixel belonging to a rendered triangle is usually determined through some combination of colors from multiple sources. The color of a pixel on the face of a triangle is commonly derived from the product of a color looked up in a texture map and another color that is interpolated among the triangle's vertices. In this case, we say that the texture color is *modulated* by the vertex color.

6.2 LIGHT SOURCES

The color that we calculate for any point on a surface is the sum of contributions from all the light sources that illuminate the surface. The standard types of light sources supported by 3D graphics systems come in four varieties: ambient, directional, point, and spot. This section describes each of these types of light sources and how they contribute to the radiation present at a point in space.

6.2.1 AMBIENT LIGHT

The *ambient* light present at a certain location is the low-intensity light that arises from the many reflections of light on all nearby surfaces in an environment. Using ambient light provides a rough approximation of the general brightness of an area and replaces the complexities of calculating all the interobject reflections in a scene.

Ambient light appears to come from every direction with equal intensity, and thus illuminates every part of an object uniformly. The color $\mathbf{A}$ of the ambient light is usually a constant in a scene, but it may also be a function of spatial position. For instance, one can use a three-dimensional texture map to store samples of the ambient light on a regular grid that permeates a region of the world.

6.2.2 DIRECTIONAL LIGHT SOURCES

A *directional* light source, also known as an *infinite* light source, is one that radiates light in a single direction from infinitely far away. Directional lights are typically used to model light sources such as the sun, whose rays can be considered parallel. Since they have no position in space, directional lights have infinite range, and the intensity of the light they radiate does not diminish over distance, as does the intensity of point lights and spot lights.

6.2.3 POINT LIGHT SOURCES

A *point* light source is one that radiates light equally in every direction from a single point in space. The intensity of light naturally decreases with distance according to the inverse square law. OpenGL and Direct3D both implement a generalization of this concept that allows us to control the intensity of light radiated by a point light source using the reciprocal of a quadratic polynomial.

Suppose that a point light source has been placed at a point $\mathbf{P}$. The intensity $\mathbf{C}$ of light reaching a point in space $\mathbf{Q}$ is given by

$$\mathbf{C} = \frac{1}{k_c + k_l d + k_q d^2}\, \mathbf{C}_0, \tag{6.3}$$

where $\mathbf{C}_0$ is the color of the light, d is the distance between the light source and $\mathbf{Q}$ (i.e., $d = \|\mathbf{P} - \mathbf{Q}\|$), and the constants k_c, k_l, and k_q are called the constant, linear, and quadratic attenuation constants.

6.2.4 SPOT LIGHT SOURCES

A *spot* light is similar to a point light but has a preferred direction of radiation. The intensity of a spot light is attenuated over distance in the same way that it is for a point light and is also attenuated by another factor, called the spot light effect.

Suppose that a spot light source has been placed at a point $\mathbf{P}$ and has a spot direction $\mathbf{U}$. The intensity $\mathbf{C}$ of light reaching a point in space $\mathbf{Q}$ is given by

$$\mathbf{C} = \frac{\max\{-\mathbf{U} \cdot \mathbf{L}, 0\}^p}{k_c + k_l d + k_q d^2}\, \mathbf{C}_0, \tag{6.4}$$

where $\mathbf{C}_0$ is the color of the light; d is the distance between the light source and $\mathbf{Q}$; k_c, k_l, and k_q are the attenuation constants; and $\mathbf{L}$ is the unit length direction pointing from $\mathbf{Q}$ toward the light source:

$$\mathbf{L} = \frac{\mathbf{P} - \mathbf{Q}}{\|\mathbf{P} - \mathbf{Q}\|}. \tag{6.5}$$

The exponent p controls how concentrated the spot light is. As shown in Figure 6.1, a large value of p corresponds to a highly focused spot light having a sharp falloff, whereas a smaller value of p corresponds to a less concentrated beam. The spot light is most intense when $\mathbf{U} = -\mathbf{L}$ and gradually falls off as the angle between $\mathbf{U}$ and $-\mathbf{L}$ increases. No radiation from a spot light reaches a point for which the angle between $\mathbf{U}$ and $-\mathbf{L}$ is greater than 90 degrees.

FIGURE
6.1
The spot light exponent p controls how concentrated the beam of a spot light is. From left to right, the spot light exponents used to illuminate the ground are 2, 10, 50, and 100.

6.3 DIFFUSE LIGHTING

A diffuse surface is one for which part of the light incident on a point on the surface is scattered in random directions. The average effect is that a certain color of light, the surface's diffuse reflection color, is reflected uniformly in every direction. This is called the *Lambertian* reflection, and because light is reflected equally in every direction, the appearance of the Lambertian reflection does not depend on the position of the observer.

As shown in Figure 6.2, a beam of light having a cross-sectional area A illuminates the same area A on a surface only if the surface is perpendicular to the direction in which the light is traveling. As the angle between the normal vector and the light direction increases, so does the surface area illuminated by the beam of light. If the angle between the normal vector and light direction is θ, then the surface area illuminated by the beam of light is equal to $A/\cos\theta$. This results in a *decrease* in the intensity of the light per unit surface area by a factor of $\cos\theta$.

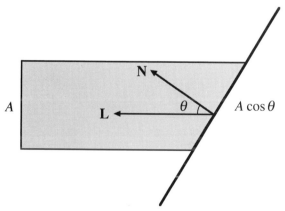

FIGURE
6.2
The surface area illuminated by a beam of light increases as the angle between the surface normal and direction to the light increases, decreasing the intensity of incident light per unit area.

The value of $\cos \theta$ is given by the dot product between the normal vector **N** and the unit direction to the light source **L**. A negative dot product means that the surface is facing away from the light source and should not be illuminated at all. Thus, we clamp the dot product to zero in our illumination calculations.

We can now begin to construct a formula that calculates the color of light **K** that is reflected toward the viewer from a given point **Q** on a surface. This formula is written in terms of the intensity $\mathbf{C}_i$ of each of n lights illuminating the point **Q**, which is constant for directional light sources and is given by Equations (6.3) and (6.4) for point and spot light sources. The reflected light is modulated by the surface's diffuse reflection color **D**. Adding the contributions from n light sources and considering the ambient intensity **A**, we can express the diffuse component of our lighting formula as

$$\mathbf{K}_{\text{diffuse}} = \mathbf{DTA} + \mathbf{DT}\sum_{i=1}^{n} \mathbf{C}_i \max\{\mathbf{N} \cdot \mathbf{L}_i, 0\}, \tag{6.6}$$

where the unit vector $\mathbf{L}_i$ points from **Q** toward the i-th light source.

6.4 TEXTURE MAPPING

One or more *texture* maps may be applied to a surface to achieve greater detail, as shown in Figure 6.3. At each point on a surface, a *texel* (texture pixel) is looked up in each texture map and combined in some way with the lighting formula. In the simplest case, a sample from a diffuse texture map is looked up and used to modulate the diffuse reflection color. More advanced applications are discussed later in this chapter.

FIGURE *Applying a texture map adds detail to a surface.*
6.3

Let the color **T** represent a filtered sample from a texture map at a point on a surface. Using this color to modulate the diffuse reflection color produces the following augmented version of Equation (6.6).

$$\mathbf{K}_{\text{diffuse}} = \mathbf{DTA} + \mathbf{DT}\sum_{i=1}^{n}\mathbf{C}_i\ \max\{\mathbf{N} \cdot \mathbf{L}_i, 0\}, \tag{6.7}$$

The actual color sampled from the texture map is determined by texture co-ordinates applied to an object. Texture coordinates are either precomputed and stored with each vertex of a triangle mesh or calculated at runtime to produce some special effect. The texture coordinates are then interpolated using Equation (4.36) across the face of a triangle when it is rendered. There may be from one to four coordinates at each vertex, and they are labeled s, t, r, and q. The next few sections describe the different varieties of texture maps and how texture coordinates are used to look up a texel in each type.

6.4.1 STANDARD TEXTURE MAPS

One, two, or three texture coordinates may be used to look up texels in one-, two-, or three-dimensional texture maps. As shown in Figure 6.4, the entire width, height, and depth of a texture map corresponds to coordinate values lying between zero and one in the s, t, and r directions.

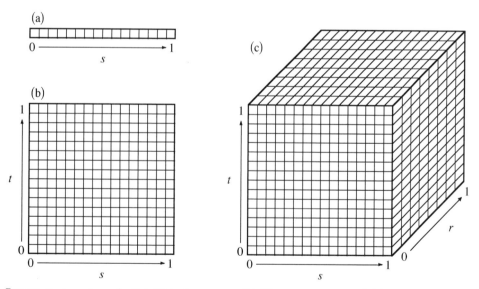

FIGURE *Texture space for (a) 1D texture maps, (b) 2D texture maps, and (c) 3D texture*
6.4 *maps.*

A one-dimensional texture map can be thought of as a two-dimensional texture map that is only a single pixel in height. Similarly, a two-dimensional texture map can be thought of as a three-dimensional texture map that is only a single pixel in depth. When t- and r-coordinates are not specified, they are assumed to be zero.

6.4.2 PROJECTIVE TEXTURE MAPS

The fourth texture coordinate is used for projective texture mapping, an application of which is described later in this section. The q-coordinate behaves in much the same way the w-coordinate does for homogeneous points and is assumed to be one when not specified. The interpolated s-, t-, and r-coordinates are divided by the interpolated q-coordinate. For a scanline whose endpoints have texture coordinates $\langle s_1, t_1, r_1, q_1 \rangle$ and $\langle s_2, t_2, r_2, q_2 \rangle$, we can use Equation (4.36) to calculate interpolated values s_3 and q_3 at some intermediate parameter $u \in [0,1]$. The quotient of these two values gives the following expression for the s-coordinate used to sample the texture map.

$$s = \frac{s_3}{q_3} = \frac{(1-u)\dfrac{s_1}{z_1} + u\dfrac{s_2}{z_2}}{(1-u)\dfrac{q_1}{z_1} + u\dfrac{q_2}{z_2}} \tag{6.8}$$

Similar expressions give the projected t and r texture coordinates.

One application of projective texture maps is the simulation of a spot light that projects an image onto the environment. As shown in Figure 6.5, the projected image becomes larger as distance from the spot light increases. The effect is achieved by using a 4×4 texture matrix to map the vertex positions of an object to texture coordinates $\langle s, t, 0, q \rangle$ such that division by q produces the correct 2D texture coordinates $\langle s, t \rangle$ used to sample the projected image.

Suppose that a spot light has been placed at the point $\mathbf{P}$ and points in the direction $\mathbf{U}$. Let the unit vectors $\mathbf{S}$ and $\mathbf{T}$ lie in the plane perpendicular to $\mathbf{U}$ such that they are aligned to the directions in which the s- and t-axes of the projected texture image should be oriented (see Figure 6.5). Each vertex position $\langle x, y, z, 1 \rangle$ belonging to a surface illuminated by the spot light must first be transformed into the coordinate system in which the spot light lies at the origin and the x-, y-, and z-axes correspond to the directions $\mathbf{S}$, $\mathbf{T}$, and $\mathbf{U}$. This can be accomplished using the inverse of the matrix whose columns are the vectors $\mathbf{S}$, $\mathbf{T}$, $\mathbf{U}$, and $\mathbf{P}$. If $\mathbf{S}$ and $\mathbf{T}$ are orthogonal (i.e., the projected image is not skewed), the transformation is given by

$$\mathbf{M}_1 = \begin{bmatrix} S_x & S_y & S_z & -\mathbf{S} \cdot \mathbf{P} \\ T_x & T_y & T_z & -\mathbf{T} \cdot \mathbf{P} \\ U_x & U_y & U_z & -\mathbf{U} \cdot \mathbf{P} \\ 0 & 0 & 0 & 1 \end{bmatrix}. \tag{6.9}$$

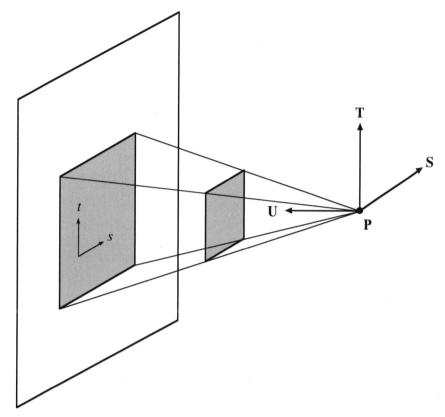

FIGURE   *A projective texture map can be used to simulate a spot light that projects an image*
6.5   *onto the environment.*

(Note that this matrix transforms into a left-handed coordinate system since
$\mathbf{S} \times \mathbf{T} = -\mathbf{U}$.)

Now we need to multiply the matrix in Equation (6.9) by a second matrix that
performs the projection. Just as we define the focal length of the view frustum,
we can define the focal length of the spot light projection in terms of an apex
angle α. The focal length e is given by

$$e = \frac{1}{\tan(\alpha/2)}. \tag{6.10}$$

Let a be the aspect ratio of the texture map, equal to its height divided by its
width. Every vertex position should be projected onto the plane lying at a distance e from the spot light, where we want to map the interval $[-1, 1]$ in the x
direction to $[0, 1]$, and we want to map the interval $[-a, a]$ in the y direction to
$[0, 1]$. The matrix

$$\mathbf{M}_2 = \begin{bmatrix} e/2 & 0 & 1/2 & 0 \\ 0 & e/2a & 1/2 & 0 \\ 0 & 0 & 0 & 0 \\ 0 & 0 & 1 & 0 \end{bmatrix} \tag{6.11}$$

performs this mapping and causes the projection to occur when the s- and t-coordinates are divided by the q-coordinate of the result. Combining the matrices given in Equations (6.9) and (6.11), the 4×4 texture matrix $\mathbf{M}$ used to implement a projected spot light image is given by $\mathbf{M} = \mathbf{M}_2\mathbf{M}_1$.

6.4.3 CUBE TEXTURE MAPS

A relatively new method of texturing an object is enabled through the use of a *cube texture map*. Cube texture maps are often used to approximate an environmental reflection on the surface of a model. Shown in Figure 6.6, a cube texture map consists of six two-dimensional components that correspond to the faces of a cube. The s-, t-, and r-coordinates represent a direction vector emanating from the center of the cube that points toward the texel to be sampled.

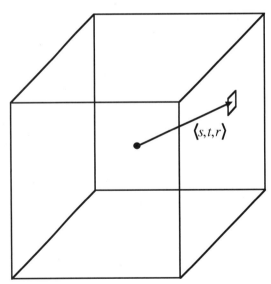

FIGURE *A cube texture map consists of six components that correspond to the faces of a cube.*
6.6

Which face to sample is determined by the sign of the coordinate having the largest absolute value. The other two coordinates are divided by the largest coordinate and remapped to the range [0, 1] using the formulas listed in Table 6.1 to produce 2D texture coordinates $\langle s', t' \rangle$. These coordinates are then used to

Table 6.1 Formulas used to calculate the 2D coordinates $\langle s', t' \rangle$ used to sample a texel in one of the six faces of a cube texture map.

Face	s'	t'
Positive x	$\dfrac{1}{2} - \dfrac{r}{2s}$	$\dfrac{1}{2} + \dfrac{t}{2s}$
Negative x	$\dfrac{1}{2} - \dfrac{r}{2s}$	$\dfrac{1}{2} + \dfrac{t}{2s}$
Positive y	$\dfrac{1}{2} + \dfrac{s}{2t}$	$\dfrac{1}{2} + \dfrac{r}{2t}$
Negative y	$\dfrac{1}{2} - \dfrac{s}{2t}$	$\dfrac{1}{2} + \dfrac{r}{2t}$
Positive z	$\dfrac{1}{2} + \dfrac{s}{2r}$	$\dfrac{1}{2} - \dfrac{t}{2r}$
Negative z	$\dfrac{1}{2} + \dfrac{s}{2r}$	$\dfrac{1}{2} + \dfrac{t}{2r}$

sample the two-dimensional texture map for the corresponding face of the cube texture map. Figure 6.7 shows the orientation of the cube map axes relative to each of the six faces.

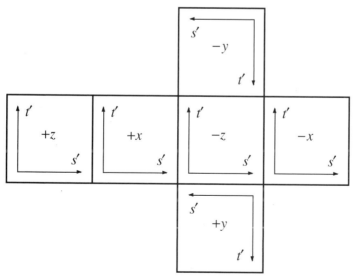

FIGURE *Orientation of the cube map axes relative to each of the six faces.*
6.7

Texture coordinates used in conjunction with cube texture maps are typically generated at runtime. For instance, environment mapping can be performed by calculating the reflection of the direction to the camera and storing it in the $\langle s, t, r \rangle$ coordinates at each vertex of a triangle mesh. The reflection direction calculation is normally implemented in hardware, so this can be done very efficiently.

An invaluable application of cube texture maps is that of normalizing vectors. A *normalization cube map* is a cube texture map that, instead of storing color images in each of its six faces, stores an array of vectors that are encoded as RGB colors using the following formulas.

$$\text{red} = \frac{x + 1}{2}$$

$$\text{green} = \frac{y + 1}{2}$$

$$\text{blue} = \frac{z + 1}{2}. \tag{6.12}$$

The vector stored at each pixel of a face of the cube map is the unit length vector $\langle s, t, r \rangle$ that causes that pixel to be sampled. The use of a normalization cube map becomes desirable when performing per-pixel lighting because interpolation of surface normals across the face of a triangle invariably produces normal vectors whose length is less than one.

6.5 SPECULAR LIGHTING

In addition to the uniform diffuse reflection, surfaces tend to reflect light strongly along the path given by the reflection of the incident direction across the surface normal. This results in the appearance of a shiny highlight on a surface called a *specularity*. Unlike the diffuse reflection, the specular reflection visible on a surface depends on the position of the viewer.

Figure 6.8 shows the normal vector **N** at a point **Q** on a surface, the unit direction to viewer vector **V**, the unit direction to light vector **L**, and the direct reflection vector **R** calculated using Equation (5.83) corresponding to the vector **L**. Specular highlights are the most intense when the reflection direction **R** points toward the viewer and decrease in intensity as the angle between **R** and the direction to the viewer **V** increases.

A model that produces a believable (but having almost no real physical basis) rendition of specular highlights uses the expression

$$\mathbf{SC} \max\{\mathbf{R} \cdot \mathbf{V}, 0\}^{m} \, (\mathbf{N} \cdot \mathbf{L} > 0) \tag{6.13}$$

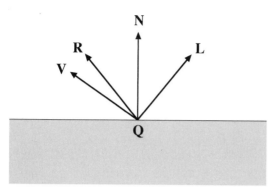

FIGURE **6.8** *The intensity of the specular reflection is related to the angle between the direction to viewer vector **V** and the direct reflection vector **R** corresponding to the direction to light vector **L**.*

to calculate the specular contribution from a single light source, where **S** is the surface's specular reflection color, **C** is the intensity of the incident light, and *m* is called the *specular exponent*. The expression $(\mathbf{N} \cdot \mathbf{L} > 0)$ is a Boolean expression that evaluates to one if true and zero otherwise. This prevents specular highlights from showing up at points on a surface that face away from the light source.

The specular exponent *m* controls the sharpness of the specular highlight. As shown in Figure 6.9, a small value of *m* produces a dull highlight that fades out over a relatively large distance, and a large value of *m* produces a sharp highlight that fades out quickly as the vectors **V** and **R** diverge.

An alternative formulation of specular highlights that requires less calculation in some cases makes use of a direction called the *halfway vector*. Shown in Figure 6.10, the halfway vector **H** is the vector lying exactly halfway between the direction to viewer vector **V** and the direction light vector **L**. Specular highlights are the most intense when **H** points in the direction of the normal vector **N**. Using this model, we replace the dot product $\mathbf{R} \cdot \mathbf{V}$ in Equation (6.13) with the dot product $\mathbf{N} \cdot \mathbf{H}$. This produces different results in terms of the rate at which

FIGURE **6.9** *The specular exponent m controls the sharpness of the specular highlight seen on a surface. From left to right, the specular exponents used to illuminate the tori are 2, 10, 50, and 100.*

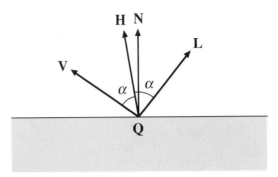

FIGURE *The angle between the normal vector **N** and the halfway vector **H** can also be used to*
6.10 *determine specular intensity.*

specular highlights diminish but still retains the general characteristics of our original model.

Adding the contributions from n light sources, we can express the specular component of our lighting formula as

$$\mathbf{K}_{\text{specular}} = \mathbf{S} \sum_{i=1}^{n} \mathbf{C}_i \max\{\mathbf{N} \cdot \mathbf{H}_i, 0\}^m (\mathbf{N} \cdot \mathbf{L}_i > 0), \qquad (6.14)$$

where $\mathbf{H}_i$ is the halfway vector for the i-th light source given by

$$\mathbf{H}_i = \frac{\mathbf{L}_i + \mathbf{V}}{\|\mathbf{L}_i + \mathbf{V}\|}. \qquad (6.15)$$

Just as a texture map can be used to modulate the diffuse component of the lighting formula, we can also use a map to modulate the specular component. Such a map is called a *gloss map* and determines the intensity of the specularity at each point on a surface. Using the color $\mathbf{G}$ to represent a filtered sample from the gloss map, we can augment the formula for the specular contribution as follows.

$$\mathbf{K}_{\text{specular}} = \mathbf{SG} \sum_{i=1}^{n} \mathbf{C}_i \max\{\mathbf{N} \cdot \mathbf{H}_i, 0\}^m (\mathbf{N} \cdot \mathbf{L}_i > 0) \qquad (6.16)$$

6.6 EMISSION

Some objects may emit light in addition to reflecting it. To give an object the appearance of emitting a uniform glow, we add an emission color $\mathbf{E}$ to our lighting formula. This emission color can also be modulated by an *emission map*, which determines the color and intensity of the glow at each point on a surface. Using the color $\mathbf{M}$ to represent a filtered sample from the emission map, the emission component of the lighting formula is given by the simple expression

$$\mathbf{K}_{\text{emission}} = \mathbf{EM}. \tag{6.17}$$

Figure 6.11 demonstrates the application of an emission map to the surface of a torus.

FIGURE *Applying an emission map to the surface of an object determines which parts of the*
6.11 *surface appear to give off a glow.*

6.7 SHADING

Information about the surface of a model, such as the positions of points on the surface and the normal vectors at those points, are stored only for each vertex of a triangle mesh. When a single triangle is rendered, information known at each vertex is interpolated across the face of the triangle, as discussed in Section 4.4.2. Conventional lighting pipelines calculate diffuse and specular illumination only at the vertices of a mesh. More modern graphics hardware enables the calculation of the entire illumination formula at every individual pixel drawn to the display. The manner in which lighting is determined for the surface of a triangle, combined with any number of texture maps, is called *shading*.

6.7.1 CALCULATING NORMAL VECTORS

To apply the lighting formula to a triangle mesh, we need to have a representation of the surface normal at each vertex. We can calculate the normal vector for a single triangle by using the cross product. The unit-length normal vector $\mathbf{N}$ of a triangle whose vertices lie at the points $\mathbf{P}_0$, $\mathbf{P}_1$, and $\mathbf{P}_2$ is given by

$$\mathbf{N} = \frac{\left(\mathbf{P}_1 - \mathbf{P}_0\right) \times \left(\mathbf{P}_2 - \mathbf{P}_0\right)}{\left\|\left(\mathbf{P}_1 - \mathbf{P}_0\right) \times \left(\mathbf{P}_2 - \mathbf{P}_0\right)\right\|}. \tag{6.18}$$

This assumes that the vertices are oriented in a counterclockwise fashion when the normal points toward the viewer, as shown in Figure 6.12.

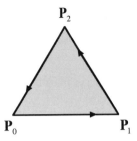

FIGURE *The vertices of a triangle should be oriented in a counterclockwise fashion when the*
6.12 *normal vector points toward the viewer.*

The normal vector at a single vertex is typically calculated by averaging the
normal vectors of all triangles that share that vertex. Using the formula

$$\mathbf{N}_{\text{vertex}} = \frac{\sum_{i=1}^{k} \mathbf{N}_i}{\left\| \sum_{i=1}^{k} \mathbf{N}_i \right\|} \tag{6.19}$$

to calculate the normal vector $\mathbf{N}_{\text{vertex}}$ for a vertex shared by k triangles results in
a vertex normal that is influenced equally by the normal vector $\mathbf{N}_i$ of each of the
triangles surrounding it.

An alternative formulation, illustrated in Figure 6.13, makes use of the fact that
the cross product of two vectors is proportional to the area of the triangle that they
form. By using the unnormalized triangle normals calculated with the equation

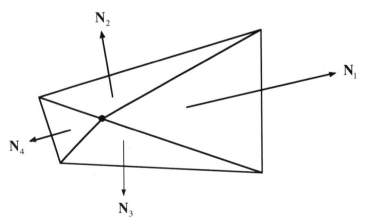

FIGURE *By averaging the unnormalized normal vectors of each triangle sharing a vertex, a*
6.13 *vertex normal can be calculated that is influenced more strongly by triangles with*
greater area.

$$\mathbf{N} = (\mathbf{P}_1 - \mathbf{P}_0) \times (\mathbf{P}_2 - \mathbf{P}_0) \tag{6.20}$$

instead of Equation (6.18) and then averaging using Equation (6.19), we can calculate a vertex normal that is more strongly influenced by triangles with greater area. This method produces more appealing vertex normals for some models.

6.7.2 GOURAUD SHADING

The interpolation of lighting values calculated at each vertex across the face of a triangle is known as *Gouraud shading*. Before the advent of graphics hardware capable of performing per-pixel lighting calculations, diffuse and specular colors were calculated only at each vertex of a triangle mesh. This method calculates the colors

$$\mathbf{K}_{\text{primary}} = \mathbf{E} + \mathbf{DA} + \mathbf{D} \sum_{i=1}^{n} \mathbf{C}_i \max\{\mathbf{N} \cdot \mathbf{L}_i, 0\}$$

$$\mathbf{K}_{\text{secondary}} = \mathbf{S} \sum_{i=1}^{n} \mathbf{C}_i \max\{\mathbf{N} \cdot \mathbf{H}_i, 0\}^m (\mathbf{N} \cdot \mathbf{L}_i > 0) \tag{6.21}$$

at each vertex and interpolates them across the face of a triangle. The color $\mathbf{K}$ of a pixel is then calculated using the equation

$$\mathbf{K} = \mathbf{K}_{\text{primary}} \circ \mathbf{T}_1 \circ \mathbf{T}_2 \circ \cdots \circ \mathbf{T}_k + \mathbf{K}_{\text{secondary}}, \tag{6.22}$$

where each $\mathbf{T}_i$ represents a color sampled from one of k texture maps, and the operation $\circ$ is one of several available texture combination operations, including modulation and addition.

6.7.3 PHONG SHADING

Instead of interpolating lighting values calculated at each vertex, a *Phong-shaded* triangle interpolates the vertex normals and evaluates the lighting formula at each pixel. Graphics hardware that can perform complex calculations on a per-pixel basis (a process called *pixel shading* or *fragment shading*) can be configured to evaluate the entire expression

$$\mathbf{K} = \mathbf{K}_{\text{emission}} + \mathbf{K}_{\text{diffuse}} + \mathbf{K}_{\text{specular}}$$

$$= \mathbf{EM} + \mathbf{DTA} + \sum_{i=1}^{n} \mathbf{C}_i \left[\mathbf{DT}(\mathbf{N} \cdot \mathbf{L}_i) + \mathbf{SG}(\mathbf{N} \cdot \mathbf{H}_i)^m (\mathbf{N} \cdot \mathbf{L}_i > 0) \right] \tag{6.23}$$

at each pixel composing the face of a triangle. In the interests of simplicity, we have omitted the maximum functions here, but it should be noted that the diffuse and specular dot products in this equation are clamped to zero. The intensity $\mathbf{C}_i$ of each of the n light sources is still calculated at each vertex and interpolated across the face of a triangle. These values and the interpolated normal vector are used to evaluate **K** at each pixel. Of course, not every component of Equation (6.23) needs to be present.

An advantage that Phong shading possesses over Gouraud shading is that it does a far better job of modeling specularity due to the fact that the dot product **N** · **H** is evaluated at every pixel. When a sharp specular highlight falls in the interior of a triangle, Gouraud shading produces poor results because the specular component calculated at the triangle's vertices is unrepresentative of the true values existing elsewhere on the face of the triangle.

A problem that arises when using Phong shading is that interpolated normal vectors do not retain the unit length that they have at the vertices. Densely tessellated models for which the normal vectors belonging to neighboring vertices differ in direction by only a small amount may not produce visually unacceptable artifacts, but most models exhibit a noticeable darkening of the specularity in the interior of each triangle. This problem is solved by using a normalization cube map (see Section 6.4.3). Normal vectors are passed into the texture engine as $\langle s, t, r \rangle$ mapping coordinates, which results in the output of unit vectors encoded as RGB colors.

6.8 BUMP MAPPING

The surface detail that an observer perceives when an object is viewed from any direction other than edge-on is generally determined by the way in which its surface is illuminated. The illumination at each pixel rendered is determined by the normal vector used during the evaluation of the lighting formula. So far, we have been limited to calculating normal vectors only at the vertices of a triangle mesh and using a smoothly interpolated normal vector elsewhere. This coarse resolution prevents us from illuminating any details that are smaller than a typical triangle in a mesh. *Bump mapping* is a technique that presents the illusion of greater detail to the viewer by using a texture map to perturb the normal vector at each pixel.

6.8.1 BUMP MAP CONSTRUCTION

High-resolution information about how the normal vector is perturbed is stored in a two-dimensional array of three-dimensional vectors called a *bump map* or *normal map*. Each vector in the bump map represents the direction in which the normal vector should point relative to the interpolated normal vector at a point inside the face of a triangle. The vector $\langle 0, 0, 1 \rangle$ represents an unperturbed normal, whereas any other vector represents a modification to the normal that affects the result of the lighting formula.

A bump map is typically constructed by extracting normal vectors from a height map whose contents represent the height of a flat surface at each pixel. To derive the normal vector corresponding to a particular pixel in the height map, we first calculate tangents in the s and t directions, which are based on the difference in height between adjacent pixels. Using the notation $H(i, j)$ to represent the value stored at coordinates $\langle i, j \rangle$ in a $w \times h$ pixel height map, we can express the tangent vectors $\mathbf{S}(i, j)$ and $\mathbf{T}(i, j)$, aligned to the s and t directions respectively, as follows.

$$\mathbf{S}(i, j) = \langle 1, 0, aH(i + 1, j) - aH(i - 1, j) \rangle$$
$$\mathbf{T}(i, j) = \langle 0, 1, aH(i, j + 1) - aH(i, j - 1) \rangle \qquad (6.24)$$

The constant a is scale factor that can be used to vary the range of the height values, controlling how pronounced the perturbed normals are. If we let S_z and T_z denote the z-components of $\mathbf{S}(i, j)$ and $\mathbf{T}(i, j)$, then the normal vector $\mathbf{N}(i, j)$ is calculated using the cross product

$$\mathbf{N}(i, j) = \frac{\mathbf{S}(i, j) \times \mathbf{T}(i, j)}{\left\| \mathbf{S}(i, j) \times \mathbf{T}(i, j) \right\|} = \frac{\langle -S_z, -T_z, 1 \rangle}{\sqrt{S_z^2 + T_z^2 + 1}} . \qquad (6.25)$$

The components of each normal vector are encoded as an RGB color using the relations given in Equation (6.12). Figure 6.14 shows a grayscale height map and the corresponding bump map calculated using Equation (6.25).

 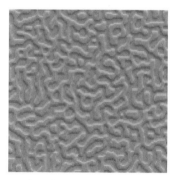

FIGURE   *A height map and the corresponding bump map containing perturbed normal*
6.14   *vectors. A pastel purple color is prevalent in the bump map since the unperturbed*
   normal vector $\langle 0, 0, 1 \rangle$ corresponds to the RGB color $\left\langle \frac{1}{2}, \frac{1}{2}, 1 \right\rangle$.

6.8.2 TANGENT SPACE

Since the vector $\langle 0, 0, 1 \rangle$ in a bump map represents an unperturbed normal, we need it to correspond to the interpolated normal vector that we would ordinarily use in the lighting formula. This can be achieved by constructing a coordinate system at each vertex in which the vertex normal always points along the positive z-axis. In addition to the normal vector, we need two vectors tangent to the surface at each vertex that form an orthonormal basis. The resulting coordinate system is called *tangent space* or *vertex space* and is shown in Figure 6.15.

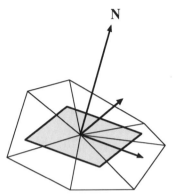

N

FIGURE   *Tangent space is aligned to the tangent plane and normal vector at a vertex.*
6.15

Once a tangent-space coordinate system has been established at each vertex of a triangle mesh, the direction to light vector **L** is calculated at each vertex and transformed into the tangent space. The tangent-space vector **L** is then interpolated across the face of a triangle. Since the vector $\langle 0, 0, 1 \rangle$ in tangent space corresponds to the normal vector, the dot product between the tangent-space direction to light **L** and a sample from a bump map produces a valid Lambertian reflection term.

The tangent vectors at each vertex must be chosen so that they are aligned to the texture space of the bump map. For surfaces generated by parametric functions, tangents can usually be calculated by simply taking derivatives with respect to each of the parameters. Arbitrary triangle meshes, however, can have bump maps applied to them in any orientation, which necessitates a more general method for determining the tangent directions at each vertex.

6.8.3 CALCULATING TANGENT VECTORS

Our goal is to find a 3×3 matrix at each vertex that transforms vectors from object space into tangent space. To accomplish this, we consider the more intuitive problem of transforming vectors in the reverse direction from tangent space into object space. Since the normal vector at a vertex corresponds to $\langle 0, 0, 1 \rangle$ in tangent space, we know that the z-axis of our tangent space always gets mapped to a vertex's normal vector.

We want our tangent space to be aligned such that the x-axis corresponds to the s direction in the bump map and the y-axis corresponds to the t direction in the bump map. That is, if **P** represents a point inside the triangle, we would like to be able to write

$$\mathbf{P} - \mathbf{E} = (s - s_{\mathrm{E}})\mathbf{T} + (t - t_{\mathrm{E}})\mathbf{B}, \tag{6.26}$$

where **T** and **B** are tangent vectors aligned to the texture map (the letter **B** stands for *binormal*), **E** is the position of one of the vertices of the triangle, and $\langle s_{\mathrm{E}}, t_{\mathrm{E}} \rangle$ are the texture coordinates at that vertex.

Suppose that we have a triangle whose vertex positions are given by the points **E**, **F**, and **G** and whose corresponding texture coordinates are given by $\langle s_{\mathrm{E}}, t_{\mathrm{E}} \rangle$, $\langle s_{\mathrm{F}}, t_{\mathrm{F}} \rangle$, and $\langle s_{\mathrm{G}}, t_{\mathrm{G}} \rangle$. Our calculations can be made much simpler by working relative to the vertex **E**, so we let

$$\mathbf{P} = \mathbf{F} - \mathbf{E}$$
$$\mathbf{Q} = \mathbf{G} - \mathbf{E} \tag{6.27}$$

and

$$\langle s_1, t_1 \rangle = \langle s_{\mathrm{F}} - s_{\mathrm{E}}, t_{\mathrm{F}} - t_{\mathrm{E}} \rangle$$
$$\langle s_2, t_2 \rangle = \langle s_{\mathrm{G}} - s_{\mathrm{E}}, t_{\mathrm{G}} - t_{\mathrm{E}} \rangle. \tag{6.28}$$

We need to solve the following equations for **T** and **B**.

$$\mathbf{P} = s_1\mathbf{T} + t_1\mathbf{B}$$
$$\mathbf{Q} = s_2\mathbf{T} + t_2\mathbf{B} \tag{6.29}$$

This is a linear system with six unknowns (three for each **T** and **B**) and six equations (the x-, y-, and z-components of the two equations). We can write this in matrix form, as follows.

$$\begin{bmatrix} P_x & P_y & P_z \\ Q_x & Q_y & Q_z \end{bmatrix} = \begin{bmatrix} s_1 & t_1 \\ s_2 & t_2 \end{bmatrix}\begin{bmatrix} T_x & T_y & T_z \\ B_x & B_y & B_z \end{bmatrix} \tag{6.30}$$

Multiplying both sides by the inverse of the $\langle s,t \rangle$ matrix, we have

$$\begin{bmatrix} T_x & T_y & T_z \\ B_x & B_y & B_z \end{bmatrix} = \frac{1}{s_1t_2 - s_2t_1}\begin{bmatrix} t_2 & -t_1 \\ -s_2 & s_1 \end{bmatrix}\begin{bmatrix} P_x & P_y & P_z \\ Q_x & Q_y & Q_z \end{bmatrix}. \tag{6.31}$$

This gives us the (unnormalized) **T** and **B** tangent vectors for the triangle whose vertices are **E**, **F**, and **G**. To find the tangent vectors for a single vertex, we average the tangents for all triangles sharing that vertex in a manner similar to the way in which vertex normals are commonly calculated. In the case that neighboring triangles have discontinuous texture mapping (see Figure 6.16), vertices along the border are generally already duplicated since they have different mapping coordinates anyway. We do not average tangents from such triangles because the result would not accurately represent the orientation of the bump map for either triangle.

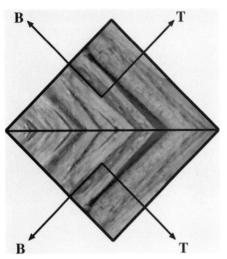

FIGURE *Neighboring triangles may have very different texture map orientations.*
6.16

Once we have the normal vector **N** and the tangent vectors **T** and **B** for a vertex, we can transform from tangent space into object space using the matrix

$$\begin{bmatrix} T_x & B_x & N_x \\ T_y & B_y & N_y \\ T_z & B_z & N_z \end{bmatrix}. \tag{6.32}$$

To transform in the opposite direction (from object space to tangent space—what we want to do to the light direction), we can simply use the inverse of this matrix. It is not necessarily true that the tangent vectors are perpendicular to each other or to the normal vector, so the inverse of this matrix is not generally equal to its transpose. It is safe to assume, however, that the three vectors will at least be *close* to orthogonal, so using the Gram-Schmidt algorithm (see Algorithm 1.16) to orthogonalize them should not cause any unacceptable distortions. Using this process, new (still unnormalized) tangent vectors **T′** and **B′** are given by

$$\mathbf{T}' = \mathbf{T} - (\mathbf{N} \cdot \mathbf{T})\mathbf{N}$$
$$\mathbf{B}' = \mathbf{B} - (\mathbf{N} \cdot \mathbf{B})\mathbf{N} - (\mathbf{T}' \cdot \mathbf{B})\mathbf{T}'. \tag{6.33}$$

Normalizing these vectors and storing them as the tangent and binormal for a vertex lets us use the matrix

$$\begin{bmatrix} T'_x & T'_y & T'_z \\ B'_x & B'_y & B'_z \\ N_x & N_y & N_z \end{bmatrix} \tag{6.34}$$

to transform the direction to light from object space into tangent space. Taking the dot product of the transformed light direction with a sample from the bump map then produces the correct Lambertian diffuse lighting value.

It is not necessary to store an extra array containing the per-vertex binormal since the cross product $\mathbf{N} \times \mathbf{T}'$ can be used to obtain $m\mathbf{B}'$, where $m = \pm1$ represents the handedness of the tangent space. The handedness value must be stored per vertex since the binormal $\mathbf{B}'$ obtained from $\mathbf{N} \times \mathbf{T}'$ may point in the wrong direction. The value of m is equal to the determinant of the matrix in Equation (6.34). One may find it convenient to store the per-vertex tangent vector $\mathbf{T}'$ as a four-dimensional entity whose w-coordinate holds the value of m. Then the binormal $\mathbf{B}'$ can be computed using the formula

$$\mathbf{B}' = \mathbf{T}'_w (\mathbf{N} \times \mathbf{T}'), \tag{6.35}$$

where the cross product ignores the w-coordinate. This works nicely for vertex programs by avoiding the need to specify an additional array containing the per-vertex m values.

6.8.4 IMPLEMENTATION

Bump mapping operations can be divided into those calculated for each vertex and those calculated for each pixel. At each vertex, we must calculate the direction to light $\mathbf{L}$ and the halfway vector $\mathbf{H}$ and transform them into tangent space using Equation (6.34). The vertex program shown in Listing 6.1 performs these calculations for a surface illuminated by a directional light source (for which $\mathbf{L}$ is constant).

Listing 6.1. This vertex program performs the calculations necessary for bump mapping. The orthonormalized tangent $\mathbf{T}'$ is read from vertex attribute array 6, and the binormal $\mathbf{B}'$ is calculated using Equation (6.35). The tangent-space direction-to-light $\mathbf{L}$ is stored in the primary color, and the tangent-space halfway vector $\mathbf{H}$ is stored in the secondary color. The bump map is bound to texture unit 0, and the ordinary texture map is bound to texture unit 1.

```
!!VP1.0

# c[0 - 3] = projection * modelview matrix
# c[4] = constant (0.5, 0.5, 0.5, 0.0)
# c[5] = object space camera position
# c[6] = object space light direction L

DP4   o[HPOS].x, c[0], v[OPOS];          # Transform vertex
DP4   o[HPOS].y, c[1], v[OPOS];
DP4   o[HPOS].z, c[2], v[OPOS];
DP4   o[HPOS].w, c[3], v[OPOS];
```

```
MOV    R0, v[NRML];                       # Load normal N
MOV    R1, v[6];                          # Load tangent T

MUL    R2.xyz, R0.zxyw, R1.yzxw;          # B = N x T
MAD    R2.xyz, R0.yzxw, R1.zxyw, -R2;
MUL    R2, R2, R1.w;                      # B *= T.w

ADD    R3, c[5], -v[OPOS];                # R3 = view direction V
DP3    R5, R3, R3;                        # Normalize V
RSQ    R5.x, R5.x;
MUL    R3.xyz, R3, R5.x;

ADD    R4, R3, c[6];                      # R4 = halfway vector H
DP3    R6, R4, R4;                        # Normalize H
RSQ    R6.x, R6.x;
MUL    R4.xyz, R4, R6.x;

DP3    R7.x, R1, c[6];                    # Transform L into
DP3    R7.y, R2, c[6];                    # tangent space
DP3    R7.z, R0, c[6];
MAD    o[COL0], R7, c[4], c[4];           # Encode as RGB

DP3    R8.x, R1, R4;                      # Transform H into
DP3    R8.y, R2, R4;                      # tangent space
DP3    R8.z, R0, R4;
MAD    o[COL1], R8, c[4], c[4];           # Encode as RGB

MOV    o[TEX0], v[TEX0];                  # Copy bump map coords
MOV    o[TEX1], v[TEX1];                  # Copy texture map coords
END
```

The dot products $\mathbf{N} \cdot \mathbf{L}$ and $\mathbf{N} \cdot \mathbf{H}$ are calculated for every pixel, where the normal vector $\mathbf{N}$ is sampled from the bump map and the vectors $\mathbf{L}$ and $\mathbf{H}$ are interpolated among the values calculated at each vertex. Since these vectors are interpolated, their magnitudes can become slightly reduced, which may cause the interiors of triangles to appear darker than they should. This effect is often not noticeable, but models lacking sufficient tessellation may require the use of normalization cube maps. For hardware having enough texture units, we can modify Listing 6.1 so that the tangent-space $\mathbf{L}$ and $\mathbf{H}$ vectors index into a cube map that effectively normalizes the texture coordinates. To accomplish this, we bind normalization cube maps to both texture units 2 and 3, and we replace the transformation of $\mathbf{L}$ and $\mathbf{H}$ with the following code. Hardware having only two texture units requires that we render using multiple passes.

```
DP3    o[TEX2].x, R1, c[6];                    # Transform L into
DP3    o[TEX2].y, R2, c[6];                    # tangent space
DP3    o[TEX2].z, R0, c[6];                    # <s,t,r> = L

DP3    o[TEX3].x, R1, R4;                       # Transform H into
DP3    o[TEX3].y, R2, R4;                       # tangent space
DP3    o[TEX3].z, R0, R4;                       # <s,t,r> = H
```

The per-pixel dot products can be calculated using either the GL_EXT_
texture_env_dot3 extension or the GL_NV_register_combiners extension. The
quantity $\mathbf{N} \cdot \mathbf{H}$ can then be raised to a power by successively squaring it, but this
allows only small power-of-two exponents. OpenGL implementations capable
of dependent texture fetches (for instance, through the GL_NV_texture_shader
extension) enable arbitrary specular exponents to be used by storing the values
$\mathbf{S}(\mathbf{N} \cdot \mathbf{H})^m$ in a one-dimensional texture map.

6.9 A PHYSICAL REFLECTION MODEL

The manner in which we have calculated the reflection of light on a surface before this point is computationally cheap and produces visually pleasing results
in many cases, but it is not an accurate model of the physically correct distribution of reflected light. Achieving greater realism requires that we use a better
model of a surface's microscopic structure and that we apply a little electromagnetic theory.

6.9.1 BIDIRECTIONAL REFLECTANCE DISTRIBUTION FUNCTIONS

In general, our goal is to model the way in which the radiant energy contained
in a beam of light is redistributed when it strikes a surface. Some of the energy
is absorbed by the surface, some may be transmitted through the surface, and
whatever energy remains is reflected. The reflected energy is usually scattered in
every direction, but not in a uniform manner. A function that takes the direction
$\mathbf{L}$ to a light source and a reflection direction $\mathbf{R}$ and returns the amount of incident light from the direction $\mathbf{L}$, which is reflected in the direction $\mathbf{R}$, is called a
bidirectional reflectance distribution function (BRDF).

The precise definition of a BRDF requires that we first introduce some termi-
nology from the field of *radiometry*, the study of the transfer of energy via radiation. The radiant power (energy per unit time) emitted by a light source or
received by a surface is called *flux* and is measured in watts (W). The power
emitted by a light source or received by a surface per unit area is called *flux
density* and is measured in watts per square meter (W · m^{-2}). The flux density
emitted by a surface is called the surface's *radiosity*, and the flux density incident on a surface is called the *irradiance* of the light.

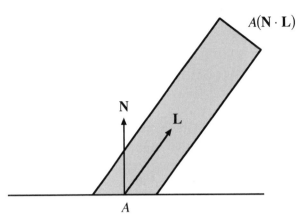

$A(\mathbf{N} \cdot \mathbf{L})$

$\mathbf{N}$

$\mathbf{L}$

A

Figure 6.17 *The flux density incident on an area A of a surface is equal to the flux density of an incident light beam scaled by a factor of $\mathbf{N} \cdot \mathbf{L}$.*

Figure 6.17 illustrates a situation in which a light source is emitting P watts of power toward a surface of area A. The power received by the surface is equal to the power emitted by the light source, but the flux densities received and emitted are different because of the Lambertian effect. The area of the beam is equal to $A(\mathbf{N} \cdot \mathbf{L})$, where $\mathbf{N}$ is the unit surface normal and $\mathbf{L}$ is the unit direction-to-light vector. The flux density Φ_E emitted by the light source is thus given by

$$\Phi_E = \frac{P}{A(\mathbf{N} \cdot \mathbf{L})}. \tag{6.36}$$

Since the flux density Φ_I incident on the surface is equal to P/A, we have the relation

$$\Phi_I = \Phi_E(\mathbf{N} \cdot \mathbf{L}). \tag{6.37}$$

The direction from which light illuminates a surface is defined in terms of solid angles, the three-dimensional analog of planar angles. As Figure 6.18 illustrates, the measure of a planar angle θ in radians is given by the arc length l swept out on a circle divided by the radius r of the circle: $\theta = l/r$. Extending this to three dimensions, the measure of a solid angle ω corresponding to an area A on the surface of a sphere of radius r is defined as $\omega = A/r^2$. The unit of solid angle measure is the *steradian*, abbreviated sr. Since the surface area of a sphere of radius r is equal to $4\pi r^2$, there are 4π steradians in the solid angle representing the entire sphere.

A differential solid angle $d\omega$ can be written in terms of the differential polar angle $d\theta$ and the differential azimuthal angle $d\phi$. As shown in Figure 6.19, the circle at the polar angle θ that lies parallel to the x-y plane and passes through the point $\langle r, \theta, \phi \rangle$ has radius $r \sin \theta$. Thus, the differential arc length in the

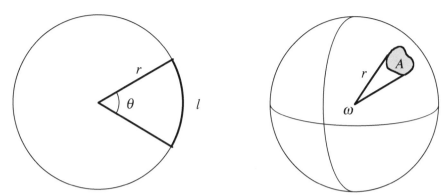

FIGURE *Planar angles are equal to the arc length that they sweep out divided by the radius of*
6.18 *the circle. Similarly, solid angles are equal to the surface area that subtends them*
divided by the square of the radius of the sphere.

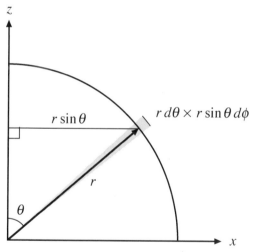

FIGURE *The differential surface area at the point $\langle r, \theta, \phi \rangle$ on a sphere is equal to $r^2 \sin \theta \, d\theta \, d\phi$.*
6.19

azimuthal direction on this circle is equal to $r \sin \theta \, d\phi$. Multiplying this by the
differential arc length $r \, d\theta$ in the polar direction gives us the following expression for the differential surface area dA.

$$dA = r^2 \sin \theta \, d\theta \, d\phi \tag{6.38}$$

Dividing by r^2 gives us the expression for the corresponding differential solid
angle $d\omega$:

$$d\omega = \sin \theta \, d\theta \, d\phi. \tag{6.39}$$

Radiance is the term used to describe the flux density of radiation per unit solid
angle and is measured in watts per square meter per steradian ($W \cdot m^{-2} \cdot sr^{-1}$). The

irradiance (flux density) Φ_I of the light received by a differential area dA on a surface is equal to the following integral of the radiance $C_I(\mathbf{L})$ received by the area, where the direction to light $\mathbf{L}$ ranges over the unit hemisphere Ω above the surface. (The angles θ and ϕ are the polar and azimuthal angles corresponding to the direction $\mathbf{L}$.)

$$\Phi_R = \int_\Omega C_I(\mathbf{L}) \, d\omega$$

$$= \int_0^{2\pi} \int_0^{\pi/2} C_I(\theta, \phi) \, d\theta \, d\phi \qquad (6.40)$$

For the same reason that the flux density received by a surface and flux density emitted by a light source are related by Equation (6.37), the radiance C_I received by a surface and the radiance C_E emitted by a light source are related by

$$C_I = C_E(\mathbf{N} \cdot \mathbf{L}) = C_E \cos \theta. \qquad (6.41)$$

We can therefore rewrite Equation (6.40) as

$$\Phi_I = \int_\Omega C_E(\mathbf{L})(\mathbf{N} \cdot \mathbf{L}) \, d\omega$$

$$= \int_0^{2\pi} \int_0^{\pi/2} C_E(\theta, \phi) \cos \theta \, d\theta \, d\phi. \qquad (6.42)$$

The *bidirectional reflectivity* $\rho(\mathbf{V}, \mathbf{L})$ at a point on a surface is a function of the direction to viewer $\mathbf{V}$ and the direction to light $\mathbf{L}$. It is equal to the ratio of the differential reflected radiance dC_R to the differential incident irradiance $d\Phi_I$:

$$\rho(\mathbf{V}, \mathbf{L}) = \frac{dC_R}{d\Phi_I} = \frac{dC_R}{C_E(\mathbf{L})(\mathbf{N} \cdot \mathbf{L}) \, d\omega}. \qquad (6.43)$$

The function $\rho(\mathbf{V}, \mathbf{L})$ is the BRDF that we use to calculate the radiance of the light reflected in a specific direction from a surface using the equation

$$DC_R = \rho(\mathbf{V}, \mathbf{L})C_E(\mathbf{L})(\mathbf{N} \cdot \mathbf{L}) \, d\omega. \qquad (6.44)$$

Directional, point, and spot light sources illuminate a point on a surface from a single direction. Thus, instead of integrating Equation (6.44) to determine the amount of light $C_R(\mathbf{V})$ from n sources reflected in the direction to viewer $\mathbf{V}$, we simply sum over the discrete directions to light $\mathbf{L}_i$:

$$C_R(\mathbf{V}) = \sum_{i=1}^{n} \rho(\mathbf{V}, \mathbf{L}_i)C_i(\mathbf{N} \cdot \mathbf{L}_i). \qquad (6.45)$$

Up to this point in our discussion of BRDFs, we have not said anything about color. In addition to the incoming and outgoing light directions, a BRDF should be a function of the wavelength of the light. Applications requiring accurate reflection models across the entire spectrum typically evaluate a BRDF at several wavelengths and then fit a curve to the resulting numbers. For real-time computer graphics, we find it sufficient to treat our BRDFs as functions that take the RGB color of the incident light and return the RGB color of the reflected light. From this point on, we assume that all operations involving a BRDF take place for each of the red, green, and blue components of light, and we write all mathematical entities having RGB components in boldface.

The diffuse and specular reflection formulas given in Equations (6.6) and (6.14) can be reproduced by defining the BRDF $\boldsymbol{\rho}$ as

$$\boldsymbol{\rho}(\mathbf{V}, \mathbf{L}) = \mathbf{D} + \mathbf{S}\frac{(\mathbf{N} \cdot \mathbf{H})^{m}}{\mathbf{N} \cdot \mathbf{L}}. \tag{6.46}$$

The term *bidirectional* means that the function $\boldsymbol{\rho}$ should be invariant when the directions $\mathbf{V}$ and $\mathbf{L}$ are exchanged. That is, $\boldsymbol{\rho}$ should satisfy the reciprocity property

$$\boldsymbol{\rho}(\mathbf{V}, \mathbf{L}) = \boldsymbol{\rho}(\mathbf{L}, \mathbf{V}) \tag{6.47}$$

required by the fact that reversing the direction that light travels along a certain path should not produce different results. The function $\boldsymbol{\rho}$ given by Equation (6.46) does not satisfy the bidirectional requirement, however, and therefore cannot be physically correct.

Another physical law violated by Equation (6.46) is conservation of energy. Any physically correct BRDF must not reflect more light from a point on a surface than is incident at that point. We can divide the reflected energy given by the BRDF $\boldsymbol{\rho}$ into diffuse and specular components by writing

$$\boldsymbol{\rho}(\mathbf{V}, \mathbf{L}) = k\mathbf{D} + (1 - k)\boldsymbol{\rho}_{s}(\mathbf{V}, \mathbf{L}), \tag{6.48}$$

where $\mathbf{D}$ is the surface's diffuse reflection color and k represents the fraction of the incident light that is diffusely reflected. The remaining fraction $1 - k$ of the incident light is either absorbed or makes up a specular reflection. These effects are modeled by the function $\boldsymbol{\rho}_{s}$, which is described in the next section.

6.9.2 COOK-TORRANCE ILLUMINATION

The Cook-Torrance illumination model produces a realistic specular reflection by treating a surface as being composed of planar microscopic facets called *microfacets*. Each microfacet is treated as a perfect reflector that obeys the reflective laws of electromagnetic theory. The roughness of a surface is characterized by the slopes of the microfacets. As shown in Figure 6.20, a rough surface is composed of microfacets having greatly varying slopes, whereas the microfacets for a relatively smooth surface have only small slopes.

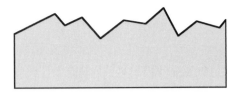

Surface roughness is characterized by how much the slopes of the microfacets vary.

Cook and Torrance use the following formula for the specular component ρ_s of the BRDF given in Equation (6.48).

$$\rho_s(\mathbf{V}, \mathbf{L}) = \mathbf{F}(\mathbf{V}, \mathbf{L}) \frac{D(\mathbf{V}, \mathbf{L}) G(\mathbf{V}, \mathbf{L})}{(\mathbf{N} \cdot \mathbf{V})(\mathbf{N} \cdot \mathbf{L})} \tag{6.49}$$

$\mathbf{F}$ is the Fresnel factor, which describes the amount of light reflected as a function of the angle of incidence; D is the microfacet distribution function, which returns the fraction of microfacets oriented in a given direction; and G is the geometrical attenuation factor, which accounts for self-shadowing of the microfacets. Since the microfacets are perfect reflectors, only those microfacets whose normal vectors point in the direction of the halfway vector $\mathbf{H}$ contribute to the specular reflection.

6.9.3 THE FRESNEL FACTOR

The interaction of an electromagnetic wave and a surface results in a reflected wave and a transmitted wave. The energy contained in the reflected wave is equal to the energy contained in the incident wave minus the energy contained in the transmitted wave (which is quickly absorbed by opaque materials). The electric field of the incident light can be decomposed into components that are polarized with respect to the plane containing the surface normal $\mathbf{N}$ and the direction to light $\mathbf{L}$. The component parallel to this plane is called p-polarized and the component perpendicular to this plane is called s-polarized. The Fresnel factors giving, for a single wavelength, the fractions F_p and F_s of the amount of light reflected for these components are

$$F_p = \frac{\tan^2(\theta_1 - \theta_2)}{\tan^2(\theta_1 + \theta_2)}$$

$$F_s = \frac{\sin^2(\theta_1 - \theta_2)}{\sin^2(\theta_1 + \theta_2)}, \tag{6.50}$$

where θ_1 is the angle of incidence and θ_2 is the wavelength-dependent angle of transmittance. For unpolarized light, we simply average these to obtain the Fresnel factor F_λ corresponding to the wavelength λ:

$$F_\lambda = \frac{1}{2}\left[\frac{\tan^2(\theta_1 - \theta_2)}{\tan^2(\theta_1 + \theta_2)} + \frac{\sin^2(\theta_1 - \theta_2)}{\sin^2(\theta_1 + \theta_2)}\right]. \tag{6.51}$$

The angle of incidence θ_1 is equal to $\cos^{-1}(\mathbf{L} \cdot \mathbf{H})$ since every microfacet contributing to the specular reflection is oriented such that its normal vector points along the halfway vector $\mathbf{H}$. It turns out that we can write the Fresnel factor in terms of $\mathbf{L} \cdot \mathbf{H}$ and the indexes of refraction η_1 and η_2 of the two materials by applying some trigonometric identities and using Snell's law. Factoring the sine function out of Equation (6.51) gives us

$$F_\lambda = \frac{1}{2}\frac{\sin^2(\theta_1 - \theta_2)}{\sin^2(\theta_1 + \theta_2)}\left[\frac{\cos^2(\theta_1 + \theta_2)}{\cos^2(\theta_1 - \theta_2)} + 1\right]. \tag{6.52}$$

Applying the trigonometric identities for sums and differences of angles to the sine factors yields

$$\frac{\sin(\theta_1 - \theta_2)}{\sin(\theta_1 + \theta_2)} = \frac{\sin\theta_1 \cos\theta_2 - \cos\theta_1 \sin\theta_2}{\sin\theta_1 \cos\theta_2 + \cos\theta_1 \sin\theta_2}$$

$$= \frac{\eta_\lambda \cos\theta_2 - \cos\theta_1}{\eta_\lambda \cos\theta_2 + \cos\theta_1}, \tag{6.53}$$

where Snell's law has been used to obtain

$$\eta_\lambda = \frac{\eta_2}{\eta_1} = \frac{\sin\theta_1}{\sin\theta_2}. \tag{6.54}$$

We can express $\cos\theta_2$ in terms of $\cos\theta_1$ and η by writing Snell's law in the form

$$\eta_1\sqrt{1 - \cos^2\theta_1} = \eta_2\sqrt{1 - \cos^2\theta_2} \tag{6.55}$$

and solving for $\cos\theta_2$:

$$\cos\theta_2 = \sqrt{1 - \frac{1}{\eta_\lambda^2}\left(1 - \cos^2\theta_1\right)}. \tag{6.56}$$

Defining the variable g as

$$g = \eta_\lambda \cos\theta_2 = \sqrt{\eta_\lambda^2 - 1 + (\mathbf{L} \cdot \mathbf{H})^2} \tag{6.57}$$

lets us express the quotient of the sine functions as

$$\frac{\sin(\theta_1 - \theta_2)}{\sin(\theta_1 + \theta_2)} = \frac{g - \mathbf{L} \cdot \mathbf{H}}{g + \mathbf{L} \cdot \mathbf{H}}. \tag{6.58}$$

A similar procedure allows us to express the cosine factors in terms of g and $\mathbf{L} \cdot \mathbf{H}$. We begin by applying angle sum and difference identities:

$$\frac{\cos(\theta_1 + \theta_2)}{\cos(\theta_1 - \theta_2)} = \frac{\cos \theta_1 \cos \theta_2 - \sin \theta_1 \sin \theta_2}{\cos \theta_1 \cos \theta_2 + \sin \theta_1 \sin \theta_2}$$

$$= \frac{\cos \theta_1 \cos \theta_2 - \eta_\lambda \sin^2 \theta_2}{\cos \theta_1 \cos \theta_2 + \eta_\lambda \sin^2 \theta_2}. \tag{6.59}$$

Again using the variable g defined in Equation (6.57), we can write this as

$$\frac{\cos(\theta_1 + \theta_2)}{\cos(\theta_1 - \theta_2)} = \frac{g \cos \theta_1 - \eta_\lambda^2 (1 - \cos^2 \theta_2)}{g \cos \theta_1 + \eta_\lambda^2 (1 - \cos^2 \theta_2)}$$

$$= \frac{g \cos \theta_1 - \eta_\lambda^2 + g^2}{g \cos \theta_1 + \eta_\lambda^2 - g^2}$$

$$= \frac{(\mathbf{L} \cdot \mathbf{H})(g + \mathbf{L} \cdot \mathbf{H}) - 1}{(\mathbf{L} \cdot \mathbf{H})(g - \mathbf{L} \cdot \mathbf{H}) + 1}. \tag{6.60}$$

The Fresnel factor can now be entirely expressed in terms of $\mathbf{L} \cdot \mathbf{H}$ and η_λ, as follows.

$$F_\lambda(\mathbf{V}, \mathbf{L}) = \frac{1}{2} \frac{(g - \mathbf{L} \cdot \mathbf{H})^2}{(g + \mathbf{L} \cdot \mathbf{H})^2} \left(\frac{\left[(\mathbf{L} \cdot \mathbf{H})(g + \mathbf{L} \cdot \mathbf{H}) - 1 \right]^2}{\left[(\mathbf{L} \cdot \mathbf{H})(g - \mathbf{L} \cdot \mathbf{H}) + 1 \right]^2} + 1 \right) \tag{6.61}$$

The RGB color Fresnel factor $\mathbf{F}(\mathbf{V}, \mathbf{L})$ simply consists of the function $F_\lambda(\mathbf{V}, \mathbf{L})$ evaluated at red, green, and blue wavelengths.

We can make a couple of observations about the behavior of the function F_λ. First, as the angle of incidence approaches 90 degrees, the value of $\mathbf{L} \cdot \mathbf{H}$ approaches zero and thus the value of F_λ approaches one. This means that at grazing angles, all the incident light is reflected, leaving none to be absorbed by the surface. Second, for normal incidence, in which the incident angle is zero, the value of $\mathbf{L} \cdot \mathbf{H}$ is one and F_λ reduces to

$$\left(F_\lambda \right)_{\mathbf{L}=\mathbf{H}} = \left(\frac{\eta_\lambda - 1}{\eta_\lambda + 1} \right)^2. \tag{6.62}$$

This gives us a convenient way of deriving an approximate value for η_λ if all that is known about a material is the specular color **S** reflected at normal incidence. Solving Equation (6.62) for η_λ yields

$$\eta_\lambda = \frac{1 + \sqrt{\left(F_\lambda\right)_{\mathbf{L}=\mathbf{H}}}}{1 - \sqrt{\left(F_\lambda\right)_{\mathbf{L}=\mathbf{H}}}}. \tag{6.63}$$

Once a value of η_λ has been calculated with this equation by setting the value of $(F_\lambda)_{\mathbf{L}=\mathbf{H}}$ at red, green, and blue wavelengths equal to the red, green, and blue components of **S**, it can be used in Equation (6.61) to calculate reflectance for any other angle of incidence.

6.9.4 The Microfacet Distribution Function

Given a halfway vector **H**, the microfacet distribution function returns the fraction of microfacets whose normal vectors point along the direction **H**. For rough surfaces, the Beckmann distribution function given by

$$D_m(\mathbf{V}, \mathbf{L}) = \frac{1}{4\pi m^2 (\mathbf{N} \cdot \mathbf{H})^4} e^{\frac{(\mathbf{N}\cdot\mathbf{H})^2 - 1}{m^2(\mathbf{N}\cdot\mathbf{H})^2}} \tag{6.64}$$

describes the distribution of microfacet orientations in terms of the root mean square slope m. Large values of m correspond to rough surfaces and thus produce a wide distribution of microfacet orientations. As shown in Figure 6.21, smaller values of m correspond to smoother surfaces and produce relatively narrow distributions, which result in a sharper specularity.

The function given by Equation (6.64) is *isotropic*, meaning that it is invariant under a rotation about the normal vector **N**. As long as the angle between the direction to viewer **V** and direction to light **L** remains constant and the angle between each of these vectors and the normal vector remains constant, the distribution of microfacets also remains constant. Many surfaces, however, possess different degrees of roughness in different directions. These surfaces are called *anisotropic* reflectors and include materials such as brushed metal, hair, and certain fabrics.

We can modify the microfacet distribution function to account for anisotropic surface roughness by changing Equation (6.64) to

$$D_{\mathbf{m}}(\mathbf{V}, \mathbf{L}) = \frac{1}{4\pi m_x m_y (\mathbf{N} \cdot \mathbf{H})^4} e^{\left(\frac{(\mathbf{T}\cdot\mathbf{P})^2}{m_x^2} + \frac{1-(\mathbf{T}\cdot\mathbf{P})^2}{m_y^2}\right)\frac{(\mathbf{N}\cdot\mathbf{H})^2-1}{(\mathbf{N}\cdot\mathbf{H})^2}}, \tag{6.65}$$

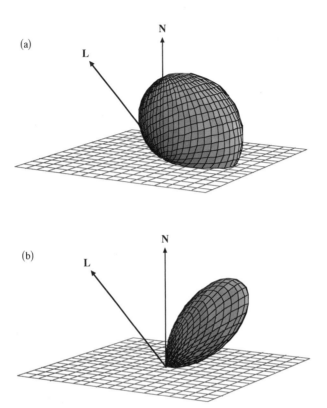

FIGURE 6.21 *Microfacet distributions given by equation (6.64) modeling (a) a rough surface using* m = 0.6 *and (b) a relatively smooth surface using* m = 0.25.

where **m** is a two-dimensional roughness vector, **T** is the tangent to the surface aligned to the direction in which the roughness is m_x, and **P** is the normalized projection of the halfway vector **H** onto the tangent plane:

$$\mathbf{P} = \frac{\mathbf{H} - (\mathbf{N} \cdot \mathbf{H})\mathbf{N}}{\left\| \mathbf{H} - (\mathbf{N} \cdot \mathbf{H})\mathbf{N} \right\|}. \tag{6.66}$$

Figure 6.22 shows a disk rendered with both isotropic and anisotropic surface roughness values.

Some surfaces exhibit roughness at multiple scales. This can be accounted for by calculating a weighted average of microfacet distribution functions,

$$D(\mathbf{V}, \mathbf{L}) = \sum_{i=1}^{n} w_i D_{\mathbf{m}_i}(\mathbf{V}, \mathbf{L}), \tag{6.67}$$

FIGURE *A disk rendered using the anisotropic distribution function given by equation (6.65).*
6.22 *For each image m_y = 0.1. From left to right the values of m_x are 0.1 (isotropic), 0.12, 0.15, and 0.2. The tangent vectors are aligned to concentric rings around the center of the disk—they are perpendicular to the radial direction at every point on the surface.*

where multiple roughness values $\mathbf{m}_i$ are used and the weights w_i sum to one. Figure 6.23 shows two objects rendered with different values of $\mathbf{m}$ and another object rendered using a weighted sum of those same values.

FIGURE *Copper vases rendered with isotropic microfacet distributions. The first two images*
6.23 *use a single roughness value of m_1 = 0.1 and m_2 = 0.25. The third image combines these using the weights w_1 = 0.4 and w_2 = 0.6.*

6.9.5 THE GEOMETRICAL ATTENUATION FACTOR

Some of the light incident on a single microfacet may be blocked by adjacent microfacets before it reaches the surface or after it has been reflected. This blocking results in a slight darkening of the specular reflection and is accounted for by the geometrical attenuation factor. Blocked light is essentially scattered in random directions and ultimately contributes to the surface's diffuse reflection.

We can derive an estimate of how much light is blocked due to surface roughness by assuming that microfacets always form V-shaped grooves. Figure 6.24(a) illustrates a situation in which light reflected by a microfacet is partially blocked by an adjacent microfacet. In this case, light is blocked after being

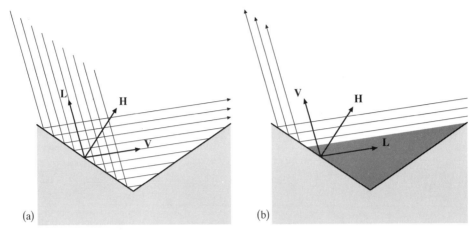

FIGURE **6.24** *(a) Light reflected by the left microfacet is partially blocked by the right microfacet. (b) Light is blocked by the right microfacet before reaching the left microfacet.*

reflected. Reversing the direction in which the light travels exhibits the case in which light is blocked before reaching the microfacet, as shown in Figure 6.24(b).

The application of a little trigonometry leads us to a formula giving the fraction of light reflected by a microfacet that still reaches the viewer after being partially blocked by an adjacent microfacet. As shown in Figure 6.25, we would like to determine the portion x of the width w of a microfacet that is visible to the viewer. We first observe that

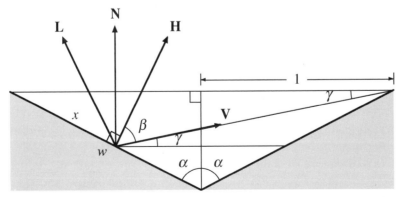

FIGURE **6.25** *The fraction of light reflected from the left microfacet that reaches the viewer is equal to x/w. The halfway vector **H** is normal to the microfacet surface since only microfacets possessing that orientation contribute to the specular reflection.*

$$w = \frac{1}{\sin \alpha} \tag{6.68}$$

and that, by the law of sines,

$$x = \frac{2 \sin \gamma}{\sin(\beta + \pi/2)}. \tag{6.69}$$

We can express each of the sine functions in Equations (6.68) and (6.69) as cosine functions that have been shifted by $\pi/2$ radians by writing

$$\sin \alpha = \cos(\pi/2 - \alpha) = \mathbf{N} \cdot \mathbf{H}$$

$$\sin(\beta + \pi/2) = \cos \beta = \mathbf{V} \cdot \mathbf{H}$$

$$\sin \gamma = \cos(\pi/2 - \gamma) = \mathbf{N} \cdot \mathbf{V}. \tag{6.70}$$

Using the dot products corresponding to each of the cosine functions lets us express the fraction of light G_1 reaching the viewer as

$$G_1 = \frac{x}{w} = \frac{2(\mathbf{N} \cdot \mathbf{H})(\mathbf{N} \cdot \mathbf{V})}{\mathbf{V} \cdot \mathbf{H}}. \tag{6.71}$$

When light is blocked before reaching a microfacet, we can calculate the fraction G_2 that still reaches the viewer by simply exchanging the vectors $\mathbf{V}$ and $\mathbf{L}$ in Figure 6.25 to obtain

$$G_2 = \frac{x}{w} = \frac{2(\mathbf{N} \cdot \mathbf{H})(\mathbf{N} \cdot \mathbf{L})}{\mathbf{V} \cdot \mathbf{H}}. \tag{6.72}$$

We have left the denominator unchanged since, by the definition of the halfway vector, the angle between $\mathbf{L}$ and $\mathbf{H}$ is equal to the angle between $\mathbf{V}$ and $\mathbf{H}$, and thus $\mathbf{L} \cdot \mathbf{H} = \mathbf{V} \cdot \mathbf{H}$.

The three possible cases pertaining to light reflected by a microfacet are that the light is completely unobstructed (the fraction of light reaching the viewer is one), that some of the reflected light is blocked, and that some of the incident light is blocked. We account for all three cases by defining the geometrical attenuation factor as the minimum fraction of light that reaches the viewer:

$$G(\mathbf{V}, \mathbf{L}) = \min\{1, G_1, G_2\}$$

$$= \min\left\{1, \frac{2(\mathbf{N} \cdot \mathbf{H})(\mathbf{N} \cdot \mathbf{V})}{\mathbf{V} \cdot \mathbf{H}}, \frac{2(\mathbf{N} \cdot \mathbf{H})(\mathbf{N} \cdot \mathbf{L})}{\mathbf{V} \cdot \mathbf{H}}\right\}. \tag{6.73}$$

6.9.6 IMPLEMENTATION

Ray tracing applications can directly apply Equation (6.49) whenever a ray intersects a surface. The calculations are too complex, however, to evaluate at every pixel when rendering a triangle mesh. For sufficiently tessellated surfaces, evaluating Equation (6.49) at each vertex produces good results, but it can be computationally expensive. A trick that avoids many of these calculations is to use texture maps essentially to store lookup tables that are indexed by quantities easily calculated at each vertex.

Adding ambient and emission terms to Equation (6.45) gives us the following formula for the color of light **K** reflected toward the viewer by a surface illuminated by n light sources.

$$\mathbf{K} = \mathbf{E} + \mathbf{DA} + \sum_{i=1}^{n} \rho(\mathbf{V}, \mathbf{L}_i)\mathbf{C}_i(\mathbf{N} \cdot \mathbf{L}_i) \tag{6.74}$$

Substituting Equation (6.48) for the BRDF ρ produces

$$\mathbf{K} = \mathbf{E} + \mathbf{DA} + k\mathbf{D}\sum_{i=1}^{n} \mathbf{C}_i(\mathbf{N} \cdot \mathbf{L}_i) + (1-k)\sum_{i=1}^{n} \rho_s(\mathbf{V}, \mathbf{L}_i)\mathbf{C}_i(\mathbf{N} \cdot \mathbf{L}_i). \tag{6.75}$$

Using Equation (6.49), we can express the specular component of **K** contributed by a single light source as

$$\mathbf{K}_{\text{specular}} = \mathbf{C}(1-k)\rho_s(\mathbf{V}, \mathbf{L})(\mathbf{N} \cdot \mathbf{L})$$

$$= \mathbf{C}(1-k)\mathbf{F}(\mathbf{V}, \mathbf{L})\frac{D_m(\mathbf{V}, \mathbf{L})G(\mathbf{V}, \mathbf{L})}{\mathbf{N} \cdot \mathbf{V}}, \tag{6.76}$$

where **C** is the color of the light and k is the fraction of light that is reflected diffusely. The only quantity that the Fresnel factor **F**(**V**, **L**) depends on is $\mathbf{L} \cdot \mathbf{H}$, and the only quantity that the isotropic microfacet distribution function $D_m(\mathbf{V}, \mathbf{L})$ depends on is $\mathbf{N} \cdot \mathbf{H}$. Given a normal-incidence specular reflection color **S** and a microfacet root mean square slope m, we can construct a texture map whose s and t coordinates correspond to $\mathbf{L} \cdot \mathbf{H}$ and $\mathbf{N} \cdot \mathbf{H}$, respectively, and whose color values represent the product $\mathbf{F}(\mathbf{V}, \mathbf{L})D_m(\mathbf{V}, \mathbf{L})$. Furthermore, we can include the constant $1 - k$ and part of the geometrical attenuation factor $G(\mathbf{V}, \mathbf{L})$ in this texture map.

Writing **F** as a function of $\mathbf{L} \cdot \mathbf{H}$ and D_m as a function of $\mathbf{N} \cdot \mathbf{H}$, we have

$$\mathbf{K}_{\text{specular}} = \mathbf{C}(1-k)\mathbf{F}(\mathbf{L} \cdot \mathbf{H})D_m(\mathbf{N} \cdot \mathbf{H})\frac{G(\mathbf{V}, \mathbf{L})}{\mathbf{N} \cdot \mathbf{V}}. \tag{6.77}$$

For the $G(\mathbf{V}, \mathbf{L})/\mathbf{N} \cdot \mathbf{V}$ factor, we can replace each $\mathbf{V} \cdot \mathbf{H}$ appearing in Equation (6.73) with $\mathbf{L} \cdot \mathbf{H}$ and plug it into Equation (6.77) to get

$$\frac{G(\mathbf{V}, \mathbf{L})}{\mathbf{N} \cdot \mathbf{V}} = \min\left\{\frac{1}{\mathbf{N} \cdot \mathbf{V}}, \frac{2(\mathbf{N} \cdot \mathbf{H})}{\mathbf{L} \cdot \mathbf{H}}, \frac{2(\mathbf{N} \cdot \mathbf{H})(\mathbf{N} \cdot \mathbf{L})}{(\mathbf{L} \cdot \mathbf{H})(\mathbf{N} \cdot \mathbf{V})}\right\}, \tag{6.78}$$

where we have assumed that $\mathbf{N} \cdot \mathbf{V}$ is positive since the surface would not be visible otherwise. The right side of Equation (6.78) has no upper bound, so we factor $2(\mathbf{N} \cdot \mathbf{H})/\mathbf{L} \cdot \mathbf{H}$ out of the minimum function to limit its range:

$$\frac{G(\mathbf{V}, \mathbf{L})}{\mathbf{N} \cdot \mathbf{V}} = \frac{2(\mathbf{N} \cdot \mathbf{H})}{\mathbf{L} \cdot \mathbf{H}} \min\left\{\frac{\mathbf{L} \cdot \mathbf{H}}{2(\mathbf{N} \cdot \mathbf{H})(\mathbf{N} \cdot \mathbf{V})}, 1, \frac{\mathbf{N} \cdot \mathbf{L}}{\mathbf{N} \cdot \mathbf{V}}\right\}. \tag{6.79}$$

We can now write the entire specular component as

$$\mathbf{K}_{\text{specular}} = 4[\mathbf{C}X(\mathbf{V}, \mathbf{L})][Y(\mathbf{N} \cdot \mathbf{H})][\mathbf{Z}(\mathbf{L} \cdot \mathbf{H})], \tag{6.80}$$

where the functions X, Y, and $\mathbf{Z}$ are given by

$$X(\mathbf{V}, \mathbf{L}) = \min\left\{\frac{\mathbf{L} \cdot \mathbf{H}}{2(\mathbf{N} \cdot \mathbf{H})(\mathbf{N} \cdot \mathbf{V})}, 1, \frac{\mathbf{N} \cdot \mathbf{L}}{\mathbf{N} \cdot \mathbf{V}}\right\}$$

$$Y(\mathbf{N} \cdot \mathbf{H}) = (1 - k)(\mathbf{N} \cdot \mathbf{H})D_m(\mathbf{N} \cdot \mathbf{H})$$

$$\mathbf{Z}(\mathbf{L} \cdot \mathbf{H}) = \frac{\mathbf{F}(\mathbf{L} \cdot \mathbf{H})}{2(\mathbf{L} \cdot \mathbf{H})}. \tag{6.81}$$

If any of the quantities $\mathbf{N} \cdot \mathbf{L}$, $\mathbf{N} \cdot \mathbf{V}$, or $\mathbf{L} \cdot \mathbf{H}$ are less than zero, then we assign a value of zero to X. Otherwise, the value of X is less than one, so we calculate the product $\mathbf{C}X$ for every vertex of a triangle mesh and store it in a color array. Listing 6.2 demonstrates how these calculations might be carried out using a vertex program. The product $Y\mathbf{Z}$ is precalculated for many values of $\mathbf{N} \cdot \mathbf{H}$ and $\mathbf{L} \cdot \mathbf{H}$ to construct a texture map resembling the image shown in Figure 6.26. The 2 appearing in the denominator of $\mathbf{Z}$ reduces the size of the product so that the texture map can represent a larger range of values. The result of multiplying a sample from the texture map by the interpolated value of $\mathbf{C}X$ supplied by the color array is scaled by 4 to produce the final specular color used to shade a pixel.

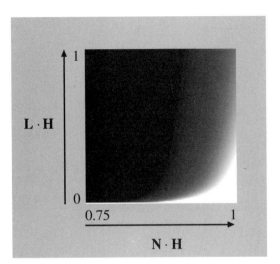

FIGURE 6.26. *A texture map representing the product Y**Z** whose factors are defined by Equation (6.81). The s-coordinate corresponds to the quantity 4(**N** · **H**) − 3, and the t-coordinate corresponds to the quantity **L** · **H**. This image was generated using the normal-incidence specular reflection color **S** = ⟨0.8, 0. 6, 0.1⟩, the microfacet root mean square slope m = 0.25, and a diffuse reflection fraction k = 0.6.*

Listing 6.2. This vertex program performs the calculations necessary for isotropic Cook-Torrance illumination. The primary color is set to **C**X, and the texture unit 0 coordinates are set to ⟨4(**N** · **H**) − 3, **L** · **H**⟩.

```
!!VP1.0

# c[0-3] = projection * modelview matrix
# c[4] = constant (1.0, 4.0, 3.0, 0.0)
# c[5] = object-space camera position
# c[6] = object-space light direction L
# c[7] = light color C

DP4   o[HPOS].x, c[0], v[OPOS];          # Transform vertex
DP4   o[HPOS].y, c[1], v[OPOS];
DP4   o[HPOS].z, c[2], v[OPOS];
DP4   o[HPOS].w, c[3], v[OPOS];

MOV   R0, v[NRML];                       # Load normal N

ADD   R2, c[5], −v[OPOS];                # R2 = view direction V
DP3   R5, R2, R2;                        # Normalize V
RSQ   R5.x, R5.x;
MUL   R2.xyz, R2, R5.x;
```

```
ADD    R3, R2, c[6];                    # R3 = halfway vector H
DP3    R6, R3, R3;                      # Normalize H
RSQ    R6.x, R6.x;
MUL    R3.xyz, R3, R6.x;

DP3    R4.x, R0, c[6];                  # R4.x = N dot L
DP3    R4.y, R0, R2;                    # R4.y = N dot V
DP3    R4.z, R0, R3;                    # R4.z = N dot H
DP3    R4.w, c[6], R3;                  # R4.w = L dot H

ADD    R5.x, R4.z, R4.z;                # R5.x = 2(N*H)
RCP    R5.x, R5.x;                      # R5.x = 1/(2(N*H))
RCP    R5.y, R4.y;                      # R5.y = 1/(N*V)
MUL    R6.x, R5.x, R4.w;                # R6.x = (L*H)/(2(N*H))
MUL    R6.x, R6.x, R5.y;                # R6.x = (L*H)/(2(N*H)(N*V))
MUL    R6.y, R5.y, R4.x;                # R6.y = (N*L)/(N*V)

MIN    R5.x, R6.x, R6.y;                # Calculate minimum
MIN    R5.x, R5.x, c[4].x;              # R5.x = min(R5.x, 1)

SLT    R6, −R4, c[4].w;                 # Dot products > 0?
MUL    R6.x, R6.x, R6.y;                # R6.x = (N*L > 0)(N*V > 0)
MUL    R6.x, R6.x, R6.w;                # R6.x *= (L*H > 0)
MUL    R5.x, R5.x, R6.x;                # R5.x *= 0 or 1

# Anisotropic case replaces code below
MUL    o[COL0], R5.x, c[7];             # R5.x * light color
MAD    o[TEX0].x, R4.z, c[4].y, −c[4].z;  # s = 4(N*H)−3
MOV    o[TEX0].y, R4.w;                 # t = L*H
END
```

For anisotropic surfaces, the microfacet distribution function $D_\mathbf{m}$ depends on the dot product $\mathbf{T} \cdot \mathbf{P}$ as well as $\mathbf{N} \cdot \mathbf{H}$. In this case, we define Y and $\mathbf{Z}$ as

$$Y(\mathbf{N} \cdot \mathbf{H}, \mathbf{T} \cdot \mathbf{P}) = \frac{1-k}{\sqrt{2}} D_\mathbf{m}(\mathbf{N} \cdot \mathbf{H}, \mathbf{T} \cdot \mathbf{P})$$

$$\mathbf{Z}(\mathbf{N} \cdot \mathbf{H}, \mathbf{L} \cdot \mathbf{H}) = \frac{(\mathbf{N} \cdot \mathbf{H})\mathbf{F}(\mathbf{L} \cdot \mathbf{H})}{\sqrt{2}(\mathbf{L} \cdot \mathbf{H})}, \tag{6.82}$$

where the 2 originally appearing in the denominator of $\mathbf{Z}$ is now split between Y and $\mathbf{Z}$. A three-dimensional texture map could be used as a lookup table for the product $Y\mathbf{Z}$, but hardware that does not support three-dimensional texture maps requires that we store the values of Y and $\mathbf{Z}$ in separate two-dimensional texture maps similar to those shown in Figure 6.27. Listing 6.3 illustrates the

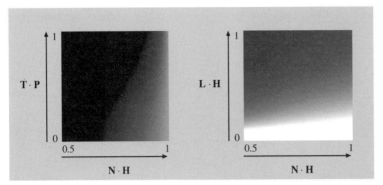

FIGURE **6.27** *Texture maps representing the values of Y (left) and Z (right) defined by Equation (6.82). The s-coordinate corresponds to the quantity $2(\mathbf{N} \cdot \mathbf{H}) - 1$ for both maps, and the t-coordinate corresponds to the quantity $\mathbf{T} \cdot \mathbf{P}$ for the Y map and $\mathbf{L} \cdot \mathbf{H}$ for the Z map. This image was generated using the same values used to generate Figure 6.26 except that the root mean square slope has been made anisotropic using $\mathbf{m} = \langle 0.25, 0.5 \rangle$.*

changes that can be made to the vertex program for the isotropic case in order to achieve anisotropic reflections.

> **Listing 6.3.** This code replaces the last four lines of Listing 6.2 with the calculations necessary for anisotropic Cook-Torrance illumination. The vertex tangent is read from attribute array 6. The texture mapping coordinates $\langle 2(\mathbf{N} \cdot \mathbf{H}) - 1, \mathbf{L} \cdot \mathbf{H} \rangle$ are assigned to texture unit 0, and the coordinates $\langle 2(\mathbf{N} \cdot \mathbf{H}) - 1, \mathbf{T} \cdot \mathbf{P} \rangle$ are assigned to texture unit 1.

```
# c[4] = constant (1.0, 2.0, 0.0, 0.0)

MAD    R7, -R4.z, R0, R3;                    # R7 = P = H - (N*H)N
DP3    R8, R7, R7;                           # Normalize P
RSQ    R8.x, R8.x;
MUL    R7.xyz, R7, R8.x;

MUL    o[COL0], R5.x, c[7];                  # R5.x * light color
MAD    o[TEX0].x, R4.z, c[4].y, -c[4].x;     # s0 = 2(N*H)-1
MOV    o[TEX0].y, R4.w;                      # t0 = L*H
MAD    o[TEX1].x, R4.z, c[4].y, -c[4].x;     # s1 = 2(N*H)-1
DP3    o[TEX1].y, v[6], R7;                  # t1 = T*P
END
```

CHAPTER 6 SUMMARY

Point Light Source Attenuation

The intensity **C** of a point light source at a distance d from its position is given by

$$\mathbf{C} = \frac{1}{k_c + k_l d + k_q d^2} \mathbf{C}_0,$$

where $\mathbf{C}_0$ is the color of the light and the constants k_c, k_l, and k_q control the attenuation.

Spot Light Source Attenuation

The intensity $\mathbf{C}$ of a spot light source at a point $\mathbf{Q}$ lying at a distance d from the light's position is given by

$$\mathbf{C} = \frac{\max\{-\mathbf{U} \cdot \mathbf{L}, 0\}^p}{k_c + k_l d + k_q d^2} \mathbf{C}_0,$$

where $\mathbf{C}_0$ is the color of the light; k_c, k_l, and k_q are the attenuation constants; $\mathbf{U}$ is the direction in which the spot light is pointing; $\mathbf{L}$ is the unit vector pointing from $\mathbf{Q}$ to the light position; and the exponent p controls the rate at which the intensity falls off as the angle between $\mathbf{U}$ and $-\mathbf{L}$ increases.

Ambient and Diffuse Lighting

The ambient and diffuse contribution to the illumination color calculated at a point $\mathbf{Q}$ on a surface is given by the expression

$$\mathbf{K}_{\text{diffuse}} = \mathbf{DA} + \mathbf{D}\sum_{i=1}^{n} \mathbf{C}_i \max\{\mathbf{N} \cdot \mathbf{L}_i, 0\},$$

where $\mathbf{D}$ is the surface's diffuse reflection color, $\mathbf{N}$ is the normal vector to the surface, $\mathbf{L}_i$ is the unit vector pointing from $\mathbf{Q}$ toward the i-th light, $\mathbf{C}_i$ is the intensity of the i-th light at the point $\mathbf{Q}$, and $\mathbf{A}$ represents the ambient light color.

Specular Lighting

The specular contribution to the illumination color calculated at a point $\mathbf{Q}$ on a surface is given by the expression

$$\mathbf{K}_{\text{specular}} = \mathbf{S}\sum_{i=1}^{n} \mathbf{C}_i \max\{\mathbf{N} \cdot \mathbf{H}_i, 0\}^m (\mathbf{N} \cdot \mathbf{L}_i > 0),$$

where $\mathbf{S}$ is the surface's specular reflection color; $\mathbf{H}_i$ is the unit halfway vector at the point $\mathbf{Q}$, which lies halfway between the direction to light $\mathbf{L}_i$ and the direction to the viewer; and m controls the sharpness of the specularity. The expression $(\mathbf{N} \cdot \mathbf{L}_i > 0)$ evaluates to one or zero, depending on whether the surface is facing the light.

Total Illumination Equation

The reflected color $\mathbf{K}$ calculated at a point $\mathbf{Q}$ on a surface illuminated by n lights is given by

$$\mathbf{K} = \mathbf{EM} + \mathbf{DTA} + \sum_{i=1}^{n} \mathbf{C}_i \Big[\mathbf{DT}(\mathbf{N} \cdot \mathbf{L}_i) + \mathbf{SG}(\mathbf{N} \cdot \mathbf{H}_i)^m (\mathbf{N} \cdot \mathbf{L}_i > 0) \Big],$$

where the dot products $\mathbf{N} \cdot \mathbf{L}$ and $\mathbf{N} \cdot \mathbf{H}$ are clamped to zero and the quantities involved are defined as follows.

$$
\begin{aligned}
\mathbf{D} &= \text{diffuse reflection color} \\
\mathbf{S} &= \text{specular reflection color} \\
m &= \text{specular exponent} \\
\mathbf{A} &= \text{ambient light color} \\
\mathbf{E} &= \text{emission color} \\
\mathbf{T} &= \text{texture map color} \\
\mathbf{G} &= \text{gloss map color} \\
\mathbf{M} &= \text{emission map color} \\
\mathbf{C}_i &= \text{color of } i\text{-th light at } \mathbf{Q} \\
\mathbf{L}_i &= \text{direction vector to } i\text{-th light} \\
\mathbf{H}_i &= \text{halfway vector for } i\text{-th light} \\
\mathbf{N} &= \text{normal vector}
\end{aligned}
$$

Bump Mapping

The tangent $\mathbf{T}$ and binormal $\mathbf{B}$ for a triangle whose vertices lie at the points $\mathbf{E}$, $\mathbf{F}$, and $\mathbf{G}$ are calculated using the formula

$$
\begin{bmatrix} T_x & T_y & T_z \\ B_x & B_y & B_z \end{bmatrix} = \frac{1}{s_1 t_2 - s_2 t_1} \begin{bmatrix} t_2 & -t_1 \\ -s_2 & s_1 \end{bmatrix} \begin{bmatrix} P_x & P_y & P_z \\ Q_x & Q_y & Q_z \end{bmatrix},
$$

where $\mathbf{P} = \mathbf{F} - \mathbf{E}$, $\mathbf{Q} = \mathbf{G} - \mathbf{E}$, and

$$\langle s_1, t_1 \rangle = \langle s_F - s_E, t_F - t_E \rangle$$

$$\langle s_2, t_2 \rangle = \langle s_G - s_E, t_G - t_E \rangle.$$

The direction-to-light vector $\mathbf{L}$ and halfway vector $\mathbf{H}$ are transformed from object space to tangent space using the matrix

$$
\begin{bmatrix} T'_x & T'_y & T'_z \\ B'_x & B'_y & B'_z \\ N_x & N_y & N_z \end{bmatrix},
$$

where $\mathbf{T}'$ and $\mathbf{B}'$ are orthogonal to $\mathbf{N}$ and each other.

Bidirectional Reflectance Distribution Functions

The radiance $\mathbf{C}_R$ of the light reflected in the direction $\mathbf{V}$ from a surface illuminated by n lights is given by

$$\mathbf{C}_R(\mathbf{V}) = \sum_{i=1}^{n} \rho(\mathbf{V}, \mathbf{L}_i)\mathbf{C}_i(\mathbf{N} \cdot \mathbf{L}_i),$$

where $\mathbf{C}_i$ is the radiance of the i-th light source. The BRDF ρ can be divided into diffuse and specular components by writing

$$\rho(\mathbf{V}, \mathbf{L}) = k\mathbf{D} + (1 - k)\rho_s(\mathbf{V}, \mathbf{L}),$$

where k is the fraction of light that is reflected diffusely.

Cook-Torrance Illumination

The specular component of the BRDF used in the Cook-Torrance illumination model is given by

$$\rho_s(\mathbf{V}, \mathbf{L}) = \mathbf{F}(\mathbf{V}, \mathbf{L}) \frac{D(\mathbf{V}, \mathbf{L})G(\mathbf{V}, \mathbf{L})}{(\mathbf{N} \cdot \mathbf{V})(\mathbf{N} \cdot \mathbf{L})},$$

where $\mathbf{F}$ is the Fresnel factor, D is the microfacet distribution function, and G is the geometrical attenuation factor.

Fresnel Factor

The Fresnel factor for a single color is given by

$$F_\lambda(\mathbf{V}, \mathbf{L}) = \frac{1}{2} \frac{(g - \mathbf{L} \cdot \mathbf{H})^2}{(g + \mathbf{L} \cdot \mathbf{H})^2} \left(\frac{\left[(\mathbf{L} \cdot \mathbf{H})(g + \mathbf{L} \cdot \mathbf{H}) - 1\right]^2}{\left[(\mathbf{L} \cdot \mathbf{H})(g - \mathbf{L} \cdot \mathbf{H}) + 1\right]^2} + 1 \right),$$

where g is defined by

$$g = \sqrt{\eta_\lambda^2 - 1 + (\mathbf{L} \cdot \mathbf{H})^2}.$$

The index of refraction η_λ can be calculated using the equation

$$\eta_\lambda = \frac{1 + \sqrt{S_\lambda}}{1 - \sqrt{S_\lambda}},$$

where $\mathbf{S}$ is the specular reflection color at normal incidence.

Microfacet Distribution Functions

The microfacet distribution function D_m for isotropic surfaces is given by

$$D_m(\mathbf{V}, \mathbf{L}) = \frac{1}{4\pi m^2 (\mathbf{N} \cdot \mathbf{H})^4} e^{\frac{(\mathbf{N} \cdot \mathbf{H})^2 - 1}{m^2 (\mathbf{N} \cdot \mathbf{H})^2}},$$

where m is the root mean square slope of the microfacets. For anisotropic surfaces, the microfacet distribution function becomes

$$D_{\mathbf{m}}(\mathbf{V}, \mathbf{L}) = \frac{1}{4\pi m_x m_y (\mathbf{N} \cdot \mathbf{H})^4} e^{\left(\frac{(\mathbf{T} \cdot \mathbf{P})^2}{m_x^2} + \frac{1 - (\mathbf{T} \cdot \mathbf{P})^2}{m_y^2}\right)\frac{(\mathbf{N} \cdot \mathbf{H})^2 - 1}{(\mathbf{N} \cdot \mathbf{H})^2}},$$

where m_x and m_y represent the root mean square slopes parallel and perpendicular to the tangent direction $\mathbf{T}$. The vector $\mathbf{P}$ is the normalized projection of the halfway vector $\mathbf{H}$ onto the tangent plane.

Geometrical Attenuation Factor

The geometrical attenuation factor is given by the formula

$$G(\mathbf{V}, \mathbf{L}) = \min\left\{1, \frac{2(\mathbf{N} \cdot \mathbf{H})(\mathbf{N} \cdot \mathbf{V})}{\mathbf{V} \cdot \mathbf{H}}, \frac{2(\mathbf{N} \cdot \mathbf{H})(\mathbf{N} \cdot \mathbf{L})}{\mathbf{V} \cdot \mathbf{H}}\right\}$$

and accounts for the incident or reflected light for a microfacet that is blocked by adjacent microfacets.

EXERCISES FOR CHAPTER 6

1. A point light source has attenuation constants $k_c = 1$, $k_l = 0$, and $k_q = \frac{1}{2}$. At what distance from the light source is the radiant intensity one-fourth that of the intensity at a distance of one meter?

2. A spot light source positioned 10 meters above the origin at the point $\mathbf{P} = \langle 0, 0, 10 \rangle$ and radiating energy in the direction $\mathbf{U} = \langle 0, 0, -1 \rangle$ is configured so that no distance attenuation takes place by setting $k_c = 1$ and $k_l = k_q = 0$. If the color of the light is white ($\mathbf{C}_0 = \langle 1, 1, 1 \rangle$) and the spot exponent is 8, then what is the radius of the circle lying in the x-y plane where the intensity of the light is 50% gray ($\mathbf{C} = \langle \frac{1}{2}, \frac{1}{2}, \frac{1}{2} \rangle$)?

3. Describe how it is possible for $\mathbf{N} \cdot \mathbf{H}$ to be a positive number when $\mathbf{N} \cdot \mathbf{L}$ is a negative number, thus necessitating the ($\mathbf{N} \cdot \mathbf{L} > 0$) term in the illumination formula.

4. Write a program that calculates vertex normals and vertex tangents for an arbitrary triangle mesh. Assume that the triangle mesh is specified such that each of n triangles indexes three entries in an array of m vertices. Each entry in the vertex array contains the position of the vertex and two-dimensional texture-mapping coordinates.

5. Implement a simple ray tracer that calculates diffuse and specular reflections using Equations (6.6) and (6.14). The ray tracer should be able to model spheres and should support directional, point, and spot light sources.

6. Extend the ray tracer from the previous exercise to implement Cook-Torrance illumination.

CHAPTER

7

Visibility Determination

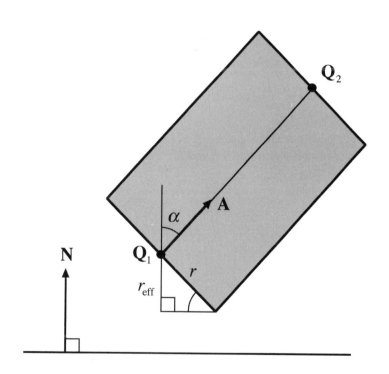

When it comes to the performance of a real-time 3D engine, the single most important component of the rendering architecture is visibility determination. Given a particular camera position and orientation, every engine must be able to efficiently determine which parts of the world are potentially visible and therefore should be rendered. This problem is usually attacked from the opposite perspective—the engine determines which parts of the world are definitely *not* visible and renders whatever is left over.

Most engines perform visibility determination at multiple levels. The general goal is to determine which world geometry cannot possibly intersect the view frustum. At the smallest scale, 3D hardware performs backface culling to eliminate individual triangles that face away from the camera. At the level above that, bounding volume tests are usually performed to determine whether an object lies completely outside the view frustum. Moderate-sized groups of geometry can be culled from the visible set by organizing areas of the world into tree structures such as binary space partitioning (BSP) trees or octrees. At the largest scale, entire regions of world geometry can be eliminated by using a technique known as a portal system.

7.1 BOUNDING VOLUME CONSTRUCTION

Bounding volumes are constructed so that they enclose all the vertices belonging to a triangle mesh, thereby ensuring that every triangle in the mesh is also contained in the bounding volume. The bounding volume should be made as small as possible so that it falls completely outside the view frustum as often as possible, thus enabling the object it contains to be culled from the visible set of geometry as often as possible.

Figure 7.1 shows a box bounding a set of points that represent the vertices of a triangle mesh. The box is aligned to the coordinate axes, but the vertices are distributed in such a way that the box enclosing them contains a lot of empty space.

As Figure 7.2 demonstrates, choosing a bounding box that is aligned to the natural axes of the data set can greatly reduce the size of the box. We present a method for determining the natural alignment in the next section.

7.1.1 PRINCIPAL COMPONENT ANALYSIS

We can reduce the size of each of our bounding volumes by determining a coordinate system that is naturally aligned to the set of vertices belonging to each triangle mesh. We can calculate these coordinate axes by using a statistical method called *principal component analysis*. Principal component analysis allows us to find a coordinate space in which a set of data composed of multiple

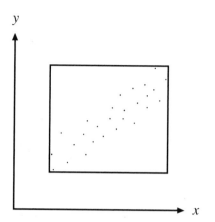

FIGURE *A bounding volume aligned to the coordinate axes is usually a poor choice for most*
7.1   *vertex distributions.*

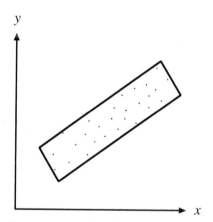

FIGURE *Using properly aligned axes produces a far superior bounding volume.*
7.2

variables, such as the x-, y-, and z-coordinates stored in an array of vertex positions, can be separated into uncorrelated components. The *primary* principal
component of the data is represented by the direction in which the data vary the
most.

To determine the natural coordinate system for an arbitrary set of N vertices
$\mathbf{P}_1, \mathbf{P}_2, \ldots, \mathbf{P}_N$, where $\mathbf{P}_i = \langle x_i, y_i, z_i \rangle$, we first calculate the mean (average) position
$\mathbf{m}$ using the formula

$$\mathbf{m} = \frac{1}{N} \sum_{i=1}^{N} \mathbf{P}_i. \tag{7.1}$$

We then construct a 3×3 matrix $\mathbf{C}$, called the *covariance matrix*, as follows.

$$\mathbf{C} = \frac{1}{N} \sum_{i=1}^{N} (\mathbf{P}_i - \mathbf{m})(\mathbf{P}_i - \mathbf{m})^{\mathsf{T}} \qquad (7.2)$$

The covariance matrix is a symmetric matrix made up of the following six unique entries.

$$C_{11} = \frac{1}{N} \sum_{i=1}^{N} (x_i - m_x)^2 \quad C_{12} = C_{21} = \frac{1}{N} \sum_{i=1}^{N} (x_i - m_x)(y_i - m_y)$$

$$C_{22} = \frac{1}{N} \sum_{i=1}^{N} (y_i - m_y)^2 \quad C_{13} = C_{31} = \frac{1}{N} \sum_{i=1}^{N} (x_i - m_x)(z_i - m_z)$$

$$C_{33} = \frac{1}{N} \sum_{i=1}^{N} (z_i - m_z)^2 \quad C_{23} = C_{32} = \frac{1}{N} \sum_{i=1}^{N} (y_i - m_y)(z_i - m_z) \qquad (7.3)$$

The entries of the covariance matrix represent the correlation between each pair of the x-, y-, and z-coordinates. An entry of zero indicates no correlation between the two coordinates used to calculate that entry. If $\mathbf{C}$ is a diagonal matrix, then all three coordinates are completely uncorrelated, meaning that the points are distributed evenly about each axis.

We want to find a basis to which we can transform our set of vertices so that the covariance matrix is diagonal. If we apply a transformation matrix $\mathbf{A}$ to each of the points $\{\mathbf{P}_i\}$, then the covariance matrix $\mathbf{C}'$ of the transformed set of points is given by

$$\mathbf{C}' = \frac{1}{N} \sum_{i=1}^{N} (\mathbf{A}\mathbf{P}_i - \mathbf{A}\mathbf{m})(\mathbf{A}\mathbf{P}_i - \mathbf{A}\mathbf{m})^{\mathsf{T}}$$

$$= \frac{1}{N} \sum_{i=1}^{N} \mathbf{A}(\mathbf{P}_i - \mathbf{m})(\mathbf{P}_i - \mathbf{m})^{\mathsf{T}} \mathbf{A}^{\mathsf{T}}$$

$$= \mathbf{A}\mathbf{C}\mathbf{A}^{\mathsf{T}}. \qquad (7.4)$$

Thus, we require an orthogonal transformation matrix $\mathbf{A}$ whose transpose diagonalizes the matrix $\mathbf{C}$. Since $\mathbf{C}$ is a real symmetric matrix, we know by Theorem 2.25 that its eigenvectors are orthogonal. The matrix whose rows consist of the eigenvectors of $\mathbf{C}$ meets our requirements and maps our vertices into a space where their coordinates are uncorrelated.

We have now turned the problem of finding the natural axes of a set of points into that of calculating the eigenvectors of the covariance matrix. To do this, we must first calculate the eigenvalues given by the roots of the characteristic polynomial, which in the case of the 3×3 covariance matrix is a cubic polynomial. Fortunately, since the covariance matrix is symmetric, it has only real eigenvalues (see Theorem 2.24), and we can therefore use the method presented in Section 5.1.2 to calculate them all explicitly. Finding the corresponding eigenvectors is then achieved by solving three homogeneous linear systems.

Example 7.1. Determine the natural axes for the following set of points.

$$\mathbf{P}_1 = \langle -1, -2, 1\rangle$$
$$\mathbf{P}_2 = \langle 1, 0, 2\rangle$$
$$\mathbf{P}_3 = \langle 2, -1, 3\rangle$$
$$\mathbf{P}_4 = \langle 2, -1, 2\rangle$$

Solution. We first calculate the average position $\mathbf{m}$:

$$\mathbf{m} = \frac{1}{4}\sum_{i=1}^{4}\mathbf{P}_i = \langle 1, -1, 2\rangle. \tag{7.5}$$

The covariance matrix $\mathbf{C}$ is then given by

$$\mathbf{C} = \begin{bmatrix} \frac{3}{2} & \frac{1}{2} & \frac{3}{4} \\ \frac{1}{2} & \frac{1}{2} & \frac{1}{4} \\ \frac{3}{4} & \frac{1}{4} & \frac{1}{2} \end{bmatrix}. \tag{7.6}$$

The eigenvalues of the covariance matrix are the roots of the characteristic polynomial:

$$\det(\mathbf{C} - \lambda\mathbf{I}) = \begin{vmatrix} \frac{3}{2} - \lambda & \frac{1}{2} & \frac{3}{4} \\ \frac{1}{2} & \frac{1}{2} - \lambda & \frac{1}{4} \\ \frac{3}{4} & \frac{1}{4} & \frac{1}{2} - \lambda \end{vmatrix}$$
$$= -\lambda^3 + \frac{5}{2}\lambda^2 - \frac{7}{8}\lambda + \frac{1}{16}. \tag{7.7}$$

Explicitly solving for the roots of the characteristic polynomial using the method presented in Section 5.1.2 gives us the following eigenvalues.

$$\lambda_1 = 2.097$$
$$\lambda_2 = 0.3055$$
$$\lambda_3 = 0.09756 \tag{7.8}$$

The eigenvectors, which we call $\mathbf{R}$, $\mathbf{S}$, and $\mathbf{T}$ here, are found by solving the linear systems $\mathbf{C} - \lambda_i\mathbf{I} = \mathbf{0}$. Omitting the details of these calculations, the unit-length eigenvectors of the matrix $\mathbf{C}$ are

$$\mathbf{R} = \begin{bmatrix} -0.833 \\ -0.330 \\ -0.443 \end{bmatrix} \quad \mathbf{S} = \begin{bmatrix} -0.257 \\ 0.941 \\ -0.218 \end{bmatrix} \quad \mathbf{T} = \begin{bmatrix} 0.489 \\ -0.0675 \\ -0.870 \end{bmatrix}, \qquad (7.9)$$

and these represent the natural axes of the set of vertices $\mathbf{P}_i$.

In the remainder of this chapter, we use the letters $\mathbf{R}$, $\mathbf{S}$, and $\mathbf{T}$ to represent the natural axes of a set of vertices. The direction $\mathbf{R}$ always represents the principal axis, which corresponds to the largest eigenvalue of the covariance matrix. The directions $\mathbf{S}$ and $\mathbf{T}$ represent the axes corresponding to the second largest and the smallest eigenvalues, respectively. That is, if λ_1, λ_2, and λ_3 are the eigenvalues corresponding to the vectors $\mathbf{R}$, $\mathbf{S}$, and $\mathbf{T}$, respectively, then $|\lambda_1| \geq |\lambda_2| \geq |\lambda_3|$.

7.1.2 BOUNDING BOX CONSTRUCTION

Given a set of vertex positions $\mathbf{P}_1$, $\mathbf{P}_2,\ldots$, $\mathbf{P}_N$ for a triangle mesh, we can now calculate the directions $\mathbf{R}$, $\mathbf{S}$, and $\mathbf{T}$ corresponding to the natural axes of the object. To construct a bounding box, we need to determine the minimum and maximum extents of the vertex set along these three directions. These extents immediately produce the six planes of the bounding box; other types of bounding volumes require a little more computation.

To find the extents, we simply compute the dot product of each vertex position $\mathbf{P}_i$ with the unit length vectors $\mathbf{R}$, $\mathbf{S}$, and $\mathbf{T}$ and take the minimum and maximum values. The six planes of the bounding box are then given by

$$\left\langle \mathbf{R}, - \min_{1 \leq i \leq N} \{\mathbf{P}_i \cdot \mathbf{R}\} \right\rangle \quad \left\langle -\mathbf{R}, \max_{1 \leq i \leq N} \{\mathbf{P}_i \cdot \mathbf{R}\} \right\rangle$$

$$\left\langle \mathbf{S}, - \min_{1 \leq i \leq N} \{\mathbf{P}_i \cdot \mathbf{S}\} \right\rangle \quad \left\langle -\mathbf{S}, \max_{1 \leq i \leq N} \{\mathbf{P}_i \cdot \mathbf{S}\} \right\rangle$$

$$\left\langle \mathbf{T}, - \min_{1 \leq i \leq N} \{\mathbf{P}_i \cdot \mathbf{T}\} \right\rangle \quad \left\langle -\mathbf{T}, \max_{1 \leq i \leq N} \{\mathbf{P}_i \cdot \mathbf{T}\} \right\rangle. \qquad (7.10)$$

Example 7.2. Calculate the six planes of the naturally aligned bounding box for the set of points given in Example 7.1.

Solution. The natural axes for this set of points are given by Equation (7.9). The dot products of each of the four points with the directions $\mathbf{R}$, $\mathbf{S}$, and $\mathbf{T}$ are listed below.

$$\begin{aligned}
\mathbf{P}_1 \cdot \mathbf{R} &= 1.05 & \mathbf{P}_1 \cdot \mathbf{S} &= -1.84 & \mathbf{P}_1 \cdot \mathbf{T} &= -1.22 \\
\mathbf{P}_2 \cdot \mathbf{R} &= -1.72 & \mathbf{P}_2 \cdot \mathbf{S} &= -0.693 & \mathbf{P}_2 \cdot \mathbf{T} &= -1.25 \\
\mathbf{P}_3 \cdot \mathbf{R} &= -2.67 & \mathbf{P}_3 \cdot \mathbf{S} &= -2.11 & \mathbf{P}_3 \cdot \mathbf{T} &= -1.56 \\
\mathbf{P}_4 \cdot \mathbf{R} &= -2.22 & \mathbf{P}_4 \cdot \mathbf{S} &= -1.89 & \mathbf{P}_4 \cdot \mathbf{T} &= -0.695
\end{aligned} \tag{7.11}$$

Using the minimum and maximum values of $\mathbf{P}_i \cdot \mathbf{R}$, the two planes perpendicular to the direction $\mathbf{R}$ are given by

$$\langle \mathbf{R}, 2.67 \rangle \quad \langle -\mathbf{R}, 1.05 \rangle. \tag{7.12}$$

Similarly, the planes perpendicular to the $\mathbf{S}$ and $\mathbf{T}$ directions are given by

$$\langle \mathbf{S}, 2.11 \rangle \quad \langle -\mathbf{S}, -0.693 \rangle$$

$$\langle \mathbf{T}, 1.56 \rangle \quad \langle -\mathbf{T}, -0.695 \rangle. \tag{7.13}$$

The dimensions of the bounding box are given by the differences between the minimum and maximum dot products in each of the directions $\mathbf{R}$, $\mathbf{S}$, and $\mathbf{T}$. The center $\mathbf{Q}$ of the bounding box is the point at which the three planes lying halfway between each pair of opposing faces intersect. We assign to the scalars a, b, and c the average extent in the $\mathbf{R}$, $\mathbf{S}$, and $\mathbf{T}$ directions, respectively, as follows.

$$a = \frac{\min\limits_{1 \le i \le N}\{\mathbf{P}_i \cdot \mathbf{R}\} + \max\limits_{1 \le i \le N}\{\mathbf{P}_i \cdot \mathbf{R}\}}{2}$$

$$b = \frac{\min\limits_{1 \le i \le N}\{\mathbf{P}_i \cdot \mathbf{S}\} + \max\limits_{1 \le i \le N}\{\mathbf{P}_i \cdot \mathbf{S}\}}{2}$$

$$c = \frac{\min\limits_{1 \le i \le N}\{\mathbf{P}_i \cdot \mathbf{T}\} + \max\limits_{1 \le i \le N}\{\mathbf{P}_i \cdot \mathbf{T}\}}{2} \tag{7.14}$$

The three planes that divide the box in half are given by $\langle \mathbf{R}, -a \rangle$, $\langle \mathbf{S}, -b \rangle$, and $\langle \mathbf{T}, -c \rangle$. Using Equation (4.20) to calculate the point of intersection provides us with the following expression for the center $\mathbf{Q}$.

$$\mathbf{Q} = a\mathbf{R} + b\mathbf{S} + c\mathbf{T} \tag{7.15}$$

7.1.3 BOUNDING SPHERE CONSTRUCTION

Bounding spheres are commonly used in tests for object visibility due to the speed with which such a test can be performed. As with all bounding volumes, we should construct bounding spheres that are as tight as possible so as to minimize its intersection with the view frustum. Achieving an absolutely optimal bounding sphere in all cases turns out to be a hard problem that we do not discuss here, but we are able to construct bounding spheres that are acceptably efficient without requiring an excessively complex algorithm.

We begin constructing a bounding sphere for a set of points $\mathbf{P}_1, \mathbf{P}_2, ..., \mathbf{P}_N$ by first calculating the principal axis $\mathbf{R}$ and locating the points $\mathbf{P}_k$ and $\mathbf{P}_l$, representing the minimum and maximum extents in that direction (i.e., we locate the points having the least and greatest dot product with $\mathbf{R}$). We then construct a sphere whose center $\mathbf{Q}$ and radius r are given by

$$\mathbf{Q} = \frac{\mathbf{P}_k + \mathbf{P}_l}{2}$$

$$r = \left\| \mathbf{P}_k - \mathbf{Q} \right\|. \tag{7.16}$$

That is, the center of the sphere lies halfway between the points producing the minimum and maximum extents in the $\mathbf{R}$ direction, and the radius is the distance from the center to either of those points.

Although it is a good approximation to the final bounding sphere, the sphere given by Equation (7.16) may not enclose all the points $\mathbf{P}_1, \mathbf{P}_2, ..., \mathbf{P}_N$. We must therefore test each of the points $\{\mathbf{P}_i\}$ to make sure they fall inside the sphere. Whenever a point is encountered that lies outside the sphere, we expand the sphere by adjusting the center $\mathbf{Q}$ and radius r to enclose the previous sphere and the exterior point, as shown in Figure 7.3. A point $\mathbf{P}_i$ lies outside the sphere if

$$\left\| \mathbf{P}_i - \mathbf{Q} \right\|^2 > r^2. \tag{7.17}$$

We expand the sphere by placing the new center $\mathbf{Q}'$ on the line connecting the previous center $\mathbf{Q}$ and the exterior point $\mathbf{P}_i$. The new sphere is then tangent to the previous sphere at a point $\mathbf{G}$ given by

$$\mathbf{G} = \mathbf{Q} - r \frac{\mathbf{P}_i - \mathbf{Q}}{\left\| \mathbf{P}_i - \mathbf{Q} \right\|}, \tag{7.18}$$

which also lies on the line containing $\mathbf{Q}$ and $\mathbf{P}_i$. The new center $\mathbf{Q}'$ is placed halfway between the points $\mathbf{G}$ and $\mathbf{P}_i$, and the new radius r' is the distance from the new center to either of these points:

$$\mathbf{Q}' = \frac{\mathbf{G} + \mathbf{P}_i}{2}$$

$$r' = \left\| \mathbf{P}_i - \mathbf{Q}' \right\|. \tag{7.19}$$

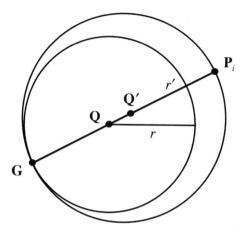

FIGURE 7.3 *The initial bounding sphere determined by the extents of the set of points in the direction of the principal axis is expanded to include any points in the set that lie outside of the sphere.*

7.1.4 BOUNDING ELLIPSOID CONSTRUCTION

An ellipsoidal bounding volume may be appropriate for a triangle mesh having an elongated shape. To determine a good bounding ellipsoid for a set of vertices $\mathbf{P}_1, \mathbf{P}_2, ..., \mathbf{P}_N$, we need to calculate the lengths of the three semi-axes of the ellipsoid aligned to the natural axes $\mathbf{R}$, $\mathbf{S}$, and $\mathbf{T}$. We can transform the problem into that of finding a bounding sphere by scaling the vertex positions in these directions so that their bounding box becomes a cube. Once the bounding sphere of the scaled set is known, we scale its radius by the reciprocal amount in each direction to derive the semi-axis lengths.

To scale the vertex positions so that they are bounded by a cube, we need to know the distance between the planes representing the minimum and maximum extents in each natural axis direction. These distances are equal to the dimensions of the standard bounding box, which are given by the differences between the minimum and maximum dot products of the points $\mathbf{P}_i$ with the vectors $\mathbf{R}$, $\mathbf{S}$, and $\mathbf{T}$. Calling these distances a, b, and c, respectively, we have

$$a = \max_{1 \leq i \leq N}\left\{\mathbf{P}_i \cdot \mathbf{R}\right\} - \min_{1 \leq i \leq N}\left\{\mathbf{P}_i \cdot \mathbf{R}\right\}$$

$$b = \max_{1 \leq i \leq N}\left\{\mathbf{P}_i \cdot \mathbf{S}\right\} - \min_{1 \leq i \leq N}\left\{\mathbf{P}_i \cdot \mathbf{S}\right\}$$

$$c = \max_{1 \leq i \leq N}\left\{\mathbf{P}_i \cdot \mathbf{T}\right\} - \min_{1 \leq i \leq N}\left\{\mathbf{P}_i \cdot \mathbf{T}\right\}. \tag{7.20}$$

To transform the vertex set into one bounded by a cube, we need to scale their positions by $1/a$ in the $\mathbf{R}$ direction, by $1/b$ in the $\mathbf{S}$ direction, and by $1/c$ in the

T direction. As stated in Equation (3.10), the matrix **M** that performs this scale is given by

$$\mathbf{M} = \begin{bmatrix} \mathbf{R} & \mathbf{S} & \mathbf{T} \end{bmatrix} \begin{bmatrix} 1/a & 0 & 0 \\ 0 & 1/b & 0 \\ 0 & 0 & 1/c \end{bmatrix} \begin{bmatrix} \mathbf{R} & \mathbf{S} & \mathbf{T} \end{bmatrix}^{\mathrm{T}}, \tag{7.21}$$

where we have replaced the inverse operation for the rightmost matrix by a transpose operation since the vectors **R**, **S**, and **T** are orthonormal.

Once each of the points $\{\mathbf{P}_i\}$ has been transformed by the matrix **M**, we calculate the bounding sphere for the set of points $\mathbf{MP}_1, \mathbf{MP}_2, ..., \mathbf{MP}_N$. Once the center **Q** of this sphere is known, we can calculate the center of the bounding ellipsoid of the original set of vertices by transforming **Q** back into the unscaled coordinate space. The ellipsoid center is simply given by $\mathbf{M}^{-1}\mathbf{Q}$, where the inverse of **M** is

$$\mathbf{M}^{-1} = \begin{bmatrix} \mathbf{R} & \mathbf{S} & \mathbf{T} \end{bmatrix} \begin{bmatrix} a & 0 & 0 \\ 0 & b & 0 \\ 0 & 0 & c \end{bmatrix} \begin{bmatrix} \mathbf{R} & \mathbf{S} & \mathbf{T} \end{bmatrix}^{\mathrm{T}}. \tag{7.22}$$

The lengths of the semi-axes of the bounding ellipsoid are calculated by scaling the radius r of the bounding sphere calculated for the points $\{\mathbf{MP}_i\}$. The semi-axis lengths corresponding to the directions **R**, **S**, and **T** are given by ar, br, and cr, respectively.

7.1.5 BOUNDING CYLINDER CONSTRUCTION

A cylindrical bounding volume is represented by its radius the two points corresponding to the centers of its endcaps. The endcaps of a cylinder bounding the set of points $\mathbf{P}_1, \mathbf{P}_2, ..., \mathbf{P}_N$ coincide with the planes of the bounding box that are perpendicular to the principal axis **R**. Most of the calculations involved in determining the bounding cylinder for a triangle mesh lie in finding the circle that bounds the projection of the points $\mathbf{P}_i$ onto the plane containing the natural axes **S** and **T**.

We find the bounding circle in a manner similar to the way we calculate bounding spheres, except that the component of each point $\mathbf{P}_i$ parallel to the **R** direction is ignored. Instead of working directly with the points $\{\mathbf{P}_i\}$, we remove the projection of each $\mathbf{P}_i$ onto **R** and work with the points $\{\mathbf{H}_i\}$ given by

$$\mathbf{H}_i = \mathbf{P}_i - (\mathbf{P}_i \cdot \mathbf{R})\mathbf{R}. \tag{7.23}$$

We first locate the points $\mathbf{H}_k$ and $\mathbf{H}_l$ that have the least and greatest dot products with the vector **S**. (Recall that the axis **S** corresponds to the second largest eigenvalue of the covariance matrix.) The initial center $\mathbf{Q}$ and radius r of the bounding circle are given by

$$\mathbf{Q} = \frac{\mathbf{H}_k + \mathbf{H}_l}{2}$$

$$r = \left\| \mathbf{H}_k - \mathbf{Q} \right\|. \tag{7.24}$$

We then proceed exactly as we would when calculating a bounding sphere. We check each point to make sure it falls inside the bounding circle. When a point $\mathbf{H}_i$ for which

$$\left\| \mathbf{H}_i - \mathbf{Q} \right\|^2 > r^2 \tag{7.25}$$

is encountered, we expand the bounding circle so that it has a new center $\mathbf{Q}'$ and new radius r' given by

$$\mathbf{Q}' = \frac{\mathbf{G} + \mathbf{H}_i}{2}$$

$$r' = \left\| \mathbf{H}_i - \mathbf{Q}' \right\|, \tag{7.26}$$

where

$$\mathbf{G} = \mathbf{Q} - r \frac{\mathbf{H}_i - \mathbf{Q}}{\left\| \mathbf{H}_i - \mathbf{Q} \right\|}. \tag{7.27}$$

The radius of the bounding cylinder is the same as the radius of the circle bounding the set of points $\{\mathbf{H}_i\}$. The center $\mathbf{Q}$ of the bounding circle lies in the plane perpendicular to the direction $\mathbf{R}$ but passing through the origin. The centers of the cylinder's endcaps are found by projecting $\mathbf{Q}$ onto the bounding box planes corresponding to the least and greatest dot products of the points $\{\mathbf{P}_i\}$ with the direction $\mathbf{R}$. Calling the endpoints $\mathbf{Q}_1$ and $\mathbf{Q}_2$, we have

$$\mathbf{Q}_1 = \mathbf{Q} + \min_{1 \le i \le N}\{\mathbf{P}_i \cdot \mathbf{R}\}\mathbf{R}$$

$$\mathbf{Q}_2 = \mathbf{Q} + \max_{1 \le i \le N}\{\mathbf{P}_i \cdot \mathbf{R}\}\mathbf{R}. \tag{7.28}$$

7.2 BOUNDING VOLUME TESTS

Now that we have seen how to construct a variety of bounding volumes, we turn our attention to the methods used to determine whether each type is visible. All the techniques presented in this section reduce the problem of intersecting a bounding volume with the view frustum to that of intersecting a point or a line segment with a properly modified view frustum. This is accomplished by moving the planes of the view frustum outward by appropriate amounts, which are determined differently for each type of bounding volume.

7.2.1 BOUNDING SPHERE TEST

A sphere of radius r intersects the view frustum if its center lies inside the view frustum or lies within a distance r of any of the six sides of the view frustum. The gray region shown in Figure 7.4(a) corresponds to the volume in which the sphere's center must lie whenever it is visible. The boundary of this region, formed by rolling the sphere around the outside edges of the view frustum, is parallel to one of the frustum planes everywhere except at the corners, where it is rounded. As Figure 7.4(b) shows, we can approximate the exact volume of visibility by moving each of the six frustum planes outward by a distance r.

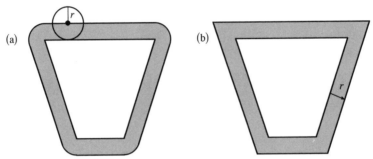

FIGURE
7.4
(a) The gray region corresponds to the volume in which the center of a sphere of radius r must lie whenever it is visible. (b) We can approximate the exact volume of visibility by moving each of the six frustum planes outward by a distance r.

Given a sphere of radius r whose center resides at the point $\mathbf{Q}$ in camera space, we compute the 4D dot products of the homogeneous extension of $\mathbf{Q}$ with the six frustum planes listed in Table 4.1. Since the frustum plane normals point inward, a negative dot product indicates that $\mathbf{Q}$ lies outside the visible volume of space. If any one of the dot products is less than or equal to $-r$, then the sphere does not intersect the view frustum at all and the object bounded by it should be culled from the visible set of geometry. Otherwise, some part of the sphere probably lies inside all six frustum planes, the exception being the case shown in Figure 7.5. Near the edges of the view frustum, some spheres that are not visible may not be culled because they do not fall far enough outside any single frustum plane. This infrequent occurrence is normally tolerated to preserve the simplicity of the visibility test. We examine a small enhancement which reduces this effect in Section 7.4.2.

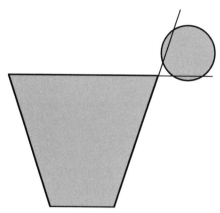

FIGURE *Near the edges of the view frustum, some spheres that are not visible are not culled*
7.5 *because they do not fall far enough outside any single frustum plane.*

7.2.2 BOUNDING ELLIPSOID TEST

When testing the visibility of a sphere, we move each of the six frustum planes
outward by the radius of the sphere and test whether the sphere's center lies on
the positive side of these modified planes. A similar method can be used to test
the visibility of an ellipsoid, but since an ellipsoid does not possess the isotropic
symmetry that a sphere does, the *effective* radius of the ellipsoid is different for
each frustum plane.

Suppose that an object is bounded by an ellipsoid whose semi-axes are given
by the mutually perpendicular vectors **R**, **S**, and **T**, as shown in Figure 7.6,
where **R**, **S**, and **T** are parallel to the principal axes of the bounded object but

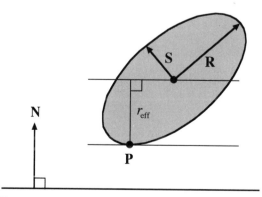

FIGURE *A bounding ellipsoid whose semi-axes are given by the mutually perpendicular*
7.6 *vectors **R**, **S**, and **T** (**T** points out of the page). The effective radius of the ellipsoid with
respect to a plane is equal to the maximum distance from the ellipsoid's center to any
point on the surface projected onto the plane's normal.*

have magnitudes equal to the semi-axis lengths of the ellipsoid. A point **P** on the surface of the ellipsoid can be expressed in terms of the three vectors **R**, **S**, and **T** as follows.

$$\mathbf{P} = \mathbf{R} \sin\theta \cos\phi + \mathbf{S} \sin\theta \sin\phi + \mathbf{T} \cos\theta \tag{7.29}$$

This expression represents a spherical coordinate system aligned to the axes of the ellipsoid. The angle θ represents the angle that the point **P** makes with the vector **T**. The angle ϕ represents the angle that the projection of **P** onto the plane containing the vectors **R** and **S** makes with the vector **R**. Over the entire surface of the ellipsoid, θ ranges from 0 to π, and ϕ ranges from 0 to 2π.

Given a unit direction vector **N**, we would like to find the point **P** on the surface of the ellipsoid whose projection onto **N** has the greatest magnitude. This would give us the effective radius r_{eff} of the ellipsoid with respect to a plane whose normal vector is **N**. Since **N** has unit length, the magnitude of the projection of **P** onto **N** is given by $\mathbf{P} \cdot \mathbf{N}$. We wish to find the angles θ and ϕ that maximize this quantity, so we set partial derivatives to zero, as follows.

$$\frac{\partial}{\partial\theta}(\mathbf{P} \cdot \mathbf{N}) = (\mathbf{R} \cdot \mathbf{N})\cos\theta\cos\phi + (\mathbf{S} \cdot \mathbf{N})\cos\theta\sin\phi - (\mathbf{T} \cdot \mathbf{N})\sin\theta = 0 \tag{7.30}$$

$$\frac{\partial}{\partial\phi}(\mathbf{P} \cdot \mathbf{N}) = -(\mathbf{R} \cdot \mathbf{N})\sin\theta\sin\phi + (\mathbf{S} \cdot \mathbf{N})\sin\theta\cos\phi = 0 \tag{7.31}$$

In our derivation of an expression for the quantity $\mathbf{P} \cdot \mathbf{N}$, we make use of the trigonometric identity

$$\tan^2\alpha + 1 = \sec^2\alpha, \tag{7.32}$$

which can be transformed into the identities

$$\sin\alpha = \frac{\tan\alpha}{\sqrt{\tan^2\alpha + 1}}$$
$$\cos\alpha = \frac{1}{\sqrt{\tan^2\alpha + 1}}. \tag{7.33}$$

Equation (7.31) can be rewritten as

$$(\mathbf{S} \cdot \mathbf{N})\cos\phi = (\mathbf{R} \cdot \mathbf{N})\sin\phi, \tag{7.34}$$

allowing us to express $\tan\phi$ as

$$\tan\phi = \frac{\mathbf{S} \cdot \mathbf{N}}{\mathbf{R} \cdot \mathbf{N}}. \tag{7.35}$$

Equation (7.30) can be rewritten as

$$(\mathbf{T} \cdot \mathbf{N}) \sin \theta = (\mathbf{R} \cdot \mathbf{N}) \cos \theta \cos \phi + (\mathbf{S} \cdot \mathbf{N}) \cos \theta \sin \phi, \qquad (7.36)$$

allowing us to express $\tan \theta$ as

$$
\begin{aligned}
\tan \theta &= \frac{\mathbf{R} \cdot \mathbf{N}}{\mathbf{T} \cdot \mathbf{N}} \cos \phi + \frac{\mathbf{S} \cdot \mathbf{N}}{\mathbf{T} \cdot \mathbf{N}} \sin \phi \\[2mm]
&= \frac{1}{\sqrt{\tan^2 \phi + 1}} \left(\frac{\mathbf{R} \cdot \mathbf{N}}{\mathbf{T} \cdot \mathbf{N}} + \tan \phi \, \frac{\mathbf{S} \cdot \mathbf{N}}{\mathbf{T} \cdot \mathbf{N}} \right) \\[2mm]
&= \frac{\mathbf{R} \cdot \mathbf{N}}{\mathbf{T} \cdot \mathbf{N}} \frac{1}{\sqrt{\tan^2 \phi + 1}} \left(1 + \tan^2 \phi \right) \\[2mm]
&= \frac{\mathbf{R} \cdot \mathbf{N}}{\mathbf{T} \cdot \mathbf{N}} \sqrt{\tan^2 \phi + 1} \\[2mm]
&= \frac{\mathbf{R} \cdot \mathbf{N}}{\mathbf{T} \cdot \mathbf{N}} \sqrt{\left(\frac{\mathbf{S} \cdot \mathbf{N}}{\mathbf{R} \cdot \mathbf{N}} \right)^2 + 1} \, , \qquad (7.37)
\end{aligned}
$$

where Equation (7.35) has been used in the last step. Using the identities given by Equation (7.33), the value of $\mathbf{P} \cdot \mathbf{N}$ can now be written as

$$
\begin{aligned}
\mathbf{P} \cdot \mathbf{N} &= (\mathbf{R} \cdot \mathbf{N}) \sin \theta \cos \phi + (\mathbf{S} \cdot \mathbf{N}) \sin \theta \sin \phi + (\mathbf{T} \cdot \mathbf{N}) \cos \theta \\[2mm]
&= \frac{1}{\sqrt{\tan^2 \theta + 1}} \left\{ \frac{\tan \theta}{\sqrt{\tan^2 \phi + 1}} \left[\mathbf{R} \cdot \mathbf{N} + (\mathbf{S} \cdot \mathbf{N}) \tan \phi \right] + \mathbf{T} \cdot \mathbf{N} \right\}. \quad (7.38)
\end{aligned}
$$

Substituting expressions from Equations (7.35) and (7.37) for $\tan \phi$ and θ gives us

$$
\begin{aligned}
\mathbf{P} \cdot \mathbf{N} &= \frac{\dfrac{\mathbf{R} \cdot \mathbf{N}}{\mathbf{T} \cdot \mathbf{N}} \left(\mathbf{R} \cdot \mathbf{N} + \dfrac{(\mathbf{S} \cdot \mathbf{N})^2}{\mathbf{R} \cdot \mathbf{N}} \right) + \mathbf{T} \cdot \mathbf{N}}{\sqrt{\left(\dfrac{\mathbf{R} \cdot \mathbf{N}}{\mathbf{T} \cdot \mathbf{N}} \right)^2 \left[\left(\dfrac{\mathbf{S} \cdot \mathbf{N}}{\mathbf{R} \cdot \mathbf{N}} \right)^2 + 1 \right] + 1}} \\[4mm]
&= \frac{(\mathbf{R} \cdot \mathbf{N})^2 + (\mathbf{S} \cdot \mathbf{N})^2 + (\mathbf{T} \cdot \mathbf{N})^2}{\mathbf{T} \cdot \mathbf{N} \sqrt{\left(\dfrac{\mathbf{R} \cdot \mathbf{N}}{\mathbf{T} \cdot \mathbf{N}} \right)^2 \left[\left(\dfrac{\mathbf{S} \cdot \mathbf{N}}{\mathbf{R} \cdot \mathbf{N}} \right)^2 + 1 \right] + 1}} \\[4mm]
&= \frac{(\mathbf{R} \cdot \mathbf{N})^2 + (\mathbf{S} \cdot \mathbf{N})^2 + (\mathbf{T} \cdot \mathbf{N})^2}{\sqrt{(\mathbf{R} \cdot \mathbf{N})^2 + (\mathbf{S} \cdot \mathbf{N})^2 + (\mathbf{T} \cdot \mathbf{N})^2}} \, , \qquad (7.39)
\end{aligned}
$$

which yields the relatively simple expression

$$r_{\text{eff}} = \mathbf{P} \cdot \mathbf{N} = \sqrt{(\mathbf{R} \cdot \mathbf{N})^2 + (\mathbf{S} \cdot \mathbf{N})^2 + (\mathbf{T} \cdot \mathbf{N})^2}. \tag{7.40}$$

Equation (7.40) provides the effective radius of an arbitrary ellipsoid with respect to a plane having unit normal direction $\mathbf{N}$. Since the near and far planes are parallel, the ellipsoid's effective radius for those two planes is the same. Thus, to test whether an ellipsoid falls outside the view frustum, we need to calculate at most five effective radii. As with the sphere test, we compute the four-dimensional dot products of the ellipsoid's center with each of the frustum plane vectors. If any single dot product is less than or equal to $-r_{\text{eff}}$, then the ellipsoid is not visible. Otherwise, the object bounded by the ellipsoid should be drawn.

7.2.3 BOUNDING CYLINDER TEST

We reduced the problem of intersecting a sphere or an ellipsoid with the view frustum to that of testing whether a point fell on the positive side of frustum planes that were offset by the bounding volume's effective radius. To intersect a cylinder with the view frustum, we instead reduce the problem to determining whether a line segment is visible in a properly expanded frustum.

As with the ellipsoid test, we must determine the effective radius of a bounding cylinder with respect to each of the view frustum planes. The effective radius depends on the cylinder's orientation and ranges from zero (when the cylinder is perpendicular to a plane) to the actual radius (when the cylinder is parallel to a plane). Suppose that we are given a cylinder of radius r whose endpoints lie at $\mathbf{Q}_1$ and $\mathbf{Q}_2$. We define the vector $\mathbf{A}$ to be the unit vector parallel to the axis of the cylinder:

$$\mathbf{A} = \frac{\mathbf{Q}_2 - \mathbf{Q}_1}{\|\mathbf{Q}_2 - \mathbf{Q}_1\|}. \tag{7.41}$$

As shown in Figure 7.7, the effective radius r_{eff} of the cylinder with respect to a plane having unit normal direction $\mathbf{N}$ is given by

$$r_{\text{eff}} = r \sin \alpha, \tag{7.42}$$

where α is the angle formed between the vectors $\mathbf{A}$ and $\mathbf{N}$. This can also be written as

$$r_{\text{eff}} = r\sqrt{1 - \cos^2 \alpha}$$

$$= r\sqrt{1 - (\mathbf{A} \cdot \mathbf{N})^2}. \tag{7.43}$$

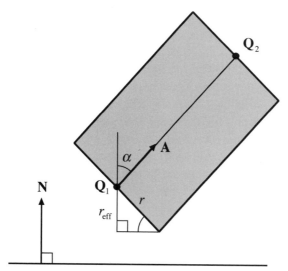

FIGURE
7.7 *The effective radius of a bounding cylinder.*

We perform the visibility test by visiting each of the six view frustum planes, beginning with the near and far planes since they are parallel and thus share the same effective radius. For each frustum plane $\mathbf{L}$, we first calculate the 4D dot products $\mathbf{L} \cdot \mathbf{Q}_1$ and $\mathbf{L} \cdot \mathbf{Q}_2$. If *both* dot products are less than or equal to the value $-r_{\text{eff}}$ corresponding to the plane $\mathbf{L}$, then we immediately know that the cylinder is not visible and the test exits. If both dot products are greater than or equal to $-r_{\text{eff}}$, then we cannot draw any conclusions and simply proceed to the next plane.

In the remaining case that one of the dot products is less than $-r_{\text{eff}}$ and the other dot product is greater than $-r_{\text{eff}}$, we calculate the point $\mathbf{Q}_3$ such that

$$\mathbf{L} \cdot \mathbf{Q}_3 = -r_{\text{eff}} \qquad (7.44)$$

and replace the exterior endpoint with it. This effectively chops off the part of the cylinder that is now known to lie outside the view frustum. To find the point $\mathbf{Q}_3$, we use the parametric line equation

$$\mathbf{Q}_3(t) = \mathbf{Q}_1 + t(\mathbf{Q}_2 - \mathbf{Q}_1), \qquad (7.45)$$

where the range $0 \leq t \leq 1$ represents the axis of the cylinder. Substituting the right side of this equation for $\mathbf{Q}_3$ in Equation (7.44) allows us to solve for the value of t:

$$t = \frac{r_{\text{eff}} + \mathbf{L} \cdot \mathbf{Q}_1}{\mathbf{L} \cdot (\mathbf{Q}_1 - \mathbf{Q}_2)}. \qquad (7.46)$$

(Note that the difference $\mathbf{Q}_1 - \mathbf{Q}_2$ has a w-coordinate of zero.) Plugging this back into Equation (7.45) gives us our new endpoint $\mathbf{Q}_3$. After replacing the exterior endpoint with it, we continue to the next plane.

If we visit all six planes of the view frustum and never encounter the case that both endpoints produce a dot product less than or equal to $-r_{\text{eff}}$, then the cylinder is probably at least partially visible. Of course, this means that we do not have to replace any endpoints for the last plane that we visit. As soon as we know that at least one endpoint $\mathbf{Q}_i$ satisfies $\mathbf{L} \cdot \mathbf{Q}_i > -r_{\text{eff}}$ for the final plane, we know that part of the cylinder intersects the view frustum.

7.2.4 BOUNDING BOX TEST

When determining whether a box intersects the view frustum, we have a choice between reducing the problem to that of testing a point or to that of testing a line segment. If the bounding box extents in the primary axis direction $\mathbf{R}$ are significantly greater than those in the $\mathbf{S}$ and $\mathbf{T}$ directions, then we may choose to test a line segment. For bounding boxes whose dimensions are roughly equal, we favor the point test.

We assume in this section that the magnitudes of the vectors $\mathbf{R}$, $\mathbf{S}$, and $\mathbf{T}$ representing the principal axes of the object bounded by the box are equal to the dimensions of the box itself. To reduce the problem of intersecting a box with the view frustum to that of testing whether its center lies inside the expanded frustum planes, we need a way to determine the box's effective radius. As shown in Figure 7.8, we can calculate the effective radius r_{eff} of a box with respect to a plane having unit normal direction $\mathbf{N}$ using the formula

$$r_{\text{eff}} = \tfrac{1}{2}\left(\left|\mathbf{R} \cdot \mathbf{N}\right| + \left|\mathbf{S} \cdot \mathbf{N}\right| + \left|\mathbf{T} \cdot \mathbf{N}\right|\right). \tag{7.47}$$

Once the effective radius is known, we proceed in exactly the same manner as we would to test an ellipsoid. For each frustum plane $\mathbf{L}$, we calculate the 4D dot product between the plane and the center $\mathbf{Q}$ of the bounding box. If for any plane $\mathbf{L} \cdot \mathbf{Q} \le -r_{\text{eff}}$, then the box is not visible.

In the case that the length of $\mathbf{R}$ is much greater than the lengths of $\mathbf{S}$ and $\mathbf{T}$, a box may not be rejected in many situations when it lies far outside the view frustum. An instance of this case is demonstrated in Figure 7.9. To circumvent this problem, we can reduce the box intersection test to a line segment intersection, as is done for cylinders.

In terms of the bounding box center $\mathbf{Q}$ and its primary axis $\mathbf{R}$, we can express the endpoints $\mathbf{Q}_1$ and $\mathbf{Q}_2$ of the line segment representing the box as

$$\mathbf{Q}_1 = \mathbf{Q} + \tfrac{1}{2}\mathbf{R}$$

$$\mathbf{Q}_2 = \mathbf{Q} - \tfrac{1}{2}\mathbf{R}. \tag{7.48}$$

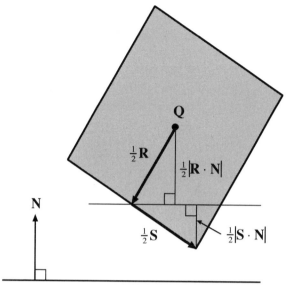

FIGURE 7.8 *Calculating the effective radius of a box.*

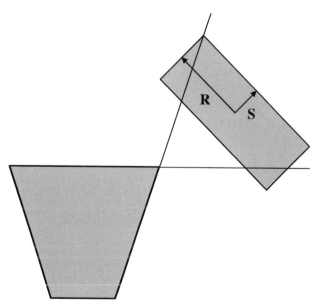

FIGURE 7.9 *This example demonstrates that using the point test for a box having one dimension much larger than the other two can result in the failure to reject a box that lies a significant distance outside the view frustum.*

The effective radius r_{eff} with respect to a plane having unit normal direction $\mathbf{N}$ is given by

$$r_{\text{eff}} = \tfrac{1}{2}\left(|\mathbf{S} \cdot \mathbf{N}| + |\mathbf{T} \cdot \mathbf{N}|\right), \tag{7.49}$$

where the $|\mathbf{R} \cdot \mathbf{N}|$ term appearing in Equation (7.47) is now absent since it is represented by the line segment connecting $\mathbf{Q}_1$ and $\mathbf{Q}_2$.

We now proceed in exactly the same manner as we would to test a cylinder. For each frustum plane $\mathbf{L}$, we first calculate the 4D dot products $\mathbf{L} \cdot \mathbf{Q}_1$ and $\mathbf{L} \cdot \mathbf{Q}_2$. If both dot products are less than or equal to the value $-r_{\text{eff}}$ corresponding to the plane $\mathbf{L}$, then we immediately know that the box is not visible and the test exits. If both dot products are greater than or equal to $-r_{\text{eff}}$, then we cannot draw any conclusions and simply proceed to the next plane. When one of the dot products is less than $-r_{\text{eff}}$ and the other dot product is greater than $-r_{\text{eff}}$, we calculate the point $\mathbf{Q}_3$ such that $\mathbf{L} \cdot \mathbf{Q}_3 = -r_{\text{eff}}$, using Equations (7.45) and (7.46), and replace the exterior endpoint with it. If we are able to visit all six frustum planes without encountering the case that both endpoints produce a dot product less than or equal to $-r_{\text{eff}}$, then the box is probably at least partially visible.

7.3 SPATIAL PARTITIONING

It is possible to increase the efficiency for which the visibility of a large number of objects is determined by organizing them into a structure whose properties allow large regions of space to be culled from the visible set of geometry using very simple tests. This practice is called *spatial partitioning* and comes in two popular varieties, which we discuss in this section: octrees and binary space partitioning trees. Both methods are usually applied only to static world geometry since computation of the data structures involved is generally too expensive to perform at runtime.

7.3.1 OCTREES

Suppose that all the geometry belonging to an entire world or to a particular region of a world is contained within a rectangular box B. An *octree* is a structure that partitions this box into eight smaller equal-sized rectangular boxes called *octants*. These smaller boxes are further subdivided into eight even smaller octants, and the process continues to some maximum number of iterations called the *depth* of the octree. Each octant is linked to the box from which it was partitioned, and each object in the world is linked to the smallest octant that completely contains it (which may be the original box B).

Figure 7.10(a) illustrates the two-dimensional analog of an octree, called a *quadtree*, constructed for an area containing a single object. Figure 7.10(b) shows how the corresponding data structure is organized. Each node in a quadtree structure has at most four subnodes—octrees can have up to eight. As this example demonstrates, if no world geometry intersects a quadrant (or an octant in an octree), then that quadrant is not subdivided. Furthermore, any quadrant that does not completely contain any objects is deleted from the tree. We always assume that any missing quadrants are empty.

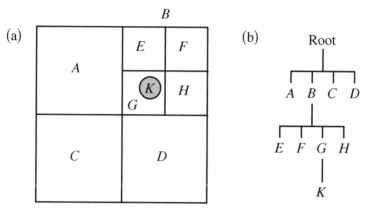

FIGURE *(a) A quadtree constructed for an area containing a single object. (b) The data*
7.10 *structure representation of the quadtree.*

Organizing geometry into a tree structure has the benefit that whenever we can determine that a node of the tree is not visible, then we immediately know that every subnode of that node is also not visible and can simultaneously be culled. (Chapter 8 discusses how a similar property of tree structures benefits collision detection.) Visibility determination for the octree begins by testing the box surrounding the root node for intersection with the view frustum. If the camera is known to always lie within the boundary of the octree, then it can be assumed that the root node is always visible. When any node's bounding box is determined to be visible, we consider each object linked to that node by testing its bounding volume for visibility. We then perform the same test for any existing subnodes of the visible node. When a node's bounding box fails the visibility test, we ignore all objects linked to that node and any subnodes belonging to that node.

We can use the fact that the bounding boxes at each level of an octree all have the same orientation to our advantage. For any given camera position and orientation, we transform the axes of the octree into camera space and calculate the five effective radii (one for the near and far planes and four corresponding to the side planes) of the box B bounding the entire structure. If r_{eff} is the effective radius of the box B with respect to a particular view frustum plane, then the effective radius of any box residing one level deeper within the tree is simply $r_{eff}/2$. This saves us from having to use Equation (7.47) to calculate effective radii for every octant at every level—calculating it once at the beginning is sufficient.

7.3.2 BINARY SPACE PARTITIONING TREES

A *binary space partitioning (BSP) tree* is a structure that divides space into two regions at each level. Unlike the planes that partition octrees, the planes partitioning a BSP tree can be arbitrarily oriented. A BSP tree is constructed for a set of objects by choosing a partitioning plane, sometimes called a *splitting plane*, and sorting the geometry into two groups: objects lying on the positive side of the plane (also called the positive *halfspace*) and objects lying on the negative side of the plane (the negative halfspace).

Traditionally, the partitioning planes of a BSP tree have been aligned to the polygons that make up the world geometry. Figure 7.11 shows a two-dimensional example of a region containing several polygons that determine the structure of the BSP tree. One polygon is chosen to represent the splitting plane at each level and the remaining polygons are sorted into positive and negative groups. Any polygons intersecting the plane are split into two polygons that lie in the positive and negative halfspaces. The positive and negative groups are then partitioned, and the process continues for each halfspace until no polygons remain.

The large number of polygons and curved surfaces used in modern 3D engines makes the traditional BSP tree impractical. In a somewhat modified ap-

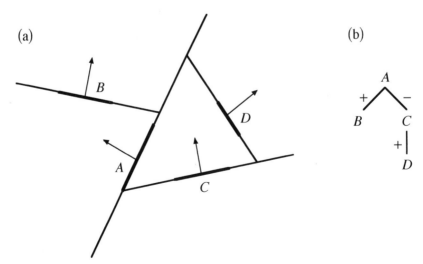

FIGURE 7.11 *(a) A traditional binary space partitioning (BSP) tree and (b) the associated data structure.*

proach, we create one splitting for each *object* instead of each polygon. As shown in Figure 7.12, the splitting plane for an object is aligned so that it is perpendicular to the object's principal axis **T** corresponding to the smallest dimension of its bounding box. This minimizes the distance that the object extends away from the splitting plane. After a splitting plane has been chosen for an object, the other objects are sorted into those that lie completely within the positive halfspace and those that lie completely within the negative halfspace. Any objects that straddle the splitting plane are added to *both* the positive and negative groups. The halfspaces are recursively partitioned until no objects remain.

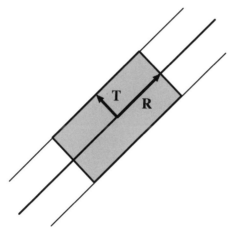

FIGURE *An object's splitting plane is aligned so that it is perpendicular to the object's*
7.12 *principal axis **T** corresponding to the smallest dimension of its bounding box.*

For each splitting plane of a BSP tree, we need to determine the visibility of each halfspace and the visibility of the object associated with the plane. This requires that we have a way to determine whether a plane **K** intersects the view frustum. The simplest approach would be to test the eight vertices of the view frustum in world space against the plane **K** by calculating the 4D dot products and comparing them to zero. If all eight dot products have the same sign (meaning that all eight points lie on the same side of the plane), then the plane does not intersect the view frustum. Fortunately, we can find a better method by transforming the plane **K** into homogeneous clip space and utilizing the cubic symmetry of the view frustum in that space (see Section 4.5.1).

A plane **K** can be transformed from world space to homogeneous clip space using the formula

$$\mathbf{K}' = [(\mathbf{PM})^{-1}]^{\mathrm{T}}\mathbf{K},$$

(7.50)

where $\mathbf{P}$ is the projection matrix and $\mathbf{M}$ is the transformation from world space to camera space. The components of each vertex of the view frustum in clip space are ± 1. The vertex producing the greatest dot product with the plane $\mathbf{K}'$ is the one having component signs that match the signs of the x-, y-, and z-components of $\mathbf{K}'$. The vertex producing the least dot product with $\mathbf{K}'$ is the one having component signs opposite those of the components of $\mathbf{K}'$. The greatest dot product $d_{\max}$ and the least dot product $d_{\min}$ are thus given by

$$d_{\max} = \left| K_x' \right| + \left| K_y' \right| + \left| K_z' \right| + K_w'$$

$$d_{\min} = -\left| K_x' \right| - \left| K_y' \right| - \left| K_z' \right| + K_w' . \tag{7.51}$$

As shown in Figure 7.13, if $d_{\max} \leq 0$, then the view frustum lies entirely on the negative side of the plane $\mathbf{K}$. This means that nothing on the *positive* side of the plane is visible. Similarly, if $d_{\min} \geq 0$, then the view frustum lies entirely on the positive side of the plane $\mathbf{K}$, and thus nothing on the *negative* side of the plane is visible. If neither of the conditions $d_{\max} \leq 0$ or $d_{\min} \geq 0$ is satisfied, then the plane $\mathbf{K}$ intersects the view frustum and we cannot cull either halfspace.

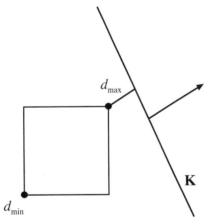

FIGURE **7.13** *Let d_{max} and d_{min} be the greatest dot product and least dot product of any frustum vertex with the plane $\mathbf{K}$. If $d_{max} \leq 0$ or $d_{min} \geq 0$, then the view frustum lies completely on one side of $\mathbf{K}$, so the other side is not visible.*

7.4 PORTAL SYSTEMS

A *portal system* is an extremely powerful technique that can be used to quickly eliminate massive regions of world geometry from the visible set. The general idea is surprisingly simple—the world is divided into many disjoint *zones* that are connected by *portals*. A portal is represented by a convex polygon through which one region can be seen from another. The advantage of a portal system is that any region of space that cannot be seen through a series of portals is never even considered for rendering. When determining what parts of a world are visible, using a portal system allows us to touch only a small fraction of the entire data set because any geometry that lies on the opposite side of an invisible portal is ignored.

Figure 7.14 illustrates how visibility determination is carried out for a portal system. We first locate the zone in which the camera resides—this zone is always considered visible. We then examine each of the portals leading out of the zone containing the camera. For each portal that intersects the view frustum, we consider the zone to which it connects visible. Each portal leading out of the connecting zone, excluding any leading back to the first zone, is then tested for visibility, but this time against a view frustum that has been reduced in size by the boundary of the portal through which we are looking. This technique is applied recursively until no new portals are visible.

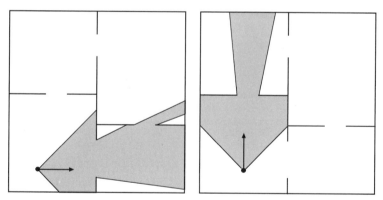

FIGURE   *Only regions of space that can be seen through a series of portals are considered*
7.14   *visible.*

The zones connected by portals may be further organized into tree structures, and the objects residing in these regions may still have bounding volumes. The visibility of large regions determined by the portal system is a large-scale culling process that should be supplemented by smaller-scale visibility determination in each zone.

7.4.1 PORTAL CLIPPING

Whenever the camera looks through a portal connecting to another zone, we know that the volume of visibility in that zone is smaller than the whole view frustum. Thus, we can reject a larger number of objects during smaller-scale visibility testing by using a smaller view frustum. The near and far planes remain the same, but the side planes of the new view frustum are replaced by a set of planes that represents the intersection of the original view frustum and the sides of any polygonal portals through which we are looking.

As a convention, the plane containing a portal must have a normal direction that points toward the camera, and the vertices of the portal must be wound counterclockwise, as shown in Figure 7.15. Consequently, portals are one-way in the sense that if a portal leads from zone X to zone Y, then the same portal does *not* lead backward from zone Y to zone X. When the camera lies on the negative side of a plane containing a portal, that portal is never considered visible. Two-way visibility between two zones requires that each zone have a portal leading to the other.

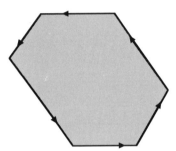

FIGURE *The vertices of a portal are wound counterclockwise about the normal of the plane*
7.15 *containing them. Here, the normal points out of the page.*

Whenever we consider a portal leading out of a zone, we are interested only in the visible area of that portal. The visible area of a portal is equal to the area that intersects the current view frustum, which may be the original view frustum or a reduced view frustum. To determine what area of a portal is visible, we *clip* its polygon against the planes bounding the current view frustum. Clipping a polygon against a plane removes the portion of the polygon lying on the negative side of the plane, resulting in a new polygon whose interior lies completely on the positive side of the plane. Clipping a polygon against every plane of the current view frustum effectively chops off any part lying outside the volume of space that is visible to the camera.

Suppose we need to clip a portal whose vertices lie at the points $\mathbf{V}_1, \mathbf{V}_2,..., \mathbf{V}_n$ and connect to form a convex polygon. When we clip this polygon against a plane $\mathbf{L}$, we produce a new convex polygon having at most $n + 1$ vertices. We begin the clipping process by classifying all the vertices into three categories: those lying on the positive side of $\mathbf{L}$, those lying on the negative side of $\mathbf{L}$, and those considered to be lying in the plane **L** itself. A vertex $\mathbf{V}_i$ is classified as lying in the plane if its dot product with **L** satisfies

$$-\varepsilon < \mathbf{L} \cdot \mathbf{V}_i \leq 0 \tag{7.52}$$

for some small constant ε (typically, $\varepsilon \approx 0.001$). This prevents problems associated with round-off error that would otherwise wreak havoc on our visibility tests by destroying the convexity of the view frustum. If no vertices lie on the positive side of the plane **L**, then the portal is not visible and we do not render anything in the zone to which it connects. If no vertices lie on the *negative* side of the plane **L**, then no clipping is necessary. Otherwise, we visit every pair of neighboring vertices looking for edges having one positive vertex and one negative vertex. As shown in Figure 7.16, new vertices are added to the polygon where edges intersect the clipping plane, and vertices lying on the negative side of the plane are removed. Vertices lying on the positive side of the clipping plane or lying in the clipping plane itself are not affected.

FIGURE *When a portal is clipped against a plane, new vertices are added where edges*
7.16 *intersect the plane, and vertices lying on the negative side of the plane are removed. Vertices lying on the positive side of the clipping plane or lying in the clipping plane itself are not affected.*

Suppose that the vertex $\mathbf{V}_i$ lies on the positive side of the clipping plane **L** and that the vertex $\mathbf{V}_{i+1}$ lies on the negative side of **L**, or equivalently,

$$\mathbf{L} \cdot \mathbf{V}_i > 0$$

$$\mathbf{L} \cdot \mathbf{V}_{i+1} \leq -\varepsilon. \tag{7.53}$$

A point $\mathbf{W}$ lying on the line segment connecting $\mathbf{V}_i$ and $\mathbf{V}_{i+1}$ can be expressed as

$$\mathbf{W}(t) = \mathbf{V}_i + t(\mathbf{V}_{i+1} - \mathbf{V}_i), \tag{7.54}$$

where the parameter t satisfies $0 \le t \le 1$. Solving for the value of t that yields $\mathbf{L} \cdot \mathbf{W}(t) = 0$, we have

$$t = \frac{\mathbf{L} \cdot \mathbf{V}_i}{\mathbf{L} \cdot (\mathbf{V}_i - \mathbf{V}_{i+1})}. \tag{7.55}$$

(Note that the difference $\mathbf{V}_i - \mathbf{V}_{i+1}$ has a w-coordinate of zero.) Substituting this value back into Equation (7.54) gives us our new vertex $\mathbf{W}$.

7.4.2 REDUCED VIEW FRUSTUMS

Given a clipped portal, we wish to calculate the planes surrounding the volume of space visible through that portal. This enables us to perform visibility determination against a view frustum that is smaller than the original view frustum, resulting in a greater number of objects being culled. Fortunately, the camera-space plane corresponding to an edge of a portal is simple to calculate. The plane $\mathbf{L}_i$ passing through the origin and the two portal vertices $\mathbf{V}_i$ and $\mathbf{V}_{i+1}$ is given by

$$\mathbf{L}_i = \left\langle \frac{\mathbf{V}_{i+1} \times \mathbf{V}_i}{\|\mathbf{V}_{i+1} \times \mathbf{V}_i\|}, 0 \right\rangle. \tag{7.56}$$

For a portal having n vertices, we use Equation (7.56) to calculate the n side planes of our reduced view frustum. (For the plane $\mathbf{L}_n$, we wrap around by setting $\mathbf{V}_{n+1} = \mathbf{V}_0$.) If the distance between any two portal vertices $\mathbf{V}_i$ and $\mathbf{V}_{i+1}$ is very small, then round-off errors can cause convexity problems, so we discard any plane $\mathbf{L}_i$ for which

$$\|\mathbf{V}_{i+1} - \mathbf{V}_i\|^2 < \varepsilon, \tag{7.57}$$

where ε is a small constant that can be adjusted to produce acceptable results.

The side planes of a reduced view frustum can meet at highly acute angles. As shown in Figure 7.17, this can influence the effectiveness of bounding volume visibility tests because objects lying far from the view frustum still may not lie on the negative side of any single frustum plane. We can eliminate this problem by detecting cases in which adjacent frustum planes meet at a small angle and adding an extra plane to the view frustum whenever such cases occur.

Figure 7.18 shows a new plane having normal direction $\mathbf{N}_3$ added to the view frustum between two adjacent planes having normal vectors $\mathbf{N}_1$ and $\mathbf{N}_2$. The vector $\mathbf{N}_3$ is constructed by first calculating the average (unnormalized) direction between $\mathbf{N}_1$ and $\mathbf{N}_2$, which is simply given by the sum $\mathbf{N}_1 + \mathbf{N}_2$. We then subtract

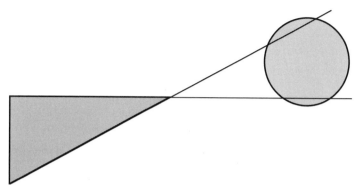

FIGURE 7.17 *Side planes of the reduced view frustum that meet at an acute angle can influence the effectiveness of bounding volume visibility tests. The bounding sphere shown here does not fail the visibility test even though it lies far outside the view frustum.*

the projection of this average onto the direction $\mathbf{N}_1 \times \mathbf{N}_2$ to ensure that the new plane contains the line at which the two original planes intersect. This gives us the following expression for $\mathbf{N}_3$.

$$\mathbf{A} = \mathbf{N}_1 + \mathbf{N}_2$$

$$\mathbf{B} = \mathbf{N}_1 \times \mathbf{N}_2$$

$$\mathbf{N}_3 = \frac{\mathbf{A} - (\mathbf{A} \cdot \mathbf{B})\mathbf{B}}{\|\mathbf{A} - (\mathbf{A} \cdot \mathbf{B})\mathbf{B}\|} \tag{7.58}$$

Since it passes through the origin in camera space, the new plane has a w-coordinate of zero.

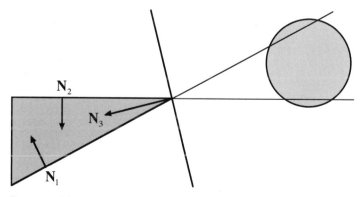

FIGURE 7.18 *Adding an extra plane where two original planes meet at an acute angle solves the visibility testing problem.*

The situation demonstrated in Figure 7.17 can be avoided by constructing an extra plane whenever two adjacent frustum planes having normals $\mathbf{N}_1$ and $\mathbf{N}_2$ satisfy the condition $\mathbf{N}_1 \cdot \mathbf{N}_2 < \alpha$, where α represents an acuteness threshold. The extra planes do not actually contribute to the shape of the view frustum since they are coincident with the lines at which previously existing planes intersect. They should be used only for visibility testing within a single zone and should not participate in the clipping of any portals leading to other zones.

CHAPTER 7 SUMMARY

Principal Components

The principal axes $\mathbf{R}$, $\mathbf{S}$, and $\mathbf{T}$ of a set of N vertices $\mathbf{P}_1$, $\mathbf{P}_2$,..., $\mathbf{P}_N$ are given by the eigenvectors of the covariance matrix $\mathbf{C}$ defined by

$$\mathbf{C} = \frac{1}{N} \sum_{i=1}^{N} (\mathbf{P}_i - \mathbf{m})(\mathbf{P}_i - \mathbf{m})^\mathsf{T},$$

where the mean position $\mathbf{m}$ is given by

$$\mathbf{m} = \frac{1}{N} \sum_{i=1}^{N} \mathbf{P}_i.$$

If λ_1, λ_2, and λ_3 are the eigenvalues corresponding to the vectors $\mathbf{R}$, $\mathbf{S}$, and $\mathbf{T}$, respectively, then $|\lambda_1| \geq |\lambda_2| \geq |\lambda_3|$.

Bounding Boxes

The two planes perpendicular to the principal axis $\mathbf{A}$ that bound the set of vertices $\mathbf{P}_1$, $\mathbf{P}_2$,..., $\mathbf{P}_N$ are given by

$$\left\langle \mathbf{A}, - \min_{1 \leq i \leq N} \{\mathbf{P}_i \cdot \mathbf{A}\} \right\rangle \quad \left\langle -\mathbf{A}, \max_{1 \leq i \leq N} \{\mathbf{P}_i \cdot \mathbf{A}\} \right\rangle.$$

The center $\mathbf{Q}$ of a bounding box is given by

$$\mathbf{Q} = k_1 \mathbf{A}_1 + k_2 \mathbf{A}_2 + k_3 \mathbf{A}_3$$

where

$$k_j = \frac{\min_{1 \leq i \leq N} \{\mathbf{P}_i \cdot \mathbf{A}_j\} + \max_{1 \leq i \leq N} \{\mathbf{P}_i \cdot \mathbf{A}_j\}}{2},$$

and $\mathbf{A}_1$, $\mathbf{A}_2$, and $\mathbf{A}_3$ are the unit-length principal axes.

The effective radius r_{eff} with respect to a plane having normal direction $\mathbf{N}$ of a bounding box, whose dimensions and orientation are described by the vectors $\mathbf{R}$, $\mathbf{S}$, and $\mathbf{T}$, is given by

$$r_{\text{eff}} = \tfrac{1}{2} \left| \mathbf{R} \cdot \mathbf{N} + \mathbf{S} \cdot \mathbf{N} + \mathbf{T} \cdot \mathbf{N} \right|.$$

Bounding Spheres

A bounding sphere for the set of vertices $\mathbf{P}_1, \mathbf{P}_2,..., \mathbf{P}_N$ is constructed by locating the points $\mathbf{P}_k$ and $\mathbf{P}_l$ that produce the least and greatest dot products with the primary axis $\mathbf{R}$ and setting the initial center $\mathbf{Q}$ and radius r to

$$\mathbf{Q} = \frac{\mathbf{P}_k + \mathbf{P}_l}{2}$$

$$r = \left\| \mathbf{P}_k - \mathbf{Q} \right\|.$$

For any point $\mathbf{P}_i$ satisfying $\| \mathbf{P}_i - \mathbf{Q} \|^2 > r^2$, we replace the center and radius with the values

$$\mathbf{Q}' = \frac{\mathbf{G} + \mathbf{P}_i}{2}$$

$$r' = \left\| \mathbf{P}_i - \mathbf{Q}' \right\|,$$

where $\mathbf{G}$ is defined as

$$\mathbf{G} = \mathbf{Q} - r \frac{\mathbf{P}_i - \mathbf{Q}}{\left\| \mathbf{P}_i - \mathbf{Q} \right\|}.$$

A bounding sphere having center $\mathbf{Q}$ and radius r is not visible if for any view frustum plane $\mathbf{L}$ we have $\mathbf{L} \cdot \mathbf{Q} \leq -r$.

Bounding Ellipsoids

A bounding ellipsoid for the set of vertices $\mathbf{P}_1, \mathbf{P}_2,..., \mathbf{P}_N$ is constructed by transforming into a space in which the box bounding the set is a cube, constructing a bounding sphere in that space, and then performing the reverse transformation to scale the sphere to the original dimensions of the bounding box.

The effective radius r_{eff} with respect to a plane having normal direction $\mathbf{N}$ of a bounding ellipsoid, whose semi-axis lengths and orientations are described by the vectors $\mathbf{R}$, $\mathbf{S}$, and $\mathbf{T}$, is given by

$$r_{\text{eff}} = \sqrt{\left(\mathbf{R} \cdot \mathbf{N} \right)^2 + \left(\mathbf{S} \cdot \mathbf{N} \right)^2 + \left(\mathbf{T} \cdot \mathbf{N} \right)^2}.$$

A bounding ellipsoid having center $\mathbf{Q}$ is not visible if for any view frustum plane $\mathbf{L}$ we have $\mathbf{L} \cdot \mathbf{Q} \leq -r_{\text{eff}}$.

Bounding Cylinders

A bounding cylinder for the set of vertices $\mathbf{P}_1, \mathbf{P}_2,..., \mathbf{P}_N$ is constructed by first calculating the points $\{\mathbf{H}_i\}$ using the formula

$$\mathbf{H}_i = \mathbf{P}_i - (\mathbf{P}_i \cdot \mathbf{R})\mathbf{R},$$

where $\mathbf{R}$ is the unit vector parallel to the primary axis. After finding a bounding circle for the points $\{\mathbf{H}_i\}$ having center $\mathbf{Q}$ and radius r, the endpoints $\mathbf{Q}_1$ and $\mathbf{Q}_2$ of the bounding cylinder are given by

$$\mathbf{Q}_1 = \mathbf{Q} + \min_{1 \leq i \leq N}\{\mathbf{P}_i \cdot \mathbf{R}\}\mathbf{R}$$

$$\mathbf{Q}_2 = \mathbf{Q} + \max_{1 \leq i \leq N}\{\mathbf{P}_i \cdot \mathbf{R}\}\mathbf{R}.$$

The effective radius r_{eff} with respect to a plane having normal direction $\mathbf{N}$ of a bounding cylinder is given by

$$r_{\text{eff}} = r\sqrt{1 - (\mathbf{A} \cdot \mathbf{N})^2},$$

where $\mathbf{A}$ is the unit vector parallel to the axis of the cylinder given by

$$\mathbf{A} = \frac{\mathbf{Q}_2 - \mathbf{Q}_1}{\|\mathbf{Q}_2 - \mathbf{Q}_1\|}.$$

A bounding cylinder is not visible if the line segment connecting the endpoints $\mathbf{Q}_1$ and $\mathbf{Q}_2$ is completely clipped away by the view frustum planes.

BINARY SPACE PARTITIONING (BSP) TREES

We can determine whether a world-space plane $\mathbf{K}$ intersects the view frustum by transforming the plane into homogeneous clip space using the formula

$$\mathbf{K}' = [(\mathbf{PM})^{-1}]^{\mathsf{T}}\mathbf{K},$$

where $\mathbf{P}$ is the projection matrix and $\mathbf{M}$ is the transformation from world space to camera space. The greatest dot product $d_{\max}$ and least dot product $d_{\min}$ of any frustum vertex with the plane $\mathbf{K}'$ are given by

$$d_{\max} = |K'_x| + |K'_y| + |K'_z| + K'_w$$

$$d_{\min} = -|K'_x| - |K'_y| - |K'_z| + K'_w.$$

If $d_{\max} \leq 0$ or $d_{\min} \geq 0$, then the view frustum lies completely on one side of $\mathbf{K}$, so the other side is not visible.

Portal Systems

When clipping a portal having vertices $\mathbf{V}_1, \mathbf{V}_2,..., \mathbf{V}_n$ against a plane $\mathbf{L}$, we add a new vertex between any two adjacent vertices $\mathbf{V}_i$ and $\mathbf{V}_{i+1}$ lying on opposite sides of $\mathbf{L}$. The new vertex $\mathbf{W}$ is given by

$$\mathbf{W} = \mathbf{V}_i + t(\mathbf{V}_{i+1} - \mathbf{V}_i),$$

where the parameter t is given by

$$t = \frac{\mathbf{L} \cdot \mathbf{V}_i}{\mathbf{L} \cdot \left(\mathbf{V}_i - \mathbf{V}_{i+1}\right)}.$$

The plane $\mathbf{L}_i$ passing through the origin and the two portal vertices $\mathbf{V}_i$ and $\mathbf{V}_{i+1}$ is given by

$$\mathbf{L}_i = \left\langle \frac{\mathbf{V}_{i+1} \times \mathbf{V}_i}{\left\|\mathbf{V}_{i+1} \times \mathbf{V}_i\right\|}, 0 \right\rangle.$$

An extra plane may be added to the view frustum to improve bounding volume visibility determination when planes having normal directions $\mathbf{N}_1$ and $\mathbf{N}_2$ meet at an acute angle. The new plane passes through the origin and has the normal direction $\mathbf{N}_3$ given by

$$\mathbf{A} = \mathbf{N}_1 + \mathbf{N}_2$$

$$\mathbf{B} = \mathbf{N}_1 \times \mathbf{N}_2$$

$$\mathbf{N}_3 = \frac{\mathbf{A} - \left(\mathbf{A} \cdot \mathbf{B}\right)\mathbf{B}}{\left\|\mathbf{A} - \left(\mathbf{A} \cdot \mathbf{B}\right)\mathbf{B}\right\|}.$$

EXERCISES FOR CHAPTER 7

1. Given two spheres S_1 and S_2 centered at the points $\mathbf{Q}_1$ and $\mathbf{Q}_2$ and having radii r_1 and r_2, respectively, determine the center $\mathbf{Q}$ and radius r of the smallest single sphere that encloses both S_1 and S_2. Account for the cases that the two spheres are disjoint, that the two spheres intersect, and that one of the spheres encloses the other.

2. Determine formulas for the center $\mathbf{Q}$ and radius r of the optimal bounding sphere for a cone whose radius (at the base) is s, whose height is h, and whose base is centered on the origin of the x-y plane, as shown in Figure 7.19. Consider the two cases that $s < h$ and $s \geq h$.

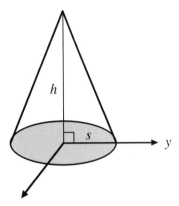

FIGURE *The cone used in Exercise 2.*
7.19

3. Determine the effective radius r_{eff} of a box whose edges are described by the vectors $\mathbf{R} = \langle 2, 0, 1 \rangle$, $\mathbf{S} = \langle 1, 0, -2 \rangle$, and $\mathbf{T} = \langle 0, 1, 0 \rangle$ with respect to a plane having unit normal direction $\mathbf{N} = \left\langle \frac{\sqrt{3}}{3}, -\frac{\sqrt{3}}{3}, \frac{\sqrt{3}}{3} \right\rangle$.

4. Write programs that construct a bounding box, a bounding sphere, a bounding ellipsoid, and a bounding cylinder given an array of n vertex positions.

5. Implement a portal system that can clip the view frustum to an arbitrary convex polygon and perform visibility tests against the reduced frustum.

8 Collision Detection

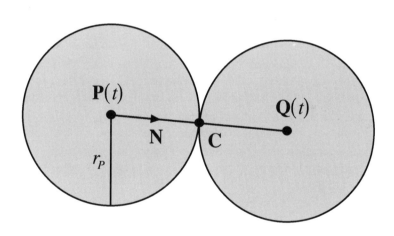

Every 3D game is filled with the action of moving objects. Except when an object is emitting a force field that affects its surroundings, interaction between two objects generally occurs when they attempt to occupy the same space at the same time. The process by which game engines determine when such events occur is called *collision detection*. Collision detection calculations typically fall into two categories. The first is detecting a collision between a moving object and static geometry belonging to the environment. The second category is detecting a collision between two objects that are both potentially in motion. This chapter discusses several techniques that can be used to determine when and where such collisions occur.

8.1 ENVIRONMENTAL COLLISIONS

With the exception of those that take place in deep space, most games need to determine when a collision occurs between a moving object and the environment. The complex geometrical shapes that moving objects may possess are usually approximated by simple bounding volumes in order to reduce the cost of collision detection calculations.

Suppose that the position of a moving object is known at the time that a frame is rendered, and that we are able to calculate the position to which the object would move if it is unobstructed before the next frame is rendered. Since the time between frames is usually small, it is commonly assumed that objects travel along straight lines during the time between frames. Thus, the general problem is determining whether the extrusion of a bounding volume along a line segment intersects some part of the environment.

Very small moving objects are often treated as points, which reduces the collision detection problem to a ray intersection. The collision detection calculations for larger moving objects can also be reduced to ray intersections in many cases by using techniques similar to those used for visibility determination. For instance, a collision between a moving sphere and a plane can be found by intersecting the path followed by the sphere's center with a plane that has been offset by the sphere's radius.

8.1.1 COLLISION OF A SPHERE AND A PLANE

The detection of a collision between a moving sphere of radius r and *any* surface that can easily be extended outward in the normal direction at each point by the distance r can be transformed into a ray intersection. The simplest example is that of a collision between a sphere and a plane. As shown in Figure 8.1, when a sphere is in contact with a plane $\mathbf{L}$ (on the positive side), the distance from the center of the sphere $\mathbf{P}$ to the plane is r, so $\mathbf{L} \cdot \mathbf{P} = r$. Writing the plane $\mathbf{L}$ as the 4D vector

$$\mathbf{L} = \langle \mathbf{N}, D \rangle, \tag{8.1}$$

the relationship $\mathbf{L} \cdot \mathbf{P} = r$ can be written as

$$\mathbf{N} \cdot \mathbf{P} + D = r. \tag{8.2}$$

If we move r to the left side of the equation, then this is equivalent to

$$\mathbf{N} \cdot \mathbf{P} + D - r = 0, \tag{8.3}$$

which is the same as stating that the point $\mathbf{P}$ lies on the plane $\mathbf{L}'$ given by

$$\mathbf{L}' = \langle \mathbf{N}, D - r \rangle. \tag{8.4}$$

The plane $\mathbf{L}'$ is parallel to $\mathbf{L}$, but it has been shifted by the distance r in the direction of its normal.

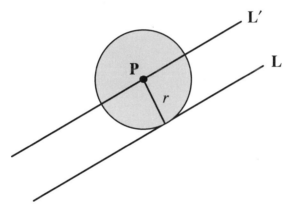

FIGURE *A sphere of radius r is in contact with a plane **L** when its center lies on the plane **L'***
8.1 *that has been shifted by a distance r.*

Suppose that the center of a sphere of radius r moves from the point $\mathbf{P}_1$ at time $t = 0$ to the point $\mathbf{P}_2$ at time $t = 1$ and that we wish to determine whether it collides with a plane $\mathbf{L}$. We assume that the sphere is not initially intersecting the plane and that the starting point $\mathbf{P}_1$ lies on the positive side of a plane since the negative side represents the interior of some structure. Thus, $\mathbf{L} \cdot \mathbf{P} \geq r$. If it is also the case that $\mathbf{L} \cdot \mathbf{P}_2 \geq r$, then the sphere remains on the positive side of the plane during the time interval $0 \leq t < 1$, in which case we know that no collision occurs.

The position $\mathbf{P}(t)$ of the sphere's center at time t is then given by

$$\mathbf{P}(t) = \mathbf{P}_1 + t\mathbf{V}, \tag{8.5}$$

where $\mathbf{V}$ is the velocity of the sphere:

$$\mathbf{V} = \mathbf{P}_2 - \mathbf{P}_1. \tag{8.6}$$

A collision occurs between the sphere and the plane $\mathbf{L} = \langle \mathbf{N}, D \rangle$ if the equation

$$\mathbf{L}' \cdot \mathbf{P}(t) = 0, \tag{8.7}$$

where $\mathbf{L}'$ is defined by Equation (8.4), has a solution t such that $0 \le t < 1$. Substituting the value given by Equation (8.5) for $\mathbf{P}(t)$, we have

$$\mathbf{L}' \cdot \mathbf{P}_1 + t\left(\mathbf{L}' \cdot \mathbf{V}\right) = 0. \tag{8.8}$$

Solving for t yields

$$t = -\frac{\mathbf{L}' \cdot \mathbf{P}_1}{\mathbf{L}' \cdot \mathbf{V}}. \tag{8.9}$$

Remember that the vector $\mathbf{V}$ represents a direction and therefore has a w-coordinate of zero, so the denominator is equal to $\mathbf{N} \cdot \mathbf{V}$. If $\mathbf{N} \cdot \mathbf{V} = 0$, then the sphere is moving parallel to the plane, so no intersection occurs. Otherwise, the sphere collides with the plane at the time t given by Equation (8.9). The point $\mathbf{C}$ at which the sphere makes contact with the plane is given by

$$\mathbf{C} = \mathbf{P}(t) - r\mathbf{N} \tag{8.10}$$

since this point lies at a distance r from the sphere's center in the direction opposite that of the plane's normal $\mathbf{N}$.

8.1.2 COLLISION OF A BOX AND A PLANE

Determining whether a moving box collides with a plane can be accomplished using a method similar to that used to determine whether a sphere collides with a plane. The difference is that we must offset the plane by the *effective* radius of the box, introduced in Section 7.2.4. Furthermore, the box can make contact with the plane at more than one point. It is possible that an edge of the box collides with the plane or that the box meets the plane directly parallel to one of its faces.

Suppose that a box has edges whose length and orientation are described by the vectors $\mathbf{R}$, $\mathbf{S}$, and $\mathbf{T}$. The effective radius r_{eff} of the box with respect to a plane having normal direction $\mathbf{N}$ is given by

$$r_{\text{eff}} = \tfrac{1}{2}\left(\left|\mathbf{R} \cdot \mathbf{N}\right| + \left|\mathbf{S} \cdot \mathbf{N}\right| + \left|\mathbf{T} \cdot \mathbf{N}\right|\right). \tag{8.11}$$

Let $\mathbf{Q}_1$ be the position of the box's center at time $t = 0$ and let $\mathbf{Q}_2$ be its position at time $t = 1$, as shown in Figure 8.2. Then the position $\mathbf{Q}(t)$ of the box is given by

$$\mathbf{Q}(t) = \mathbf{Q}_1 + t\mathbf{V}, \tag{8.12}$$

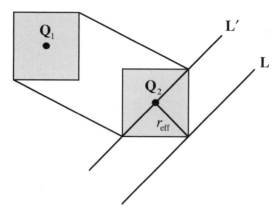

FIGURE *Whether a moving box collides with a plane can be determined by shifting the plane*
8.2 *by the box's effective radius.*

where **V** is the velocity of the box:

$$\mathbf{V} = \mathbf{Q}_2 - \mathbf{Q}_1. \tag{8.13}$$

To find an intersection with the plane $\mathbf{L} = \langle \mathbf{N}, D \rangle$, we calculate

$$t = -\frac{\mathbf{L}' \cdot \mathbf{Q}_1}{\mathbf{L}' \cdot \mathbf{V}}, \tag{8.14}$$

where $\mathbf{L}'$ is the plane parallel to $\mathbf{L}$ that has been offset by a distance r_{eff}:

$$\mathbf{L}' = \langle \mathbf{L}, D - r_{\text{eff}} \rangle. \tag{8.15}$$

Again, we assume that the box is not initially intersecting the plane and that its center lies on the positive side of $\mathbf{L}'$ at time $t = 0$ (i.e., $\mathbf{L}' \cdot \mathbf{Q}_1 \geq 0$). Therefore, if the condition $\mathbf{L}' \cdot \mathbf{Q}_2 \geq 0$ is also satisfied, then the box remains on the positive side of the plane $\mathbf{L}$ and no collision occurs.

Once we have determined that a collision between the box and the plane has occurred (because the value of t given by Equation (8.14) satisfies $0 \leq t < 1$), we must determine the point or set of points at which contact has been made. If all three of the quantities $|\mathbf{R} \cdot \mathbf{N}|$, $|\mathbf{S} \cdot \mathbf{N}|$, and $|\mathbf{T} \cdot \mathbf{N}|$ are nonzero, then no edge of the box is parallel to the plane $\mathbf{L}$. In this case, the collision must occur at one of the box's vertices. We can find a general formula for the position of the vertex that makes contact with the plane by examining expressions for all eight of the box's vertices. The position $\mathbf{Z}$ of each vertex of the box is given by

$$\mathbf{Z} = \mathbf{Q}(t) \pm \tfrac{1}{2}\mathbf{R} \pm \tfrac{1}{2}\mathbf{S} \pm \tfrac{1}{2}\mathbf{T}. \tag{8.16}$$

To find the vertex closest to the plane, we choose signs such that the dot product $\mathbf{L} \cdot \mathbf{Z}$ is minimized. This occurs when the quantities $\pm \mathbf{R} \cdot \mathbf{N}$, $\pm \mathbf{S} \cdot \mathbf{N}$, and

$\pm\mathbf{T} \cdot \mathbf{N}$ are all negative, so if any one is positive, we choose the corresponding negative sign in Equation (8.16). The point of contact $\mathbf{C}$ is then given by

$$\mathbf{C} = \mathbf{Q}(t) - \tfrac{1}{2}\Big[\operatorname{sgn}(\mathbf{R} \cdot \mathbf{N})\mathbf{R} + \operatorname{sgn}(\mathbf{S} \cdot \mathbf{N})\mathbf{S} + \operatorname{sgn}(\mathbf{T} \cdot \mathbf{N})\mathbf{T}\Big], \qquad (8.17)$$

where the function $\operatorname{sgn}(x)$ returns the sign of x:

$$\operatorname{sgn}(x) = \begin{cases} 1, & \text{if } x \geq 0; \\ -1, & \text{if } x < 0. \end{cases} \qquad (8.18)$$

In the case that exactly one of the quantities $|\mathbf{R} \cdot \mathbf{N}|$, $|\mathbf{S} \cdot \mathbf{N}|$, and $|\mathbf{T} \cdot \mathbf{N}|$ is zero, the corresponding axis of the box is parallel to the plane and any collision must occur at an edge. The endpoints $\mathbf{C}_1$ and $\mathbf{C}_2$ of the edge are given by modifying Equation (8.17) so that both signs are chosen for the term containing the zero dot product. For instance, if $|\mathbf{T} \cdot \mathbf{N}|$, then we have

$$\mathbf{C}_{1,2} = \mathbf{Q}(t) - \tfrac{1}{2}\Big[\operatorname{sgn}(\mathbf{R} \cdot \mathbf{N})\mathbf{R} + \operatorname{sgn}(\mathbf{S} \cdot \mathbf{N})\mathbf{S} \pm \mathbf{T}\Big]. \qquad (8.19)$$

This modification is taken one step further when two of the quantities $|\mathbf{R} \cdot \mathbf{N}|$, $|\mathbf{S} \cdot \mathbf{N}|$, and $|\mathbf{T} \cdot \mathbf{N}|$ are zero. In this case, the collision occurs at a face of the box whose vertices are given by modifying Equation (8.17) so that both signs are chosen for both of the terms containing zero dot products. For instance, if $|\mathbf{S} \cdot \mathbf{N}| = 0$ and $|\mathbf{T} \cdot \mathbf{N}| = 0$, then the vertices $\mathbf{C}_1$, $\mathbf{C}_2$, $\mathbf{C}_3$, and $\mathbf{C}_4$ of the face in contact with the plane are given by

$$\mathbf{C}_{1,2,3,4} = \mathbf{Q}(t) - \tfrac{1}{2}\Big[\operatorname{sgn}(\mathbf{R} \cdot \mathbf{N})\mathbf{R} \pm \mathbf{S} \pm \mathbf{T}\Big]. \qquad (8.20)$$

8.1.3 SPATIAL PARTITIONING

Being able to determine whether an object collides with a plane is essential to fast collision detection in a spatially partitioned environment. Since regions of octrees and BSP trees are separated by planes, we can usually tell that a moving object does not collide with large parts of the world without having to perform collision detection tests with the actual geometry in those regions.

Suppose that an object moves from the point $\mathbf{P}_1$ to the point $\mathbf{P}_2$ during a single frame. Let $\mathbf{L} = \langle \mathbf{N}, D \rangle$ represent a plane that partitions the world geometry in some way, and suppose that the moving object has an effective radius of r_{eff} with respect to that plane. We say that the object lies completely on the positive side of the plane $\mathbf{L}$ if its position $\mathbf{P}$ satisfies

$$\mathbf{L} \cdot \mathbf{P} \geq r_{\text{eff}}, \qquad (8.21)$$

and we say that the object lies completely on the negative side of the plane $\mathbf{L}$ if its position $\mathbf{P}$ satisfies

$$\mathbf{L} \cdot \mathbf{P} \leq -r_{\text{eff}}. \tag{8.22}$$

If both of the points $\mathbf{P}_1$ and $\mathbf{P}_2$ represent positions of the object for which it lies completely on the positive side of the plane, then we know that no part of the object ever crosses into the negative side of the plane $\mathbf{L}$. Similarly, if both of the points $\mathbf{P}_1$ and $\mathbf{P}_2$ represent positions of the object for which it lies completely on the negative side of the plane, then we know that no part of the object ever crosses into the positive side of the plane $\mathbf{L}$. When these cases occur, we can avoid performing collision detection calculations between the moving object and any geometry that lies on the opposite side of the plane $\mathbf{L}$.

8.2 INTEROBJECT COLLISIONS

This section discusses techniques for detecting collisions between two moving objects. Since we can always subtract one object's velocity from the other, the problem can always be reduced to that of detecting collisions between one moving object and one stationary object. Thus, we present methods for detecting collisions between a moving sphere or box and a stationary sphere or box.

8.2.1 COLLISION OF TWO SPHERES

Suppose that two spheres are in motion and have a constant linear velocity during a time interval beginning at $t = 0$ and ending at $t = 1$. We assume that the spheres are not already intersecting and that neither sphere contains the other. Let the points $\mathbf{P}_1$ and $\mathbf{P}_2$ represent the initial and final positions of the first sphere's center, and let $\mathbf{Q}_1$ and $\mathbf{Q}_2$ be the initial and final positions of the second sphere's center, as shown in Figure 8.3. We define the velocity vectors $\mathbf{V}_P$ and $\mathbf{V}_Q$ as

$$\mathbf{V}_P = \mathbf{P}_2 - \mathbf{P}_1$$
$$\mathbf{V}_Q = \mathbf{Q}_2 - \mathbf{Q}_1. \tag{8.23}$$

The position $\mathbf{P}(t)$ of the first sphere's center and the position $\mathbf{Q}(t)$ of the second sphere's center are then given by

$$\mathbf{P}(t) = \mathbf{P}_1 + t\mathbf{V}_P$$
$$\mathbf{Q}(t) = \mathbf{Q}_1 + t\mathbf{V}_Q. \tag{8.24}$$

Let r_P and r_Q be the radii of the two spheres. We wish to determine whether the distance d between the centers $\mathbf{P}(t)$ and $\mathbf{Q}(t)$ is ever equal to $r_P + r_Q$ at some time $t \in [0,1)$. If so, then the spheres are tangent to each other at time t and a collision has taken place. We examine the squared distance between $\mathbf{P}(t)$ and $\mathbf{Q}(t)$ given by

$$d^2 = \|\mathbf{P}(t) - \mathbf{Q}(t)\|^2. \tag{8.25}$$

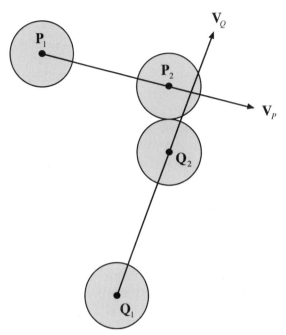

FIGURE *Detecting a collision between two moving spheres.*
8.3

Substituting the values given by Equation (8.24) for $\mathbf{P}(t)$ and $\mathbf{Q}(t)$, we have

$$d^2 = \|\mathbf{P}_1 + t\mathbf{V}_P - \mathbf{Q}_1 - t\mathbf{V}_Q\|^2. \qquad (8.26)$$

For convenience, we define

$$\mathbf{A} = \mathbf{P}_1 - \mathbf{Q}_1$$
$$\mathbf{B} = \mathbf{V}_P - \mathbf{V}_Q \qquad (8.27)$$

so that Equation (8.26) can be written as

$$d^2 = \|\mathbf{A} + t\mathbf{B}\|^2$$
$$= A^2 + 2t(\mathbf{A} \cdot \mathbf{B}) + t^2 B^2. \qquad (8.28)$$

Using the quadratic formula to solve for t gives us the formulas

$$t_1 = \frac{-(\mathbf{A} \cdot \mathbf{B}) - \sqrt{(\mathbf{A} \cdot \mathbf{B})^2 - B^2(A^2 - d^2)}}{B^2}$$

$$t_2 = \frac{-(\mathbf{A} \cdot \mathbf{B}) + \sqrt{(\mathbf{A} \cdot \mathbf{B})^2 - B^2(A^2 - d^2)}}{B^2}. \qquad (8.29)$$

Setting $d = r_P + r_Q$ gives us the times t_1 and t_2 when the two spheres are tangent, if ever. It is possible that the value inside the radical is negative, in which case the spheres never collide. It is also possible that $B^2 = 0$, meaning that either both spheres are stationary or that both are traveling in the same direction at the same speed and thus cannot collide.

Since B^2 is not negative, the value of t_1 is always less than or equal to the value of t_2. The time t_1 represents the instant at which the spheres are tangent while they are still approaching each other. The time t_2, however, represents the instant at which the spheres are tangent while they are moving away from each other. Since we assume that the spheres are not intersecting to begin with, we are only interested in the time t_1 when they first collide. Thus, we only need to calculate the following time t to determine when a collision occurs.

$$t = \frac{-(\mathbf{A} \cdot \mathbf{B}) - \sqrt{(\mathbf{A} \cdot \mathbf{B})^2 - B^2\left[A^2 - (r_P + r_Q)^2\right]}}{B^2} \tag{8.30}$$

If t does not fall in the range [0, 1), then no collision occurs during our time interval of interest.

It is possible to determine that a collision cannot occur without evaluating Equation (8.30). The time t at which the squared distance d^2 is minimized can be found by setting the derivative of the right side of Equation (8.28) to zero, as follows.

$$2B^2t + 2(\mathbf{A} \cdot \mathbf{B}) = 0 \tag{8.31}$$

Solving for t produces the following time at which the distance between the centers of the spheres is the least.

$$t = -\frac{\mathbf{A} \cdot \mathbf{B}}{B^2} \tag{8.32}$$

Plugging this time into Equation (8.28) yields the smallest distance ever separating the centers of the two spheres:

$$d^2 = A^2 - \frac{(\mathbf{A} \cdot \mathbf{B})^2}{B^2}. \tag{8.33}$$

If $d^2 > (r_P + r_Q)^2$, then we know that the two spheres can never collide.

Once we have determined that a collision has occurred at time t, we can calculate the centers $\mathbf{P}(t)$ and $\mathbf{Q}(t)$ of the two spheres at that time by plugging t into Equations (8.24). As shown in Figure 8.4, the point of contact $\mathbf{C}$ lies on the line segment connecting $\mathbf{P}(t)$ and $\mathbf{Q}(t)$ at a distance r_P from $\mathbf{P}(t)$, and is thus given by

$$\mathbf{C} = \mathbf{P}(t) + r_P\mathbf{N}, \tag{8.34}$$

where $\mathbf{N}$ is the unit length normal vector pointing from $\mathbf{P}(t)$ to $\mathbf{Q}(t)$:

$$\mathbf{N} = \frac{\mathbf{Q}(t) - \mathbf{P}(t)}{\left\|\mathbf{Q}(t) - \mathbf{P}(t)\right\|}. \tag{8.35}$$

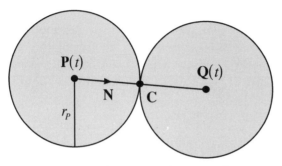

FIGURE *The point of contact **C** where two spheres meet lies on the line connecting their*
8.4 *centers at the time of the collision.*

8.2.2 COLLISION OF A SPHERE AND A BOX

Suppose that the center of a sphere of radius r moves with constant velocity from the point $\mathbf{P}_1$ at time $t = 0$ to the point $\mathbf{P}_2$ at time $t = 1$. Let the vectors $\mathbf{R}$, $\mathbf{S}$, and $\mathbf{T}$ represent the lengths and orientations of the edges of a box whose center moves from the point $\mathbf{Q}_1$ at time $t = 0$ to the point $\mathbf{Q}_2$ at time $t = 1$, as shown in Figure 8.5. As before, we assume that the sphere and the box do not initially intersect and that neither contains the other.

Because a significant amount of work is necessary to determine that *no* collision has taken place between a sphere and a box, it is a common practice to first determine whether a collision occurs with a sphere that encloses the box using the method described in Section 8.2.1. (The sphere enclosing the box has radius $\frac{1}{2}\|\mathbf{R} + \mathbf{S} + \mathbf{T}\|$.) If the sphere moving from the point $\mathbf{P}_1$ to the point $\mathbf{P}_2$ does not collide with the sphere bounding the box as its center moves from the point $\mathbf{Q}_1$ to the point $\mathbf{Q}_2$, then no collision can possibly occur with the box.

The problem of determining whether a sphere and a box collide can be reduced to that of determining whether the sphere collides with a stationary axis-aligned box by making the appropriate coordinate transformations. First, we subtract the velocity of the box from that of the sphere to obtain the velocity $\mathbf{V}$ of the sphere in the reference frame in which the box is stationary:

$$\mathbf{V} = (\mathbf{P}_2 - \mathbf{P}_1) - (\mathbf{Q}_2 - \mathbf{Q}_1). \tag{8.36}$$

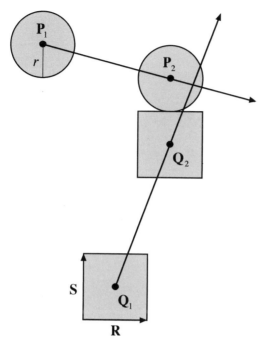

FIGURE *Detecting a collision between a moving sphere and a moving box.*
8.5

The position $\mathbf{P}(t)$ of the sphere in this reference frame is given by

$$\mathbf{P}(t) = \mathbf{P}_1 + t\mathbf{V}, \tag{8.37}$$

and the box always remains centered at the point $\mathbf{Q}_1$.

We now wish to perform a transformation that aligns the stationary box to the coordinate axes. Since the vectors $\mathbf{R}$, $\mathbf{S}$, and $\mathbf{T}$ are orthogonal, the 3×3 matrix whose rows are given by the corresponding unit-length vectors

$$\hat{\mathbf{R}} = \frac{\mathbf{R}}{\|\mathbf{R}\|}, \hat{\mathbf{S}} = \frac{\mathbf{S}}{\|\mathbf{S}\|}, \text{ and } \hat{\mathbf{T}} = \frac{\mathbf{T}}{\|\mathbf{T}\|} \tag{8.38}$$

rotates the box so that the edges represented by the directions $\mathbf{R}$, $\mathbf{S}$, and $\mathbf{T}$ get mapped to the x-, y-, and z-axes, respectively. We can also perform a translation that maps the vertex $\mathbf{G}$ of the box given by

$$\mathbf{G} = \mathbf{Q}_1 - \tfrac{1}{2}(\mathbf{R} + \mathbf{S} + \mathbf{T}) \tag{8.39}$$

to the origin by using the following 4×4 transformation matrix.

$$\mathbf{M} = \begin{bmatrix} \hat{R}_x & \hat{R}_y & \hat{R}_z & -\hat{\mathbf{R}} \cdot \mathbf{G} \\ \hat{S}_x & \hat{S}_y & \hat{S}_z & -\hat{\mathbf{S}} \cdot \mathbf{G} \\ \hat{T}_x & \hat{T}_y & \hat{T}_z & -\hat{\mathbf{T}} \cdot \mathbf{G} \\ 0 & 0 & 0 & 1 \end{bmatrix} \tag{8.40}$$

After transformation by the matrix $\mathbf{M}$, the box occupies the volume bounded by the six planes below.

$$x = 0 \qquad x = \|\mathbf{R}\|$$

$$y = 0 \qquad y = \|\mathbf{S}\|$$

$$z = 0 \qquad z = \|\mathbf{T}\| \tag{8.41}$$

The initial center $\mathbf{P}'_1$ of the sphere in the transformed coordinate space is given by

$$\mathbf{P}'_1 = \mathbf{M}\mathbf{P}_1, \tag{8.42}$$

and the velocity $\mathbf{V}'$ of the sphere is given by

$$\mathbf{V}' = \mathbf{M}_{3\times3}\mathbf{V}. \tag{8.43}$$

The 4D extension of the vector $\mathbf{V}$ has a w-coordinate of zero since it represents a direction, so the velocity is transformed only by the 3×3 rotation portion of the matrix $\mathbf{M}$.

Our task is now to determine whether the moving sphere, whose center $\mathbf{P}'(t)$ at time t is given by

$$\mathbf{P}'(t) = \mathbf{P}'_1 + t\mathbf{V}', \tag{8.44}$$

collides with the stationary axis-aligned box. Such a collision may occur on one of the box's faces, at a point along one of the box's edges, or at one of the box's vertices. When the sphere is in contact with the box, its center lies at a distance r from some point on the box's surface. Thus, we need to calculate at what time, if any, the sphere's center intersects the set of points that lie at exactly the distance r outside the box. As illustrated in Figure 8.6, this set is composed of six planar faces, twelve cylindrical components that correspond to the edges of the box, and eight spherical components that correspond to the vertices of the box. Since the box is axis-aligned, each of these 26 components has a simple mathematical representation.

The six faces lying at a distance r from the box can be described by the plane equations and associated bounding conditions listed in Table 8.1. At most three of these faces need to be considered for intersection with the moving sphere's

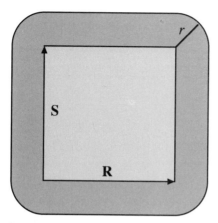

FIGURE *To determine whether a sphere collides with a box, we expand the box by the sphere's*
8.6 *radius r and intersect the line segment followed by the sphere's center with the*
expanded surface.

path since any face having a nonnegative dot product with the velocity $\mathbf{V}'$ is facing away from the sphere and may be rejected because it cannot contain the
point where the sphere first makes contact with the box.

The twelve cylindrical components of radius r whose axes are coincident
with the box's edges are listed in Table 8.2. Each component represents one-
quarter of a cylinder whose axis is parallel to one of the x-, y-, or z-axes. The
bounding conditions restrict the surface of the quarter-cylinder to the area
falling between two adjacent faces. Any quarter-cylinder that corresponds to an
edge lying between two rejected faces may also be rejected since every point on
its surface must face away from the path of the moving sphere. Since there must
be a set of three pairwise adjacent faces that are always rejected, at least three
quarter-cylinders can also be rejected in every case. Thus, the greatest number
of quarter-cylinders that will ever need to be tested for intersection with the
moving sphere's path is nine.

Table 8.1 The six faces of a box expanded by a radius *r*.

Face	Plane	Normal	Conditions	
1	$x = -r$	$\langle -1, 0, 0 \rangle$	$0 \leq y \leq \|\mathbf{S}\|$	$0 \leq z \leq \|\mathbf{T}\|$
2	$x = \|\mathbf{R}\| + r$	$\langle 1, 0, 0 \rangle$	$0 \leq y \leq \|\mathbf{S}\|$	$0 \leq z \leq \|\mathbf{T}\|$
3	$y = -r$	$\langle 0, -1, 0 \rangle$	$0 \leq x \leq \|\mathbf{R}\|$	$0 \leq z \leq \|\mathbf{T}\|$
4	$y = \|\mathbf{S}\| + r$	$\langle 0, 1, 0 \rangle$	$0 \leq x \leq \|\mathbf{R}\|$	$0 \leq z \leq \|\mathbf{T}\|$
5	$z = -r$	$\langle 0, 0, -1 \rangle$	$0 \leq x \leq \|\mathbf{R}\|$	$0 \leq y \leq \|\mathbf{S}\|$
6	$z = \|\mathbf{T}\| + r$	$\langle 0, 0, 1 \rangle$	$0 \leq x \leq \|\mathbf{R}\|$	$0 \leq y \leq \|\mathbf{S}\|$

Table 8.2 The twelve cylindrical components of a box expanded by a radius *r*. The shared faces indicate which two faces listed in Table 8.1 are shared by the edge corresponding to each cylinder.

Cylinder	Shared Faces	Conditions		
$x^2 + y^2 = r^2$	1 and 3	$x < 0$	$y < 0$	$0 \leq z \leq \|\mathbf{T}\|$
$(x - \|\mathbf{R}\|)^2 + y^2 = r^2$	2 and 3	$x > \|\mathbf{R}\|$	$y < 0$	$0 \leq z \leq \|\mathbf{T}\|$
$(x - \|\mathbf{R}\|)^2 + (y - \|\mathbf{S}\|)^2 = r^2$	2 and 4	$x > \|\mathbf{R}\|$	$y > \|\mathbf{S}\|$	$0 \leq z \leq \|\mathbf{T}\|$
$x^2 + (y - \|\mathbf{S}\|)^2 = r^2$	1 and 4	$x < 0$	$y > \|\mathbf{S}\|$	$0 \leq z \leq \|\mathbf{T}\|$
$x^2 + z^2 = r^2$	1 and 5	$x < 0$	$z < 0$	$0 \leq y \leq \|\mathbf{S}\|$
$(x - \|\mathbf{R}\|)^2 + z^2 = r^2$	2 and 5	$x > \|\mathbf{R}\|$	$z < 0$	$0 \leq y \leq \|\mathbf{S}\|$
$(x - \|\mathbf{R}\|)^2 + (z - \|\mathbf{T}\|)^2 = r^2$	2 and 6	$x > \|\mathbf{R}\|$	$z > \|\mathbf{T}\|$	$0 \leq y \leq \|\mathbf{S}\|$
$x^2 + (z - \|\mathbf{T}\|)^2 = r^2$	1 and 6	$x < 0$	$z > \|\mathbf{T}\|$	$0 \leq y \leq \|\mathbf{S}\|$
$y^2 + z^2 = r^2$	3 and 5	$y < 0$	$z < 0$	$0 \leq x \leq \|\mathbf{R}\|$
$(y - \|\mathbf{S}\|)^2 + z^2 = r^2$	4 and 5	$y > \|\mathbf{S}\|$	$z < 0$	$0 \leq x \leq \|\mathbf{R}\|$
$(y - \|\mathbf{S}\|)^2 + (z - \|\mathbf{T}\|)^2 = r^2$	4 and 6	$y > \|\mathbf{S}\|$	$z > \|\mathbf{T}\|$	$0 \leq x \leq \|\mathbf{R}\|$
$y^2 + (z - \|\mathbf{T}\|)^2 = r^2$	3 and 6	$y < 0$	$z > \|\mathbf{T}\|$	$0 \leq x \leq \|\mathbf{R}\|$

The eight spherical components of radius *r* centered at the box's vertices are listed in Table 8.3. The bounding conditions eliminate all but one-eighth of each sphere's surface. Any eighth-sphere corresponding to a vertex shared by three rejected faces may also be rejected since every point on its surface must face away from the path of the moving sphere. At least one vertex's eighth-sphere can always be rejected, leaving at most seven to test for an intersection with the moving sphere's path.

Table 8.3 The eight spherical components of a box expanded by a radius *r*. The shared faces indicate which three faces listed in Table 8.1 are shared by the vertex corresponding to each sphere.

Sphere	Shared Faces	Conditions		
$x^2 + y^2 + z^2 = r^2$	1, 3, and 5	$x < 0$	$y < 0$	$z < 0$
$(x - \|\mathbf{R}\|)^2 + y^2 + z^2 = r^2$	2, 3, and 5	$x > \|\mathbf{R}\|$	$y < 0$	$z < 0$
$(x - \|\mathbf{R}\|)^2 + (y - \|\mathbf{S}\|)^2 + z^2 = r^2$	2, 4, and 5	$x > \|\mathbf{R}\|$	$y > \|\mathbf{S}\|$	$z < 0$
$x^2 + (y - \|\mathbf{S}\|)^2 + z^2 = r^2$	1, 4, and 5	$x < 0$	$y > \|\mathbf{S}\|$	$z < 0$
$x^2 + y^2 + (z - \|\mathbf{T}\|)^2 = r^2$	1, 3, and 6	$x < 0$	$y < 0$	$z > \|\mathbf{T}\|$
$(x - \|\mathbf{R}\|)^2 + y^2 + (z - \|\mathbf{T}\|)^2 = r^2$	2, 3, and 6	$x > \|\mathbf{R}\|$	$y < 0$	$z > \|\mathbf{T}\|$
$(x - \|\mathbf{R}\|)^2 + (y - \|\mathbf{S}\|)^2 + (z - \|\mathbf{T}\|)^2 = r^2$	2, 4, and 6	$x > \|\mathbf{R}\|$	$y > \|\mathbf{S}\|$	$z > \|\mathbf{T}\|$
$x^2 + (y - \|\mathbf{S}\|)^2 + (z - \|\mathbf{T}\|)^2 = r^2$	1, 4, and 6	$x < 0$	$y > \|\mathbf{S}\|$	$z > \|\mathbf{T}\|$

We determine whether the moving sphere collides with the box by considering the path $\mathbf{P}'(t)$ followed by the sphere's center and attempting to find an intersection of this path with the expanded box. First, we intersect this path with at most three eligible planes from Table 8.1. (Recall that any face for which the dot product of the normal and the velocity $\mathbf{V}'$ is nonnegative can be rejected.) If no intersection occurs, we next try to find an intersection of the path with at most nine eligible cylinders from Table 8.2. If we still have not found an intersection, then we finally test at most seven spheres from Table 8.3. If no intersection is found with any of these objects, then the moving sphere does not collide with the box.

The intersection between the path $\mathbf{P}'(t)$ and one of the faces listed in Table 8.1 is found by substituting one of the x-, y-, or z-components of $\mathbf{P}'(t)$ into a particular plane equation and solving for the time t. The following example demonstrates how an intersection with the first face listed in Table 8.1 can be found.

Example 8.1. Determine whether the path $\mathbf{P}'(t) = \mathbf{P}'_1 + t\mathbf{V}'$ intersects the area of the plane described by the equation $x = -r$ bounded by the conditions $0 \leq y \leq \|\mathbf{S}\|$ and $0 \leq z \leq \|\mathbf{T}\|$.

Solution. Substituting the x-component of the path $\mathbf{P}'(t)$ for the variable x in the plane equation gives us

$$\left(\mathbf{P}'_1\right)_x + tV'_x = -r. \tag{8.45}$$

Solving for t, we have the following expression for the time t_0 at which a collision potentially occurs.

$$t_0 = -\frac{r + \left(\mathbf{P}'_1\right)_x}{V'_x} \tag{8.46}$$

(Note that if V'_x is zero, then this face would have already been rejected since the dot product of the face's normal $\langle -1, 0, 0 \rangle$ with $\mathbf{V}'$ would be zero.) If t_0 does not fall into the range $[0, 1)$, then no collision occurs during the time interval to which we are restricted. Otherwise, we must check that the y- and z-components of the point $\mathbf{P}'(t_0)$ satisfy the following inequalities.

$$0 \leq \left(\mathbf{P}'_1\right)_y + t_0 V'_y \leq \|\mathbf{S}\|$$

$$0 \leq \left(\mathbf{P}'_1\right)_z + t_0 V'_z \leq \|\mathbf{T}\| \tag{8.47}$$

An intersection with the box's face occurs only if both inequalities are satisfied.

Once it has been determined that the path of the sphere's center intersects a face of the expanded box, it is not necessary to proceed any further. If the sphere's center does not collide with any of the six faces, we next test the box's edges by intersecting the line segment given by $\mathbf{P}'(t)$ with the cylinders listed in Table 8.2. As with the planes, we find such an intersection by substituting the x-, y-, and z-components of $\mathbf{P}'(t)$ into the equation describing a particular cylinder and solve for the time t. The following example demonstrates how an intersection with the first cylinder listed in Table 8.2 can be found.

Example 8.2. Determine whether the path $\mathbf{P}'(t) = \mathbf{P}'_1 + t\mathbf{V}'$ intersects the area of the cylinder described by the equation $x^2 + y^2 = r^2$ bounded by the conditions $x < 0$, $y < 0$, and $0 \leq z \leq \|\mathbf{T}\|$.

Solution. Substituting the x- and y-components of the path $\mathbf{P}'(t)$ for the variables x and y in the cylinder equation gives us

$$\left(\mathbf{P}'_1 + t\mathbf{V}'\right)^2_x + \left(\mathbf{P}'_1 + t\mathbf{V}'\right)^2_y = r^2. \tag{8.48}$$

Expanding terms, this yields the following quadratic equation in t.

$$\left(V'^2_x + V'^2_y\right)t^2 + 2\left[\left(\mathbf{P}'_1\right)_x V'_x + \left(\mathbf{P}'_1\right)_y V'_y\right]t + \left(\mathbf{P}'_1\right)^2_x + \left(\mathbf{P}'_1\right)^2_y - r^2 = 0 \tag{8.49}$$

We can quickly determine whether the line segment intersects the infinite cylinder by examining the discriminant $D = b^2 - 4ac$, where

$$a = V'^2_x + V'^2_y$$

$$b = 2\left[\left(\mathbf{P}'_1\right)_x V'_x + \left(\mathbf{P}'_1\right)_y V'_y\right]$$

$$c = \left(\mathbf{P}'_1\right)^2_x + \left(\mathbf{P}'_1\right)^2_y - r^2. \tag{8.50}$$

If $D \leq 0$, then no intersection occurs. (In the case that $D = 0$, the sphere grazes the edge of the box.) If $D > 0$, then the smaller time of intersection t_0 is given by

$$t_0 = \frac{-b - \sqrt{D}}{2a} \tag{8.51}$$

since a is positive. The larger value of t_0 is not meaningful to us because it represents the intersection of the line segment with the back side of the cylinder from the perspective of the starting point $\mathbf{P}'_1$. If the value of t_0 given by Equation (8.51) does not fall into the range $[0, 1)$, then no intersection occurs during the time interval to which we are restricted. If an intersection does occur at a valid time, then we must check that the point $\mathbf{P}'(t_0)$ falls within the segment of the cylinder corresponding to the edge of the box by verifying the inequality

$$0 \leq \left(\mathbf{P}_1'\right)_z + t_0 V_z' \leq \|\mathbf{T}\|. \tag{8.52}$$

Since the expanded box is a convex volume, it is not necessary for us to verify that the remaining two bounding conditions ($x < 0$ and $y < 0$) are satisfied. Any point found at this stage where the segment $\mathbf{P}'(t)$ intersects a cylinder cannot lie behind one of the box's expanded faces.

If an intersection of the path $\mathbf{P}'(t)$ and a cylinder is found, then we are finished. Otherwise, we proceed to the box's vertices and search for an intersection with one of the spheres listed in Table 8.3. Again, we determine a point of intersection by substituting the components of $\mathbf{P}'(t)$ into the equations describing the surface we are testing. The following example demonstrates how an intersection can be found with the first sphere listed in Table 8.3.

Example 8.3. Determine whether the path $\mathbf{P}'(t) = \mathbf{P}_1' + t\mathbf{V}'$ intersects the area of the sphere described by the equation $x^2 + y^2 + z^2 = r^2$ bounded by the conditions $x < 0$, $y < 0$, and $z < 0$.

Solution. Substituting the x-, y-, and z-components of the path $\mathbf{P}'(t)$ for the variables x, y, and z in the sphere equation gives us

$$\left(\mathbf{P}_1' + t\mathbf{V}'\right)_x^2 + \left(\mathbf{P}_1' + t\mathbf{V}'\right)_y^2 + \left(\mathbf{P}_1' + t\mathbf{V}'\right)_z^2 = r^2. \tag{8.53}$$

As discussed in Section 5.2.3, a ray-sphere intersection is determined by solving the quadratic equation $at^2 + bt + c = 0$, where

$$a = V'^2$$

$$b = 2\left(\mathbf{P}_1' \cdot \mathbf{V}'\right)$$

$$c = \mathbf{P}_1'^2 - r^2. \tag{8.54}$$

Examining the discriminant $D = b^2 - 4ac$ tells us whether an intersection occurs. If $D > 0$, then the smaller time of intersection t_0 is given by

$$t_0 = \frac{-b - \sqrt{D}}{2a}. \tag{8.55}$$

If $0 \leq t_0 < 1$, then a collision has occurred. It is not necessary that we check the point $\mathbf{P}'(t_0)$ against the bounding conditions because any path $\mathbf{P}'(t)$ that intersects a sphere at a point lying *inside* the expanded box must also intersect a plane or a cylinder at an earlier time. Thus, we know that the point $\mathbf{P}'(t_0)$ lies on the one-eighth of the sphere that contributes to the surface of the expanded box.

If an intersection between the path $\mathbf{P}'(t)$ and the expanded box occurs at time t_0, then the position of the sphere's center and box's center in the untransformed coordinate space at that time are calculated by simply evaluating $\mathbf{P}(t)$ and $\mathbf{Q}(t)$ at t_0. To calculate the actual point of contact $\mathbf{C}$, we first need to determine the normal vector of the collision. If the sphere collided with a face of the box, then the normal vector $\mathbf{N}'$ in the transformed coordinate space is the vector listed in Table 8.1 for that face. If the sphere collided with a quarter-cylinder representing an edge of the box or a one-eighth sphere representing a vertex of the box, then the normal vector $\mathbf{N}'$ is given by the gradient of the function describing the surface evaluated at the point $\mathbf{P}'(t_0)$. Since the 3×3 rotation portion of the matrix $\mathbf{M}$ is orthogonal, the normal vector $\mathbf{N}$ in the untransformed coordinate space is given by

$$\mathbf{N} = \mathbf{M}^{\mathrm{T}}\mathbf{N}'. \tag{8.56}$$

The point of contact $\mathbf{C}$ can now be determined by calculating

$$\mathbf{C} = \mathbf{P}(t_0) - r\mathbf{N}. \tag{8.57}$$

8.2.3 COLLISION OF TWO BOXES

Suppose that we have two arbitrarily oriented boxes, labeled P and Q, moving with a constant linear velocity, as illustrated in Figure 8.7. Let the points $\mathbf{P}_1$ and $\mathbf{P}_2$ represent the initial position (at time $t = 0$) and the final position (at time $t = 1$) of the first box's center, and let the points $\mathbf{Q}_1$ and $\mathbf{Q}_2$ represent the initial and final positions of the second box's center. Let the first box have edges described by the vectors $\mathbf{R}_P$, $\mathbf{S}_P$, and $\mathbf{T}_P$, and let the second box have edges described by the vectors $\mathbf{R}_Q$, $\mathbf{S}_Q$, and $\mathbf{T}_Q$. Again, we assume that the two boxes do not initially intersect and that neither contains the other.

Due to the amount of computation necessary to perform a collision test between two moving boxes, it is usually a good idea to first perform a collision test between the two spheres bounding the boxes. If the spheres do not collide, then there is no need to proceed with the more complicated box collision test.

There are several ways in which two boxes can collide. We can classify the types of collisions into the following four categories.

(a) A vertex of one box collides with a face of the other box. This includes cases in which a vertex of one box collides with an edge of the other box or collides with a vertex of the other box.

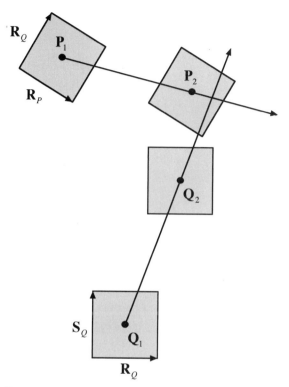

FIGURE *Detecting a collision between two moving boxes.*
8.7

(b) An edge of one box collides with a face of the other box. This includes cases in which an edge of one box collides with an edge of the other box and the two edges are parallel.

(c) A face of one box collides with a face of the other box, and the faces are parallel.

(d) An edge of one box collides with an edge of the other box at a single point, and neither edge is parallel to any face of the other box.

The first three possibilities can all be detected by performing collision tests between one box and the faces of the other box using the box-plane test discussed in Section 8.1.2. These tests must be performed in both directions—box P needs to be tested against the faces of box Q, and box Q needs to be tested against the faces of box P. This sounds like a lot of work, but at most half of the faces represent surfaces where a collision can potentially occur. The technique presented in this section begins with the box-plane tests. In most cases, either a collision occurs at this stage or it is determined that a collision definitely cannot occur between the two boxes. In certain instances, however, it is necessary to continue the algorithm to search for a collision of type (d) listed previously, that two edges collide at a single point, and neither edge is parallel to any face of the other box.

Our collision detection method performs calculations from two perspectives. We first transform to a coordinate system in which box P is stationary and axis-aligned. The second perspective is that in which box Q is stationary and axis-aligned. In a manner identical to that used for the sphere-box collision test, we can transform to a coordinate space in which box P is stationary and axis-aligned by setting the velocity $\mathbf{V}$ of box Q to

$$\mathbf{V} = (\mathbf{Q}_2 - \mathbf{Q}_1) - (\mathbf{P}_2 - \mathbf{P}_1) \tag{8.58}$$

and transforming each box using the matrix

$$\mathbf{M} = \begin{bmatrix} (\hat{\mathbf{R}}_P)_x & (\hat{\mathbf{R}}_P)_y & (\hat{\mathbf{R}}_P)_z & -\hat{\mathbf{R}}_P \cdot \mathbf{G}_P \\ (\hat{\mathbf{S}}_P)_x & (\hat{\mathbf{S}}_P)_y & (\hat{\mathbf{S}}_P)_z & -\hat{\mathbf{S}}_P \cdot \mathbf{G}_P \\ (\hat{\mathbf{T}}_P)_x & (\hat{\mathbf{T}}_P)_y & (\hat{\mathbf{T}}_P)_z & -\hat{\mathbf{T}}_P \cdot \mathbf{G}_P \\ 0 & 0 & 0 & 1 \end{bmatrix}, \tag{8.59}$$

where $\hat{\mathbf{R}}_P$, $\hat{\mathbf{S}}_P$, and $\hat{\mathbf{T}}_P$ are the unit vectors defined by

$$\hat{\mathbf{R}}_P = \frac{\mathbf{R}_P}{\|\mathbf{R}_P\|}, \quad \hat{\mathbf{S}}_P = \frac{\mathbf{S}_P}{\|\mathbf{S}_P\|}, \quad \text{and } \hat{\mathbf{T}}_P = \frac{\mathbf{T}_P}{\|\mathbf{T}_P\|}, \tag{8.60}$$

and the point $\mathbf{G}_P$ is given by

$$\mathbf{G}_P = \mathbf{P}_1 - \tfrac{1}{2}\left(\mathbf{R}_P + \mathbf{S}_P + \mathbf{T}_P\right). \tag{8.61}$$

Box P now occupies the volume bounded by the following six planes.

$$\langle -1, 0, 0, 0 \rangle \quad \langle 1, 0, 0, -\|\mathbf{R}_P\| \rangle$$

$$\langle 0, -1, 0, 0 \rangle \quad \langle 0, 1, 0, -\|\mathbf{S}_P\| \rangle$$

$$\langle 0, 0, -1, 0 \rangle \quad \langle 0, 0, 1, -\|\mathbf{T}_P\| \rangle \tag{8.62}$$

(Note that these are equivalent to the planes given by Equation (8.41).) The initial center $\mathbf{Q}_1'$ of box Q in the transformed coordinate space is given by

$$\mathbf{Q}_1' = \mathbf{M}\mathbf{Q}_1, \tag{8.63}$$

and the edges of box Q are described by the vectors $\mathbf{R}_Q'$, $\mathbf{S}_Q'$, and $\mathbf{T}_Q'$ given by

$$\mathbf{R}'_Q = \mathbf{M}_{3\times3}\mathbf{R}_Q$$

$$\mathbf{S}'_Q = \mathbf{M}_{3\times3}\mathbf{S}_Q$$

$$\mathbf{T}'_Q = \mathbf{M}_{3\times3}\mathbf{T}_Q. \tag{8.64}$$

The position $\mathbf{Q}'(t)$ of the center of box Q is given by

$$\mathbf{Q}'(t) = \mathbf{Q}'_1 + t\mathbf{V}', \tag{8.65}$$

where $\mathbf{V}'$ is the transformed velocity:

$$\mathbf{V}' = \mathbf{M}_{3\times3}\mathbf{V}. \tag{8.66}$$

We now need to decide which faces of the transformed box P need to participate in our collision detection calculations. Any face of box P having a normal vector whose dot product with the velocity $\mathbf{V}'$ is not positive can be eliminated since it faces away from the other box. This leaves at most three faces of box P that we need to consider. We can also eliminate faces for which the box Q initially lies completely on the negative side of the corresponding plane $\mathbf{L} = \langle \mathbf{N}, D \rangle$. This can be determined by first calculating the effective radius r_{eff} of the box Q with respect to $\mathbf{L}$, a calculation that requires significantly less work due to the simplicity of the planes given by Equations (8.62). If $\mathbf{L} \cdot \mathbf{Q}'_1 \le -r_{\text{eff}}$, then the box lies on the negative side of $\mathbf{L}$. It is possible that all six faces of box P are eliminated at this stage. In this case, the boxes are moving away from each other and no collision occurs.

For each remaining eligible face F of box P, we perform a box-plane collision test between box Q and the plane $\mathbf{L}$ containing F. If box Q initially lies completely on the positive side of the plane $\mathbf{L}$ (i.e., $\mathbf{L} \cdot \mathbf{Q}'_1 \ge r_{\text{eff}}$) and no collision occurs with the entire plane, then the two boxes themselves do not collide and we immediately exit the box-box collision test. (If box Q initially intersects the plane $\mathbf{L}$, then we cannot exit at this point.) Otherwise, we need to determine whether the collision with the plane $\mathbf{L}$ actually occurs inside the face F. If the collision occurs at a single point $\mathbf{C}$, then we need to determine whether that point falls between both pairs of opposite faces perpendicular to F. For instance, suppose that a collision test reveals that the box Q collides with the plane $\langle -1, 0, 0, 0 \rangle$ at the point $\mathbf{C}$. Then we must verify that the conditions

$$0 \le C_y \le \|\mathbf{S}_P\|$$

$$0 \le C_z \le \|\mathbf{T}_P\| \tag{8.67}$$

are satisfied since the collision did not occur inside the face F otherwise. If a collision has indeed occurred inside the face F, then there is no need to proceed further because no earlier collision can occur with a different face.

If the box Q collides with the plane $\mathbf{L}$ at an edge bounded by the endpoints $\mathbf{C}_1$ and $\mathbf{C}_2$, then we must determine whether any part of the line segment connecting the endpoints lies within the face F. This is done by clipping the line segment to the four planes perpendicular to F, as illustrated in Figure 8.8. For each plane $\mathbf{K}$ perpendicular to $\mathbf{L}$, we calculate $\mathbf{K} \cdot \mathbf{C}_1$ and $\mathbf{K} \cdot \mathbf{C}_2$. If both quantities are positive, then the segment falls outside the face F and no collision has occurred. If both quantities are negative, then we take no action and proceed to the next plane. If one is positive and the other is negative, then we replace the endpoint lying on the positive side of the plane $\mathbf{K}$ with the point where the line segment intersects the plane and proceed to the next plane. If after visiting all four planes, the line segment has not been completely clipped away, then a collision has occurred and it is not necessary to proceed any further.

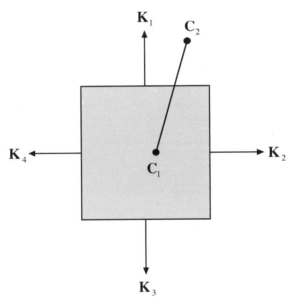

FIGURE 8.8 *If an edge of a box collides with a plane containing the face F, then the line segment connecting the edge's endpoints $\mathbf{C}_1$ and $\mathbf{C}_2$ must be clipped to the four perpendicular faces, which lie in the planes $\mathbf{K}_1$, $\mathbf{K}_2$, $\mathbf{K}_3$, and $\mathbf{K}_4$, to determine whether any part of it lies within the face F.*

In the remaining case that the box Q collides with the plane $\mathbf{L}$ at a face bounded by the vertices $\mathbf{C}_1$, $\mathbf{C}_2$, $\mathbf{C}_3$, and $\mathbf{C}_4$, then we must determine whether any part of the polygon composed by these vertices lies within the face F. This is done by clipping the polygon to the four planes perpendicular to F using a technique such as that discussed in Section 9.2.2. Note that for this to work correctly, consecutive vertices in the list $\mathbf{C}_1$, $\mathbf{C}_2$, $\mathbf{C}_3$, $\mathbf{C}_4$ must be adjacent to each other. This can be ensured by choosing signs in Equation (8.20) as follows.

$$\mathbf{C}_1 = \mathbf{Q}'(t) - \tfrac{1}{2}\left[\operatorname{sgn}(\mathbf{R}'_Q \cdot \mathbf{N})\mathbf{R}'_Q + \mathbf{S}'_Q + \mathbf{T}'_Q\right]$$

$$\mathbf{C}_2 = \mathbf{Q}'(t) - \tfrac{1}{2}\left[\operatorname{sgn}(\mathbf{R}'_Q \cdot \mathbf{N})\mathbf{R}'_Q - \mathbf{S}'_Q + \mathbf{T}'_Q\right]$$

$$\mathbf{C}_3 = \mathbf{Q}'(t) - \tfrac{1}{2}\left[\operatorname{sgn}(\mathbf{R}'_Q \cdot \mathbf{N})\mathbf{R}'_Q - \mathbf{S}'_Q - \mathbf{T}'_Q\right]$$

$$\mathbf{C}_4 = \mathbf{Q}'(t) - \tfrac{1}{2}\left[\operatorname{sgn}(\mathbf{R}'_Q \cdot \mathbf{N})\mathbf{R}'_Q + \mathbf{S}'_Q - \mathbf{T}'_Q\right] \tag{8.68}$$

Also note that the planes to which the polygon is being clipped face outward, so they should be negated during the clipping process. If after clipping to all four planes, the polygon has not been completely clipped away, then a collision has occurred and it is not necessary to proceed any further.

Once we have tested for collisions between box Q and the faces of box P, we next reverse the roles of the two boxes and test for collisions between the box P and the faces of box Q. If we still have not found a collision or determined that a collision cannot occur up to this point, then the possibility that an edge-edge collision takes place, where neither edge is parallel to any face of the other box, must be investigated.

As we perform the collision tests between box Q and the faces of box P (and vice versa), we record which vertex of box Q collided with each plane $\mathbf{L}$ containing a face of box P, even if it occurred in the past where $t < 0$. If we made it to this point in the algorithm, then the point of contact with each plane lies outside the corresponding face of box P. Furthermore, no axis of box Q can be parallel to any axis of box P, so box Q did not collide with any plane $\mathbf{L}$ at an edge or face.

For each pair of planes $\mathbf{L}_1 = \langle \mathbf{N}_1, D_1 \rangle$ and $\mathbf{L}_2 = \langle \mathbf{N}_2, D_2 \rangle$ of box P, we consider the edge of box Q connecting the vertices $\mathbf{C}_1$ and $\mathbf{C}_2$ that collided with the planes $\mathbf{L}_1$ and $\mathbf{L}_2$, respectively. Let E_Q denote the edge of box Q connecting the vertices $\mathbf{C}_1$ and $\mathbf{C}_2$, and let E_P denote the edge of box P coinciding with the intersection of the planes $\mathbf{L}_1$ and $\mathbf{L}_2$. If the extrusion of edge E_Q along the direction of the velocity $\mathbf{V}$ intersects edge E_P, then a collision occurs where these two edges make contact. The normal $\mathbf{N}_3$ to the plane containing the extrusion of edge E_Q is given by

$$\mathbf{N}_3 = \mathbf{V} \times (\mathbf{C}_2 - \mathbf{C}_1), \tag{8.69}$$

and thus the 4D plane vector $\mathbf{L}_3$ of the extruded edge is

$$\mathbf{L}_3 = \langle \mathbf{N}_3, -\mathbf{N}_3 \cdot \mathbf{C}_1 \rangle. \tag{8.70}$$

The point $\mathbf{A}$ at which the three planes $\mathbf{L}_1$, $\mathbf{L}_2$, and $\mathbf{L}_3$ intersect is given by Equation (4.20). All we have to do now is make sure that this point falls within the path traveled by edge E_Q during the time $0 \le t < 1$. Define the vector $\mathbf{W}$ as

$$\mathbf{W} = \mathbf{N}_3 \times (\mathbf{C}_2 - \mathbf{C}_1). \qquad (8.71)$$

As shown in Figure 8.9, $\mathbf{W}$ lies in the plane of the extrusion of E_Q, is perpendicular to edge E_Q, and points away from the vector $\mathbf{V}$. A collision occurs between edges E_P and E_Q at the point $\mathbf{A}$ if

$$\mathbf{W} \cdot (\mathbf{A} - \mathbf{V} - \mathbf{C}_1) > 0. \qquad (8.72)$$

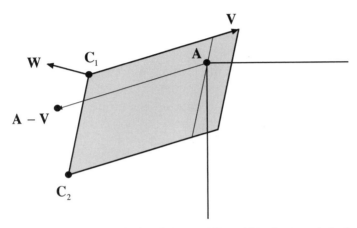

FIGURE *Determining whether the point* **A** *lies within the extruded edge.*
8.9

CHAPTER 8 SUMMARY

Collision of a Sphere and a Plane

A sphere of radius r whose center moves from the point $\mathbf{P}_1$ at time $t = 0$ to the point $\mathbf{P}_2$ at time $t = 1$ collides with a plane $\mathbf{L} = \langle \mathbf{N}, D \rangle$ at time

$$t = -\frac{\mathbf{L}' \cdot \mathbf{P}_1}{\mathbf{L}' \cdot \mathbf{V}},$$

where $\mathbf{L}' = \langle \mathbf{N}, D - r \rangle$.

Collision of a Box and a Plane

A box described by the vectors $\mathbf{R}$, $\mathbf{S}$, and $\mathbf{T}$ whose center moves from the point $\mathbf{Q}_1$ at time $t = 0$ to the point $\mathbf{Q}_2$ at time $t = 1$ collides with a plane $\mathbf{L} = \langle \mathbf{N}, D \rangle$ at time

$$t = -\frac{\mathbf{L}' \cdot \mathbf{Q}_1}{\mathbf{L}' \cdot \mathbf{V}},$$

where $\mathbf{L}' = \langle \mathbf{L}, D - r_{\text{eff}} \rangle$ and r_{eff} is the effective radius of the box, given by

$$r_{\text{eff}} = \tfrac{1}{2}\left(\left|\mathbf{R} \cdot \mathbf{N}\right| + \left|\mathbf{S} \cdot \mathbf{N}\right| + \left|\mathbf{T} \cdot \mathbf{N}\right|\right).$$

When a box collides with the plane at a point, the position $\mathbf{C}$ of the vertex making contact with the plane is given by

$$\mathbf{C} = \mathbf{Q}(t) - \tfrac{1}{2}\left[\operatorname{sgn}(\mathbf{R} \cdot \mathbf{N})\mathbf{R} + \operatorname{sgn}(\mathbf{S} \cdot \mathbf{N})\mathbf{S} + \operatorname{sgn}(\mathbf{T} \cdot \mathbf{N})\mathbf{T}\right],$$

where $\mathbf{Q}(t) = \mathbf{Q}_1 + t(\mathbf{Q}_2 - \mathbf{Q}_1)$.

Collision of Two Spheres

A sphere of radius r_P moving from the point $\mathbf{P}_1$ at time $t = 0$ to the point $\mathbf{P}_2$ at time $t = 1$ collides with another sphere of radius r_Q moving from the point $\mathbf{Q}_1$ to the point $\mathbf{Q}_2$ at time

$$t = \frac{-(\mathbf{A} \cdot \mathbf{B}) - \sqrt{(\mathbf{A} \cdot \mathbf{B})^2 - B^2\left[A^2 - \left(r_P + r_Q\right)^2\right]}}{B^2},$$

where

$\mathbf{A} = \mathbf{P}_1 - \mathbf{Q}_1$

$\mathbf{B} = (\mathbf{P}_2 - \mathbf{P}_1) - (\mathbf{Q}_2 - \mathbf{Q}_1)$.

EXERCISES FOR CHAPTER 8

1. Determine the time t when a sphere having a radius of two meters collides with the plane $x = 10$ m if its center lies at the origin at time $t = 0$ and it moves with a constant velocity of $\langle 2, 0, 1 \rangle$ m/s.
2. Write a program that determines whether two spheres collide within a given time interval. The program should take as parameters the initial positions and velocities of the two spheres. If a collision occurs, the program should calculate the point of contact at that time.
3. Write a vectorized implementation of the sphere-box collision test that performs ray intersections in parallel. The program should be able to calculate intersections with four parallel cylinders from Table 8.2 simultaneously and four spheres from Table 8.3 simultaneously.

CHAPTER

9 Polygonal Techniques

This chapter discusses several techniques involving the manipulation of polygonal models. These techniques can be employed to achieve a large number of special effects, including surface decals, particle systems, and real-time shadows.

9.1 DEPTH VALUE OFFSET

Many games need to render special effects such as scorch marks on a wall or footprints on the ground that are not an original part of a scene but are created during game play. (A method for creating these is discussed in Section 9.2.) These types of decorative additions are usually decaled onto an existing surface and thus consist of polygons that are coplanar with other polygons in a scene. The problem is that pixels rendered as part of one polygon rarely have exactly the same interpolated depth value as pixels rendered as part of a coplanar polygon. The result is an undesired pattern in which parts of the original surface show through the decaled polygons.

The goal is to find a way to offset a polygon's depth in a scene without changing its projected screen coordinates or altering its texture mapping perspective. Most 3D graphics systems contain some kind of polygon offset function to help achieve this goal. However, these solutions generally lack fine control and usually incur a per-vertex performance cost. In this section, we present an alternative method that modifies the projection matrix to achieve the depth offset effect.

9.1.1 PROJECTION MATRIX MODIFICATION

Let us first examine the effect of the standard OpenGL perspective projection matrix on an eye space point $\mathbf{P} = (P_x, P_y, P_z, 1)$. To simplify the matrix given in Equation (4.50) a bit, we assume that the view frustum is centered about the z-axis so that the left and right planes intersect the near plane at $x = \pm n/e$ and the top and bottom planes intersect the near plane at $y = \pm an/e$, where e is the focal length and a is the aspect ratio. Calling the distance to the near clipping plane n and the distance to the far clipping plane f, we have

$$
\begin{bmatrix}
e & 0 & 0 & 0 \\
0 & e/a & 0 & 0 \\
0 & 0 & -\dfrac{f+n}{f-n} & -\dfrac{2fn}{f-n} \\
0 & 0 & -1 & 0
\end{bmatrix}
\begin{bmatrix}
P_x \\ P_y \\ P_z \\ 1
\end{bmatrix}
=
\begin{bmatrix}
eP_x \\
(e/a)P_y \\
-\dfrac{f+n}{f-n}P_z - \dfrac{2fn}{f-n} \\
-P_z
\end{bmatrix}.
\tag{9.1}
$$

To finish the projection, we need to divide this result by its w-coordinate, which has the value $-P_z$. The resulting point $\mathbf{P}'$ is given by

$$
\mathbf{P}' = \begin{bmatrix} -\dfrac{eP_x}{P_z} \\[2ex] -\dfrac{(e/a)P_y}{P_z} \\[2ex] \dfrac{f+n}{f-n} + \dfrac{2fn}{P_z(f-n)} \end{bmatrix}.
\tag{9.2}
$$

It is clear from Equation (9.2) that preserving the value of $-P_z$ for the w-coordinate will guarantee the preservation of the projected x- and y-coordinates as well. From this point forward, we shall concern ourselves only with the lower-right 2 × 2 portion of the projection matrix, since this is the only part that affects the z- and w-coordinates.

The projected z-coordinate may be altered without disturbing the w-coordinate by introducing a factor of $1 + \varepsilon$, for some small ε, as follows.

$$
\begin{bmatrix} -(1+\varepsilon)\dfrac{f+n}{f-n} & -\dfrac{2fn}{f-n} \\[2ex] -1 & 0 \end{bmatrix} \cdot \begin{bmatrix} P_z \\[1ex] 1 \end{bmatrix} = \begin{bmatrix} -(1+\varepsilon)\dfrac{f+n}{f-n}P_z - \dfrac{2fn}{f-n} \\[2ex] -P_z \end{bmatrix}
\tag{9.3}
$$

After dividing by w, we arrive at the following value for the projected z-coordinate.

$$
\begin{aligned}
P_z' &= (1+\varepsilon)\frac{f+n}{f-n} + \frac{2fn}{P_z(f-n)} \\[2ex]
&= \frac{f+n}{f-n} + \frac{2fn}{P_z(f-n)} + \varepsilon\frac{f+n}{f-n}
\end{aligned}
\tag{9.4}
$$

Comparing this to the z-coordinate in Equation (9.2), we see that we have found a way to offset projected depth values by a constant $\varepsilon\frac{f+n}{f-n}$.

9.1.2 OFFSET VALUE SELECTION

Due to the nonlinear nature of the z-buffer, the constant offset given in Equation (9.4) corresponds to a larger difference far from the camera than it does near the camera. Although this constant offset may work well for some applications, there is no single solution that works for every application at all depths. The best we can do is choose an appropriate ε given a camera space offset δ and a depth value P_z that collectively represents the object that we are offsetting. To determine a formula for ε, we examine the result of applying the standard projection matrix from Equation (9.1) to a point whose z-coordinate has been offset by some small δ as follows.

$$\begin{bmatrix} -\dfrac{f+n}{f-n} & -\dfrac{2fn}{f-n} \\ -1 & 0 \end{bmatrix} \cdot \begin{bmatrix} P_z + \delta \\ 1 \end{bmatrix} = \begin{bmatrix} -\dfrac{f+n}{f-n}(P_z + \delta) - \dfrac{2fn}{f-n} \\ -(P_z + \delta) \end{bmatrix} \qquad (9.5)$$

Dividing by w, we have the following value for the projected z-coordinate.

$$\begin{aligned} P_z' &= \frac{f+n}{f-n} + \frac{2fn}{(P_z + \delta)(f - n)} \\ &= \frac{f+n}{f-n} + \frac{2fn}{P_z(f-n)} + \frac{2fn}{f-n}\left(\frac{1}{P_z + \delta} - \frac{1}{P_z}\right) \end{aligned} \qquad (9.6)$$

Equating this result to Equation (9.4) and simplifying a bit, we end up with

$$\varepsilon = -\frac{2fn}{f+n}\left(\frac{\delta}{P_z(P_z + \delta)}\right). \qquad (9.7)$$

A good value of δ for a particular application can be found with a little experimentation. It should be kept in mind that δ is a camera space offset, and thus becomes less effective as P_z gets larger. For an m-bit integer depth buffer, we want to make sure that

$$|\varepsilon| \geq \frac{1}{2^m - 1}\left(\frac{f - n}{f + n}\right) \qquad (9.8)$$

since smaller values of ε will not yield an offset significant enough to alter the integer depth value. Substituting the right side of Equation (9.7) for ε and solving for δ gives us

$$\delta \geq \frac{kP_z^2}{1 - kP_z} \qquad (9.9)$$

or

$$\delta \leq \frac{-kP_z^2}{1 + kP_z}, \qquad (9.10)$$

where the constant k is given by

$$k = \frac{f - n}{2fn(2^m - 1)}. \qquad (9.11)$$

Equation (9.9) gives us the minimum effective value for δ when offsetting a polygon toward the camera (the usual case) and Equation (9.10) gives us the maximum effective value for δ when offsetting a polygon away from the camera.

9.1.3 IMPLEMENTATION

Listing demonstrates how the projection matrix shown in Equation (9.3) may be implemented under OpenGL. The function `LoadOffsetMatrix` takes the same six values that are passed to the OpenGL function `glFrustum`. It also takes the values for δ and P_z that are used to calculate ε.

> **Listing 9.1.** This code modifies the OpenGL projection matrix so that it off-sets depth values by the constant ε given by Equation (9.7).
>
> ```
> void LoadOffsetMatrix(GLdouble l, GLdouble r,
>     GLdouble b, GLdouble t,
>     GLdouble n, GLdouble f,
>     GLfloat delta, GLfloat pz)
> {
>     GLfloat matrix[16];
>
>     // Set up standard perspective projection
>     glMatrixMode(GL_PROJECTION);
>     glFrustum(l, r, b, t, n, f);
>
>     // Retrieve the projection matrix
>     glGetFloatv(GL_PROJECTION_MATRIX, matrix);
>
>     // Calculate epsilon with equation (9.7)
>     GLfloat epsilon = -2.0F * f * n * delta /
>         ((f + n) * pz * (pz + delta));
>
>     // Modify entry (3,3) of the projection matrix
>     matrix[10] *= 1.0F + epsilon;
>
>     // Send the projection matrix back to OpenGL
>     glLoadMatrix(matrix);
> }
> ```

9.2 DECAL APPLICATION

Effects such as scorch marks on walls or footprints on the ground are commonly implemented by creating a new object, called a *decal*, that coincides with an existing surface and rendering it using a depth offset technique such as that discussed in Section 9.1. Applying a decal to the interior of a planar surface is simple, but difficulties arise when applying decals to the more complex surfaces used in today's games to represent curved objects and terrain patches. In this section, we present a general method for applying a decal to an arbitrarily shaped surface and concurrently clipping the decal to the surface's boundary. The example shown in Figure 9.1 was generated using the technique presented in this section.

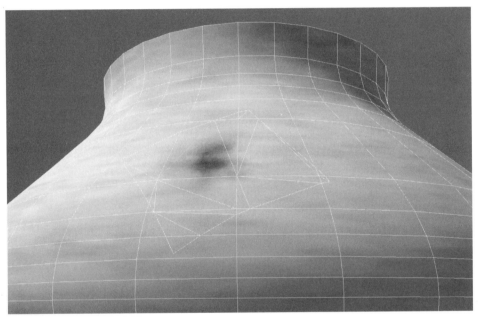

FIGURE *A scorch mark decal applied to a curved surface.*
9.1

9.2.1 DECAL MESH CONSTRUCTION

We begin with a point **P** that lies on an existing surface and a unit normal direction **N** that is perpendicular to the surface at that point. The point **P** represents the center of the decal and may be the point at which a projectile has hit the surface or the point where a character's foot has stepped on the ground. A unit tangent direction **T** must also be chosen to determine the orientation of the decal. This configuration is illustrated in Figure 9.2.

Given the point **P** and the directions **N** and **T**, we have an oriented plane that is tangent to the surface geometry at **P**. We can carve a rectangle out of this plane that represents the area of our decal by constructing four boundary planes that are parallel to the normal direction **N**. Let w and h be the width and height

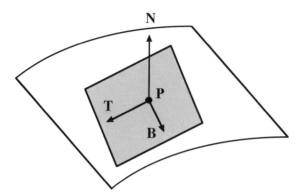

FIGURE *The configuration of a decal.*
9.2

of the decal. Then the 4D vectors corresponding to the four border planes are given by

$$left = \left(\mathbf{T}, \frac{w}{2} - \mathbf{T} \cdot \mathbf{P} \right)$$

$$right = \left(-\mathbf{T}, \frac{w}{2} + \mathbf{T} \cdot \mathbf{P} \right)$$

$$bottom = \left(\mathbf{B}, \frac{h}{2} - \mathbf{B} \cdot \mathbf{P} \right)$$

$$top = \left(-\mathbf{B}, \frac{h}{2} + \mathbf{B} \cdot \mathbf{P} \right), \qquad (9.12)$$

where $\mathbf{B} = \mathbf{N} \times \mathbf{T}$. We generate a triangle mesh for the decal object by clipping nearby surfaces to the four boundary planes. We also want to clip to front and back planes to avoid bleeding through to parts of the same surface mesh that may be inside the boundary planes but far in front of or behind the point $\mathbf{P}$. The 4D vectors corresponding to the front and back planes are given by

$$front = (-\mathbf{N}, d + \mathbf{N} \cdot \mathbf{P})$$

$$back = (\mathbf{N}, d - \mathbf{N} \cdot \mathbf{P}), \qquad (9.13)$$

where d is the maximum distance that any vertex in the decal may be from the tangent plane passing through the point $\mathbf{P}$.

The mesh construction algorithm proceeds as follows. First, we identify which surfaces in the world could be affected by the decal. This may be determined by locating each surface whose bounding volume reaches within a certain distance of the point **P**. For each potentially affected surface, we individually examine every triangle in the surface's mesh. Let **M** denote the unit normal direction corresponding to the plane of a triangle in the mesh. We throw out any triangles for which $\mathbf{N} \cdot \mathbf{M} < \varepsilon$ for some fixed positive value ε since these triangles are facing away from the decal's normal direction **N**. The remaining triangles are clipped to the planes given by Equations (9.12) and (9.13) and stored in a new triangle mesh.

When a triangle overlaps any of the planes and needs to be clipped, we interpolate the normal vectors as well as the vertex positions so that we can later apply coloring to the clipped vertices that reflect the angle between each vertex's normal direction and the decal's normal direction. This has the effect of smoothly fading the decal texture in relation to each triangle's orientation relative to the plane of the decal. We assign an alpha value to each vertex using the equation

$$alpha = \frac{\dfrac{\mathbf{N} \cdot \mathbf{R}}{\|\mathbf{R}\|} - \varepsilon}{1 - \varepsilon}, \tag{9.14}$$

where **R** is the (possibly unnormalized due to interpolation) normal vector corresponding to the vertex. This maps the dot product range $[\varepsilon, 1]$ to the alpha value range $[0, 1]$.

Texture mapping coordinates are applied to the resulting triangle mesh by measuring the distance from each vertex to the planes passing through the point **P** and having normal directions **T** and **B**. Let **Q** be the position of a vertex in the decal's triangle mesh. Then the texture coordinates s and t are given by

$$s = \frac{\mathbf{T} \cdot (\mathbf{Q} - \mathbf{P})}{w} + \frac{1}{2}$$

$$t = \frac{\mathbf{B} \cdot (\mathbf{Q} - \mathbf{P})}{b} + \frac{1}{2}. \tag{9.15}$$

9.2.2 POLYGON CLIPPING

Each triangle belonging to a surface that could be affected by the decal is treated as a convex polygon and clipped to each of the six boundary planes, one at a time. Clipping a convex polygon having n vertices to a plane results in a new convex polygon having at most $n + 1$ vertices. Thus, polygons that have been clipped against all six planes may possess as many as nine vertices. Once the clipping process is complete, each polygon is treated as a triangle fan and added to the decal's triangle mesh.

To clip a convex polygon against an arbitrary plane, we first classify all the vertices belonging to the polygon into two categories: those lying on the negative side of the plane and those lying on the positive side of the plane or in the plane itself. (This differs from the method used to clip portals in Section 7.4.1 in that we do not have a separate classification for vertices lying in the plane.) If all the polygon's vertices lie on the negative side of the plane, then the polygon is discarded. Otherwise, we visit every pair of neighboring vertices in the polygon looking for edges that intersect the clipping plane. As shown in Figure 9.3, new vertices are added to the polygon where such intersections occur, and vertices lying on the negative side of the plane are removed.

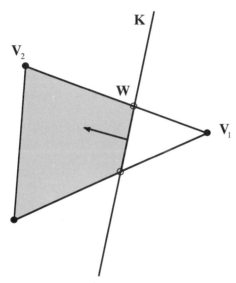

FIGURE *When a polygon is clipped against a plane, new vertices are added where edges*
9.3 *intersect the plane, and vertices lying on the negative side of the plane are removed.*

Suppose that the vertex $\mathbf{V}_1$ lies on the positive side of the clipping plane $\mathbf{K}$ and that the vertex $\mathbf{V}_2$ lies on the negative side of $\mathbf{K}$. A point $\mathbf{W}$ lying on the line segment connecting $\mathbf{V}_1$ and $\mathbf{V}_2$ can be expressed as

$$\mathbf{W}(t) = \mathbf{V}_1 + t(\mathbf{V}_2 - \mathbf{V}_1), \tag{9.16}$$

where the parameter t satisfies $0 \leq t \leq 1$. The value of t for which $\mathbf{K} \cdot \mathbf{W}(t) = 0$ is given by

$$t = \frac{\mathbf{K} \cdot \mathbf{V}_1}{\mathbf{K} \cdot (\mathbf{V}_1 - \mathbf{V}_2)}. \tag{9.17}$$

(Note that the difference $\mathbf{V}_1 - \mathbf{V}_2$ has a w-coordinate of zero.) Substituting this value of t back into Equation (9.16) gives us our new vertex $\mathbf{W}$.

9.3 BILLBOARDING

Many special effects are implemented by applying a two-dimensional texture map to a flat polygon that is always oriented to face the camera. This technique is called *billboarding* and is an effective way to create the illusion that a flat object has volume. This section examines methods for calculating the vertices of billboard polygons in different situations.

9.3.1 UNCONSTRAINED QUADS

An unconstrained quad is a four-sided rectangular polygon that is free to rotate in any direction. Unconstrained quads are typically used to create special effects such as particle systems, smoke trails, and lens flare coronas.

We billboard an unconstrained quad by forcing its vertices to lie in a plane that is perpendicular to the direction in which the camera is pointing. Let the vectors $\mathbf{R}$ and $\mathbf{U}$ denote the unit-length world space right direction and up direction of the current camera view. (These correspond to the camera space x- and y-axes, respectively.) The quad that we wish to billboard is defined by the following quantities.

(a) The world space position $\mathbf{P}$ corresponding to the center of the quad.
(b) The width w and height h of the quad. These may be changed over time to produce the effect of an expanding or shrinking billboard.
(c) The angle θ by which the quad should be rotated relative to the camera's orientation. This may be changed over time to produce the effect of a spinning billboard. If θ is constant, then the quad rotates with the camera about the view direction.

Using these quantities, we define the vectors $\mathbf{X}$ and $\mathbf{Y}$ as follows.

$$\mathbf{X} = \left(\frac{w}{2}\cos\theta\right)\mathbf{R} + \left(\frac{w}{2}\sin\theta\right)\mathbf{U}$$

$$\mathbf{Y} = \left(-\frac{h}{2}\sin\theta\right)\mathbf{R} + \left(\frac{h}{2}\cos\theta\right)\mathbf{U} \tag{9.18}$$

The rotation θ is typically quantized to some number of possible angles so that a lookup table may be used for the sine and cosine functions. Of course, if $\theta = 0$, then the expressions for the vectors $\mathbf{X}$ and $\mathbf{Y}$ reduce to

$$\mathbf{X} = \frac{w}{2}\mathbf{R}$$

$$\mathbf{Y} = \frac{h}{2}\mathbf{U}. \tag{9.19}$$

As illustrated in Figure 9.4, the four vertices $\mathbf{Q}_1$, $\mathbf{Q}_2$, $\mathbf{Q}_3$, and $\mathbf{Q}_4$ of the quad are given by

$$\mathbf{Q}_1 = \mathbf{P} + \mathbf{X} + \mathbf{Y} \qquad \mathbf{Q}_2 = \mathbf{P} - \mathbf{X} + \mathbf{Y}$$

$$\mathbf{Q}_3 = \mathbf{P} - \mathbf{X} - \mathbf{Y} \qquad \mathbf{Q}_4 = \mathbf{P} + \mathbf{X} - \mathbf{Y}. \tag{9.20}$$

These vertices are arranged in a counterclockwise winding order so that the front of the quad faces the camera. The corresponding two-dimensional texture mapping coordinates are given by

$$\langle s_1, t_1 \rangle = \langle 1, 1 \rangle \qquad \langle s_2, t_2 \rangle = \langle 0, 1 \rangle$$

$$\langle s_3, t_3 \rangle = \langle 0, 0 \rangle \qquad \langle s_4, t_4 \rangle = \langle 1, 0 \rangle. \tag{9.21}$$

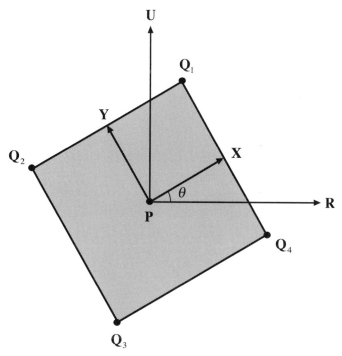

FIGURE *Calculating the vertices of an unconstrained billboarded quad.*
9.4

Billboarded quads whose vertices derive from the vectors $\mathbf{X}$ and $\mathbf{Y}$ given by Equations (9.18) are always aligned to the plane of the camera. As Figure 9.5 demonstrates, this alignment can differ significantly from the plane perpendicular to the true direction from the quad's center to the camera position. When

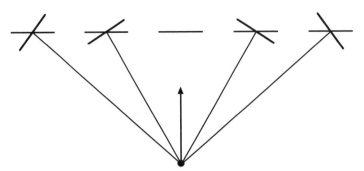

FIGURE 9.5 *A billboarded quad that is aligned to the plane of the camera may differ significantly from a quad that directly faces the camera position.*

hundreds or thousands of small particles are being rendered, one may wish to use Equation (9.18) for efficiency, but large quads may look better if oriented to face the actual camera position instead of the plane of the camera.

We align a quad so that it faces the camera position by presenting a more computationally expensive formulation of the vectors $\mathbf{X}$ and $\mathbf{Y}$. Let the vector $\mathbf{C}$ denote the world space camera position. Assuming that the center $\mathbf{P}$ of the quad does not lie on the line containing $\mathbf{C}$ and running in the direction $\mathbf{U}$, we can calculate

$$\mathbf{Z} = \frac{\mathbf{C} - \mathbf{P}}{\left\| \mathbf{C} - \mathbf{P} \right\|}$$

$$\mathbf{A} = \frac{\mathbf{U} \times \mathbf{Z}}{\left\| \mathbf{U} \times \mathbf{Z} \right\|}$$

$$\mathbf{B} = \mathbf{Z} \times \mathbf{A}. \tag{9.22}$$

The vector $\mathbf{Z}$ is the unit vector that points from the quad's center toward the camera position. Calculating the cross product with $\mathbf{U}$ produces orthogonal vector $\mathbf{A}$ lying in the plane of the billboard. If $\mathbf{U} \times \mathbf{Z}$ is close to zero, then we can use the alternate formula

$$\mathbf{B} = \frac{\mathbf{Z} \times \mathbf{R}}{\left\| \mathbf{Z} \times \mathbf{R} \right\|}$$

$$\mathbf{A} = \mathbf{B} \times \mathbf{Z}. \tag{9.23}$$

The vectors $\mathbf{A}$ and $\mathbf{B}$ form an orthogonal pair of unit vectors that we can use to express the vectors $\mathbf{X}$ and $\mathbf{Y}$:

$$\mathbf{X} = \left(\frac{w}{2}\cos\theta\right)\mathbf{A} + \left(\frac{w}{2}\sin\theta\right)\mathbf{B}$$

$$\mathbf{Y} = \left(-\frac{h}{2}\sin\theta\right)\mathbf{A} + \left(\frac{h}{2}\cos\theta\right)\mathbf{B}. \tag{9.24}$$

Using these in Equation (9.20) produces the vertices of the billboarded quad.

9.3.2 CONSTRAINED QUADS

We now consider how to orient a quad that is constrained to rotate only about the z-axis. An example of how such a quad might be used is to render the fire texture for a torch. In this case, the fire is always pointing upward, but the plane of the quad rotates to face the camera. As long as the camera does not view the quad from sharply above or below, this produces the convincing illusion that the fire has volume.

Suppose that the camera resides at the world space point $\mathbf{C}$. For a quad centered at the point $\mathbf{P}$, we define the vector $\mathbf{X}$ as

$$\mathbf{X} = \langle P_y - C_y, C_x - P_x, 0 \rangle. \tag{9.25}$$

As shown in Figure 9.6, this vector is constructed by taking the difference between the camera position and the center of the quad, projecting it onto the x-y plane, and rotating it 90 degrees counterclockwise about the z-axis. If $\|\mathbf{X}\| = 0$, then the camera is either directly above or directly below the quad. In

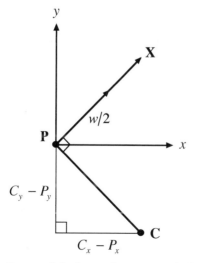

FIGURE *Calculating the vertices of a billboarded quad that is constrained to rotate about the*
9.6 *z-axis.*

this case, the quad is being viewed on edge and therefore should not be rendered. Otherwise, we calculate the four vertices $\mathbf{Q}_1$, $\mathbf{Q}_2$, $\mathbf{Q}_3$, and $\mathbf{Q}_4$ of the quad as follows.

$$\mathbf{Q}_1 = \mathbf{P} + \frac{w}{2}\frac{\mathbf{X}}{\|\mathbf{X}\|} + \left\langle 0, 0, \frac{b}{2}\right\rangle \qquad \mathbf{Q}_2 = \mathbf{P} - \frac{w}{2}\frac{\mathbf{X}}{\|\mathbf{X}\|} + \left\langle 0, 0, \frac{b}{2}\right\rangle$$

$$\mathbf{Q}_3 = \mathbf{P} - \frac{w}{2}\frac{\mathbf{X}}{\|\mathbf{X}\|} - \left\langle 0, 0, \frac{b}{2}\right\rangle \qquad \mathbf{Q}_4 = \mathbf{P} + \frac{w}{2}\frac{\mathbf{X}}{\|\mathbf{X}\|} - \left\langle 0, 0, \frac{b}{2}\right\rangle \qquad (9.26)$$

The texture mapping coordinates are the same as those for an unconstrained quad given by Equations (9.21).

9.3.3 POLYLINE QUADSTRIPS

A polyline defined by a series of N points $\mathbf{P}_1$, $\mathbf{P}_2$,..., $\mathbf{P}_N$ can be given some thickness r by constructing a quadstrip that traces the polyline in the manner shown in Figure 9.7. One application of such a quadstrip is to render a lightning bolt whose path is defined by a set of points. Another application is to render a motion-blurred particle for which a number of intermediate positions have been calculated between its position on the previous frame and its current position.

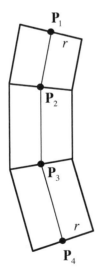

FIGURE *A quadstrip of radius r that traces a polyline.*
9.7

For each point $\mathbf{P}_i$ defining the polyline, we generate two quadstrip vertices lying at a distance r from $\mathbf{P}_i$. The direction of the line on which these vertices and the point $\mathbf{P}_i$ lie should be orthogonal to both the direction to the camera position and the tangent direction of the polyline at $\mathbf{P}_i$. The unit direction $\mathbf{Z}_i$ to the camera is given by

$$\mathbf{Z}_i = \frac{\mathbf{C} - \mathbf{P}_i}{\|\mathbf{C} - \mathbf{P}_i\|}, \tag{9.27}$$

where $\mathbf{C}$ is the camera position. A unit tangent vector $\mathbf{T}_i$ may be calculated for the point $\mathbf{P}_i$ using the formula

$$\mathbf{T}_i = \frac{\mathbf{P}_{i+1} - \mathbf{P}_{i-1}}{\|\mathbf{P}_{i+1} - \mathbf{P}_{i-1}\|}, \tag{9.28}$$

or in the case that $\mathbf{P}_i$ is an endpoint,

$$\mathbf{T}_1 = \frac{\mathbf{P}_2 - \mathbf{P}_1}{\|\mathbf{P}_2 - \mathbf{P}_1\|}$$

$$\mathbf{T}_N = \frac{\mathbf{P}_N - \mathbf{P}_{N-1}}{\|\mathbf{P}_N - \mathbf{P}_{N-1}\|}. \tag{9.29}$$

The two quadstrip vertices $\mathbf{G}_i$ and $\mathbf{H}_i$ corresponding to the point $\mathbf{P}_i$ are then given by

$$\mathbf{G}_i = \mathbf{P}_i + r(\mathbf{T}_i \times \mathbf{Z}_i)$$

$$\mathbf{H}_i = \mathbf{P}_i - r(\mathbf{T}_i \times \mathbf{Z}_i). \tag{9.30}$$

Each edge of the quadstrip constructed using the vertices $\mathbf{G}_1, \mathbf{H}_1, \mathbf{G}_2, \mathbf{H}_2, \ldots, \mathbf{G}_N, \mathbf{H}_N$ is perpendicular to the direction to the camera. Figure 9.8 demonstrates a lightning bolt generated using this technique.

9.4 STENCIL SHADOWS

This section describes a technique that can be used to render an extremely accurate shadow for any closed triangle mesh. By a *closed* triangle mesh, we mean one for which each edge is shared by an even number of triangles. This requirement disallows any holes in the mesh that would enable us to see the interior of a model's surface.

The method works by first precomputing the list of all edges in the triangle mesh and for each edge, noting which two triangles share that edge. (Edges shared by more than two triangles are duplicated.) When rendering the shadow for a particular light source, we determine whether each triangle is facing toward the light source or away from it. Any edge shared by one triangle that is facing the light source and another triangle facing away from the light source is then considered part of the mesh's silhouette. Each edge on the silhouette is

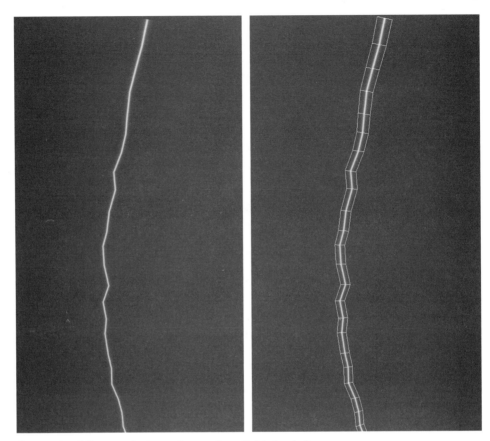

FIGURE   *A polyline quadstrip used to render a lightning bolt.*
9.8

extruded away from the light source, forming a quad. The set of all quads corresponding to the silhouette edges bounds a region of space called the *shadow volume*.

By employing specific stencil buffer operations, the shadow volume is rendered in such a way that ones (1s) are written to the stencil buffer at the exact locations where the shadow is cast on the environment. The details of this technique are discussed below.

9.4.1 EDGE LIST CONSTRUCTION

Suppose that we have an indexed triangle mesh consisting of an array of N vertices $\mathbf{V}_1, \mathbf{V}_2, \ldots, \mathbf{V}_N$ and an array of M triangles $T_1, T_2, \ldots, T_M$. Each triangle simply indicates which three vertices it uses by storing three integer indexes i_1, i_2, and i_3.

We say that an index i_p precedes an index i_q if the number p immediately precedes the number q in the cyclic chain $1 \rightarrow 2 \rightarrow 3 \rightarrow 1$. For instance, i_2 precedes i_3 and i_3 precedes i_1, but i_2 does not precede i_1.

The indexes i_1, i_2, and i_3 are ordered such that the positions of the vertices $\mathbf{V}_{i_1}$, $\mathbf{V}_{i_2}$, and $\mathbf{V}_{i_3}$ to which they refer are wound counterclockwise about the triangle's normal vector. Suppose that two triangles share an edge whose endpoints are the vertices $\mathbf{V}_a$ and $\mathbf{V}_b$, as shown in Figure 9.9. The consistent winding rule enforces the property that for one of the triangles, the index referring to $\mathbf{V}_a$ precedes the index referring to $\mathbf{V}_b$, and that for the other triangle, the index referring to $\mathbf{V}_b$ precedes the index referring to $\mathbf{V}_a$.

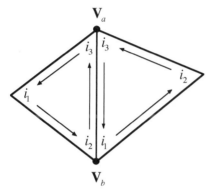

FIGURE **9.9** *When consistent winding is enforced, it is always the case that the indexes referring to the vertices $\mathbf{V}_a$ and $\mathbf{V}_b$ of exactly one of the two triangles sharing an edge satisfies the property that the index referring to $\mathbf{V}_a$ precedes the index referring to $\mathbf{V}_b$.*

The edges of a triangle mesh can be identified by making a single pass through the triangle list. For any triangle having vertex indexes i_1, i_2, and i_3, we create an edge record for every instance in which $i_1 < i_2$, $i_2 < i_3$, or $i_3 < i_1$ and store the index of the current triangle in the edge record. This procedure creates exactly one edge for every pair of triangles that share two vertices $\mathbf{V}_a$ and $\mathbf{V}_b$, duplicating any edges that are shared by multiple pairs of triangles.

Once we have identified all the edges, we make a second pass through the triangle list to find the second triangle that shares each edge. This is done by locating triangles for which $i_1 > i_2$, $i_2 > i_3$, or $i_3 > i_1$ and matching it to an edge having the same vertex indexes that has not yet been supplied with a second triangle index (thus allowing for duplicated edges).

Listing 9.2 demonstrates how the construction of an edge list may be implemented.

Listing 9.2. This code examines an array of indexed triangles and constructs an array of edge records that refer back to the triangles that share them. The return value is the number of edges written to the array edgeArray.

```
Struct Edge
{
    unsigned short   vertexIndex[2];
    unsigned short   triangleIndex[2];
};

Struct Triangle
{
    unsigned short   index[3];
};

long BuildEdges(long triangleCount, const Triangle *triangleArray,
    Edge **edgeArray)
{
    // Allocate enough space to hold all edges
    *edgeArray = new Edge[triangleCount * 3];

    long edgeCount = 0;
    Edge *edge = *edgeArray;

    // First pass: find edges
    const Triangle *triangle = triangleArray;
    for (long a = 0; a < triangleCount; a++)
    {
        long i1 = triangle->index[0];
        long i2 = triangle->index[1];
        long i3 = triangle->index[2];

        if (i1 < i2)
        {
            edge->vertexIndex[0] = i1;
            edge->vertexIndex[1] = i2;
            edge->triangleIndex[0] = a;
            edge->triangleIndex[1] = -1;
            edgeCount++;
            edge++;
        }

        if (i2 < i3)
        {
```

```
                    edge ->vertexIndex[0] = i2;
                    edge ->vertexIndex[1] = i3;
                    edge ->triangleIndex[0] = a;
                    edge ->triangleIndex[1] = -1;
                    edgeCount++;
                    edge++;
            }

            if (i3 < i1)
            {
                    edge ->vertexIndex[0] = i3;
                    edge ->vertexIndex[1] = i1;
                    edge ->triangleIndex[0] = a;
                    edge ->triangleIndex[1] = -1;
                    edgeCount++;
                    edge++;
            }

            triangle++;
    }

    // Second pass: match triangles to edges
    triangle = triangleArray;
    for (long a = 0; a < triangleCount; a++)
    {
        long i1 = triangle->index[0];
        long i2 = triangle->index[1];
        long i3 = triangle->index[2];

        if (i1 > i2)
        {
            edge = *edgeArray;
            for (long b = 0; b < edgeCount; b++)
            {
                if ((edge ->vertexIndex[0] == i2) &&
                    (edge ->vertexIndex[1] == i1) &&
                    (edge ->triangleIndex[1] == -1))
                {
                    edge ->triangleIndex[1] = a;
                    break;
                }
                edge++;
            }
        }
    }
```

```
        if (i2 > i3)
        {
            edge = *edgeArray;
            for (long b = 0; b < edgeCount; b++)
            {
                if ((edge->vertexIndex[0] == i3) &&
                    (edge->vertexIndex[1] == i2) &&
                    (edge->triangleIndex[1] == −1))
                {
                    edge->triangleIndex[1] = a;
                    break;
                }
                edge++;
            }
        }

        if (i3 > i1)
        {
            edge = *edgeArray;
            for (long b = 0; b < edgeCount; b++)
            {
                if ((edge->vertexIndex[0] == i1) &&
                    (edge->vertexIndex[1] == i3) &&
                    (edge->triangleIndex[1] == −1))
                {
                    edge->triangleIndex[1] = a;
                    break;
                }
                edge++;
            }
        }

        triangle++;
    }

    return (edgeCount);
}
```

9.4.2 SHADOW RENDERING

Armed with the edge list for a triangle mesh, we determine the silhouette of a model with respect to a particular light source by first calculating the dot product of each triangle's normal vector $\mathbf{N}$ with the direction to the light source $\mathbf{D}$. For a triangle whose vertex indexes are i_1, i_2, and i_3, the (unnormalized) outward-pointing normal direction is always given by

$$\mathbf{N} = (\mathbf{V}_{i_2} - \mathbf{V}_{i_1}) \times (\mathbf{V}_{i_2} - \mathbf{V}_{i_1}) \tag{9.31}$$

since the vertices are assumed to be wound counterclockwise. The triangle is facing the light source if $\mathbf{N} \cdot \mathbf{D} > 0$ and is facing away from it otherwise.

The silhouette is determined by traversing the edge list and examining the directions in which the two triangles sharing each edge face. Any edge shared by one triangle facing toward the light source and the other triangle facing away from the light source is part of the silhouette. As the silhouette edges are identified, they are extruded away from the light source to form a quad and stored in an array to be rendered. (The order in which the quads are stored is inconsequential.) The quad must be wound counterclockwise, so we must be careful to put the vertices in the correct order. Suppose that a silhouette edge has endpoints given by the vertices $\mathbf{V}_a$ and $\mathbf{V}_b$. If the first triangle associated with the edge is facing toward the light source, then the vertices of the quad are given by

$$\mathbf{Q}_1 = \mathbf{V}_b \qquad\qquad \mathbf{Q}_2 = \mathbf{V}_a$$

$$\mathbf{Q}_3 = \mathbf{V}_a - m\mathbf{D} \quad \mathbf{Q}_4 = \mathbf{V}_b - m\mathbf{D}, \qquad\qquad (9.32)$$

where m is the length of the shadow and we are assuming that $\mathbf{D}$ has unit length. If the first triangle associated with the edge is facing *away from* the light source, then the vertices of the quad are given by

$$\mathbf{Q}_1 = \mathbf{V}_a \qquad\qquad \mathbf{Q}_2 = \mathbf{V}_b$$

$$\mathbf{Q}_3 = \mathbf{V}_b - m\mathbf{D} \quad \mathbf{Q}_4 = \mathbf{V}_a - m\mathbf{D}. \qquad\qquad (9.33)$$

The vertices $\mathbf{Q}_3$ and $\mathbf{Q}_4$ may be placed at the points where the quad intersects a plane $\mathbf{L}$ by setting

$$m_a = \frac{\mathbf{L} \cdot \mathbf{V}_a}{\mathbf{L} \cdot \mathbf{D}}$$

$$m_b = \frac{\mathbf{L} \cdot \mathbf{V}_b}{\mathbf{L} \cdot \mathbf{D}} \qquad\qquad (9.34)$$

and replacing occurrences of $\mathbf{V}_a - m\mathbf{D}$ with $\mathbf{V}_a - m_a\mathbf{D}$ and occurrences of $\mathbf{V}_b - m\mathbf{D}$ with $\mathbf{V}_b - m_b\mathbf{D}$. This can be done to prevent a shadow from extending beyond a wall or beneath the floor of a room.

9.4.3 IMPLEMENTATION

Now that we have an array of quads bounding the shadow volume of a triangle mesh, we can render the shadow itself by using stencil operations. The trick is to render the shadow volume twice, the first time rendering only front faces, and the second time rendering only back faces. On the first pass, we increment the value in the stencil buffer whenever the z-buffer test passes. On the second pass, we decrement the value in the stencil buffer whenever the z-buffer test passes. For any pixels in shadow, the z-buffer test fails on the second pass, leaving a 1 in the stencil buffer. Listing 9.3 demonstrates how to implement these operations in OpenGL.

Listing 9.3. This code shows how to program OpenGL to perform the stencil operations necessary to render shadows.

```
// Disable writes to the color buffer and z-buffer
glColorMask(GL_FALSE, GL_FALSE, GL_FALSE, GL_FALSE);
glDepthMask(GL_FALSE);

// Make sure stencil test always passes
glStencilFunc(GL_ALWAYS, 0, 255);

// Draw front faces
glCullFace(GL_BACK);
glStencilOp(GL_KEEP, GL_KEEP, GL_INCR);
glDrawArrays(...);

// Draw back faces
glCullFace(GL_FRONT);
glStencilOp(GL_KEEP, GL_KEEP, GL_DECR);
glDrawArrays(...);

// Re-enable color buffer and z-buffer writes
glColorMask(GL_TRUE, GL_TRUE, GL_TRUE, GL_TRUE);
glDepthMask(GL_TRUE);
glCullFace(GL_BACK);
```

Once we have drawn to the stencil buffer, we can darken the area where the stencil buffer values are nonzero by drawing an alpha-blended quad over the entire screen. The stencil test can be programmed in OpenGL using the following function calls.

```
glStencilOp(GL_KEEP, GL_KEEP, GL_KEEP);
glStencilFunc(GL_NOTEQUAL, 0, 255);
```

Figure 9.10 shows the result of this operation for a character whose shadow volume was determined using the technique presented in this section. Also shown are the corresponding silhouette edges of the shadow volume.

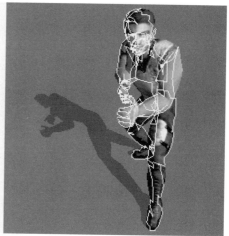

FIGURE
9.10
The shadow for this character was rendered by extruding the silhouette edges visible in the image on the right and applying the stencil operations shown in Listing 9.3.

9.5 POLYGON REDUCTION

When a model consisting of a large number of triangles is rendered far from the camera, it is likely that many of the triangles make no perceptible contribution to the resulting image. By reducing the number of rendered triangles as the distance from the camera to the model increases, we can reduce the amount of computation needed to process the mesh as well as the amount of data sent to the graphics hardware.

A common method used to reduce the number of triangles in a mesh is the edge collapse technique. This method works by locating edges within a triangle mesh whose removal would not cause a large change in the shape of the model. The process of removing an edge is called an *edge collapse* and is performed by merging the edge's two endpoints. As illustrated in Figure 9.11, one endpoint remains stationary and the other endpoint is moved to the same location as the first. Thus, there are two ways in which an edge can be collapsed, depending on which endpoint remains stationary. The two triangles sharing the collapsed edge are eliminated and any triangles using the moved vertex are stretched to fill in the space left behind. Of course, since the two endpoints now occupy the same location, the one that was moved can simply be eliminated. Thus, a single edge collapse results in the removal of two triangles, one edge, and one vertex from the mesh.

We decide which edges to collapse in a triangle mesh by calculating two *costs* for each edge. A cost is assigned to each endpoint of an edge based on how

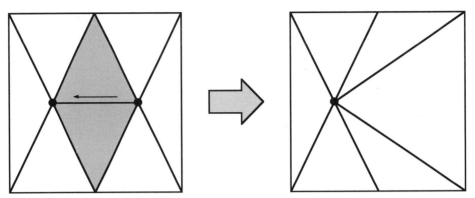

FIGURE   *An edge collapse merges the two endpoints of the edge and eliminates the triangles*
9.11   *that share the edge.*

much the appearance of the triangle mesh would be altered if the edge is collapsed by removing that endpoint. Endpoints having the lowest collapse cost determine which edges are the first to be eliminated. If it is known that an edge should definitely *not* be eliminated, then the collapse costs of its endpoints can be set to some large value to indicate this.

There are many possible ways to calculate edge collapse costs. The method presented in this section assigns costs based on a combination of the edge's length and the flatness of the triangle mesh on both sides of the edge around the endpoint being considered for elimination. Suppose that we wish to calculate the cost of eliminating the vertex $\mathbf{V}_1$ in Figure 9.12 by collapsing it into the vertex $\mathbf{V}_2$. We first calculate the normal vector $\mathbf{N}$ for the vertex $\mathbf{V}_1$ by averaging the normals of the surrounding triangles (see Chapter 6, Section 6.7.1). We then define the vector $\mathbf{D}$ to be

$$\mathbf{D} = \frac{\mathbf{N} \times \mathbf{E}}{\|\mathbf{N} \times \mathbf{E}\|}, \tag{9.35}$$

where $\mathbf{E}$ is the direction pointing from $\mathbf{V}_1$ to $\mathbf{V}_2$:

$$\mathbf{E} = \mathbf{V}_2 - \mathbf{V}_1. \tag{9.36}$$

The direction $\mathbf{D}$ is perpendicular to both the normal to the surface at $\mathbf{V}_1$ and the edge that we are considering. It will be used to determine on which side of the edge a point lies.

It should be noted that if *any* of the edges leading away from the vertex $\mathbf{V}_1$ are not shared by two triangles, then $\mathbf{V}_1$ should not be eliminated because doing so would change the shape of the triangle mesh's boundary. If $\mathbf{V}_1$ does lie in the interior of the mesh, then for each of the two triangles sharing the edge that connects $\mathbf{V}_1$ and $\mathbf{V}_2$ we examine the vertex $\mathbf{V}_3$ of the triangle that does not lie on

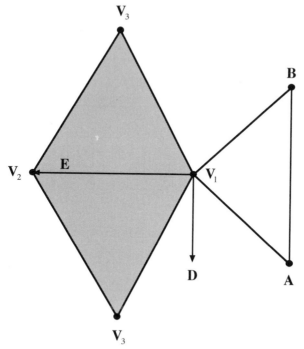

FIGURE   *Calculating the collapse cost.*
9.12

the edge to determine whether the triangle lies on the positive side or negative side of the edge. If the condition

$$\mathbf{D} \cdot (\mathbf{V}_3 - \mathbf{V}_1) \geq 0 \tag{9.37}$$

is satisfied, then the triangle lies on the positive side of the edge; otherwise, it lies on the negative side of the plane. We must have one of each, so if both triangles lie on the positive side or both triangles lie on the negative side, then the edge should not be collapsed.

Let $\mathbf{T}_{pos}$ represent the unit-length normal vector of the triangle lying on the positive side of the edge, and let $\mathbf{T}_{neg}$ represent the unit-length normal vector of the triangle lying on the negative side of the edge. We estimate the flatness of the triangle mesh on either side of the edge being considered for collapse by comparing the normal vectors $\mathbf{T}_{pos}$ and $\mathbf{T}_{neg}$ to those of the other triangles using the vertex $\mathbf{V}_1$. As we examine these triangles, we maintain a value d corresponding to the smallest dot product found between the normal of any triangle occupying space on the positive side of the edge and the vector $\mathbf{T}_{pos}$ and between the normal of any triangle occupying space on the negative side of the edge and the vector $\mathbf{T}_{neg}$. A value of d near one indicates that the mesh is mostly flat on either side of the edge, but a small value of d indicates that large angles exist between triangles sharing the vertex $\mathbf{V}_1$. If d falls below some threshold corresponding to the maximum surface roughness allowed, then the edge connecting $\mathbf{V}_1$ and $\mathbf{V}_2$ should not be collapsed. Otherwise, we assign the cost c to the edge using the formula

$$c = (1 - d)\|\mathbf{E}\|. \tag{9.38}$$

To clarify the procedure for calculating the value of d, suppose that a triangle has vertices $\mathbf{V}_1$, $\mathbf{A}$, and $\mathbf{B}$ (where neither $\mathbf{A}$ nor $\mathbf{B}$ is equal to $\mathbf{V}_2$), and has the unit-length normal vector $\mathbf{T}$. We classify the vertices $\mathbf{A}$ and $\mathbf{B}$ as lying on the positive side of the edge, on the negative side of the edge, or on the edge itself by examining the dot products

$$a = \mathbf{D} \cdot (\mathbf{A} - \mathbf{V}_1)$$
$$b = \mathbf{D} \cdot (\mathbf{B} - \mathbf{V}_1). \tag{9.39}$$

The quantities a and b represent the distances from the plane containing the edge and having normal vector $\mathbf{D}$ to the points $\mathbf{A}$ and $\mathbf{B}$. If $a > \varepsilon$ or $b > \varepsilon$ for some small distance ε, then we consider the corresponding points to lie on the positive side of the edge. Similarly, if $a < -\varepsilon$ or $b < -\varepsilon$, then we consider the corresponding point to lie on the negative side of the edge. Points lying within the distance ε of the edge are considered to be lying on the edge itself. If either $\mathbf{A}$ or $\mathbf{B}$ lies on the positive side of the edge, then we replace the minimum dot product d with the dot product $\mathbf{T} \cdot \mathbf{T}_{pos}$ if it is smaller:

$$d \leftarrow \min\{d, \mathbf{T} \cdot \mathbf{T}_{pos}\}. \tag{9.40}$$

If either $\mathbf{A}$ or $\mathbf{B}$ lies on the negative side of the edge, then we replace d with the dot product $\mathbf{T} \cdot \mathbf{T}_{neg}$ if it is smaller:

$$d \leftarrow \min\{d, \mathbf{T} \cdot \mathbf{T}_{neg}\}. \tag{9.41}$$

It is possible that both of the operations given by Equations (9.40) and (9.41) may be performed for a single triangle.

The edge collapse cost calculation presented in this section allows the collapse of an edge such as that shown in Figure 9.13. As long as the triangle mesh is reasonably flat on both sides of the edge, a collapse may occur along an edge between two triangles having largely differing orientations.

Figure 9.14 shows the original triangle mesh for a character model and the same model after 30% of its triangles have been eliminated using the edge collapse technique. Notice how edges in regions of high triangle concentration and regions of relative flatness were the first edges chosen to be removed.

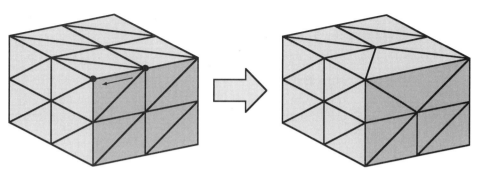

FIGURE
9.13 *The edge collapse cost calculation allows the collapse of an edge between two triangles having largely differing orientations as long as the triangle mesh is reasonably flat on both sides of the edge.*

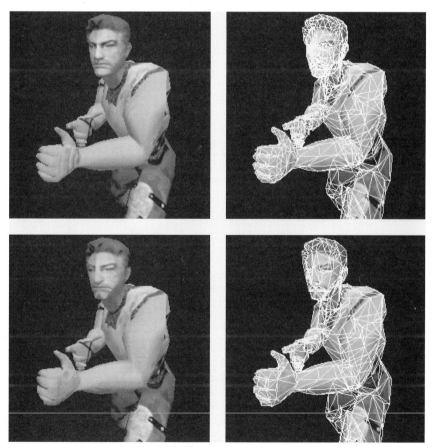

FIGURE
9.14 *The top pair of images shows a character model and the wire frame of its triangle mesh. The bottom pair of images shows the same model after 30% of its triangles have been eliminated.*

CHAPTER 9 SUMMARY

Depth Value Offset

To offset the depth of a vertex whose z-coordinate is roughly P_z by a distance δ, the (3, 3) entry of the perspective projection matrix should be multiplied by $1 + \varepsilon$, where

$$\varepsilon = -\frac{2fn}{f + n}\left(\frac{\delta}{P_z(P_z + \delta)}\right).$$

Decal Application

A decal of width w and height h centered at the point $\mathbf{P}$, having normal direction $\mathbf{N}$ and tangent direction $\mathbf{T}$, should be clipped to the planes

$$left = \left(\mathbf{T}, \frac{w}{2} - \mathbf{T} \cdot \mathbf{P}\right) \quad right = \left(-\mathbf{T}, \frac{w}{2} + \mathbf{T} \cdot \mathbf{P}\right)$$

$$bottom = \left(\mathbf{B}, \frac{h}{2} - \mathbf{B} \cdot \mathbf{P}\right) \quad top = \left(-\mathbf{B}, \frac{h}{2} + \mathbf{B} \cdot \mathbf{P}\right)$$

$$front = \left(-\mathbf{N}, d + \mathbf{N} \cdot \mathbf{P}\right) \quad back = \left(\mathbf{N}, d - \mathbf{N} \cdot \mathbf{P}\right),$$

where $\mathbf{B} = \mathbf{N} \times \mathbf{T}$ and d is the maximum distance that any vertex in the decal may be from the tangent plane passing through the point $\mathbf{P}$. The texture coordinates for a decal vertex $\mathbf{Q}$ are given by

$$s = \frac{\mathbf{T} \cdot (\mathbf{Q} - \mathbf{P})}{w} + \frac{1}{2}$$

$$t = \frac{\mathbf{B} \cdot (\mathbf{Q} - \mathbf{P})}{h} + \frac{1}{2}.$$

Billboarding

The vertices of an unconstrained billboarded quad of width w, height h, and orientation θ centered at the point $\mathbf{P}$ may be calculated using

$$\mathbf{Q}_1 = \mathbf{P} + \mathbf{X} + \mathbf{Y} \quad \mathbf{Q}_2 = \mathbf{P} - \mathbf{X} + \mathbf{Y}$$

$$\mathbf{Q}_3 = \mathbf{P} - \mathbf{X} - \mathbf{Y} \quad \mathbf{Q}_4 = \mathbf{P} + \mathbf{X} - \mathbf{Y},$$

where

$$\mathbf{X} = \left(\frac{w}{2}\cos\theta\right)\mathbf{R} + \left(\frac{w}{2}\sin\theta\right)\mathbf{U}$$

$$\mathbf{Y} = \left(-\frac{h}{2}\sin\theta\right)\mathbf{R} + \left(\frac{h}{2}\cos\theta\right)\mathbf{U}$$

and the directions $\mathbf{R}$ and $\mathbf{U}$ are the world space right and up directions of the camera view. The vertices of a billboarded quad constrained to rotate only about the z-axis are given by

$$\mathbf{Q}_1 = \mathbf{P} + \frac{\mathbf{X}}{\|\mathbf{X}\|} + \left\langle 0, 0, \frac{h}{2}\right\rangle \quad \mathbf{Q}_2 = \mathbf{P} - \frac{\mathbf{X}}{\|\mathbf{X}\|} + \left\langle 0, 0, \frac{h}{2}\right\rangle$$

$$\mathbf{Q}_3 = \mathbf{P} - \frac{\mathbf{X}}{\|\mathbf{X}\|} - \left\langle 0, 0, \frac{h}{2}\right\rangle \quad \mathbf{Q}_4 = \mathbf{P} + \frac{\mathbf{X}}{\|\mathbf{X}\|} - \left\langle 0, 0, \frac{h}{2}\right\rangle,$$

where

$$\mathbf{X} = \frac{w}{2}\left\langle -\left(C_y - P_y\right), C_x - P_x, 0\right\rangle,$$

and $\mathbf{C}$ is the world-space camera position.

EXERCISES FOR CHAPTER 9

1. Suppose that the distance to the near plane is $n = 1$ and the distance to the far plane is $f = 100$ for a particular view frustum. Calculate by what value the (3, 3) entry of the projection matrix should be multiplied in order to offset a model centered at a depth of $z = -20$ toward the camera by a distance of 0.2.

2. Calculate the least distance d by which the model in exercise 1 can be offset toward the camera if a 16-bit z-buffer is used.

3. Write a program that applies a decal to a surface. Assume that the decal is described by its center $\mathbf{P}$, a normal direction $\mathbf{N}$, a tangent direction $\mathbf{T}$, its width w, and its height h. The program should construct a decal object by clipping an arbitrary triangle mesh to the planes bounding the decal and should then calculate texture coordinates for each vertex in the decal object.

4. Implement a particle system for which each particle is rendered as a square, textured quad centered at the particle's position. Each particle should be described by its position $\mathbf{P}$ in space, its velocity $\mathbf{V}$, its radius r (equal to both its width and height), and its orientation θ.

5. Write a program that renders a stencil shadow for a triangle mesh illuminated by a single light source. Assume that the triangle mesh is specified such that each of n triangles indexes three entries in an array of m vertices. The program should precalculate an edge list, determine the edges belonging to the model's silhouette with respect to the light source, and render the extruded silhouette edges using the stencil buffer operations shown in Listing 9.3.

CHAPTER

10

Linear Physics

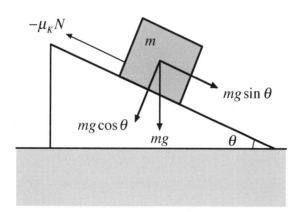

imulating the accurate motion and interaction of dynamic objects adds a pervasive feeling of realism to a game and can usually be achieved without overly complex mathematics. This chapter and the next discuss several general topics in classical mechanics that apply to game programming. We begin with an examination of linear motion, which refers to any motion that is not taking place in a rotating environment.

10.1 POSITION FUNCTIONS

A *position function* provides the 3D position of an object as a function of time. Time is usually measured relative to some starting point when the position of an object is known. For instance, suppose that an object is traveling in a straight line with a constant velocity $\mathbf{v}_0$. If the position of the object at time $t = 0$ is known to be $\mathbf{x}_0$, then its position $\mathbf{x}(t)$ at any time afterward is given by

$$\mathbf{x}(t) = \mathbf{x}_0 + \mathbf{v}_0 t. \tag{10.1}$$

A *velocity function* describes the 3D velocity of an object as a function of time. The velocity function $\mathbf{v}(t)$ of an object is given by the derivative of the position function with respect to time. The time derivative is commonly denoted by placing a dot above the function being differentiated:

$$\mathbf{v}(t) = \dot{\mathbf{x}}(t) = \frac{d}{dt}\mathbf{x}(t). \tag{10.2}$$

Since the velocity of the object whose position is given by Equation (10.1) is constant, its velocity function $\mathbf{v}(t)$ is simply given by

$$\mathbf{v}(t) = \mathbf{v}_0. \tag{10.3}$$

An object undergoing a constant acceleration $\mathbf{a}_0$ has the velocity function

$$\mathbf{v}(t) = \mathbf{v}_0 + \mathbf{a}_0 t. \tag{10.4}$$

The *acceleration function* $\mathbf{a}(t)$ of an object, which describes the object's 3D acceleration as a function of time, is given by the derivative of the velocity function:

$$\mathbf{a}(t) = \dot{\mathbf{v}}(t) = \ddot{\mathbf{x}}(t) = \frac{d^2}{dt^2}\mathbf{x}(t). \tag{10.5}$$

We can integrate any velocity function to determine the distance d that an object has traveled between times t_1 and t_2 as follows.

$$d = \int_{t_1}^{t_2} \mathbf{v}(t)\,dt \tag{10.6}$$

Integrating Equation (10.4) from time zero to time t, we have

$$d = \int_0^t \left(\mathbf{v}_0 + \mathbf{a}_0 t\right) dt$$

$$= \mathbf{v}_0 t + \tfrac{1}{2}\mathbf{a}_0 t^2. \tag{10.7}$$

Adding the distance d to an initial position $\mathbf{x}_0$, the position function $\mathbf{x}(t)$ of a uniformly accelerating object is given by

$$\mathbf{x}(t) = \mathbf{x}_0 + \mathbf{v}_0 t + \tfrac{1}{2}\mathbf{a}_0 t^2. \tag{10.8}$$

It is often the case that we are aware of the forces acting on an object and we want to find a function that predicts the future position of the object. The sum of the forces $\mathbf{F}_1, \mathbf{F}_2, \ldots, \mathbf{F}_N$ acting on an object is equal to the object's mass m times its acceleration $\mathbf{a}(t)$:

$$\sum_{i=1}^N \mathbf{F}_i(t) = m\mathbf{a}(t) = m\ddot{\mathbf{x}}(t). \tag{10.9}$$

Each force $\mathbf{F}_i(t)$ may be a constant, a function of the object's position, or a function of the object's velocity. Equation (10.9) is a second-order differential equation whose solution $\mathbf{x}(t)$ is the object's position function. The next section reviews the general solutions to second-order differential equations, and solutions to specific force equations are discussed at various places throughout this chapter and the next.

10.2 Second-Order Differential Equations

A second-order linear ordinary differential equation in the function $x(t)$ is one of the following form.

$$\frac{d^2}{dt^2}x(t) + a\frac{d}{dt}x(t) + bx(t) = f(t) \tag{10.10}$$

Using prime symbols to denote derivatives, we can write this in a slightly more compact form as

$$x''(t) + ax'(t) + bx(t) = f(t). \tag{10.11}$$

In this chapter, a and b are always constants, but in general they may be functions of t.

10.2.1 HOMOGENEOUS EQUATIONS

The function $f(t)$ is identically zero in many situations, in which case the differential equation is called *homogeneous*. Before attempting to find a solution $x(t)$ to the equation

$$x''(t) + ax'(t) + bx(t) = 0, \tag{10.12}$$

we make a couple of important observations. First, suppose that the functions $x_1(t)$ and $x_2(t)$ are solutions to Equation (10.12). Then the functions $Ax_1(t)$ and $Bx_2(t)$ are also solutions, where A and B are arbitrary constants. Furthermore, the function $Ax_1(t) + Bx_2(t)$ is also a solution to Equation (10.12) since we can write

$$Ax_1''(t) + Bx_2''(t) + a\left[Ax_1'(t) + Bx_2'(t)\right] + b\left[Ax_1(t) + Bx_2(t)\right]$$

$$= A\left[x_1''(t) + ax_1'(t) + bx_1(t)\right] + B\left[x_2''(t) + ax_2'(t) + bx_2(t)\right]$$

$$= A \cdot 0 + B \cdot 0 = 0. \tag{10.13}$$

A general solution $x(t)$ to Equation (10.12) becomes evident on making the substitution

$$x(t) = e^{rt}. \tag{10.14}$$

The first and second derivatives of $x(t)$ are given by

$$x'(t) = re^{rt}$$

$$x''(t) = r^2 e^{rt}, \tag{10.15}$$

and substitution into Equation (10.12) yields

$$r^2 e^{rt} + are^{rt} + be^{rt} = 0. \tag{10.16}$$

Multiplying both sides by e^{-rt} eliminates the exponentials and we have

$$r^2 + ar + b = 0. \tag{10.17}$$

Equation (10.17) is called the *auxiliary equation* and has the solutions

$$r_1 = -\frac{a}{2} + \frac{1}{2}\sqrt{a^2 - 4b}$$

$$r_2 = -\frac{a}{2} - \frac{1}{2}\sqrt{a^2 - 4b}. \tag{10.18}$$

Unless $r_1 = r_2$, the general solution to Equation (10.12) is thus given by

$$x(t) = Ae^{r_1 t} + Be^{r_2 t}. \tag{10.19}$$

Example 10.1. Solve the differential equation

$$x''(t) + 5x'(t) + 6x(t) = 0. \tag{10.20}$$

Solution. The auxiliary equation is

$$r^2 - 5r + 6 = 0, \tag{10.21}$$

which has the solutions $r_1 = 2$ and $r_2 = 3$. The general solution to Equation (10.20) is therefore given by

$$x(t) = Ae^{2t} + Be^{3t}, \tag{10.22}$$

where A and B are arbitrary constants.

If $r_1 = r_2$, then it must be true that $a^2 = 4b$, so Equation (10.12) can be written as

$$x''(t) + ax'(t) + \frac{a^2}{4} x(t) = 0. \tag{10.23}$$

It is a simple task to verify that the function

$$x(t) = te^{-(a/2)t} \tag{10.24}$$

is a solution to Equation (10.23), so the general solution to Equation (10.12) when $r_1 = r_2$ is given by

$$x(t) = Ae^{rt} + Bte^{rt}, \tag{10.25}$$

where we have set $r = r_1 = r_2$.

If $a^2 - 4b < 0$, then the roots of the auxiliary equation are complex. The solution given by Equation (10.19) is still correct, but it requires the use of complex arithmetic. We can express the solution entirely in terms of real-valued functions by using the formula

$$e^{\alpha+\beta i} = e^{\alpha}(\cos \beta + i \sin \beta) \tag{10.26}$$

(see Appendix A, Section A.4). Assuming that a and b are real numbers, the roots r_1 and r_2 of the auxiliary equation are complex conjugates, so we may write

$$r_1 = \alpha + \beta i$$
$$r_2 = \alpha - \beta i, \tag{10.27}$$

where

$$\alpha = -\frac{a}{2}$$

$$\beta = \frac{1}{2}\sqrt{4b - a^2}. \tag{10.28}$$

The solution given by Equation (10.19) can now be written as

$$x(t) = Ae^{(\alpha+\beta i)t} + Be^{(\alpha-\beta i)t}$$

$$= Ae^{\alpha t}(\cos \beta t + i \sin \beta t) + be^{\alpha t}(\cos \beta t - i \sin \beta t)$$

$$= e^{\alpha t}[(A + B)\cos \beta t + (A - B)i \sin \beta t]. \tag{10.29}$$

This solution can be expressed using two real constants C_1 and C_2 by setting

$$A = \tfrac{1}{2}(C_1 + C_2 i)$$

$$B = \tfrac{1}{2}(C_1 - C_2 i). \tag{10.30}$$

Plugging these values into Equation (10.29) yields

$$x(t) = e^{\alpha t}(C_1 \cos \beta t + C_2 \sin \beta t). \tag{10.31}$$

Example 10.2. Solve the differential equation

$$x''(t) + 4x(t) = 0. \tag{10.32}$$

Solution. The auxiliary equation is

$$r^2 + 4 = 0, \tag{10.33}$$

which has the solutions $r_1 = 2i$ and $r_2 = -2i$. The solution to Equation (10.32) given by

$$x(t) = Ae^{2it} + Be^{-2it} \tag{10.34}$$

is valid, but we can also express the solution entirely in terms of real-valued functions by using Equation (10.31) with $\alpha = 0$ and $\beta = 2$ as

$$x(t) = C_1 \cos 2t + C_2 \sin 2t, \tag{10.35}$$

where C_1 and C_2 are arbitrary constants.

Equation (10.31) can be transformed into an alternate solution involving only a single trigonometric function by introducing the constant $D = \sqrt{C_1^2 + C_2^2}$ and writing

$$x(t) = De^{\alpha t}\left(\frac{C_1}{D}\cos \beta t + \frac{C_2}{D}\sin \beta t\right). \tag{10.36}$$

Suppose that C_1 and C_2 are the lengths of the legs of a right triangle and that δ is the angle opposite the side of length C_1 (see Figure 10.1). Then D is the length of the hypotenuse, so

$$\frac{C_1}{D} = \sin \delta$$

$$\frac{C_2}{D} = \cos \delta. \tag{10.37}$$

Plugging these into Equation (10.36) yields

$$x(t) = D \cos \beta t \sin \delta + D \sin \beta t \cos \delta. \tag{10.38}$$

Using an angle sum identity (see Appendix B, Section B.4), this is equivalent to

$$x(t) = D \sin(\beta t + \delta). \tag{10.39}$$

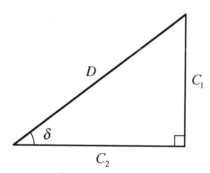

FIGURE   *In this triangle, sin δ = C_1/D and cos δ = C_2/D. This enables us to write Equation (10.36)*
10.1   *in the form given by Equation (10.39).*

10.2.2 NONHOMOGENEOUS EQUATIONS

Differential equations of the form

$$x''(t) + ax'(t) + bx(t) = f(t), \tag{10.40}$$

for which the function $f(t)$ is not identically zero, are called *nonhomogeneous*. The solution to a nonhomogeneous differential equation has the form

$$x(t) = g(t) + p(t), \tag{10.41}$$

where the function $g(t)$ is the general solution to the corresponding homogeneous equation

$$x''(t) + ax'(t) + bx(t) = 0. \tag{10.42}$$

The function $p(t)$ is called a *particular solution* to the nonhomogeneous equation and satisfies

$$p''(t) + ap'(t) + bp(t) = f(t). \tag{10.43}$$

To see that $g(t) + p(t)$ is in fact a solution to Equation (10.40), we simply plug it in:

$$g''(t) + p''(t) + a[g'(t) + p'(t)] + b[g(t) + p(t)]$$
$$= g''(t) + ag'(t) + bg(t) + p''(t) + ap'(t) + bp(t)$$
$$= 0 + f(t) = f(t). \tag{10.44}$$

There are several methods for finding the particular solution to a nonhomogeneous differential equation. The method that we present in this section is called the method of *undetermined coefficients* and is sufficient for the nonhomogeneous equations encountered later in this chapter. The general idea on which the method of undetermined coefficients is based is to guess at the form of the particular solution $p(t)$ using the knowledge that we possess about the form of the function $f(t)$. It is usually effective to choose $p(t)$ to be a sum of terms that have the same form as $f(t)$ or whose derivatives have the same form as $f(t)$. Each term is multiplied by an unknown coefficient for which we attempt to find a solution by plugging $p(t)$ into the nonhomogeneous equation. If coefficients can be determined for which $p(t)$ satisfies Equation (10.40), then a particular solution has been found. The following examples illustrate this technique in detail.

Example 10.3. Solve the differential equation

$$x''(t) + 5x'(t) + 6x(t) = 12t - 4. \tag{10.45}$$

Solution. We have already found the general solution $g(t)$ to the homogeneous equation in Example 10.1:

$$g(t) = Ae^{2t} + Be^{3t}. \tag{10.46}$$

The nonhomogeneous portion of Equation (10.45) is a linear polynomial, so we presume that the particular solution has the form

$$p(t) = Dt^2 + Et + F, \tag{10.47}$$

where the coefficients D, E, and F need to be determined. Plugging $p(t)$ into Equation (10.45) produces

$$12t - 4 = 2D + 5(2Dt + E) + 6(Dt^2 + Et + F)$$
$$= 6Dt^2 + (10D + 6E)t + 2D + 5E + 6F. \tag{10.48}$$

Equating the coefficients of like terms from each side, we find that

$$D = 0, \ E = 2, \ \text{and} \ F = -1. \tag{10.49}$$

Thus, the function $p(t) = 2t - 1$ is a particular solution to Equation (10.45). The complete solution is given by

$$x(t) = g(t) + p(t)$$
$$= Ae^{2t} + Be^{3t} + 2t - 1, \tag{10.50}$$

where A and B are arbitrary constants.

Example 10.4. Solve the differential equation

$$x''(t) + 4x(t) = 12 \ \sin \ t. \tag{10.51}$$

Solution. We have already found the general solution $g(t)$ to the homogeneous equation in Example 10.2:

$$g(t) = A \ \cos \ 2t + B \ \sin \ 2t. \tag{10.52}$$

Equivalently, we could write $g(t)$ in the form

$$g(t) = C \ \sin(2t + \delta). \tag{10.53}$$

Since the nonhomogeneous portion of Equation (10.51) is a sine function, we presume that the particular solution has the form

$$p(t) = D \ \sin \ t + E \ \cos \ t, \tag{10.54}$$

where the coefficients D and E need to be determined. Plugging $p(t)$ into Equation (10.51) produces

$$12 \ \sin \ t = -D \ \sin \ t - E \ \cos \ t + 4(D \ \sin \ t + E \ \cos \ t)$$
$$= 3D \ \sin \ t + 3E \ \cos \ t. \tag{10.55}$$

Equating the coefficients of the sine and cosine terms from each side, we find that

$$D = 4 \ \text{and} \ E = 0. \tag{10.56}$$

Thus, the function $p(t) = 4 \ \sin \ t$ is a particular solution to Equation (10.51). The complete solution is given by

$$x(t) = A \ \cos \ 2t + B \ \sin \ 2t + 4 \ \sin \ t \tag{10.57}$$

or, equivalently,

$$x(t) = C \ \sin(2t + \delta) + 4 \ \sin \ t, \tag{10.58}$$

where A, B, C, and δ are arbitrary constants.

10.2.3 INITIAL CONDITIONS

In every solution to a second-order differential equation presented so far, there have been two arbitrary constants. These constants allow for the specification of certain *initial conditions* that dictate the values of $x(t)$ and $x'(t)$ when $t = 0$. Suppose that the initial value of $x(t)$ is required to be x_0 and the initial value of $x'(t)$ is required to be v_0. Then the arbitrary constants appearing in the function $x(t)$ can be determined by examining the following system of equations.

$$x(0) = x_0$$
$$x'(0) = v_0 \tag{10.59}$$

This is demonstrated in the following examples.

Example 10.5. Solve the differential equation

$$x''(t) + 5x'(t) + 6x(t) = 0 \tag{10.60}$$

subject to the initial conditions

$$x(0) = 3$$
$$x'(0) = 0. \tag{10.61}$$

Solution. The general solution to the differential equation has already been found in Example 10.1:

$$x(t) = Ae^{2t} + Be^{3t}. \tag{10.62}$$

The derivative of $x(t)$ is given by

$$x'(t) = 2Ae^{2t} + 3Be^{3t}. \tag{10.63}$$

Imposing the initial conditions given by Equation (10.61), we have

$$x(0) = A + B = 3$$
$$x'(0) = 2A + 3B = 0. \tag{10.64}$$

Solving this linear system yields

$$A = 9 \text{ and } B = -6. \tag{10.65}$$

Thus, the solution to the differential equation that satisfies the initial conditions is given by

$$x(t) = 9e^{2t} - 6e^{3t}. \tag{10.66}$$

Example 10.6. Solve the differential equation

$$x''(t) + 4x(t) = 12 \sin t \tag{10.67}$$

subject to the initial conditions

$$x(0) = 0$$
$$x'(0) = 6. \tag{10.68}$$

Solution. The general solution to the differential equation has already been found in Example 10.4:

$$x(t) = A \cos 2t + B \sin 2t + 4 \sin t. \tag{10.69}$$

The derivative of $x(t)$ is given by

$$x'(t) = -2A \sin 2t + 2B \cos 2t + 4 \cos t. \tag{10.70}$$

Imposing the initial conditions given by Equation (10.68), we have

$$x(0) = A = 0$$
$$x'(0) = 2B + 4 = 6, \tag{10.71}$$

from which we immediately deduce that $B = 1$. Thus, the solution to the differential equation that satisfies the initial conditions is given by the simplified function

$$x(t) = \sin 2t + 4 \sin t. \tag{10.72}$$

10.3 PROJECTILE MOTION

In this section, we examine the motion of objects that are influenced only by the force of gravity. The convention used in this chapter is that the z-axis points upward in world space, so the downward acceleration of gravity $\mathbf{g}$ is the vector

$$\mathbf{g} = \langle 0, 0, -g \rangle, \tag{10.73}$$

where the scalar g is approximately 9.8 m/s^2 on the surface of the earth. An object in a gravitational field experiences a downward force of $m\mathbf{g}$.

The position $\mathbf{x}(t)$ of a projectile having initial position $\mathbf{x}_0$ and initial velocity $\mathbf{v}_0$ at time $t = 0$ is given by

$$\mathbf{x}(t) = \mathbf{x}_0 + \mathbf{v}_0 t + \tfrac{1}{2}\, \mathbf{g} t^2. \tag{10.74}$$

Since the x- and y-components of $\mathbf{g}$ are zero, only the z-component of Equation (10.74) is quadratic. Using $x(t)$, $y(t)$, and $z(t)$ to represent the components of $\mathbf{x}(t)$, we have

$$x(t) = x_0 + v_x t$$

$$y(t) = y_0 + v_y t$$

$$z(t) = z_0 + v_z t - \tfrac{1}{2} g t^2, \tag{10.75}$$

where x_0, y_0, and z_0 are the components of the initial position and v_x, v_y, and v_z are the components of the initial velocity.

When a projectile attains its maximum height, its vertical velocity is zero. We can determine the time t at which this occurs by solving the equation

$$\dot{z}(t) = v_z - gt = 0. \tag{10.76}$$

Thus, a projectile reaches its maximum height at time

$$t = \frac{v_z}{g}. \tag{10.77}$$

Plugging this time into the function $z(t)$ gives us the following expression for the maximum height h attained by a projectile.

$$h = z_0 + \frac{v_z^2}{2g} \tag{10.78}$$

Example 10.7. A projectile is launched from a platform 10 meters above the ground with an initial speed of 50 m/s in a direction forming an angle of 70 degrees with the horizontal plane (see Figure 10.2). What is the maximum height above the ground attained by the projectile?

Solution. The projectile's initial height z_0 and initial upward velocity v_z are given by

$$z_0 = 10 \text{ m}$$

$$v_z = 50 \sin 70° \approx 47.0 \text{ m/s}. \tag{10.79}$$

Plugging these values into Equation (10.78) and using the value 9.8 m/s^2 for g, we have $h \approx 123$ m.

The horizontal distance that a projectile travels before returning to the height from which it was launched is called the projectile's range. If a projectile is launched from a horizontal plane at $z_0 = 0$, then the time t at which it lands is given by the solution to the equation

$$v_z t - \tfrac{1}{2} g t^2 = 0. \tag{10.80}$$

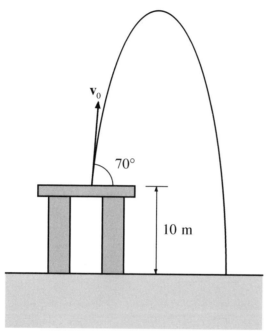

FIGURE *The path of the projectile used in Example 10.7.*
10.2

One solution to this equation is $t = 0$, corresponding to the time when the projectile was launched. The other solution is

$$t = \frac{2v_z}{g},$$ (10.81)

and as we would expect, this is twice as long as it takes for the projectile to reach its maximum height. If we assume that the projectile follows a path lying in the x-z plane, then plugging this time into the function $x(t)$ and subtracting the initial x-coordinate x_0 gives us the following expression for the range r of a projectile.

$$r = \frac{2v_x v_y}{g}$$ (10.82)

Example 10.8. A projectile is launched with an initial speed of 30 m/s in a direction forming an angle of 40 degrees with the ground (see Figure 10.3). Assuming the ground is flat down range, how far does the projectile travel before landing?

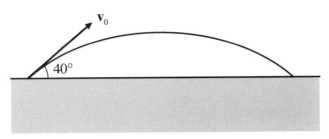

FIGURE   *The path of the projectile used in Example 10.8.*
10.3

Solution. We assume that the projectile is launched from the origin and that the path of the projectile lies in the x-z plane. The v_x and v_z components of the initial velocity are given by

$$v_x = 30 \ \cos \ 40° \approx 23.0 \ \text{m/s}$$

$$v_z = 30 \ \sin \ 40° \approx 19.3 \ \text{m/s}. \tag{10.83}$$

Plugging these values into Equation (10.82) and using the value 9.8 m/s^2 for g, the range of the projectile is 90.4 meters.

Given an initial speed s at which a projectile is launched, we can determine at which angle the initial velocity vector should point in order for the projectile to reach a particular maximum height or to have a particular range. For motion in the x-z plane, the components of the initial velocity are given by

$$v_x = s \ \cos \ \alpha$$

$$v_z = s \ \sin \ \alpha, \tag{10.84}$$

where α is the angle formed between the initial trajectory and the horizontal plane. Given a desired maximum height h, we can plug the value of v_z into Equation (10.78) and solve for α to obtain

$$\alpha = \sin^{-1}\left(\frac{1}{s} \ \sqrt{2g(h - z_0)}\right). \tag{10.85}$$

Given a desired range r, we can plug the values of v_x and v_z into Equation (10.82) as follows.

$$r = \frac{2s^2}{g} \sin \alpha \cos \alpha = \frac{s^2}{g} \sin 2\alpha \tag{10.86}$$

Solving for α gives us

$$\alpha = \frac{1}{2} \sin^{-1} \frac{rg}{s^2}. \tag{10.87}$$

Since $\sin(\pi - \alpha) = \sin \alpha$, there are two angles that produce the range r in Equation (10.86): the angle α given by Equation (10.87) and its complementary angle $\pi/2 - \alpha$. If the values inside the inverse sine functions in Equations (10.85) and (10.87) are greater than one, then the initial speed s is not great enough to achieve the desired maximum height or range.

Example 10.9. A projectile is launched from the ground with an initial speed of 65 m/s (see Figure 10.4). Assuming that the ground is flat, at what angle α should the projectile be launched so that it lands 400 meters down range?

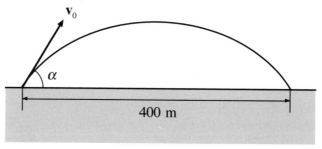

FIGURE *The angle of the projectile used in Example 10.9.*
10.4

Solution. Plugging the values $s = 65$ and $r = 400$ into Equation (10.87), we have $\alpha \approx 34°$. The complementary angle $\beta = 56°$ would also result in the projectile traveling a distance of 400 m. If we use the angle α, then the initial velocity is given by

$$v_x = 65 \cos 34° \approx 53.9 \text{ m/s}$$
$$v_z = 65 \sin 34° \approx 36.3 \text{ m/s}. \tag{10.88}$$

10.4 RESISTED MOTION

In the previous section, we neglected any kind of resistance to the motion of an object. In reality, an object's velocity is slowed by the medium through which it is moving, whether it be air, water, or some other substance. A precise physical formulation of resisted motion is complicated, but a decent approximation is achieved by assuming that resistance produces a force that acts in the direction opposite that in which an object is moving and is proportional to the magnitude of the object's velocity.

The force equation for an object of mass m influenced by gravity and experiencing resistance from the surrounding medium is given by

$$m\mathbf{g} - mk\dot{\mathbf{x}}(t) = m\ddot{\mathbf{x}}(t),$$ (10.89)

where mk is a constant describing the strength of the resistance. This can be rewritten as the following second-order nonhomogeneous differential equation.

$$\ddot{\mathbf{x}}(t) + k\dot{\mathbf{x}}(t) = \mathbf{g}$$ (10.90)

The method of undetermined coefficients provides the following particular solution to Equation (10.90).

$$\mathbf{x}(t) = \frac{\mathbf{g}}{k}t$$ (10.91)

Adding the general solution to the homogeneous differential equation, we have

$$\mathbf{x}(t) = \mathbf{A} + \mathbf{B}e^{-kt} + \frac{\mathbf{g}}{k}t,$$ (10.92)

where the vectors $\mathbf{A}$ and $\mathbf{B}$ are arbitrary constants that can be determined by establishing initial conditions. Specifying the initial position $\mathbf{x}_0$ and initial velocity $\mathbf{v}_0$, we have

$$\mathbf{x}(0) = \mathbf{x}_0$$

$$\dot{\mathbf{x}}(0) = \mathbf{v}_0.$$ (10.93)

Setting these equal to the values given by the functions $\mathbf{x}(t)$ and $\dot{\mathbf{x}}(t)$ at time $t = 0$ gives us the system

$$\mathbf{A} + \mathbf{B} = \mathbf{x}_0$$

$$-k\mathbf{B} + \frac{\mathbf{g}}{k} = \mathbf{v}_0,$$ (10.94)

from which we can derive the following expressions for $\mathbf{A}$ and $\mathbf{B}$.

$$\mathbf{A} = \mathbf{x}_0 - \frac{\mathbf{g}}{k^2} + \frac{\mathbf{v}_0}{k}$$

$$\mathbf{B} = \frac{\mathbf{g}}{k^2} - \frac{\mathbf{v}_0}{k}$$ (10.95)

The position function $\mathbf{x}(t)$ for an object moving through a resistive medium is given by

$$\mathbf{x}(t) = \mathbf{x}_0 + \frac{\mathbf{g}}{k}t + \frac{k\mathbf{v}_0 - \mathbf{g}}{k^2}\left(1 - e^{-kt}\right).$$ (10.96)

The velocity function $\mathbf{v}(t)$ is given by the derivative of $\mathbf{x}(t)$:

$$\mathbf{v}(t) = \dot{\mathbf{x}}(t) = \frac{\mathbf{g}}{k} + \left(\mathbf{v}_0 - \frac{\mathbf{g}}{k} \right) e^{-kt}. \tag{10.97}$$

Over time, the velocity of an object whose motion is being resisted approaches a constant called the *terminal velocity*. The terminal velocity $\mathbf{v}_T$ is given by the limit of the velocity function $\mathbf{v}(t)$ as t tends to infinity:

$$\mathbf{v}_T = \lim_{t \to \infty} \mathbf{v}(t) = \frac{\mathbf{g}}{k}. \tag{10.98}$$

Although it is not apparent from Equation (10.96), the position function for an object moving through a resistive medium does converge to the familiar Equation (10.74) as the constant k approaches zero. This can be seen by evaluating the limit

$$\mathbf{x}(t) = \lim_{k \to 0} \left[\mathbf{x}_0 + \frac{\mathbf{g}}{k}t + \frac{k\mathbf{v}_0 - \mathbf{g}}{k^2} \left(1 - e^{-kt} \right) \right]. \tag{10.99}$$

Replacing the exponential function with its power series (see Appendix D, Equation (D.11)), we have

$$\mathbf{x}(t) = \lim_{k \to 0} \left[\mathbf{x}_0 + \frac{\mathbf{g}}{k}t + \frac{k\mathbf{v}_0 - \mathbf{g}}{k^2} \left(kt - \frac{k^2 t^2}{2!} + \frac{k^3 t^3}{3!} - \frac{k^4 t^4}{4!} + - \cdots \right) \right]$$

$$= \lim_{k \to 0} \left[\mathbf{x}_0 + \frac{\mathbf{g}}{k}t + \left(k\mathbf{v}_0 - \mathbf{g} \right) \left(\frac{t}{k} - \frac{t^2}{2!} + \frac{kt^3}{3!} - \frac{k^2 t^4}{4!} + - \cdots \right) \right]$$

$$= \lim_{k \to 0} \left[\mathbf{x}_0 + \mathbf{v}_0 t - \tfrac{1}{2}k\mathbf{v}_0 t^2 + \tfrac{1}{2}\mathbf{g}t^2 + \left(k\mathbf{v}_0 - \mathbf{g} \right) \left(\frac{kt^3}{3!} - \frac{k^2 t^4}{4!} + - \cdots \right) \right]$$

$$= \mathbf{x}_0 + \mathbf{v}_0 t + \tfrac{1}{2}\mathbf{g}t^2. \tag{10.100}$$

10.5 FRICTION

Friction is the well-known force that arises when two surfaces come in contact. We discuss two types of friction in this section: kinetic friction and static friction. Kinetic friction occurs between two surfaces that are in motion relative to each other and has the effect of resisting that motion. Static friction refers to the force that holds a stationary object in place when it is in contact with another surface.

The forces resisting the motion of one object sliding across the surface of another object are very complex, but it turns out that the net kinetic frictional force F_K can usually be approximated quite accurately using the simple formula

$$F_K = -\mu_K N, \tag{10.101}$$

where N is the normal component of the force by which the object is bound to the surface (usually gravity), and μ_K is called the *coefficient of kinetic friction*. The minus sign appears in Equation (10.101) because the kinetic friction force always acts in the direction opposite that in which an object is moving across a surface. The coefficient of kinetic friction μ_K is a positive constant that depends on the types of the surfaces in contact with each other. Typical values of μ_K for various surfaces are listed in Table 10.1.

Table 10.1 Typical values of the coefficient of kinetic friction μ_K and coefficient of static friction μ_S.

Surfaces	μ_K	μ_S
Aluminum on aluminum	1.4	1.1
Aluminum on steel	0.47	0.61
Copper on steel	0.36	0.53
Steel on steel	0.57	0.74
Nickel on nickel	0.53	1.1
Glass on glass	0.40	0.94
Copper on glass	0.53	0.68
Oak on oak (parallel to grain)	0.48	0.62
Oak on oak (perpendicular to grain)	0.32	0.54
Rubber on concrete (dry)	0.90	1.0
Rubber on concrete (wet)	0.25	0.30

Example 10.10. Suppose that a 10-kg block is sliding down a plane that is inclined at an angle of 30 degrees. If the coefficient of kinetic friction is $\mu_K = 0.5$, determine the block's acceleration.

Solution. Let m be the mass of the block, and let θ be the angle by which the plane is inclined. As shown in Figure 10.5, the block is acted on by a gravitational force and a resisting force due to friction. The gravitational force can be divided into components that are parallel to the plane and perpendicular to the plane. The parallel component F_G is given by

$$F_G = mg \sin \theta \tag{10.102}$$

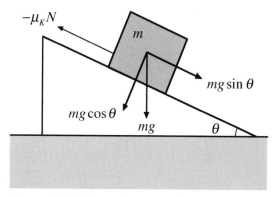

FIGURE   *The block used in Example 10.10.*
10.5

and pulls the block across the plane. The perpendicular component produces the force holding the block to the plane:

$$N = mg \, \cos \, \theta. \tag{10.103}$$

The force F_K due to kinetic friction is given by

$$F_K = -\mu_K N = -\mu_K mg \, \cos \, \theta \tag{10.104}$$

and acts in the direction opposite that of F_G. The acceleration a of the block is equal to the net force acting on it divided by its mass:

$$a = \frac{F_G + F_K}{m} = g \sin \theta - \mu_K g \cos \theta. \tag{10.105}$$

Plugging in the angle of inclination and coefficient of kinetic friction, we obtain the result

$$a = \left(9.8 \, \text{m/s}^2\right) \cdot \frac{1}{2} - 0.5 \cdot \left(9.8 \, \text{m/s}^2\right) \cdot \frac{\sqrt{3}}{2} \approx 0.656 \, \text{m/s}^2. \tag{10.106}$$

Notice that the mass of the block is inconsequential.

The static friction force prevents an object on a surface from moving by opposing any tangential force that may be acting on it. The maximum force F_S that can be exerted due to static friction is given by

$$F_S = -\mu_S N, \tag{10.107}$$

where N is the normal force and μ_S is called the *coefficient of static friction.* Again, we use a minus sign to indicate that the force acts in the direction opposite that of any force trying to move the object. Typical values of μ_S for various surfaces are listed in Table 10.1.

As soon as a force on an object exceeds the maximum value of F_S given by Equation (10.107), the object begins to move and the static friction force is replaced by the kinetic friction force F_K. It is often the case that $F_K < F_S$, so less force is required to move an object once it has been set in motion than was required to initiate the motion.

Example 10.11. A block is resting on a horizontal plane for which the coefficient of static friction is given by $\mu_S = 0.5$. Determine by what angle the plane needs to be inclined before the block begins sliding under the influence of gravity.

Solution. We need to determine when the component of the gravitation force that is parallel to the plane exceeds the static friction force. This occurs when

$$mg \sin \theta = \mu_S N = \mu_S mg \cos \theta, \qquad (10.108)$$

where θ is the angle of inclination. Solving for θ, we have

$$\theta = \tan^{-1} \mu_s \approx 26.6°. \qquad (10.109)$$

CHAPTER 10 SUMMARY

Force Equation
The acceleration $\mathbf{a}(t)$ of an object multiplied by its mass m is equal to the sum of the forces acting on it:

$$\sum_{i=1}^{N} \mathbf{F}_i(t) = m\mathbf{a}(t) = m\ddot{\mathbf{x}}(t).$$

Second-Order Differential Equations
The general solution to the homogeneous second-order differential equation

$$x''(t) + ax'(t) + bx(t) = 0$$

is given by

$$x(t) = Ae^{r_1 t} + Be^{r_2 t},$$

where

$$r_1 = -\frac{a}{2} + \frac{1}{2}\sqrt{a^2 - 4b}$$

$$r_2 = -\frac{a}{2} - \frac{1}{2}\sqrt{a^2 - 4b}.$$

If $r_1 = r_2 = r$, then the general solution is given by

$$x(t) = Ae^{rt} + Bte^{rt}.$$

If r_1 and r_2 are complex numbers, then the general solution can also be written as

$$x(t) = e^{\alpha t}(C_1 \cos \beta t + C_2 \sin \beta t),$$

where

$$\alpha = -\frac{a}{2}$$

$$\beta = \frac{1}{2}\sqrt{4b - a^2}.$$

This is equivalent to the solution

$$x(t) = D \sin(\beta t + \delta),$$

where

$$D = \sqrt{C_1^2 + C_2^2}$$

$$\delta = \sin^{-1}\frac{C_1}{D}.$$

Projectile Motion

The position $\mathbf{x}(t)$ of a projectile is given by the function

$$\mathbf{x}(t) = \mathbf{x}_0 + \mathbf{v}_0 t + \tfrac{1}{2}\mathbf{g}t^2,$$

where $\mathbf{x}_0$ is the initial position, $\mathbf{v}_0$ is the initial velocity, and $\mathbf{g} = \langle 0, 0, -g \rangle$ is the acceleration of gravity. The maximum height b attained by the projectile is given by

$$b = z_0 + \frac{v_z^2}{2g},$$

and the range r of the projectile is given by

$$r = \frac{2v_x v_y}{g}.$$

Resisted Motion

The position function $\mathbf{x}(t)$ for an object moving through a resistive medium is given by

$$\mathbf{x}(t) = \mathbf{x}_0 + \frac{\mathbf{g}}{k} t + \frac{k\mathbf{v}_0 - \mathbf{g}}{k^2} \left(1 - e^{-kt}\right),$$

where k represents the intensity of the damping force. The terminal velocity $\mathbf{v}_T$ is given by

$$\mathbf{v}_T = \frac{\mathbf{g}}{k}.$$

Friction

The force of kinetic friction F_K is given by

$$F_K = -\mu_K N,$$

where μ_K is the coefficient of kinetic friction. The kinetic friction force acts in the direction opposite that of the motion.

The maximum force of static friction F_S is given by

$$F_S = -\mu_S N,$$

where μ_S is the coefficient of static friction. The static friction force acts in the direction opposite that of any tangential force trying to move an object.

EXERCISES FOR CHAPTER 10

1. Solve the differential equation

   $$x''(t) - 6x'(t) + 9x(t) = 9t + 3.$$

2. Solve the differential equation

   $$x''(t) + 16x(t) = 0$$

   subject to the initial conditions $x(0) = 3$ and $x'(0) = 1$.
3. A projectile is launched from a platform 20 meters above the ground with an initial speed of 20 m/s in a direction forming an angle of 45 degrees with the horizontal plane. What is the maximum height above the ground attained by the projectile?

4. For what period of time does the projectile in exercise 3 travel before it lands on the ground?

5. A rock is dropped from rest at 50 meters above the ground and allowed to fall straight down through a resistive medium. Suppose that $k = 1$ s^{-1} and use Newton's method (see Section 5.1.4) to approximate the time t when the rock hits the ground.

6. An object of mass M is hanging from a rope that runs over a frictionless pulley and connects to another object of mass m lying on an inclined plane that forms an angle θ with the horizontal (see Figure 10.6). The coefficient of kinetic friction on the incline is μ_K. Assuming that M is much larger than m, determine the downward acceleration a of the hanging object. [*Hint.* Both masses are being accelerated, so the sum of the forces acting on the system should be set equal to $(M + m)a$.]

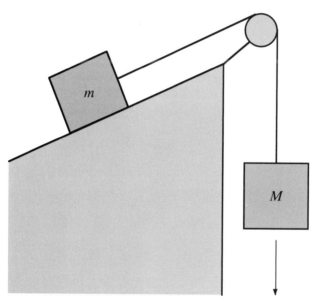

FIGURE *The system used in Exercise 6.*
10.6

11 Rotational Physics

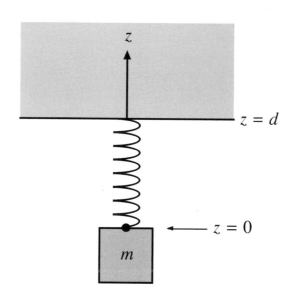

his chapter continues the survey of physics that begins in chapter 10. We now enter the domain of rotational mechanics to examine the behavior of rotating objects and the forces experienced in a rotating environment. Rotational physics has a wide range of applications in game programming, ranging from modeling the interaction between players and objects in the environment to space combat simulations. Virtually any object that is flying through the air or otherwise not resting on a surface is probably rotating, and thus would benefit from an accurate simulation of its motion.

11.1 ROTATING ENVIRONMENTS

This section discusses the physics that apply to an object in a rotating environment. A rotating environment refers to any frame of reference that is rotating about some axis and includes everything from a merry-go-round to the planet Earth. We begin with the introduction of angular velocity, and then we investigate the forces experienced by an object in the rotating reference frame.

11.1.1 ANGULAR VELOCITY

Suppose that a particle of mass m is rotating about an axis parallel to the unit vector $\mathbf{A}$ because it is attached to the axis by a string of length r (see Figure 11.1). Let the vectors $\mathbf{X}$ and $\mathbf{Y}$ be unit vectors lying in the plane perpendicular to $\mathbf{A}$ such that the axes $\mathbf{X}$, $\mathbf{Y}$, and $\mathbf{A}$ form a right-handed coordinate system (i.e., $\mathbf{X} \times \mathbf{Y} = \mathbf{A}$). Let $\theta(t)$ represent the counterclockwise angle that the projection of the string onto the $\mathbf{X}$-$\mathbf{Y}$ plane makes with the vector $\mathbf{X}$ at time t. The *angular velocity* of the particle is defined to be the rate at which this angle is changing, and is usually denoted by ω:

$$\omega(t) = \dot{\theta}(t) = \frac{d}{dt}\theta(t). \tag{11.1}$$

The angular velocity is often written as a vector that is parallel to the axis of rotation $\mathbf{A}$ and has the magnitude $|\omega(t)|$. The vector angular velocity $\boldsymbol{\omega}(t)$ is defined as

$$\boldsymbol{\omega}(t) = \omega(t)\mathbf{A} = \dot{\theta}(t)\mathbf{A}. \tag{11.2}$$

The speed at which a rotating particle moves through space is calculated by multiplying the particle's angular velocity by its distance from the axis of rotation. For the particle shown in Figure 11.1, the speed $v(t)$ is given by

$$v(t) = |\omega(t)r|. \tag{11.3}$$

However, this tells us nothing about the direction the particle is moving. Let the vector function $\mathbf{r}(t)$ represent the position of the particle relative to a fixed

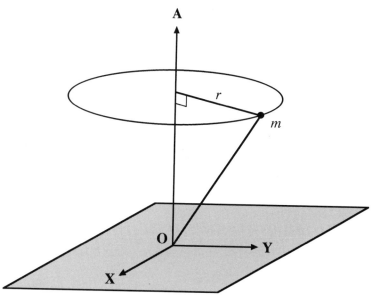

FIGURE
11.1
The angular velocity of a particle is a vector that is parallel to the axis of rotation and whose magnitude is equal to the rate of change of the angle formed in the plane perpendicular to the axis.

origin lying on the axis of rotation. As illustrated in Figure 11.2, the linear velocity vector $\mathbf{v}(t)$ of the particle is given by

$$\mathbf{v}(t) = \boldsymbol{\omega}(t) \times \mathbf{r}(t) \tag{11.4}$$

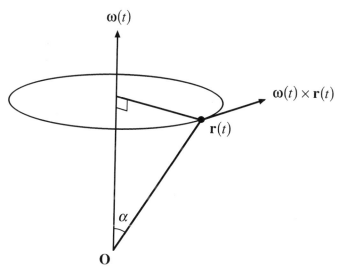

FIGURE   *The linear velocity $\boldsymbol{v}(t)$ is equal to the cross product of the angular velocity $\boldsymbol{\omega}(t)$ and*
11.2   *the position $\boldsymbol{r}(t)$.*

since the distance from the particle to the axis of rotation is equal to $\|\mathbf{r}(t)\| \sin \alpha$ and the velocity $\mathbf{v}(t)$ is always perpendicular to the direction pointing toward the axis.

11.1.2 THE CENTRIFUGAL FORCE

We continue to consider the example in which a particle is fastened by a string to the axis about which it is rotating. The linear acceleration $\mathbf{a}(t)$ of the particle is equal to the derivative of its linear velocity with respect to time. Taking the time derivative of the function $\mathbf{v}(t)$ given by Equation (11.4), we have

$$\mathbf{a}(t) = \dot{\mathbf{v}}(t) = \dot{\boldsymbol{\omega}}(t) \times \mathbf{r}(t) + \boldsymbol{\omega}(t) \times \dot{\mathbf{r}}(t). \tag{11.5}$$

Since $\mathbf{r}(t)$ is equal to the linear velocity $\mathbf{v}(t)$ of the particle, we can write

$$\mathbf{a}(t) = \dot{\boldsymbol{\omega}}(t) \times \mathbf{r}(t) + \boldsymbol{\omega}(t) \times [\boldsymbol{\omega}(t) \times \mathbf{r}(t)]. \tag{11.6}$$

If the angular velocity is constant, then the $\dot{\boldsymbol{\omega}}(t) \times \mathbf{r}(t)$ term of the acceleration is zero. The $\boldsymbol{\omega}(t) \times [\boldsymbol{\omega}(t) \times \mathbf{r}(t)]$ term, however, is always present and points in the direction from the particle toward the axis of rotation (see Figure 11.3). This part of the acceleration arises from the tension in the string connecting the particle to the axis of rotation. The particle itself experiences an equal but opposite force known as the *centrifugal force*. The centrifugal force, given by

$$\mathbf{F}_{\text{centrifugal}} = -m(\boldsymbol{\omega}(t) \times [\boldsymbol{\omega}(t) \times \mathbf{r}(t)]), \tag{11.7}$$

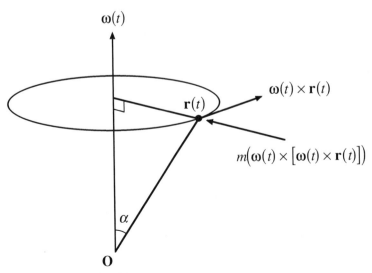

FIGURE *The centrifugal force.*
11.3

is responsible for the well-known effect that causes objects in a rotating system to move away from the center of rotation. In the case that $\mathbf{r}(t)$ and $\boldsymbol{\omega}(t)$ are perpendicular, the centrifugal force can be expressed as the scalar

$$F_{\text{centrifugal}} = m\omega^2 r = \frac{mv^2}{r}, \tag{11.8}$$

where r is the radial distance from the particle to the axis of rotation.

11.1.3 THE CORIOLIS FORCE

We now consider a somewhat more complicated situation in which a particle is moving on the surface of a rotating object. Suppose that a particle of mass m is rotating about some axis with angular velocity $\boldsymbol{\omega}(t)$. Further suppose that the particle is also moving *relative* to the rotating system with a velocity $\mathbf{v}_r(t)$. Then the velocity $\mathbf{v}(t)$ of the particle for a stationary observer outside the system is given by

$$\mathbf{v}(t) = \boldsymbol{\omega}(t) \times \mathbf{r}(t) + \mathbf{v}_r(t), \tag{11.9}$$

where $\mathbf{r}(t)$ is the position of the particle relative to some origin lying on the axis of rotation. Since the velocity $\mathbf{v}_r(t)$ is rotating with the system, a stationary observer sees the particle accelerating with respect to a fixed coordinate system according to the function

$$\mathbf{a}_f(t) = \boldsymbol{\omega}(t) \times \mathbf{v}_r(t) + \mathbf{a}_r(t), \tag{11.10}$$

where $\mathbf{a}_r(t) = \dot{\mathbf{v}}_r(t)$ is the acceleration of the particle in the rotating reference frame. The total linear acceleration $\mathbf{a}(t)$ of the particle is thus given by

$$\begin{aligned}\mathbf{a}(t) = \dot{\mathbf{v}}(t) &= \dot{\boldsymbol{\omega}}(t) \times \mathbf{r}(t) + \boldsymbol{\omega}(t) \times \dot{\mathbf{r}}(t) + \mathbf{a}_f(t)\\ &= \dot{\boldsymbol{\omega}}(t) \times \mathbf{r}(t) + \boldsymbol{\omega}(t) \times \dot{\mathbf{r}}(t) + \boldsymbol{\omega}(t) \times \mathbf{v}_r(t) + \mathbf{a}_r(t).\end{aligned} \tag{11.11}$$

Since $\dot{\mathbf{r}}(t)$ is equal to the linear velocity $\mathbf{v}(t)$ of the particle, we can write

$$\mathbf{a}(t) = \dot{\boldsymbol{\omega}}(t) \times \mathbf{r}(t) + \boldsymbol{\omega}(t) \times [\boldsymbol{\omega}(t) \times \mathbf{r}(t)] + 2\boldsymbol{\omega}(t) \times \mathbf{v}_r(t) + \mathbf{a}_r(t). \tag{11.12}$$

The force $\mathbf{F}(t)$ experienced by the particle is therefore

$$\begin{aligned}\mathbf{F}(t) = m\mathbf{a}(t) &= m\dot{\boldsymbol{\omega}}(t) \times \mathbf{r}(t) + m\boldsymbol{\omega}(t) \times [\boldsymbol{\omega}(t) \times \mathbf{r}(t)]\\ &\quad + 2m\boldsymbol{\omega}(t) \times \mathbf{v}_r(t) + m\mathbf{a}_r(t).\end{aligned} \tag{11.13}$$

In the reference frame of the rotating system, the force $\mathbf{F}_r(t)$ on the object appears to be the following.

$$\begin{aligned}\mathbf{F}_r(t) = m\mathbf{a}_r(t) &= \mathbf{F}(t) - m\dot{\boldsymbol{\omega}}(t) \times \mathbf{r}(t) - m\boldsymbol{\omega}(t) \times [\boldsymbol{\omega}(t) \times \mathbf{r}(t)]\\ &\quad - 2m\boldsymbol{\omega}(t) \times \mathbf{v}_r(t)\end{aligned} \tag{11.14}$$

As expected, the centrifugal force shows up again, but there is also a new force, called the *Coriolis force*, which acts on the particle in a direction perpendicular to its velocity in the rotating reference frame (see Figure 11.4). The Coriolis force, given by

$$\mathbf{F}_{\text{Coriolis}} = -2m\,\boldsymbol{\omega}(t) \times \mathbf{v}_r(t), \tag{11.15}$$

arises only when the particle is moving within the rotating system. It is this force that is responsible for the large-scale cyclonic motion of certain weather phenomena. For instance, hurricanes rotate counterclockwise in the northern hemisphere and clockwise in the southern hemisphere because the cross product in Equation (11.15) changes sign at the equator.

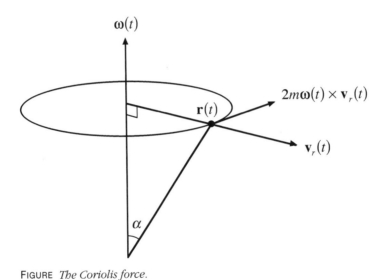

FIGURE *The Coriolis force.*
11.4

11.2 RIGID BODY MOTION

We define a *rigid body* to be a system of particles that are absolutely fixed with respect to each other and thus share the same angular velocity. A solid object can be thought of as a collection of an infinite number of particles, each having an infinitesimal mass. Since the particles composing a rigid body do not move with respect to each other, the centrifugal and Coriolis forces do not apply when the object is rotating. The only motions that a rigid body may undergo are the linear motion associated with the path along which it travels through space and the angular motion that it experiences because it is rotating about some axis. In this section, we investigate the rotational properties of a rigid body and the effects of external forces on this rotation.

11.2.1 CENTER OF MASS

When a rigid body rotates freely in the absence of any external forces, it does so about an axis that passes through the body's center of mass. The center of mass is the point within the rigid body at which a force could be applied in any direction without causing any net torque when that point is considered the origin.

Suppose that a rigid body is composed of some number of particles whose position and mass are known. The total mass M of the system of particles is given by

$$M = \sum_{\alpha} m_{\alpha},$$

(11.16)

where m_{α} is the mass of the α-th particle and the summation is taken over all of the particles belonging to the system. Let $\mathbf{r}_{\alpha}$ denote the position of the α-th particle. The center of mass $\mathbf{C}$ of the system is defined to be

$$\mathbf{C} = \frac{1}{M} \sum_{\alpha} m_{\alpha} \mathbf{r}_{\alpha}.$$

(11.17)

For a solid object, we compute the total mass of a continuous volume using the integral

$$M = \int_{V} dm(\mathbf{r}),$$

(11.18)

where $dm(\mathbf{r})$ represents the differential mass at the position $\mathbf{r}$ and V is the volume occupied by the object. If the density at the position $\mathbf{r}$ is described by the function $\rho(\mathbf{r})$, then this integral can be written as

$$M = \int_{V} \rho(\mathbf{r}) \, dV.$$

(11.19)

The center of mass for a solid object is then computed using the integral

$$\mathbf{C} = \frac{1}{M} \int_{V} \mathbf{r}\rho(\mathbf{r}) \, dV.$$

(11.20)

Example 11.1. Calculate the center of mass of a cone of radius R, height h, and constant density ρ, whose base is centered at the origin on the x-y plane (see Figure 11.5).

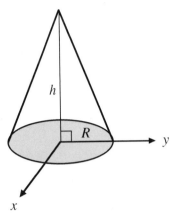

FIGURE *The cone used in Example 11.1.*
11.5

Solution. We use cylindrical coordinates. The radius $r(z)$ of a cross section of the cone at a height z above the x-y plane is given by

$$r(z) = (h - z)\frac{R}{h}.$$ (11.21)

We calculate the total mass of the cone using Equation (11.19) to integrate over the volume it occupies. The differential volume dV in cylindrical coordinates is given by

$$dV = r\, dr\, d\phi\, dz,$$ (11.22)

so the integral that we need to evaluate is

$$M = \int_0^h \rho\pi[r(z)]^2\, dz,$$ (11.23)

where the integrand represents the differential mass of a disk at height z above the x-y plane. Replacing $r(z)$ with the value given by Equation (11.21), we have

$$M = \rho\pi\frac{R^2}{h^2}\int_0^h (h - z)^2\, dz$$

$$= \tfrac{1}{3}\rho\pi R^2 h.$$ (11.24)

Due to the cylindrical symmetry of the cone, the x- and y-components of the center of mass are clearly zero. The z-component of the center of mass is found by applying Equation (11.20):

$$C_z = \frac{1}{M} \int_0^b \int_0^{2\pi} \int_0^{r(z)} \rho z r \, dr \, d\phi \, dz. \tag{11.25}$$

Evaluating the integral over ϕ leaves us with

$$C_z = \frac{2\rho\pi}{M} \int_0^b \int_0^{r(z)} z r \, dr \, dz. \tag{11.26}$$

We next integrate over r and replace $r(z)$ with the value given by Equation (11.21):

$$C_z = \frac{\rho\pi R^2}{Mb^2} \int_0^b z(b - z)^2 \, dz$$

$$= \frac{\rho\pi R^2}{Mb^2} \int_0^b \left(b^2 z - 2bz^2 + z^3 \right) dz. \tag{11.27}$$

Finally, integrating over b, we obtain

$$C_z = \frac{\rho\pi R^2 b^2}{12M} = \frac{b}{4}. \tag{11.28}$$

Thus, the center of mass of the cone is given by $\mathbf{C} = \langle 0, 0, b/4 \rangle$.

11.2.2 ANGULAR MOMENTUM AND TORQUE

Recall that the linear momentum $\mathbf{p}$ of a particle having mass m moving at a velocity $\mathbf{v}$ is given by $\mathbf{p} = m\mathbf{v}$. Just as angular velocity is the rotational analog of linear velocity, there exists a quantity called *angular momentum*, which serves as the rotational analog of linear momentum.

Suppose that a particle of mass m is rotating about some axis with an angular velocity of $\boldsymbol{\omega}(t)$ and that the position of the particle is given by the function $\mathbf{r}(t)$. The *angular momentum* $\mathbf{L}(t)$ of the particle is defined to be

$$\mathbf{L}(t) = \mathbf{r}(t) \times \mathbf{p}(t), \tag{11.29}$$

where $\mathbf{p}(t) = m\mathbf{v}(t)$ is the linear momentum of the particle.

Differentiating both sides of Equation (11.29) gives us

$$\dot{\mathbf{L}}(t) = \dot{\mathbf{r}}(t) \times \mathbf{p}(t) + \mathbf{r}(t) \times \dot{\mathbf{p}}(t). \tag{11.30}$$

Since $\dot{\mathbf{r}}(t) = \mathbf{v}(t)$, the vectors $\dot{\mathbf{r}}(t)$ and $\mathbf{p}(t)$ point in the same direction, so the cross product $\dot{\mathbf{r}}(t) \times \mathbf{p}(t)$ is zero. Thus,

$$\dot{\mathbf{L}}(t) = \mathbf{r}(t) \times \dot{\mathbf{p}}(t) = \mathbf{r}(t) \times m\dot{\mathbf{v}}(t). \tag{11.31}$$

The vector $m\dot{\mathbf{v}}(t)$ is equal to the net force $\mathbf{F}(t)$ acting on the particle, so we can write

$$\dot{\mathbf{L}}(t) = \mathbf{r}(t) \times \mathbf{F}(t). \tag{11.32}$$

The quantity on the right side of Equation (11.32) is called the *torque* $\boldsymbol{\tau}(t)$ being applied to the particle:

$$\boldsymbol{\tau}(t) = \mathbf{r}(t) \times \mathbf{F}(t). \tag{11.33}$$

Torque is the rotational analog to linear force and induces an angular acceleration. If the net torque acting on a particle is zero, then the angular momentum remains constant because

$$\dot{\mathbf{L}}(t) = \boldsymbol{\tau}(t). \tag{11.34}$$

11.2.3 THE INERTIA TENSOR

Angular momentum is related to angular velocity in a much more complicated way than linear momentum is related to linear velocity. In fact, the angular momentum vector and the associated angular velocity vector do not necessarily point in the same direction. The relationship between these two quantities is the topic of this section.

The angular momentum of a rigid body composed of a set of particles is equal to the sum

$$\mathbf{L}(t) = \sum_{\alpha} \mathbf{r}_{\alpha}(t) \times \mathbf{p}_{\alpha}(t), \tag{11.35}$$

where $\mathbf{r}_{\alpha}(t)$ represents the position of the α-th particle, $\mathbf{p}_{\alpha}(t)$ represents the momentum of the α-th particle, and the summation is taken over all the particles belonging to the system. Since the linear momentum $\mathbf{p}_{\alpha}(t)$ can be written as

$$\mathbf{p}_{\alpha}(t) = m_{\alpha}\mathbf{v}_{\alpha}(t) = m_{\alpha}\boldsymbol{\omega}(t) \times \mathbf{r}_{\alpha}(t), \tag{11.36}$$

the angular momentum becomes

$$\mathbf{L}(t) = \sum_{\alpha} m_{\alpha}\mathbf{r}_{\alpha}(t) \times \left[\boldsymbol{\omega}(t) \times \mathbf{r}_{\alpha}(t)\right]. \tag{11.37}$$

Using the vector identity given by Theorem 1.9(f),

$$\mathbf{P} \times (\mathbf{Q} \times \mathbf{P}) = \mathbf{P} \times \mathbf{Q} \times \mathbf{P} = P^2\mathbf{Q} - (\mathbf{P} \cdot \mathbf{Q})\mathbf{P}, \tag{11.38}$$

the angular momentum can also be written as

$$\mathbf{L}(t) = \sum_{\alpha} m_{\alpha}\left(r_{\alpha}^2(t)\boldsymbol{\omega}(t) - \left[\mathbf{r}_{\alpha}(t) \cdot \boldsymbol{\omega}(t)\right]\mathbf{r}_{\alpha}(t)\right). \tag{11.39}$$

Dropping the function-of-t notation for the moment, we can express the i-th component of $\mathbf{L}$ by

$$L_i = \sum_\alpha m_\alpha \left[r_\alpha^2 \omega_i - (\mathbf{r}_\alpha)_i \sum_{j=1}^{3} (\mathbf{r}_\alpha)_j \omega_j \right]. \tag{11.40}$$

We can express the quantity ω_i as

$$\omega_i = \sum_{j=1}^{3} \omega_j \delta_{ij}, \tag{11.41}$$

where δ_{ij} is the Kronecker delta defined by Equation (1.42). This substitution allows us to write L_i as

$$L_i = \sum_\alpha m_\alpha \sum_{j=1}^{3} \left[r_\alpha^2 \omega_j \delta_{ij} - (\mathbf{r}_\alpha)_i (\mathbf{r}_\alpha)_j \omega_j \right]$$

$$= \sum_{j=1}^{3} \omega_j \sum_\alpha m_\alpha \left[\delta_{ij} r_\alpha^2 - (\mathbf{r}_\alpha)_i (\mathbf{r}_\alpha)_j \right]. \tag{11.42}$$

The sum over α can be interpreted as the (i, j) entry of a 3×3 matrix $\mathcal{I}$:

$$\mathcal{I}_{ij} = \sum_\alpha m_\alpha \left[\delta_{ij} r_\alpha^2 - (\mathbf{r}_\alpha)_i (\mathbf{r}_\alpha)_j \right]. \tag{11.43}$$

This allows us to express L_i as

$$L_i = \sum_{j=1}^{3} \omega_j \mathcal{I}_{ij}, \tag{11.44}$$

and thus the angular momentum $\mathbf{L}(t)$ can be written as

$$\mathbf{L}(t) = \mathcal{I} \boldsymbol{\omega}(t). \tag{11.45}$$

The entity $\mathcal{I}$ is called the *inertia tensor* and relates the angular velocity of a rigid body to its angular momentum. The inertia tensor also relates the torque $\boldsymbol{\tau}(t)$ acting on a rigid body to the body's angular acceleration $\boldsymbol{\alpha}(t) = \dot{\boldsymbol{\omega}}(t)$. Differentiating both sides of Equation (11.45) gives us

$$\dot{\mathbf{L}}(t) = \boldsymbol{\tau}(t) = \mathcal{I} \boldsymbol{\alpha}(t). \tag{11.46}$$

Written as a 3×3 matrix, the inertia tensor is given by

$$\boldsymbol{\mathcal{I}} = \begin{bmatrix} \sum_{\alpha} m_{\alpha}\left(r_{\alpha}^2 - x_{\alpha}^2\right) & -\sum_{\alpha} m_{\alpha}x_{\alpha}y_{\alpha} & -\sum_{\alpha} m_{\alpha}x_{\alpha}z_{\alpha} \\ -\sum_{\alpha} m_{\alpha}x_{\alpha}y_{\alpha} & \sum_{\alpha} m_{\alpha}\left(r_{\alpha}^2 - y_{\alpha}^2\right) & -\sum_{\alpha} m_{\alpha}y_{\alpha}z_{\alpha} \\ -\sum_{\alpha} m_{\alpha}x_{\alpha}z_{\alpha} & -\sum_{\alpha} m_{\alpha}y_{\alpha}z_{\alpha} & \sum_{\alpha} m_{\alpha}\left(r_{\alpha}^2 - z_{\alpha}^2\right) \end{bmatrix}, \tag{11.47}$$

where $x_{\alpha} = (\mathbf{r}_{\alpha})_1$, $y_{\alpha} = (\mathbf{r}_{\alpha})_2$, and $z_{\alpha} = (\mathbf{r}_{\alpha})_3$. Clearly, $\boldsymbol{\mathcal{I}}$ is a symmetric matrix. The diagonal entries $\mathcal{I}_{11}$, $\mathcal{I}_{22}$, and $\mathcal{I}_{33}$ are called the *moments of inertia* with respect to the *x*-, *y*-, and *z*-axes, respectively. The off-diagonal entries are called the *products of inertia*.

For a continuous mass distribution, Equation (11.43) is formulated as the integral

$$\mathcal{I}_{ij} = \int_V \left(\delta_{ij}r^2 - r_i r_j\right) dm(\mathbf{r}), \tag{11.48}$$

where $dm(\mathbf{r})$ represents the differential mass at the position $\mathbf{r}$ and V is the volume occupied by the rigid body. If the density at the position $\mathbf{r}$ is described by the function $\rho(\mathbf{r})$, then this integral can be written as

$$\mathcal{I}_{ij} = \int_V \left(\delta_{ij}r^2 - r_i r_j\right)\rho(\mathbf{r}) \, dV. \tag{11.49}$$

Example 11.2. Calculate the moment of inertia about the *z*-axis of a solid sphere of radius R that is centered at the origin and has a uniform density ρ.

Solution. The moment of inertia about the *z*-axis is equal to the entry of the inertia tensor $\boldsymbol{\mathcal{I}}$. We need to evaluate the integral

$$\mathcal{I}_{33} = \int_V \left(r^2 - z^2\right)\rho \, dV. \tag{11.50}$$

The quantity $r^2 - z^2$ is equal to the squared distance from the *z*-axis, which in spherical coordinates is equal to $r^2 \sin^2 \theta$, where θ is the polar angle. The differential volume dV in spherical coordinates is given by

$$dV = r^2 \sin \theta \, dr \, d\theta \, d\phi, \tag{11.51}$$

so Equation (11.50) becomes

$$\mathcal{I}_{33} = \int_0^{2\pi} \int_0^{\pi} \int_0^R \left(r^2 \sin^2 \theta\right)\rho r^2 \sin \theta \, dr \, d\theta \, d\phi$$

$$= \rho \int_0^{2\pi} \int_0^{\pi} \int_0^R r^4 \sin^3 \theta \, dr \, d\theta \, d\phi. \tag{11.52}$$

Evaluating the integrals over r and ϕ, we have

$$\mathcal{I}_{33} = \tfrac{2}{5}\,\pi\rho R^5 \int_0^{\pi} \sin^3\theta\,d\theta = \tfrac{2}{5}\,\pi\rho R^5 \int_0^{\pi}\left(1 - \cos^2\theta\right)\sin\theta\,d\theta. \qquad (11.53)$$

By making the substitutions $u = -\cos\theta$ and $du = \sin\theta\,d\theta$, we can evaluate the remaining integral as follows.

$$\mathcal{I}_{33} = \tfrac{2}{5}\,\pi\rho R^5 \int_{-1}^{1}\left(1 - u^2\right)du$$

$$= \tfrac{8}{15}\,\pi\rho R^5 \qquad (11.54)$$

The volume of the sphere is given by $V = \tfrac{4}{3}\,\pi R^3$, so we can write the moment of inertia as

$$\mathcal{I}_{33} = \tfrac{2}{5}\,\rho V R^2 = \tfrac{2}{5}\,m R^2, \qquad (11.55)$$

where $m = \rho V$ is the mass of the sphere.

Due to the symmetry of the sphere, its moments of inertia about the x- and y-axes are also equal to $\tfrac{2}{5}\,mR^2$. Furthermore, the products of inertia are zero, so the inertia tensor $\mathcal{I}$ of a sphere has the form

$$\mathcal{I} = \begin{bmatrix} \tfrac{2}{5}\,mR^2 & 0 & 0 \\ 0 & \tfrac{2}{5}\,mR^2 & 0 \\ 0 & 0 & \tfrac{2}{5}\,mR^2 \end{bmatrix}. \qquad (11.56)$$

Consequently, the angular momentum of a rotating sphere may be written in terms of a scalar moment of inertia $I = \tfrac{2}{5}\,mR^2$:

$$\mathbf{L}(t) = I\,\boldsymbol{\omega}(t). \qquad (11.57)$$

Example 11.3. Calculate the inertia tensor of a solid cylinder of radius R and height h that is aligned to the z-axis, centered at the origin, and has a uniform density ρ (see Figure 11.6).

Solution. We first calculate the moment of inertia about the z-axis using cylindrical coordinates to evaluate the integral

$$\mathcal{I}_{33} = \int_V \left(s^2 - z^2\right)\rho\,dV. \qquad (11.58)$$

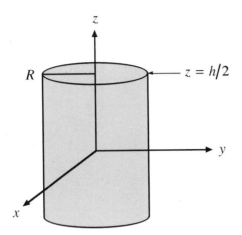

FIGURE *The cylinder used in Example 11.3.*
11.6

(We have used s^2 to represent the squared distance from the origin to avoid confusion with the radial distance r in cylindrical coordinates.) The quantity $s^2 - z^2$ is equal to the squared distance from the z-axis, which in cylindrical coordinates is simply r^2. The differential volume dV in cylindrical coordinates is given by

$$dV = r\, dr\, d\phi\, dz, \tag{11.59}$$

so Equation (11.58) becomes

$$\mathcal{I}_{33} = \rho \int_{-h/2}^{h/2} \int_0^{2\pi} \int_0^R r^2\, dr\, d\phi\, dz$$

$$= \tfrac{1}{2}\pi\rho h R^4. \tag{11.60}$$

The volume of the cylinder is given by $V = \pi h R^2$, so we can write the moment of inertia as

$$\mathcal{I}_{33} = \tfrac{1}{2}\rho V R^2 = \tfrac{1}{2} m R^2, \tag{11.61}$$

where $m = \rho V$ is the mass of the cylinder. Since a cylinder is symmetric about the z-axis, we must have $\mathcal{I}_{11} = \mathcal{I}_{22}$. We can calculate the moment of inertia about the x-axis by evaluating the integral

$$\mathcal{I}_{11} = \int_V \left(s^2 - x^2 \right) \rho\, dV. \tag{11.62}$$

Making the substitutions $s^2 = r^2 + z^2$ and $x^2 = r^2 \cos^2 \phi$, we have

$$\mathcal{I}_{11} = \rho \int_{-b/2}^{b/2} \int_0^{2\pi} \int_0^R \left(r^2 + z^2 - r^2 \cos^2 \phi \right) r \, dr \, d\phi \, dz$$

$$= \rho \int_{-b/2}^{b/2} \int_0^{2\pi} \int_0^R r^3 \sin^2 \phi \, dr \, d\phi \, dz + \rho \int_{-b/2}^{b/2} \int_0^{2\pi} \int_0^R z^2 r \, dr \, d\phi \, dz. \quad (11.63)$$

Evaluating the integrals for the variables r and z in the first term and evaluating all three integrals in the second term gives us

$$\mathcal{I}_{11} = \tfrac{1}{4} \rho b R^4 \int_0^{2\pi} \sin^2 \phi \, d\phi + \tfrac{1}{12} \pi \rho b^3 R^2. \quad (11.64)$$

Using the trigonometric identity

$$\sin^2 \phi = \frac{1 - \cos 2\phi}{2} \quad (11.65)$$

(see Appendix B, Section B.4), we can evaluate the remaining integral:

$$\int_0^{2\pi} \sin^2 \phi \, d\phi = \int_0^{2\pi} \left(\tfrac{1}{2} - \tfrac{1}{2} \cos 2\phi \right) d\phi$$

$$= \tfrac{1}{2} \phi - \tfrac{1}{4} \sin 2\phi \Big]_0^{2\pi}$$

$$= \pi. \quad (11.66)$$

The moment of inertia about the x- and y-axes is therefore given by

$$\mathcal{I}_{11} = \mathcal{I}_{22} = \tfrac{1}{4} \pi \rho b R^4 + \tfrac{1}{12} \pi \rho b^3 R^2$$

$$= \tfrac{1}{4} m R^2 + \tfrac{1}{12} m b^2. \quad (11.67)$$

The product of inertia $\mathcal{I}_{12}$ is equal to the integral

$$\mathcal{I}_{12} = \int_V -xy\rho \, dV = -\rho \int_{-b/2}^{b/2} \int_0^{2\pi} \int_0^R r^3 \sin \phi \cos \phi \, dr \, d\phi \, dz. \quad (11.68)$$

Since

$$\int_0^{2\pi} \sin\phi \cos\phi\, d\phi = 0,$$ (11.69)

it is the case that $\mathcal{I}_{12} = \mathcal{I}_{21} = 0$. It can also be shown that all of the other products of inertia are equal to zero, so the inertia tensor $\mathcal{I}$ of a cylinder has the form

$$\mathcal{I} = \begin{bmatrix} \frac{1}{4}mR^2 + \frac{1}{12}mb^2 & 0 & 0 \\ 0 & \frac{1}{4}mR^2 + \frac{1}{12}mb^2 & 0 \\ 0 & 0 & \frac{1}{2}mR^2 \end{bmatrix},$$ (11.70)

where $m = \rho V$ is the mass of the cylinder.

Nonzero products of inertia arise when we consider a solid box that rotates about an axis passing through one of its vertices. The significance of an inertia tensor that is not diagonal is discussed in Section 11.2.4.

Example 11.4. Calculate the inertia tensor of a solid box having dimensions a, b, and c that is aligned to the coordinate axes, has one vertex at the origin, and has a uniform density ρ (see Figure 11.7).

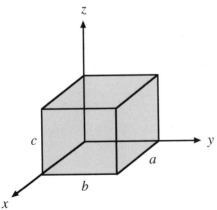

FIGURE   *The box used in Example 11.4.*
11.7

Solution. The moment of inertia about the x-axis $\mathcal{I}_{11}$ is given by the integral

$$\mathcal{I}_{11} = \int_V \left(r^2 - x^2 \right) \rho \, dV$$

$$= \rho \int_0^c \int_0^b \int_0^a \left(y^2 + z^2 \right) dx \, dy \, dz$$

$$= \rho ac \int_0^b y^2 \, dy + \rho ab \int_0^c z^2 \, dz$$

$$= \tfrac{1}{3} \rho ab^3 c + \tfrac{1}{3} \rho abc^3$$

$$= \tfrac{1}{3} \rho abc \left(b^2 + c^2 \right). \tag{11.71}$$

The volume of the box is given by $V = abc$, so we can write the moment of inertia as

$$\mathcal{I}_{11} = \tfrac{1}{3} m \left(b^2 + c^2 \right), \tag{11.72}$$

where $m = \rho V$ is the mass of the box. Similar calculations yield the moments of inertia about the y- and z-axes:

$$\mathcal{I}_{22} = \tfrac{1}{3} m \left(a^2 + c^2 \right)$$

$$\mathcal{I}_{33} = \tfrac{1}{3} m \left(a^2 + b^2 \right). \tag{11.73}$$

The product of inertia $\mathcal{I}_{12}$ is given by the integral

$$\mathcal{I}_{12} = -\int_V xy \rho \, dV$$

$$= -\rho \int_0^c \int_0^b \int_0^a xy \, dx \, dy \, dz$$

$$= -\rho c \int_0^b \int_0^a xy \, dx \, dy$$

$$= -\tfrac{1}{4} \rho a^2 b^2 c = -\tfrac{1}{4} mab. \tag{11.74}$$

Similar calculations yield the remaining two unique products of inertia:

$$\mathcal{I}_{13} = -\tfrac{1}{4} mac$$

$$\mathcal{I}_{23} = -\tfrac{1}{4} mbc. \tag{11.75}$$

The inertia tensor $\mathcal{I}$ of a box is therefore given by

$$\mathcal{I} = \begin{bmatrix} \frac{1}{3}m(b^2 + c^2) & -\frac{1}{4}mab & -\frac{1}{4}mac \\ -\frac{1}{4}mab & \frac{1}{3}m(a^2 + c^2) & -\frac{1}{4}mbc \\ -\frac{1}{4}mac & -\frac{1}{4}mbc & \frac{1}{3}m(a^2 + b^2) \end{bmatrix}, \tag{11.76}$$

where $m = \rho V$ is the mass of the box.

11.2.4 PRINCIPAL AXES OF INERTIA

Because the angular momentum $\mathbf{L}(t)$ and angular velocity $\boldsymbol{\omega}(t)$ are related by the equation

$$\mathbf{L}(t) = \mathcal{I}\boldsymbol{\omega}(t), \tag{11.77}$$

the two vectors are parallel precisely when $\boldsymbol{\omega}(t)$ is an eigenvector of the inertia tensor $\mathcal{I}$. Since the inertia tensor is a symmetric matrix, it has three real eigenvalues and the associated eigenvectors are orthogonal (see Chapter 2, Section 2.5). The eigenvalues of the inertia tensor are called the *principal moments of inertia*, and the associated eigenvectors are called the *principal axes of inertia*. If a rigid body is rotating about one of its principal axes of inertia, then its angular momentum is given by

$$\mathbf{L}(t) = I\boldsymbol{\omega}(t), \tag{11.78}$$

where I is the principal moment of inertia associated with the principal axis.

If the inertia tensor is a diagonal matrix, as it is for a sphere and a cylinder, then the principal moments of inertia are the same as the diagonal entries and the principal axes of inertia are simply the x-, y-, and z-axes. If the inertia tensor is not a diagonal matrix, then we must calculate its eigenvalues and eigenvectors to determine the principal axes, as demonstrated in the following example.

Example 11.5. Determine the principal axes of inertia for a solid cube having side length a that is aligned to the coordinate axes and has one vertex at the origin.

Solution. The inertia tensor $\mathcal{I}$ for a box is given by Equation (11.76). Setting the lengths in all three dimensions equal to each other produces the inertia tensor for a cube:

$$\mathcal{I} = \begin{bmatrix} \frac{2}{3}ma^2 & -\frac{1}{4}ma^2 & -\frac{1}{4}ma^2 \\ -\frac{1}{4}ma^2 & \frac{2}{3}ma^2 & -\frac{1}{4}ma^2 \\ -\frac{1}{4}ma^2 & -\frac{1}{4}ma^2 & \frac{2}{3}ma^2 \end{bmatrix}. \tag{11.79}$$

The determinant

$$\begin{vmatrix} \frac{2}{3}ma^2 - I & -\frac{1}{4}ma^2 & -\frac{1}{4}ma^2 \\ -\frac{1}{4}ma^2 & \frac{2}{3}ma^2 - I & -\frac{1}{4}ma^2 \\ -\frac{1}{4}ma^2 & -\frac{1}{4}ma^2 & \frac{2}{3}ma^2 - I \end{vmatrix} = 0, \qquad (11.80)$$

yields the characteristic polynomial whose roots are the eigenvalues of $\mathcal{I}$. Since the determinant is not affected by adding a multiple of one row to another row, we can subtract row 1 from row 2 to simplify our calculations:

$$\begin{vmatrix} \frac{2}{3}ma^2 - I & -\frac{1}{4}ma^2 & -\frac{1}{4}ma^2 \\ -\frac{11}{12}ma^2 + I & \frac{11}{12}ma^2 - I & 0 \\ -\frac{1}{4}ma^2 & -\frac{1}{4}ma^2 & \frac{2}{3}ma^2 - I \end{vmatrix} = 0. \qquad (11.81)$$

Factoring $\frac{11}{12}ma^2 - I$ out of row 2 and setting $b = \frac{1}{4}ma^2$ gives us

$$\left(\frac{11}{3}b - I\right)\begin{vmatrix} \frac{8}{3}b - I & -b & -b \\ -1 & 1 & 0 \\ -b & -b & \frac{8}{3}b - I \end{vmatrix} = 0. \qquad (11.82)$$

Evaluating the resulting determinant, we have

$$0 = \left(\frac{11}{3}b - I\right)\left[\left(\frac{8}{3}b - I\right)^2 - b\left(\frac{8}{3}b - I\right) - 2b^2\right]$$

$$= \left(\frac{11}{3}b - I\right)\left(I^2 - \frac{13}{3}bI + \frac{22}{9}b^2\right)$$

$$= \left(\frac{11}{3}b - I\right)\left(\frac{11}{3}b - I\right)\left(\frac{2}{3}b - I\right). \qquad (11.83)$$

The principal moments of inertia I_1, I_2, and I_3 are thus given by

$$I_1 = \frac{11}{3}b = \frac{11}{12}ma^2$$

$$I_2 = \frac{11}{3}b = \frac{11}{12}ma^2$$

$$I_3 = \frac{2}{3}b = \frac{1}{6}ma^2. \qquad (11.84)$$

To find the principal axis of inertia corresponding to the eigenvalue I_3, we need to solve the homogeneous linear system

$$\begin{bmatrix} \frac{2}{3}ma^2 - I_3 & -\frac{1}{4}ma^2 & -\frac{1}{4}ma^2 \\ -\frac{1}{4}ma^2 & \frac{2}{3}ma^2 - I_3 & -\frac{1}{4}ma^2 \\ -\frac{1}{4}ma^2 & -\frac{1}{4}ma^2 & \frac{2}{3}ma^2 - I_3 \end{bmatrix} \begin{bmatrix} x \\ y \\ z \end{bmatrix} = \mathbf{0}. \tag{11.85}$$

Again using the constant $b = \frac{1}{4}ma^2$ and substituting the value $I_3 = \frac{2}{3}b$, we have

$$\begin{bmatrix} 2b & -b & -b \\ -b & 2b & -b \\ -b & -b & 2b \end{bmatrix} \begin{bmatrix} x \\ y \\ z \end{bmatrix} = \mathbf{0}. \tag{11.86}$$

The reduced form of this system is

$$\begin{bmatrix} 1 & 0 & -1 \\ 0 & 1 & -1 \\ 0 & 0 & 0 \end{bmatrix} \begin{bmatrix} x \\ y \\ z \end{bmatrix} = \mathbf{0}, \tag{11.87}$$

and thus $x = y = z$. This tells us that the vector $\langle 1, 1, 1 \rangle$, a diagonal of the cube, represents the principal axis corresponding to the principal moment of inertia I_3. The principal axes corresponding to the eigenvalues I_1 and I_2 are found by solving the system

$$\begin{bmatrix} \frac{8}{3}b - I_1 & -b & -b \\ -b & \frac{8}{3}b - I_1 & -b \\ -b & -b & \frac{8}{3}b - I_1 \end{bmatrix} \begin{bmatrix} x \\ y \\ z \end{bmatrix} = \mathbf{0}. \tag{11.88}$$

Every entry of this matrix is the same, so the reduced form of the system is

$$\begin{bmatrix} 1 & 1 & 1 \\ 0 & 0 & 0 \\ 0 & 0 & 0 \end{bmatrix} \begin{bmatrix} x \\ y \\ z \end{bmatrix} = \mathbf{0}. \tag{11.89}$$

Therefore, the y- and z-components of each principal axis may be chosen arbitrarily (but not such that both are zero). The value of x is then given by $x = -y - z$. Any vector of the form $\langle -y - z, y, z \rangle$ is perpendicular to the vector $\langle 1, 1, 1 \rangle$, so the principal axes corresponding to the principal moments of inertia given by I_1 and I_2 can be any orthogonal pair in the plane perpendicular to the cube's diagonal.

If a rigid body is not rotating about one of its principal axes, then the angular velocity vector $\boldsymbol{\omega}(t)$ and the angular momentum vector $\mathbf{L}(t)$ are not parallel. In this situation, the vector $\mathbf{L}(t)$ rotates about the axis $\boldsymbol{\omega}(t)$ at the rate

$$\dot{\mathbf{L}}(t) = \boldsymbol{\omega}(t) \times \mathbf{L}(t) \not\equiv 0. \tag{11.90}$$

Thus, an angular acceleration results that has the effect of changing the axis of rotation. Since $\dot{\mathbf{L}}(t) = \boldsymbol{\mathcal{I}}\boldsymbol{\alpha}(t)$, the angular acceleration $\boldsymbol{\alpha}(t)$ is given by

$$\boldsymbol{\alpha}(t) = \boldsymbol{\mathcal{I}}^{-1}\dot{\mathbf{L}}(t) = \boldsymbol{\mathcal{I}}^{-1}[\boldsymbol{\omega}(t) \times \mathbf{L}(t)]. \tag{11.91}$$

To counter this angular acceleration and prevent the axis of rotation from changing, a torque equal in magnitude to $\boldsymbol{\omega}(t) \times \mathbf{L}(t)$ must be applied in the opposite direction. Therefore, the motion of a rotating rigid body can be described by the equation

$$\sum_{i=1}^{N} \boldsymbol{\tau}_i(t) - \boldsymbol{\omega}(t) \times \mathbf{L}(t) = \boldsymbol{\mathcal{I}}\boldsymbol{\alpha}(t) = \boldsymbol{\mathcal{I}}\ddot{\boldsymbol{\theta}}(t), \tag{11.92}$$

where $\boldsymbol{\tau}_1, \boldsymbol{\tau}_2,..., \boldsymbol{\tau}_N$ represent the external torques acting on the body. Equation (11.92) is the rotational analog of Equation (10.9).

11.3 OSCILLATORY MOTION

The motion of an object is *oscillatory* if it repeats over a period of time by moving back and forth through the same region of space. Such behavior is often caused by a restoring force, which may be constant or may act on a object with greater magnitude as the object moves further away from some equilibrium position. We examine oscillatory motion in this chapter because it shares some characteristics with rotational motion, such as angular velocity. The motion of a pendulum, discussed in Section 11.3.2, is an example of an object that rotates about a point with an oscillatory nature.

11.3.1 SPRING MOTION

Oscillatory motion is exhibited by an object having mass m that is attached to the end of a spring whose natural length is d (see Figure 11.8). Suppose that the spring is aligned to the z-axis and that one end is attached to an immovable object at $z = d$. Let the mass be attached to the other end, which coincides with the origin. Ignoring gravity for the moment, when the spring is stretched or compressed so that its length is greater than or less than d, a restoring force is exerted by the spring that is proportional to the displacement of the mass from its

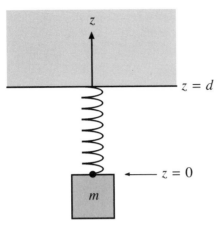

FIGURE *A mass attached to the end of a spring.*
11.8

natural resting position. If the position of the mass along the z-axis is z, then the restoring force F in that direction is given by

$$F = -kz. \tag{11.93}$$

This formula is known as *Hooke's law*. The constant k is a property of the spring corresponding to its stiffness. A larger value of k means that more work is required to move the mass attached to the end of the spring.

The position of a mass attached to the end of a spring can be determined as a function of time by examining the differential equation

$$m\ddot{z}(t) = -kz(t). \tag{11.94}$$

The general solution to this equation is

$$z(t) = A \sin \omega t + B \cos \omega t, \tag{11.95}$$

where $\omega = \sqrt{k/m}$ is called the *angular frequency* of the oscillations, measured in radians per unit time. The frequency f corresponding to the number of oscillations per unit time, measured in hertz (Hz) when the unit of time is the second, is related to the angular frequency by the equation

$$f = \frac{\omega}{2\pi}. \tag{11.96}$$

The period P of the oscillations is equal to the time that passes between each repetition of the motion and is given by the reciprocal of the frequency:

$$P = \frac{2\pi}{\omega} = 2\pi \sqrt{\frac{m}{k}}. \tag{11.97}$$

The constants A and B in Equation (11.95) must be determined by imposing initial conditions. Suppose that the initial position of the mass is z_0 and the initial velocity of the mass is v_0. Since

$$z(0) = B$$
$$\dot{z}(0) = A\omega, \qquad\qquad\qquad (11.98)$$

we can easily deduce

$$A = \frac{v_0}{\omega}$$

$$B = z_0. \qquad\qquad\qquad (11.99)$$

As discussed in Chapter 10, Section 10.2.1, we may express Equation (11.95) in the form

$$z(t) = C \sin(\omega t + \delta), \qquad\qquad\qquad (11.100)$$

where

$$C = \sqrt{\frac{v_0^2}{\omega^2} + z_0^2}$$

$$\delta = \sin^{-1} \frac{z_0}{C}. \qquad\qquad\qquad (11.101)$$

The constant C represents the *amplitude* of the oscillations and corresponds to the largest distance that the mass is ever displaced from its equilibrium position. The constant δ represents the *phase* of the oscillations and corresponds to the initial position of the mass.

Example 11.6. Determine the frequency and amplitude of a 2-kg mass attached to a spring having a restoring constant of $k = 3$ kg/s^2. Suppose that the mass was previously being pulled downward and that it is released at time $t = 0$ with an initial displacement of $z_0 = -4$ and an initial velocity of $v_0 = -1$ m/s.

Solution. The angular frequency ω is given by

$$\omega = \sqrt{\frac{k}{m}} = \frac{\sqrt{6}}{2} \text{ rad/s}. \qquad\qquad\qquad (11.102)$$

Dividing by 2π radians gives us the frequency f in oscillations per second:

$$f = \frac{\omega}{2\pi} = \frac{\sqrt{6}}{4\pi} \approx 0.195 \text{ Hz}. \qquad\qquad\qquad (11.103)$$

The amplitude C of the oscillations can be found by using Equation (11.101):

$$C = \sqrt{\frac{v_0^2}{\omega^2} + z_0^2} = \frac{5\sqrt{6}}{3} \approx 4.08 \text{ m.} \tag{11.104}$$

Suppose that a mass m attached to the end of a vertical spring is now acted upon by gravity. Adding the constant downward gravitational force $-mg$ to Equation (11.94) gives us

$$m\ddot{z}(t) = -kz(t) - mg. \tag{11.105}$$

The restoring force of the spring and the gravitational force are balanced when they are equal in magnitude and act in opposite directions. Thus, the spring experiences no net force when

$$-kz(t) = mg. \tag{11.106}$$

Solving for $z(t)$ gives us the equilibrium position of the hanging mass:

$$z(t) = -\frac{mg}{k}. \tag{11.107}$$

If the mass lies at the position $z = -mg/k$ and has no velocity, then it will never move.

Equation (11.107) is in fact a particular solution to the Equation (11.105). Adding this to the general solution to the homogeneous problem given by Equation (11.95), we have

$$z(t) = A \sin \omega t + B \cos \omega t - \frac{mg}{k}. \tag{11.108}$$

Imposing the same initial conditions as before, $z(0) = z_0$ and $z(0) = v_0$, produces the same value for A but a different value for B:

$$A = \frac{v_0}{\omega}$$

$$B = z_0 + \frac{mg}{k}. \tag{11.109}$$

When we write Equation (11.108) in the form

$$z(t) = C \sin(\omega t + \delta) - \frac{mg}{k}, \tag{11.110}$$

the amplitude C and phase δ do not change and are still given by Equation (11.101). Thus, gravity only has the effect of stretching the spring out by a distance mg/k. Otherwise, the oscillations are exactly the same as those not influenced by gravity.

11.3.2 PENDULUM MOTION

Suppose that an object of mass m under the influence of gravity is attached to a massless rod of length L hanging from a fixed point coinciding with the origin, as shown in Figure 11.9. We assume that the rod is able to pivot freely about its fixed end and that the mass is able to move in the x-z plane. Let I be the moment of inertia of the object with respect to the y-axis (about which the mass rotates). If all of the mass is concentrated at a single point, then $I = mL^2$.

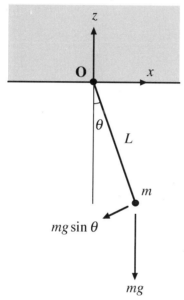

FIGURE *The plane pendulum.*
11.9

Let $\mathbf{r}(t)$ represent the position of the object. Gravity pulls downward on the object with the force $m\mathbf{g}$, exerting a torque $\boldsymbol{\tau}(t)$ given by

$$\boldsymbol{\tau}(t) = \mathbf{r}(t) \times m\mathbf{g}. \tag{11.111}$$

The resulting angular acceleration $\boldsymbol{\alpha}(t)$ is

$$\boldsymbol{\alpha}(t) = \frac{\boldsymbol{\tau}(t)}{I} = \frac{\mathbf{r}(t) \times m\mathbf{g}}{I}. \tag{11.112}$$

Since $\tau(t)$ and $\boldsymbol{\alpha}(t)$ are always perpendicular to the x-z plane in which the pendulum rotates, we can write them as scalar quantities $\tau(t)$ and $\alpha(t)$. Equation (11.112) can then be written as

$$\alpha(t) = \ddot{\theta}(t) = -\frac{mgL}{I} \sin \theta(t), \tag{11.113}$$

where $\theta(t)$ is the counterclockwise angle between the pendulum and the negative z-axis.

Equation (11.113) cannot be solved analytically for the function $\theta(t)$ due to the presence of the sine function. We can, however, transform the equation into a form that can be solved by replacing $\sin \theta(t)$ with the first term of its power series:

$$\ddot{\theta}(t) = -\frac{mgL}{I} \theta(t). \tag{11.114}$$

Equation (11.114) approximates the motion of a pendulum for which the angle $\theta(t)$ is always small. The solution to Equation (11.114) is given by

$$\theta(t) = A \sin (\omega t + \delta), \tag{11.115}$$

where the angular frequency ω is

$$\omega = \sqrt{\frac{mgL}{I}}, \tag{11.116}$$

and the constants A and δ are determined by initial conditions. The period P of the oscillations is given by

$$P = \frac{2\pi}{\omega} = 2\pi \sqrt{\frac{I}{mgL}}. \tag{11.117}$$

For a point mass, we have

$$\omega = \sqrt{\frac{g}{L}}$$

$$P = 2\pi \sqrt{\frac{L}{g}}. \tag{11.118}$$

CHAPTER 11 SUMMARY

Centrifugal Force

The centrifugal force experienced by an object in a rotating environment is given by

$$\mathbf{F}_{\text{centrifugal}} = -m(\boldsymbol{\omega}(t) \times [\boldsymbol{\omega}(t) \times \mathbf{r}(t)]),$$

where $\boldsymbol{\omega}(t)$ is the angular velocity and $\mathbf{r}(t)$ is the position of the object relative to an origin through which the axis of rotation passes. In the case that $\boldsymbol{\omega}(t)$ and $\mathbf{r}(t)$ are perpendicular, the centrifugal force can be expressed as the scalar

$$F_{\text{centrifugal}} = m\omega^2 r = \frac{mv^2}{r}.$$

Coriolis Force

The Coriolis force experienced by an object in a rotating environment is given by

$$\mathbf{F}_{\text{Coriolis}} = -2m\boldsymbol{\omega}(t) \times \mathbf{v}_r(t),$$

where $\mathbf{v}_r(t)$ is the velocity of the object relative to the rotating reference frame.

Center of Mass

The center of mass $\mathbf{C}$ of a solid object whose density at the point $\mathbf{r}$ is $\rho(\mathbf{r})$ is given by

$$\mathbf{C} = \frac{1}{M} \int_V \mathbf{r}\rho(\mathbf{r})\, dV,$$

where M is the total mass of the object.

Angular Momentum

The angular momentum $\mathbf{L}(t)$ of a particle is given by

$$\mathbf{L}(t) = \mathbf{r}(t) \times \mathbf{p}(t),$$

where $\mathbf{r}(t)$ is the position of the object relative to an origin through which the axis of rotation passes, and $\mathbf{p}(t) = m\mathbf{v}(t)$ is the linear momentum of the particle.

Torque

The torque $\boldsymbol{\tau}(t)$ acting on a particle is given by

$$\boldsymbol{\tau}(t) = \mathbf{r}(t) \times \mathbf{F}(t),$$

where $\mathbf{F}(t)$ is the force applied at the position $\mathbf{r}(t)$. The net torque acting on a particle is equal to the time rate of change of its angular momentum:

$$\dot{\mathbf{L}}(t) = \tau(t)$$

Inertia Tensor

The (i, j) entry of the inertia tensor $\mathcal{I}$ of a rigid body is given by

$$\mathcal{I}_{ij} = \int_V \left(\delta_{ij} r^2 - r_i r_j\right)\rho(\mathbf{r})\, dV,$$

where $\rho(\mathbf{r})$ is the density at the point $\mathbf{r}$.

The inertia tensor relates the angular velocity to the angular momentum and the angular acceleration to the torque:

$$\mathbf{L}(t) = \mathcal{I}\boldsymbol{\omega}(t)$$

$$\tau(t) = \mathcal{I}\boldsymbol{\alpha}(t).$$

Spring Motion

The position $z(t)$ of a mass m attached to oscillating spring having restoration constant k is given by

$$z(t) = C\sin(\omega t + \delta),$$

where

$$C = \sqrt{\frac{mv_0^2}{k} + z_0^2}$$

$$\delta = \sin^{-1}\frac{z_0}{C},$$

z_0 is the initial position, and v_0 is the initial velocity.

Pendulum Motion

A pendulum consisting of a mass m suspended from a rod of length L obeys the equation of motion

$$\alpha(t) = \ddot{\theta}(t) = -\frac{mgL}{I}\sin\theta(t),$$

where $\theta(t)$ is the angle formed with the vertical direction, and I is the moment of inertia of the mass. Small oscillations of the pendulum have an angular frequency ω given by

$$\omega = \sqrt{\frac{mgL}{I}}.$$

EXERCISES FOR CHAPTER 11

1. An ant is walking radially outward with a velocity v on the surface of a disk rotating counterclockwise with an angular velocity ω. At a distance r from the center of the disk, what is the total magnitude F of the forces experienced by the ant?

2. Suppose that a block of mass m is resting on the surface of a rotating disk at a distance r from the axis of rotation. If the coefficient of static friction at the surface is μ_S, determine the angular velocity at which the disk must rotate to cause the block to begin sliding outward.

3. Calculate the center of mass $\mathbf{C}$ of a cylinder of radius R and height h whose base is resting at the origin on the x-y plane if the density is given by $\rho(\mathbf{r}) = 1 + r_z/h$.

4. Calculate the moment of inertia about the z-axis for the annular cylinder of inner radius R_1, outer radius R_2, and height h shown in Figure 11.10. Let m be the mass of the cylinder, and assume a uniform density ρ.

5. Calculate the inertia tensor about the center of mass of a box having dimensions a, b, and c in the x, y, and z directions. Let m be the mass of the box and assume a uniform density ρ.

6. Suppose that an object of mass m is hanging from a rope of negligible mass that is wrapped around a cylindrical spool many times (see Figure 11.11). If the cylinder has mass M and radius R, determine at what rate a

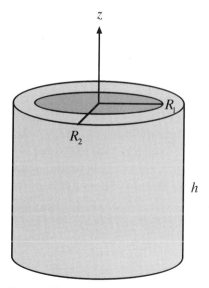

FIGURE *The annular cylinder used in Exercise 4.*
11.10

the object accelerates downward under the influence of gravity. Assume that the rope does not slip as it unwinds from the spool. [*Hint.* As gravity pulls on the object, it creates a tension T in the rope that is counteracted by the cylinder, so the force equation is $ma = mg - T$. The tension T exerts a torque on the cylinder that induces an angular acceleration α. Use the fact that $a = R\alpha$.]

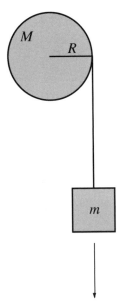

FIGURE   *The system used in Exercise 6.*
11.11

7. A spherical ball of mass m and radius R is placed on an incline that forms an angle θ with the ground (see Figure 11.12). The coefficient of static friction at the surface is μ_s. If the ball rolls down the incline under the influence of gravity without slipping, determine its acceleration a. [*Hint.* Two forces are acting on the ball, gravity and the frictional force, whose sum is equal to ma. The frictional force also exerts torque on the ball, inducing an angular acceleration α. Use the fact that $a = R\alpha$ as the ball rolls down the incline.]

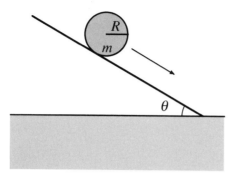

FIGURE *The ball used in Exercise 7.*
11.12

8. Suppose that a box of uniform density having mass m is resting on the ground where the coefficient of static friction is μ_S (see Figure 11.13). The box has a square base of length and width d, and the box's height is h. Determine the minimum height z at which a force $F < \mu_S mg$ applied directly to the horizontal center of a side of the box would cause the box to begin toppling over. [*Hint.* Equate the torques induced by the pull of gravity on the center of mass and the force F about the bottom edge on the side opposite that where the force is applied.]

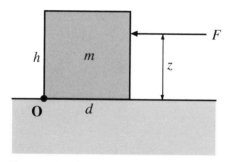

FIGURE *The box used in Exercise 8.*
11.13

12 Fluid Simulation

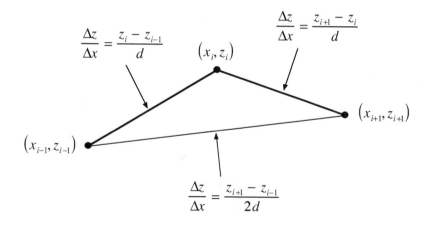

$$\frac{\Delta z}{\Delta x} = \frac{z_i - z_{i-1}}{d}$$

$$\frac{\Delta z}{\Delta x} = \frac{z_{i+1} - z_i}{d}$$

$$(x_i, z_i)$$

$$(x_{i+1}, z_{i+1})$$

$$(x_{i-1}, z_{i-1})$$

$$\frac{\Delta z}{\Delta x} = \frac{z_{i+1} - z_{i-1}}{2d}$$

The worlds presented by many games contain regions covered by a fluid surface. Whether it be a pool of water, a vat of deadly acid, or a pit of molten lava, we would like the fluid surface to behave in a physically realistic manner. To accomplish this, we need to be able to model the way in which disturbances propagate through the fluid as waves. In this chapter, we introduce the well-known wave equation and apply it to real-time simulation of fluid surfaces.

12.1 THE WAVE EQUATION

The wave equation is a partial differential equation that describes the motion of each point on a one-dimensional string or a two-dimensional surface experiencing a constant tension. We can derive the one-dimensional wave equation by considering a flexible elastic string that is tightly bound between two fixed endpoints lying on the x-axis (see Figure 12.1). We assume that the string has a constant linear density (mass per unit length) ρ and experiences a constant tension T which acts in the tangential direction.

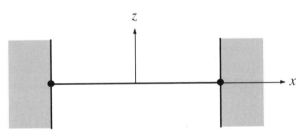

FIGURE **12.1** *A string having linear density ρ is tightly bound between two endpoints and experiences a constant tension T.*

Let the function $z(x,t)$ represent the vertical displacement of the string at the horizontal position x and at time t. When the string is displaced in the z direction, the tension produces a force at each point along the string that results in an acceleration. Newton's second law dictates that the net force $\mathbf{F}(x, t)$ experienced by a small segment of the string lying between $x = s$ and $x = s + \Delta x$ at any time t is equal to the product of its mass and its acceleration $\mathbf{a}(x, t)$. Since the linear density of the string is ρ, the mass of the segment is equal to $\rho \Delta x$ and we have

$$\mathbf{a}(x, t) = \frac{\mathbf{F}(x, t)}{\rho \Delta x}. \tag{12.1}$$

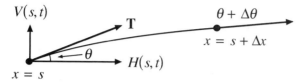

FIGURE   *The forces experienced at each endpoint of the segment lying between $x = s$ and*
12.2   *$x = s + \Delta x$ can be divided into horizontal and vertical components.*

As shown in Figure 12.2, we can divide the force experienced by each endpoint of the segment lying between $x = s$ and $x = s + \Delta x$ into horizontal and vertical components $H(x, t)$ and $V(x, t)$. Let θ represent the angle between the tangent to the string and the x-axis at the endpoint where $x = s$. Since the tension T acts in the tangential direction, the horizontal component $H(s, t)$ and vertical component $V(s, t)$ are given by

$$H(s, t) = T \cos \theta$$

$$V(s, t) = T \sin \theta. \tag{12.2}$$

Let $\theta + \Delta\theta$ represent the angle between the tangent to the string and the x-axis at the endpoint where $x = s + \Delta x$. The horizontal component $H(s + \Delta x, t)$ and vertical component $V(s + \Delta x, t)$ of the tension experienced at this endpoint are given by

$$H(s + \Delta x, t) = T \cos(\theta + \Delta\theta)$$

$$V(s + \Delta x, t) = T \sin(\theta + \Delta\theta). \tag{12.3}$$

For small motions, we assume that the net horizontal force is zero so that the segment accelerates only in the vertical direction. Thus, for the segment lying between $x = s$ and $x = s + \Delta x$, we require that

$$H(s + \Delta x, t) - H(s, t) = 0 \tag{12.4}$$

Consequently, the function H is independent of x, so we can write $H(t)$ instead of $H(x, t)$.

The net vertical force acting on the segment lying between $x = s$ and $x = s + \Delta x$ produces an acceleration that is given by the z-component of Equation (12.1). Since the vertical acceleration is equal to the second derivative of the position function $z(x, t)$, we have

$$a_z(s, t) = \frac{\partial^2}{\partial t^2} z(s, t) = \frac{V(s + \Delta x, t) - V(s, t)}{\rho \Delta x}. \tag{12.5}$$

Multiplying both sides by the density ρ and taking the limit as Δx approaches zero gives us

$$\rho \frac{\partial^2}{\partial t^2} z(s, t) = \lim_{\Delta x \to 0} \frac{V(s + \Delta x, t) - V(s, t)}{\Delta x}. \tag{12.6}$$

The right side of Equation (12.6) is equal to the definition of the partial derivative of V with respect to x evaluated at s, so we can rewrite it as

$$\rho \frac{\partial^2}{\partial t^2} z(s, t) = \frac{\partial}{\partial x} V(s, t). \tag{12.7}$$

Using the values of $H(t)$ and $V(s, t)$ given by Equations (12.2), we can express $V(s, t)$ in terms of $H(t)$ as follows.

$$V(s, t) = H(t) \tan\theta \tag{12.8}$$

Since θ is the angle formed between the tangent to the string and the x-axis, $\tan \theta$ is equal to the slope of the function $z(x, t)$ at s. Therefore,

$$V(s, t) = H(t) \frac{\partial}{\partial x} z(s, t), \tag{12.9}$$

and Equation (12.7) becomes

$$\rho \frac{\partial^2}{\partial t^2} z(s, t) = \frac{\partial}{\partial x} \left[H(t) \frac{\partial}{\partial x} z(s, t) \right]. \tag{12.10}$$

Since $H(t)$ does not depend on x, we can write

$$\rho \frac{\partial^2}{\partial t^2} z(s, t) = H(t) \frac{\partial^2}{\partial x^2} z(s, t). \tag{12.11}$$

For small motions, $\cos \theta$ is close to one, so we approximate $H(t)$ with the tension T. Letting $c^2 = T/\rho$, we now arrive at the one-dimensional wave equation:

$$\frac{\partial^2 z}{\partial t^2} = c^2 \frac{\partial^2 z}{\partial x^2}. \tag{12.12}$$

The two-dimensional wave equation is obtained by adding a second spatial term to Equation (12.12), as follows.

$$\frac{\partial^2 z}{\partial t^2} = c^2 \left(\frac{\partial^2 z}{\partial x^2} + \frac{\partial^2 z}{\partial y^2} \right) \tag{12.13}$$

The constant c has dimensions of distance per unit time and thus represents a velocity. A fact that we do not prove here is that c is actually the velocity at which waves propagate along a string or through a surface. This makes sense since the wave speed increases with tension experienced by the medium and decreases with the density of the medium.

Equation (12.13) does not account for any forces other than the surface tension. Thus, the average amplitude of the waves on the surface never diminishes, as it does for a real-world fluid. We can add a viscous damping force to the equation by introducing a force that acts in the direction opposite that of the velocity of a point on the surface to obtain

$$\frac{\partial^2 z}{\partial t^2} = c^2 \left(\frac{\partial^2 z}{\partial x^2} + \frac{\partial^2 z}{\partial y^2} \right) - \mu \frac{\partial z}{\partial t}, \tag{12.14}$$

where the nonnegative constant μ represents the viscosity of the fluid. The value of μ generally controls how long it takes for waves on a surface to calm down. A small value of μ allows waves to exist for a long time, as with water, but a large value of μ causes waves to diminish rapidly, as for a thick oil.

12.2 APPROXIMATING DERIVATIVES

The two-dimensional wave equation with viscous damping given by Equation (12.14) can be solved analytically using separation of variables. The solution, however, is quite complex and would require a significant amount of computation for a real-time simulation. We instead choose to use a numerical technique to model the propagation of waves over a fluid surface.

Suppose that our fluid surface is represented by a triangle mesh whose vertices are arranged on an $n \times m$ regular grid, as shown in Figure 12.3. Let d be the distance between adjacent vertices in both the x and y directions, and let t be the time interval between consecutive calculations of the fluid's state. We denote the displacement of a vertex in the mesh by $z(i, j, k)$, where i and j are integers satisfying $0 \le i < n$ and $0 \le j < m$ that represent the spatial coordinates, and k is a nonnegative integer that represents the temporal coordinate. That is, $z(i, j, k)$ is equal to the displacement of the vertex lying at the point $\langle id, jd \rangle$ at the time kt.

We impose the boundary condition that the vertices lying on the edge of the surface are fixed at a displacement of zero. The displacement of the interior points can be calculated by using Equation (12.14) and approximating the derivatives using the differences in the displacements of adjacent vertices. As illustrated in Figure 12.4, we can approximate the x-axis–aligned tangent to the surface at a vertex having coordinates (i, j) by calculating the average ratio of Δz to Δx between that vertex and its immediate neighbors in the x direction.

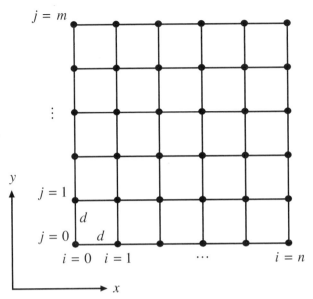

FIGURE *A fluid surface is represented by a triangle mesh whose vertices are arranged on an*
12.3 *n × m regular grid.*

Using this technique and the fact that $\Delta x = d$, we define the derivative $\partial z/\partial x$ as
follows.

$$\frac{\partial}{\partial x} z(i, j, k) = \frac{\dfrac{z(i, j, k) - z(i-1, j, k)}{d} + \dfrac{z(i+1, j, k) - z(i, j, k)}{d}}{2}$$

$$= \frac{z(i+1, j, k) - z(i-1, j, k)}{2d} \tag{12.15}$$

We define the derivative $\partial z/\partial y$ at the vertex having coordinates (i, j) in a similar
manner by calculating the average ratio of Δz to Δy between that vertex and its immediate neighbors in the y direction. As with the x direction, $\Delta y = d$, so we have

$$\frac{\partial}{\partial y} z(i, j, k) = \frac{z(i, j+1, k) - z(i, j-1, k)}{2d}. \tag{12.16}$$

We can define the temporal derivative $\partial z/\partial t$ by calculating the average difference in the displacement of a vertex between the current time and the previous
and succeeding times at which the displacement is evaluated. The time between
evaluations is t, so the average ratio of Δz to Δt is given by

$$\frac{\partial}{\partial t} z(i, j, k) = \frac{z(i, j, k+1) - z(i, j, k-1)}{2t}. \tag{12.17}$$

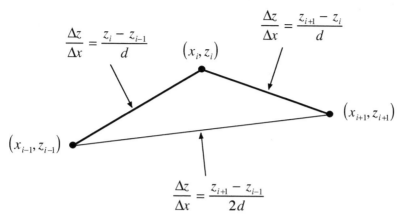

$$\frac{\Delta z}{\Delta x} = \frac{z_i - z_{i-1}}{d}$$

$$\left(x_i, z_i\right)$$

$$\frac{\Delta z}{\Delta x} = \frac{z_{i+1} - z_i}{d}$$

$$\left(x_{i+1}, z_{i+1}\right)$$

$$\left(x_{i-1}, z_{i-1}\right)$$

$$\frac{\Delta z}{\Delta x} = \frac{z_{i+1} - z_{i-1}}{2d}$$

FIGURE **12.4** *The x-axis aligned tangent to the surface can be approximated by calculating the average ratio of Δz to Δx between that vertex and its immediate neighbors.*

Second derivatives can be approximated by employing the same method used to approximate the first derivatives. This is done by calculating the average ratios of the differences between the first derivatives to one of the spatial or temporal coordinates. To illustrate, we consider the second derivative at the vertex having coordinates (i, j) with respect to x. The average difference $\Delta(\partial z/\partial x)$ between first derivatives at this vertex is given by

$$\Delta\left[\frac{\partial}{\partial x} z(i, j, k)\right] = \frac{\frac{\partial}{\partial x} z(i + 1, j, k) - \frac{\partial}{\partial x} z(i - 1, j, k)}{2}. \qquad (12.18)$$

Substituting the value given by Equation (12.15) for the derivatives with respect to x, we have the following.

$$\Delta\left[\frac{\partial}{\partial x} z(i, j, k)\right] = \frac{\dfrac{z(i + 2, j, k) - z(i, j, k)}{2d} - \dfrac{z(i, j, k) - z(i - 2, j, k)}{2d}}{2}$$

$$= \frac{z(i + 2, j, k) - 2z(i, j, k) + z(i - 2, j, k)}{4d} \qquad (12.19)$$

Dividing by d gives us the ratio of $\Delta(\partial z/\partial x)$ to Δx, which we use to define the second derivative:

$$\frac{\partial^2}{\partial x^2} z(i, j, k) = \frac{z(i + 2, j, k) - 2z(i, j, k) + z(i - 2, j, k)}{4d^2}. \qquad (12.20)$$

This formula requires that we use the displacements of neighbors lying two vertices away from the vertex where we wish to calculate the second derivative. Fortunately, the adjacent neighbors are not used, so we can scale the coordinate system about the vertex lying at (i, j) by one-half. Using the nearest neighbors and cutting the distance Δx in half, we obtain the following equivalent formula for the second derivative with respect to x.

$$\frac{\partial^2}{\partial x^2} z(i, j, k) = \frac{z(i + 1, j, k) - 2z(i, j, k) + z(i - 1, j, k)}{d^2} \tag{12.21}$$

The following similar formulas give the second derivatives with respect to the spatial coordinate y and the temporal coordinate t.

$$\frac{\partial^2}{\partial y^2} z(i, j, k) = \frac{z(i, j + 1, k) - 2z(i, j, k) + z(i, j - 1, k)}{d^2} \tag{12.22}$$

$$\frac{\partial^2}{\partial t^2} z(i, j, k) = \frac{z(i, j, k + 1) - 2z(i, j, k) + z(i, j, k - 1)}{t^2} \tag{12.23}$$

12.3 EVALUATING SURFACE DISPLACEMENT

Using the first derivative with respect to t given by Equation (12.17) and the second derivatives given by Equations (12.21), (12.22), and (12.23), the two-dimensional wave equation with viscous damping given by Equation (12.14) can be written as follows for the vertex having coordinates (i, j).

$$\frac{z(i, j, k + 1) - 2z(i, j, k) + z(i, j, k - 1)}{t^2} =$$

$$c^2 \frac{z(i + 1, j, k) - 2z(i, j, k) + z(i - 1, j, k)}{d^2}$$

$$+ c^2 \frac{z(i, j + 1, k) - 2z(i, j, k) + z(i, j - 1, k)}{d^2}$$

$$- \mu \frac{z(i, j, k + 1) - z(i, j, k - 1)}{2t} \tag{12.24}$$

We would like to be able to determine the future displacement $z(i, j, k + 1)$ occurring after the time interval t has passed, given that we already know the current displacement $z(i, j, k)$ and the previous displacement $z(i, j, k - 1)$. Solving Equation (12.24) for $z(i, j, k + 1)$ yields

$$z(i, j, k + 1) = \frac{4 - 8c^2t^2/d^2}{\mu t + 2} z(i, j, k) + \frac{\mu t - 2}{\mu t + 2} z(i, j, k - 1)$$

$$+ \frac{2c^2t^2/d^2}{\mu t + 2} \left[z(i + 1, j, k) + z(i - 1, j, k) + z(i, j + 1, k) + z(i, j - 1, k) \right],$$

$$(12.25)$$

which provides exactly what we need. The constants preceding each term can be precomputed, leaving only three multiplications and four additions to be calculated at each vertex in the mesh.

If the wave velocity c is too fast or the time interval t is too long, then successive iterations of Equation (12.25) cause the displacements to diverge toward infinity. To keep the displacements finite, we need to determine the exact conditions under which Equation (12.25) is stable. These conditions are revealed when we impose the requirement that any vertex displaced and held away from an otherwise flat surface should move toward the surface when released.

Suppose that we have an $n \times m$ array of vertices for which $z(i, j, 0) = 0$ and $z(i, j, 1) = 0$ for every vertex except the one having coordinates (i_0, j_0). Let the vertex at (i_0, j_0) be held in place such that $z(i_0, j_0, 0) = h$ and $z(i_0, j_0, 1) = h$, where h is a nonzero displacement. Now suppose that the vertex at (i_0, j_0) is released at time $2t$. When $z(i_0, j_0, 2)$ is evaluated, the third term of Equation (12.25) is zero, so we have

$$z(i_0, j_0, 2) = \frac{4 - 8c^2t^2/d^2}{\mu t + 2} z(i_0, j_0, 1) + \frac{\mu t - 2}{\mu t + 2} z(i_0, j_0, 0)$$

$$= \frac{2 - 8c^2t^2/d^2 + \mu t}{\mu t + 2} h. \qquad (12.26)$$

For the vertex to move toward the surrounding flat surface, its displacement must be smaller at time $2t$ than it was at time t. Thus, we must require that

$$\left| z(i_0, j_0, 2) \right| < \left| z(i_0, j_0, 1) \right| = \left| h \right|. \qquad (12.27)$$

Plugging in the value given by Equation (12.26) for $z(i_0, j_0, 2)$, we have

$$\left| \frac{2 - 8c^2t^2/d^2 + \mu t}{\mu t + 2} \right| \left| h \right| < \left| h \right|. \qquad (12.28)$$

Thus,

$$-1 < \frac{2 - 8c^2t^2/d^2 + \mu t}{\mu t + 2} < 1. \qquad (12.29)$$

Solving for c, we find

$$0 < c < \frac{d}{2t}\sqrt{\mu t + 2}. \tag{12.30}$$

This tells us that for any given distance d between adjacent vertices and any time interval t between consecutive iterations of Equation (12.25), the wave velocity c must be less than the maximum value imposed by Equation (12.30).

Alternatively, we may calculate a maximum time interval t given the distance d and the wave velocity c. Multiplying both sides of Equation (12.29) by $-(\mu t + 2)$ and simplifying yields

$$0 < \frac{4c^2}{d^2} t^2 < \mu t + 2. \tag{12.31}$$

The left inequality simply requires that $t > 0$, a condition that we would naturally impose in any case. The right inequality yields the quadratic expression

$$\frac{4c^2}{d^2} t^2 - \mu t - 2 < 0. \tag{12.32}$$

Using the quadratic equation, the roots of the polynomial are given by

$$t = \frac{\mu \pm \sqrt{\mu^2 + 32c^2/d^2}}{8c^2/d^2}. \tag{12.33}$$

Since the coefficient of the quadratic term in Equation (12.32) is positive, the corresponding parabola is concave upward, and the polynomial is therefore negative when t lies in between the two roots. The value under the radical in Equation (12.33) is larger than μ, so the lesser of the two roots is negative and can be discarded. We can now express the restriction on the time interval t as

$$0 < t < \frac{\mu + \sqrt{\mu^2 + 32c^2/d^2}}{8c^2/d^2}. \tag{12.34}$$

Using a value for the wave velocity c falling outside the range given by Equation (12.30) or a value for the time interval t falling outside the range given by Equation (12.34) results in an exponential explosion of the vertex displacements.

12.4 IMPLEMENTATION

An implementation of Equation (12.25) for a fluid surface requires that we store two buffers, each containing an $n \times m$ array of vertex positions. At each frame, one of the buffers contains the current vertex positions, and the other buffer contains the previous vertex positions. When we evaluate new displacements, we replace each vertex in the buffer containing the previous vertex positions with the new vertex position. The buffer containing the current vertex positions then becomes the buffer containing the previous vertex positions, so we actually alternate which buffer is used to render each frame.

To perform lighting calculations, we need to know the correct normal vector at each vertex and possibly the correct tangent vector at each vertex. At the vertex having coordinates (i, j), the (unnormalized) x-axis–aligned tangent vector $\mathbf{T}$ and y-axis–aligned tangent vector $\mathbf{B}$ are given by

$$\mathbf{T} = \left\langle 1, 0, \frac{\partial}{\partial x} z(i, j, k) \right\rangle$$

$$\mathbf{B} = \left\langle 0, 1, \frac{\partial}{\partial y} z(i, j, k) \right\rangle. \tag{12.35}$$

Substituting the formulas for the partial derivatives given by Equations (12.15) and (12.16), we have

$$\mathbf{T} = \left\langle 1, 0, \frac{z(i + 1, j, k) - z(i - 1, j, k)}{2d} \right\rangle$$

$$\mathbf{B} = \left\langle 0, 1, \frac{z(i, j + 1, k) - z(i, j - 1, k)}{2d} \right\rangle. \tag{12.36}$$

The (also unnormalized) normal vector $\mathbf{N}$ is then simply given by $\mathbf{N} = \mathbf{T} \times \mathbf{B}$, which can be expressed as follows.

$$\mathbf{N} = \begin{vmatrix} \mathbf{i} & \mathbf{j} & \mathbf{k} \\ 1 & 0 & \dfrac{z(i + 1, j, k) - z(i - 1, j, k)}{2d} \\ 0 & 1 & \dfrac{z(i, j + 1, k) - z(i, j - 1, k)}{2d} \end{vmatrix}$$

$$= \left\langle -\frac{z(i + 1, j, k) - z(i - 1, j, k)}{2d}, -\frac{z(i, j + 1, k) - z(i, j - 1, k)}{2d}, 1 \right\rangle \tag{12.37}$$

Multiplying the vectors $\mathbf{T}$, $\mathbf{B}$, and $\mathbf{N}$ by $2d$ does not change the direction in which they point but does eliminate the divisions, yielding the following formulas.

$$\mathbf{T} = \langle 2d, 0, z(i+1, j, k) - z(i-1, j, k) \rangle$$

$$\mathbf{B} = \langle 0, 2d, z(i, j+1, k) - z(i, j-1, k) \rangle$$

$$\mathbf{N} = \langle z(i-1, j, k) - z(i+1, j, k), z(i, j-1, k) - z(i, j+1, k), 2d \rangle \quad (12.38)$$

Listing 12.1 demonstrates how a fluid surface simulation might be implemented. It is important to realize that the time interval between evaluations of the fluid displacement must be constant. The frame rate for most games varies considerably, so some mechanism should be used to ensure that the position of the surface is updated only after enough time has passed in situations when the frame rate is high.

When an object interacts with the fluid surface (e.g., a rock is thrown into it), it should cause a disturbance. The surface can be displaced by explicitly modifying the current and previous positions of the vertices surrounding the point where the interaction takes place. Displacing the vertex nearest to the point of impact and, by a lesser amount, the eight nearest neighbors generally produces pleasing results.

Listing 12.1. This code implements a two-buffer surface displacement algorithm. The constructor of the `Fluid` class takes the size of the vertex array, the distance d between adjacent vertices, the time interval t, the wave velocity c, and the viscosity μ. The `renderBuffer` member variable indicates which buffer should be rendered for the current frame—it alternates between 0 and 1 during each call to the `Fluid::Evaluate` function.

```
struct Vector3D
{
    float    x, y, z;

    Vector3D& Set(float r, float s, float t)
    {
        x = r;
        y = s;
        z = t;
        return (*this);
    }
};

class Fluid
{
    private:

            long        width;
            long        height;
```

```
                Vector3D   *buffer[2];
                long       renderBuffer;

                Vector3D   *normal;
                Vector3D   *tangent;

                float      k1, k2, k3;

        public:

                Fluid(long n, long m, float d, float t, float c, float mu);
                ~Fluid();

                void Evaluate(void);
    };

    Fluid::Fluid(long n, long m, float d, float t, float c, float mu)
    {
        width = n;
        height = m;
        long count = n * m;

        buffer[0] = new Vector3D[count];
        buffer[1] = new Vector3D[count];
        renderBuffer = 0;

        normal = new Vector3D[count];
        tangent = new Vector3D[count];

        // Precompute constants for Equation (12.25)
        float f1 = c * c * t * t / (d * d);
        float f2 = 1.0F / (mu * t + 2);
        k1 = (4.0F - 8.0F * f1) * f2;
        k2 = (mu * t - 2) * f2;
        k3 = 2.0F * f1 * f2;

        // Initialize buffers
        long a = 0;
        for (long j = 0; j < m; j++)
        {
            float y = d * j;
            for (long i = 0; i < n; i++)
            {
                buffer[0][a].Set(d * i, y, 0.0F);
                buffer[1][a] = buffer[0][a];
                normal[a].Set(0.0F, 0.0F, 2.0F * d);
```

```
                        tangent[a].Set(2.0F * d, 0.0F, 0.0F);
                        a++;
                }
        }
}

Fluid::~Fluid()
{
    delete[] tangent;
    delete[] normal;
    delete[] buffer[1];
    delete[] buffer[0];
}

void Fluid::Evaluate(void)
{
    // Apply equation (12.25)
    for (long j = 1; j < height − 1; j++)
    {
        const Vector3D *crnt = buffer[renderBuffer] + j * width;
        Vector3D *prev = buffer[1 − renderBuffer] + j * width;
        for (long i = 1; i < width − 1; i++)
        {
            prev[i].z = k1 * crnt[i].z + k2 * prev[i].z +
                k3 * (crnt[i + 1].z + crnt[i − 1].z +
                crnt[i + width].z + crnt[i − width].z);
        }
    }

    // Swap buffers
    renderBuffer = 1 − renderBuffer;

    // Calculate normals and tangents
    for (long j = 1; j < height − 1; j++)
    {
        const Vector3D *next = buffer[renderBuffer] + j * width;
        Vector3D *nrml = normal + j * width;
        Vector3D *tang = tangent + j * width;
        for (long i = 1; i < width − 1; i++)
        {
            nrml[i].x = next[i − 1].z − next[i + 1].z;
            nrml[i].y = next[i − width].z − next[i + width].z;
            tang[i].z = next[i + 1].z − next[i − 1].z;
        }
    }
}
```

CHAPTER 12 SUMMARY

The Wave Equation

The two-dimensional wave equation for a surface experiencing a viscous damping force is

$$\frac{\partial^2 z}{\partial t^2} = c^2 \left(\frac{\partial^2 z}{\partial x^2} + \frac{\partial^2 z}{\partial y^2} \right) - \mu \frac{\partial z}{\partial t} .$$

The constant c is the speed at which waves propagate through the medium, and the constant μ represents the viscosity of the medium.

Approximating Derivatives

The first derivative of a function $z(x)$ can be approximated by the formula

$$\frac{d}{dx} z(x) \approx \frac{z(x + d) - z(x - d)}{2d} ,$$

where d represents some constant step size. The second derivative of $z(x)$ can be approximated by the formula

$$\frac{d^2}{dx^2} z(x) \approx \frac{z(x + d) - 2z(x) + z(x - d)}{d^2} .$$

Evaluating Surface Displacement

The future displacement $z(i, j, k + 1)$ of a point on the surface of a fluid after a time t has passed is calculated using the equation

$$z(i, j, k + 1) = \frac{4 - 8c^2 t^2 / d^2}{\mu t + 2} z(i, j, k) + \frac{\mu t - 2}{\mu t + 2} z(i, j, k - 1)$$

$$+ \frac{2c^2 t^2 / d^2}{\mu t + 2} \left[z(i + 1, j, k) + z(i - 1, j, k) + z(i, j + 1, k) + z(i, j - 1, k) \right],$$

where d is the distance between neighboring vertices in the triangle mesh.

STABILITY OF NUMERICAL METHOD

Given a constant time step t, the wave speed c must satisfy

$$0 < c < \frac{d}{2t}\sqrt{\mu t + 2}.$$

Given a constant wave speed c, the time step t must satisfy

$$0 < t < \frac{\mu + \sqrt{\mu^2 + 32c^2/d^2}}{8c^2/d^2}.$$

EXERCISES FOR CHAPTER 12

1. Suppose that the surface displacement of each vertex in a triangle mesh is evaluated 20 times per second. If the distance between neighboring vertices is 0.1 m and the viscous damping constant is $\mu = 1\ \mathrm{s}^{-1}$, what is the maximum wave speed for which Equation (12.25) is numerically stable?

2. Suppose that the distance between neighboring vertices of a surface mesh is 0.1 m and the viscous damping constant is $\mu = 1\ \mathrm{s}^{-1}$, as in the previous exercise. What is the maximum time interval between consecutive evaluations that allows a stable wave speed of 2 m/s?

APPENDIX

A

Complex Numbers

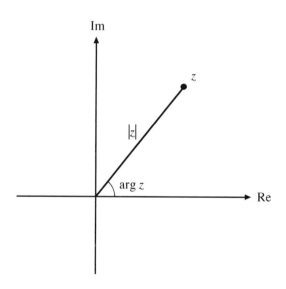

A.1 DEFINITION

The set of complex numbers $\mathbb{C}$ is a field containing the set of real numbers $\mathbb{R}$ and the "imaginary" number i. The number i is defined to be the square root of -1:

$$i = \sqrt{-1}. \tag{A.1}$$

Thus, the square root of any negative number $-n$ can be written as

$$\sqrt{-n} = i\sqrt{n}. \tag{A.2}$$

A *complex number* z is one of the form

$$z = a + bi, \tag{A.3}$$

where a and b are real numbers. The number a is called the *real part* of z, denoted by $\text{Re}(z)$, and the number b is called the *imaginary part* of z, denoted by $\text{Im}(z)$. If $b = 0$, then the number z is purely real. If $a = 0$, then the number z is purely imaginary.

A.2 ADDITION AND MULTIPLICATION

The sum of two complex numbers $a + bi$ and $c + di$ is given by

$$(a + bi) + (c + di) = (a + c) + (b + d)i. \tag{A.4}$$

The product of two complex numbers can be calculated by using the distributive property and the fact that $i^2 = -1$. The product of $a + bi$ and $c + di$ is given by

$$(a + bi)(c + di) = (ac - bd) + (ad + bc)i. \tag{A.5}$$

Addition and multiplication of complex numbers are both commutative and associative. This means that for any three complex numbers z_1, z_2, and z_3, the following properties hold.

(a) $z_1 + z_2 = z_2 + z_1$
(b) $(z_1 + z_2) + z_3 = z_1 + (z_2 + z_3)$
(c) $z_1 z_2 = z_2 z_1$
(d) $(z_1 z_2)z_3 = z_1(z_2 z_3)$

A.3 CONJUGATES AND INVERSES

The *conjugate* of a complex number $z = a + bi$ is denoted by $\bar{z}$ and is defined as

$$\bar{z} = a - bi. \tag{A.6}$$

The conjugate of z has the same components as the number z itself except that the imaginary part is negated. Taking the product of z and its conjugate $\bar{z}$ yields

$$z\bar{z} = (a + bi)(a - bi) = a^2 + b^2. \tag{A.7}$$

Thus, the product $z\bar{z}$ is a real number that reflects the magnitude of the number z. We use this to define the absolute value of a complex number, which is sometimes called the *modulus*. The modulus of a complex number $z = a + bi$ is denoted by $|z|$ and is defined as

$$|z| = \sqrt{z\bar{z}} = \sqrt{a^2 + b^2}. \tag{A.8}$$

If z is purely real, then this definition reduces to that of the ordinary absolute value for a real number.

Let $z_1 = a + bi$ and $z_2 = c + di$ be complex numbers such that $z_2 \neq 0$. We can determine the value of the quotient z_1/z_2 by multiplying the numerator and denominator by the conjugate of z_2. This gives us

$$\frac{z_1}{z_2} = \frac{a + bi}{c + di} = \frac{a + bi}{c + di} \cdot \frac{c - di}{c - di} = \frac{(a + bi)(c - di)}{c^2 + d^2} = z_1 \frac{\bar{z}_2}{|z_2|^2}. \tag{A.9}$$

We now have a way to define the inverse of a nonzero complex number z, which we denote by z^{-1}, as follows.

$$z^{-1} = \frac{\bar{z}}{|z|^2} \tag{A.10}$$

As shown below, the product of a complex number z and its inverse is one.

$$zz^{-1} = \frac{z\bar{z}}{|z|^2} = \frac{z\bar{z}}{z\bar{z}} = 1 \tag{A.11}$$

A.4 THE DEMOIVRE FORMULA

A fascinating property of complex numbers ties exponential and trigonometric functions together. For any real number x representing a radian angle of measure, we have the following identity.

$$e^{ix} = \cos x + i \sin x \tag{A.12}$$

This equation is known as the *DeMoivre formula* and can be used to derive a multitude of trigonometric identities (see Appendix B, Section B.4). The formula can be verified by expanding the function e^{ix} into its power series and collecting real and imaginary terms, as shown in Appendix D, Section D.3.

The *complex plane* is a 2D coordinate system having a real axis and an imaginary axis that are perpendicular to each other. As shown in Figure A.1, a complex number z can be uniquely identified by its absolute value and the angle that it forms with the real axis in the complex plane. This angle is called the *argument* of a complex number and is denoted by arg z. One possible value of the argument of $z = a + bi$ is given by

$$\arg z = \begin{cases} \tan^{-1} \dfrac{b}{a}, & \text{if } a \geq 0; \\ \tan^{-1} \dfrac{b}{a} + \pi \, \text{sgn}(b), & \text{if } a < 0, \end{cases} \tag{A.13}$$

where the function sgn(b) returns the sign of b:

$$\text{sgn}(b) = \begin{cases} 1, & \text{if } b \geq 0; \\ -1, & \text{if } b < 0. \end{cases} \tag{A.14}$$

Any angle differing from the value given by Equation (A.13) by a multiple of 2π is also correct.

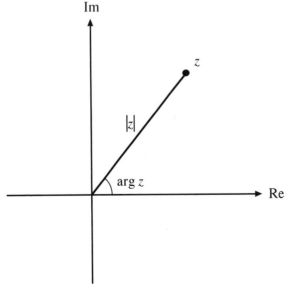

FIGURE **A.1** *A complex number can be expressed in terms of its distance from the origin and the angle that it forms with the real axis in the complex plane.*

We can now express any complex number z as

$$z = re^{i\theta},$$ (A.15)

where $r = |z|$ and $\theta = \arg z$. Since the sine and cosine functions have a period of 2π, we know that

$$e^{i\theta} = e^{i(\theta + 2\pi k)}$$ (A.16)

for any integer k.

The DeMoivre formula is useful for raising a complex number to a power. The quantity z^n can be written as

$$z^n = r^n e^{in\theta} = r^n(\cos n\theta + i \sin n\theta).$$ (A.17)

In particular, we can calculate the n-th roots of a complex number z by writing

$$z^{1/n} = \left(re^{i(\theta + 2\pi k)}\right)^{1/n} = \sqrt[n]{r}\left(\cos \frac{\theta + 2\pi k}{n} + i \sin \frac{\theta + 2\pi k}{n}\right),$$ (A.18)

where k is an integer. Choosing $k = 0, 1,..., n - 1$ produces all n roots of the number z. A root ρ is called *primitive* if the smallest positive power m yielding $\rho^m = z$ is $m = n$.

The n-th roots of unity can be calculated using the formula

$$e^{2\pi k i/n} = \cos \frac{2\pi k}{n} + i \sin \frac{2\pi k}{n}$$ (A.19)

since $r = 1$ and $\theta = 0$ in this case. For example, the three cube roots of unity ρ_0, ρ_1, and ρ_2 are given by

$$\rho_0 = 1$$

$$\rho_1 = \cos \frac{2\pi}{3} + i \sin \frac{2\pi}{3} = -\frac{1}{2} + i \frac{\sqrt{3}}{2}$$

$$\rho_2 = \cos \frac{4\pi}{3} + i \sin \frac{4\pi}{3} = -\frac{1}{2} - i \frac{\sqrt{3}}{2}.$$ (A.20)

Note that ρ_1 and ρ_2 are both primitive roots of unity and that $\rho_1^2 = \rho_2$ and $\rho_2^2 = \rho_1$. In general, a primitive n-th root of unity generates all the n-th roots of unity when raised to the powers $1, 2,..., n$.

B Trigonometry Reference

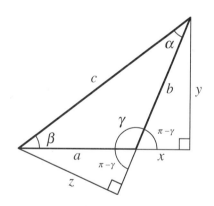

B.1 FUNCTION DEFINITIONS

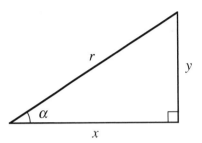

FIGURE *Equation (B.1) defines the trigonometric functions in terms of the angle α shown in*
B.1 *this triangle.*

For the angle α shown in Figure B.1, the trigonometric functions are defined as follows.

$$\sin \alpha = \frac{y}{r} \quad \cos \alpha = \frac{x}{r}$$

$$\tan \alpha = \frac{y}{x} \quad \cot \alpha = \frac{x}{y}$$

$$\sec \alpha = \frac{r}{x} \quad \csc \alpha = \frac{r}{y} \tag{B.1}$$

The relationships among the trigonometric functions listed below follow immediately from the definitions.

$$\tan \alpha = \frac{\sin \alpha}{\cos \alpha} \quad \cot \alpha = \frac{1}{\tan \alpha}$$

$$\sec \alpha = \frac{1}{\cos \alpha} \quad \csc \alpha = \frac{1}{\sin \alpha} \tag{B.2}$$

B.2 SYMMETRY AND PHASE SHIFTS

The cosine function is an *even* function, meaning that it is symmetric about the y-axis. The sine and tangent functions are *odd* functions, meaning that they are symmetric about the origin. We thus have the following identities.

$$\sin(-\alpha) = -\sin \alpha$$

$$\cos(-\alpha) = \cos \alpha$$

$$\tan(-\alpha) = -\tan \alpha \tag{B.3}$$

The cosine function produces the same value at an angle α that the sine function does at the angle $\alpha + \pi/2$. That is, the graph of the cosine function is identical to the graph of the sine function shifted to the left by $\pi/2$ radians. We can thus formulate the following phase shift identities.

$$\sin(\alpha + \pi/2) = \cos \alpha$$

$$\cos(\alpha + \pi/2) = -\sin \alpha$$

$$\tan(\alpha + \pi/2) = -\cot \alpha \tag{B.4}$$

Using the symmetry properties given by Equation (B.3), we can also state

$$\sin(\pi/2 - \alpha) = \cos \alpha$$

$$\cos(\pi/2 - \alpha) = \sin \alpha$$

$$\tan(\pi/2 - \alpha) = \cot \alpha. \tag{B.5}$$

Shifting the sine or cosine function by a value of π simply negates the values of the function. This gives us

$$\sin(\alpha + \pi) = -\sin \alpha$$

$$\cos(\alpha + \pi) = -\cos \alpha$$

$$\tan(\alpha + \pi) = \tan \alpha. \tag{B.6}$$

Again using the symmetry properties of the functions, we can also state

$$\sin(\pi - \alpha) = \sin \alpha$$

$$\cos(\pi - \alpha) = -\cos \alpha$$

$$\tan(\pi - \alpha) = -\tan \alpha. \tag{B.7}$$

B.3 PYTHAGOREAN IDENTITIES

The following identities arise directly from the definitions given in Equation (B.1) and the fact that $x^2 + y^2 = r^2$.

$$\sin^2 \alpha + \cos^2 \alpha = 1$$

$$\tan^2 \alpha + 1 = \sec^2 \alpha$$

$$\cot^2 \alpha + 1 = \csc^2 \alpha \tag{B.8}$$

If the angle α satisfies $0 \le \alpha \le \pi/2$, then we can write

$$\sin \alpha = \sqrt{1 - \cos^2 \alpha}$$

$$\cos \alpha = \sqrt{1 - \sin^2 \alpha}$$

$$\tan \alpha = \sqrt{\sec^2 \alpha - 1}. \tag{B.9}$$

B.4 EXPONENTIAL IDENTITIES

The DeMoivre formula states

$$e^{\alpha i} = \cos \alpha + i \sin \alpha. \tag{B.10}$$

This relationship can be used to derive several trigonometric identities simply by applying the laws of exponents. The angle sum and difference identities are given by the equation

$$e^{(\alpha + \beta)i} = e^{\alpha i}e^{\beta i}. \tag{B.11}$$

Expanding this using Equation (B.10) yields

$$\cos(\alpha + \beta) + i \sin(\alpha + \beta) = (\cos \alpha + i \sin \alpha)(\cos \beta + i \sin \beta). \tag{B.12}$$

By equating the real and imaginary components of one side to those of the other, we can infer the following.

$$\sin(\alpha + \beta) = \sin \alpha \cos \beta + \cos \alpha \sin \beta$$

$$\cos(\alpha + \beta) = \cos \alpha \cos \beta - \sin \alpha \sin \beta \tag{B.13}$$

The angle difference identities are derived by negating β as follows.

$$\sin(\alpha - \beta) = \sin \alpha \cos \beta - \cos \alpha \sin \beta$$

$$\cos(\alpha - \beta) = \cos \alpha \cos \beta + \sin \alpha \sin \beta \tag{B.14}$$

When the angles α and β are the same, the angle sum identities become

$$\sin 2\alpha = 2 \sin \alpha \cos \alpha$$

$$\cos 2\alpha = \cos^2 \alpha - \sin^2 \alpha. \tag{B.15}$$

Using the fact that $\sin^2 \alpha + \cos^2 \alpha = 1$, we can rewrite $\cos 2\alpha$ in the following ways.

$$\cos 2\alpha = 1 - 2 \sin^2 \alpha$$

$$\cos 2\alpha = 2 \cos^2 \alpha - 1 \tag{B.16}$$

Solving these for $\sin^2 \alpha$ and $\cos^2 \alpha$ gives us

$$\sin^2 \alpha = \frac{1 - \cos 2\alpha}{2}$$

$$\cos^2 \alpha = \frac{1 + \cos 2\alpha}{2}. \tag{B.17}$$

B.5 INVERSE FUNCTIONS

The inverse $f^{-1}(x)$ of a trigonometric function $f(\alpha)$ returns the angle α for which $f(\alpha) = x$. The domains and ranges of the inverse trigonometric functions are listed in the following table.

Function	Domain	Range
$\sin^{-1} x$	$[-1,1]$	$[-\pi/2, \pi/2]$
$\cos^{-1} x$	$[-1,1]$	$[0, \pi]$
$\tan^{-1} x$	$\mathbb{R}$	$[-\pi/2, \pi/2]$

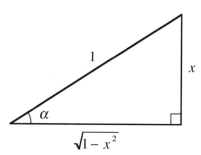

FIGURE *A triangle representing the inverse sine function.*
B.2

As shown in Figure B.2, the inverse sine of x is equal to the acute angle α in a triangle having an opposite side of length x and a hypotenuse of length 1. Since we know that the third side of the triangle has length $\sqrt{1 - x^2}$, we can derive the values of the other trigonometric functions at the angle $\sin^{-1} x$, as follows.

$$\cos\left(\sin^{-1} x\right) = \sqrt{1 - x^2}$$

$$\tan\left(\sin^{-1} x\right) = \frac{x}{\sqrt{1 - x^2}} \tag{B.18}$$

Applying the same technique for the inverse cosine and inverse tangent functions, we have the following.

$$\sin\left(\cos^{-1} x\right) = \sqrt{1 - x^2}$$

$$\tan\left(\cos^{-1} x\right) = \frac{\sqrt{1 - x^2}}{x}$$

$$\sin\left(\tan^{-1} x\right) = \frac{x}{\sqrt{x^2 + 1}}$$

$$\cos\left(\tan^{-1} x\right) = \frac{1}{\sqrt{x^2 + 1}} \tag{B.19}$$

B.6 LAWS OF SINES AND COSINES

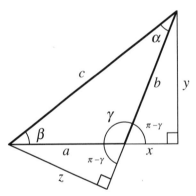

FIGURE A *triangle illustrating the laws of sines and cosines.*
B.3

Consider the triangle shown in Figure B.3 and observe the following.

$$\sin \alpha = \frac{z}{c}$$

$$\sin \beta = \frac{y}{c} \tag{B.20}$$

Solving these for c allows us to form the equality

$$\frac{z}{\sin \alpha} = \frac{y}{\sin \beta}. \tag{B.21}$$

The following observations may also be made.

$$\sin(\pi - \gamma) = \frac{z}{a}$$

$$\sin(\pi - \gamma) = \frac{y}{b} \tag{B.22}$$

Thus, $z/a = y/b$. Multiplying the left side of Equation (B.21) by a/z and the right side of Equation (B.21) by b/y yields the *law of sines*:

$$\frac{a}{\sin \alpha} = \frac{b}{\sin \beta}. \tag{B.23}$$

The same relationship can be derived for the pair of angles α and γ or the pair of angles β and γ, so we can write

$$\frac{a}{\sin \alpha} = \frac{b}{\sin \beta} = \frac{c}{\sin \gamma}. \tag{B.24}$$

Now observe the following Pythagorean relationships in the triangle shown in Figure B.3.

$$x^2 + y^2 = b^2$$

$$(a + x)^2 + y^2 = c^2 \tag{B.25}$$

Solving the first Equation for y^2 and substituting into the second equation gives us

$$c^2 = (a + x)^2 + b^2 - x^2$$

$$= a^2 + b^2 + 2ax. \tag{B.26}$$

The value of x can be replaced by observing

$$\cos(\pi - \gamma) = \frac{x}{b}. \tag{B.27}$$

Since $\cos(\pi - \gamma) = -\cos \gamma$, we have

$$x = -b \cos \gamma. \tag{B.28}$$

Plugging this into Equation (B.26) produces the *law of cosines*:

$$c^2 = a^2 + b^2 - 2ab \cos \gamma. \tag{B.29}$$

Of course, this reduces to the Pythagorean theorem when γ is a right angle since $\cos \pi/2 = 0$.

APPENDIX

C

Coordinate Systems

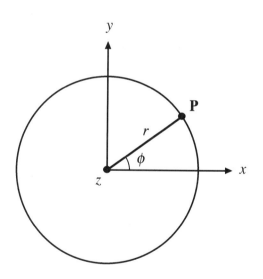

C.1 Cylindrical Coordinates

A point **P** in cylindrical coordinates is represented by the quantities r, ϕ, and z. As shown in Figure C.1, r is equal to the radial distance between **P** and the z-axis, and ϕ is equal to the counterclockwise-oriented angle formed between the x-axis and the line connecting the projection of **P** onto the x-y plane to the origin.

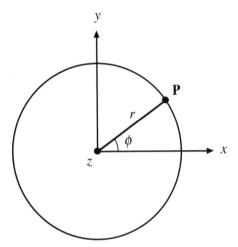

FIGURE *Cylindrical coordinates. The z-axis points out of the page.*
C.1

The z-coordinate in both Cartesian and cylindrical coordinates has the same meaning. The x and y Cartesian coordinates corresponding to a point having cylindrical coordinates $\langle r, \phi, z \rangle$ are given by

$$x = r \cos \phi$$
$$y = r \sin \phi. \tag{C.1}$$

If Cartesian coordinates x and y are known, then the corresponding cylindrical coordinates r and ϕ are given by

$$r = \sqrt{x^2 + y^2}$$

$$\phi = \operatorname{sgn}(y) \cos^{-1} \frac{x}{r}, \tag{C.2}$$

where the function $\operatorname{sgn}(y)$ returns the sign of y:

$$\operatorname{sgn}(y) = \begin{cases} 1, & \text{if } y \geq 0; \\ -1, & \text{if } y < 0. \end{cases} \tag{C.3}$$

The angle ϕ can also be expressed as

$$\phi = \begin{cases} \tan^{-1}\dfrac{y}{x}, & \text{if } x \geq 0; \\[2mm] \tan^{-1}\dfrac{y}{x} + \pi\,\text{sgn}(y), & \text{if } x < 0. \end{cases} \tag{C.4}$$

In both Equations (C.2) and (C.4), the calculated value of ϕ satisfies $-\pi \leq \phi \leq \pi$.

C.2 SPHERICAL COORDINATES

A point **P** in spherical coordinates is represented by the quantities r, θ, and ϕ. As shown in Figure C.2, r is equal to the distance from the origin to the point **P**. The angle θ is called the *polar angle* and represents the angle formed between the z-axis and the line connecting **P** to the origin. The polar angle θ always satisfies $0 \leq \theta \leq \pi$. The angle ϕ is called the *azimuthal angle*, or simply the *azimuth*, and represents the angle formed between the x-axis and the line connecting the projection of **P** onto the x-y plane to the origin (just as in cylindrical coordinates).

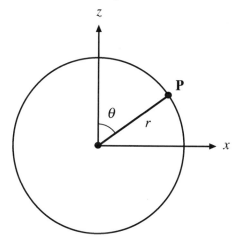

FIGURE *Spherical coordinates.*
C.2

The Cartesian coordinates $\langle x, y, z \rangle$ corresponding to a point having spherical coordinates $\langle r, \theta, \phi \rangle$ are given by

$$x = r \sin\theta \cos\phi$$

$$y = r \sin\theta \sin\phi$$

$$z = r \cos\theta. \tag{C.5}$$

Conversion from Cartesian coordinates to spherical coordinates can be accomplished by using the following relations.

$$r = \sqrt{x^2 + y^2 + z^2}$$

$$\theta = \cos^{-1}\frac{z}{r}$$

$$\phi = \text{sgn}(y)\cos^{-1}\frac{x}{\sqrt{x^2 + y^2}} \tag{C.6}$$

The azimuthal angle ϕ can also be calculated using Equation (C.4).

APPENDIX

D

Taylor Series

$$f(x) = f(c) + f'(c)(x - c) + \frac{f''(c)}{2!}(x - c)^2 + \frac{f'''(c)}{3!}(x - c)^3 + \cdots$$

$$= \sum_{k=0}^{\infty} \frac{f^{(k)}(c)}{k!}(x - c)^k.$$

D.1 DERIVATION

Let $f(x)$ be a function whose first n derivatives exist on some interval I. Suppose that we wish to approximate $f(x)$ near the value $x = c$ in I using a degree n polynomial $p_n(x)$ so that

$$p_n(x) = a_0 + a_1(x - c) + a_2(x - c)^2 + \cdots + a_n(x - c)^n \approx f(x) \qquad \text{(D.1)}$$

whenever x is small. The derivatives of $p_n(x)$ evaluated at $x = c$ are the following.

$$p_n'(c) = a_1$$
$$p_n''(c) = 2a_2$$
$$\vdots$$
$$p_n^{(n)}(c) = n!\, a_n \qquad \text{(D.2)}$$

We can determine the coefficients a_i by requiring that

$$p_n(c) = f(c)$$
$$p_n'(c) = f'(c)$$
$$p_n''(c) = f''(c)$$
$$\vdots$$
$$p_n^{(n)}(c) = f^{(n)}(c). \qquad \text{(D.3)}$$

The polynomial $p_n(x)$ is thus given by

$$p_n(x) = f(c) + f'(c)(x - c) + \frac{f''(c)}{2!}(x - c)^2 + \cdots + \frac{f^{(n)}(c)}{n!}(x - c)^n. \qquad \text{(D.4)}$$

We define the error term $r_n(x)$ to be the difference between the approximation $p_n(x)$ and the actual function value $f(x)$ so that

$$f(x) = f(c) + f'(c)(x - c) + \frac{f''(c)}{2!}(x - c)^2 + \cdots$$
$$+ \frac{f^{(n)}(c)}{n!}(x - c)^n + r_n(x). \qquad \text{(D.5)}$$

Let $g(z)$ be the function defined by

$$g(z) = f(x) - f(z) - f'(z)(x - z) - \frac{f''(z)}{2!}(x - z)^2 - \cdots$$

$$- \frac{f^{(n)}(z)}{n!}(x - z)^n - \frac{(x - z)^{n+1}}{(x - c)^{n+1}} r_n(x). \tag{D.6}$$

It is easily verified that $g(x) = 0$ and, using Equation (D.5), that $g(c) = 0$. The derivative of $g(z)$ simplifies significantly to the following.

$$g'(z) = -\frac{f^{(n+1)}(z)}{n!}(x - z)^n + (n + 1)\frac{(x - z)^n}{(x - c)^{n+1}} r_n(x) \tag{D.7}$$

By Rolle's theorem, there exists a z_0 between x and c such that $g'(z_0) = 0$. Evaluating $g'(z_0)$ and solving for $r_n(x)$ yields

$$r_n(x) = \frac{f^{(n+1)}(z_0)}{(n + 1)!}(x - c)^{n+1}. \tag{D.8}$$

If a function $f(x)$ is infinitely differentiable, then we may state

$$\lim_{n \to \infty} r_n(x) = 0. \tag{D.9}$$

We can therefore express any such function $f(x)$ as the infinite series

$$f(x) = f(c) + f'(c)(x - c) + \frac{f''(c)}{2!}(x - c)^2 + \frac{f'''(c)}{3!}(x - c)^3 + \cdots$$

$$= \sum_{k=0}^{\infty} \frac{f^{(k)}(c)}{k!}(x - c)^k. \tag{D.10}$$

D.2 POWER SERIES

Equation (D.10) can be used to derive power series expansions for common functions by using $c = 0$. Because the exponential function e^x is equal to its own derivative and $e^0 = 1$, its power series is given by

$$e^x = 1 + x + \frac{x^2}{2!} + \frac{x^3}{3!} + \frac{x^4}{4!} + \cdots$$

$$= \sum_{k=0}^{\infty} \frac{x^k}{k!}. \tag{D.11}$$

For the sine function, we first observe the following.

$$f(x) = \sin x \qquad f(0) = 0$$
$$f'(x) = \cos x \qquad f'(0) = 1$$
$$f''(x) = -\sin x \qquad f''(0) = 0$$
$$f'''(x) = -\cos x \qquad f'''(0) = -1 \tag{D.12}$$

The power series for the sine function is thus given by

$$\sin x = x - \frac{x^3}{3!} + \frac{x^5}{5!} - \frac{x^7}{7!} + - \cdots$$

$$= \sum_{k=0}^{\infty} \frac{(-1)^k x^{2k+1}}{(2k+1)!}. \tag{D.13}$$

Similarly, the power series for the cosine function is given by

$$\cos x = 1 - \frac{x^2}{2!} + \frac{x^4}{4!} - \frac{x^6}{6!} + - \cdots$$

$$= \sum_{k=0}^{\infty} \frac{(-1)^k x^{2k}}{(2k)!}. \tag{D.14}$$

Another interesting function is

$$f(x) = \frac{1}{1+x} \tag{D.15}$$

because it is the derivative of $\ln(1 + x)$ on the interval $(0, \infty)$. The first few derivatives of $f(x)$ are the following.

$$f'(x) = \frac{-1}{(1+x)^2}$$

$$f''(x) = \frac{2}{(1+x)^3}$$

$$f'''(x) = \frac{-6}{(1+x)^4} \tag{D.16}$$

In general, the k-th derivative of $f(x)$ is given by

$$f^{(k)}(x) = \frac{(-1)^k k!}{(1 + x)^{k+1}}, \tag{D.17}$$

which when evaluated at $x = 0$ produces $f^{(k)}(0) = (-1)^k k!$. Thus, the power series for the function $f(x)$ is given by

$$\frac{1}{1 + x} = 1 - x + x^2 - x^3 + - \cdots$$

$$= \sum_{k=0}^{\infty} (-1)^k x^k. \tag{D.18}$$

This series converges on the interval $(-1, 1)$. Integrating both sides, we arrive at the following power series for the natural logarithm of $1 + x$ on the same interval.

$$\ln(1 + x) = x - \frac{x^2}{2} + \frac{x^3}{3} - \frac{x^4}{4} + - \cdots$$

$$= \sum_{k=0}^{\infty} \frac{(-1)^k x^{k+1}}{k + 1} \tag{D.19}$$

D.3 THE DEMOIVRE FORMULA

The DeMoivre formula expresses the following relationship between the exponential function and the sine and cosine functions.

$$e^{ix} = \cos x = i \sin x \tag{D.20}$$

This can be verified by examining the power series of the function e^{ix}:

$$e^{ix} = \sum_{k=0}^{\infty} \frac{i^k x^k}{k!}. \tag{D.21}$$

Using the fact that $i^2 = -1$, $i^3 = -i$, and $i^4 = 1$, we can collect the real and imaginary terms of this series as follows.

$$e^{ix} = \sum_{k=0}^{\infty} \frac{(-1)^k x^{2k}}{(2k)!} + i \sum_{k=0}^{\infty} \frac{(-1)^k x^{2k+1}}{(2k + 1)!} \tag{D.22}$$

Comparing this to Equations (D.13) and (D.14) confirms the result.

APPENDIX

Answers to Exercises

$$
\begin{bmatrix}
\dfrac{2n}{r-l} & 0 & \dfrac{r+l}{r-l} & 0 \\[2.5ex]
0 & \dfrac{2n}{t-b} & \dfrac{t+b}{t-b} & 0 \\[2.5ex]
0 & 0 & -\dfrac{f}{f-n} & -\dfrac{nf}{f-n} \\[2.5ex]
0 & 0 & -1 & 0
\end{bmatrix}
$$

CHAPTER 1

1. (a) -2 (b) $\langle 2, 1, -6 \rangle$ (c) $\left\langle -\frac{4}{9}, -\frac{4}{9}, -\frac{2}{9} \right\rangle$
2. $\mathbf{e}'_1 = \mathbf{e}_1, \mathbf{e}'_2 = \mathbf{e}_2, \mathbf{e}'_3 = \langle 1, -1, -2 \rangle$

CHAPTER 2

1. (a) 22 (b) -1 (c) 1 (d) 0

2. (a) $\begin{bmatrix} \frac{1}{2} & 0 & 0 \\ 0 & \frac{1}{3} & 0 \\ 0 & 0 & \frac{1}{4} \end{bmatrix}$
(b) $\begin{bmatrix} 1 & 0 & 0 \\ \frac{3}{8} & \frac{1}{2} & -\frac{1}{8} \\ -\frac{3}{8} & 0 & \frac{1}{8} \end{bmatrix}$

(c) $\begin{bmatrix} \cos\theta & 0 & \sin\theta \\ 0 & 1 & 0 \\ -\sin\theta & 0 & \cos\theta \end{bmatrix}$
(d) $\begin{bmatrix} 1 & 0 & 0 & -4 \\ 0 & 1 & 0 & -3 \\ 0 & 0 & 1 & -7 \\ 0 & 0 & 0 & 1 \end{bmatrix}$

3. $\begin{bmatrix} x \\ y \\ z \end{bmatrix} = a \begin{bmatrix} 1 \\ -2 \\ 1 \end{bmatrix}$

4. $\lambda_1 = -1, \lambda_2 = 2, \lambda_3 = 5$

CHAPTER 3

1. $\mathbf{R}_x = \begin{bmatrix} 1 & 0 & 0 \\ 0 & \frac{\sqrt{3}}{2} & -\frac{1}{2} \\ 0 & \frac{1}{2} & \frac{\sqrt{3}}{2} \end{bmatrix}, \mathbf{R}_y = \begin{bmatrix} \frac{\sqrt{3}}{2} & 0 & \frac{1}{2} \\ 0 & 1 & 0 \\ -\frac{1}{2} & 0 & \frac{\sqrt{3}}{2} \end{bmatrix}, \mathbf{R}_z = \begin{bmatrix} \frac{\sqrt{3}}{2} & -\frac{1}{2} & 0 \\ \frac{1}{2} & \frac{\sqrt{3}}{2} & 0 \\ 0 & 0 & 1 \end{bmatrix}$

2. $\mathbf{q} = \pm\left(\frac{\sqrt{3}}{2} + \left\langle 0, \frac{3}{10}, \frac{2}{5} \right\rangle \right)$

CHAPTER 4

1. Any scalar multiple of $\langle 2, 1, 0, -4 \rangle$

2. 63.1 degrees

3. Left: $\left\langle \frac{\sqrt{2}}{2}, 0, -\frac{\sqrt{2}}{2}, 0 \right\rangle$; Right: $\left\langle -\frac{\sqrt{2}}{2}, 0, -\frac{\sqrt{2}}{2}, 0 \right\rangle$;

   Bottom: $\left\langle 0, \frac{4}{5}, -\frac{3}{5}, 0 \right\rangle$; Top: $\left\langle 0, -\frac{4}{5}, -\frac{3}{5}, 0 \right\rangle$

4.
$$\begin{bmatrix} \frac{2n}{r-l} & 0 & \frac{r+l}{r-l} & 0 \\ 0 & \frac{2n}{t-b} & \frac{t+b}{t-b} & 0 \\ 0 & 0 & -\frac{f}{f-n} & -\frac{nf}{f-n} \\ 0 & 0 & -1 & 0 \end{bmatrix}$$

CHAPTER 5

2. 5.3271783

3. $x_{n+1} = \frac{1}{p} x_n \left(p + 1 - r x^p \right)$

4. $\left(V_x^2 + V_y^2 - \frac{r^2}{b^2} V_z^2 \right) t^2 + 2\left[Q_x V_x + Q_y V_y + \frac{r}{b} V_z \left(r - \frac{r}{b} Q_z \right) \right] t$

$\quad + Q_x^2 + Q_y^2 + \frac{r}{b} Q_z \left(2r - \frac{r}{b} Q_z \right) - r^2 = 0$

5. $\langle -0.212, 0.636, -0.742 \rangle$
7. 49 degrees

CHAPTER 6

1. 3.16 meters
2. 4.35 meters

CHAPTER 7

1. If neither sphere encloses the other, $r = \frac{1}{2}\left(d + r_1 + r_2 \right)$ and

   $\mathbf{Q} = \mathbf{Q}_1 + \frac{r - r_1}{d} \left(\mathbf{Q}_2 - \mathbf{Q}_1 \right)$, where $d = \|\mathbf{Q}_2 - \mathbf{Q}_1\|$.

2. If $s < b$, $r = \dfrac{s^2 + b^2}{2b}$ and $\mathbf{Q} = \langle 0, 0, b - r \rangle$.

    If $s \geq b$, $r = s$ and $\mathbf{Q} = \langle 0, 0, 0 \rangle$.

3. $r_{\text{eff}} = \dfrac{5\sqrt{3}}{6} \approx 1.443$

CHAPTER 8

1. $t = 4$ s

CHAPTER 9

1. 1.001
2. 0.003

CHAPTER 10

1. $x(t) = Ae^{3t} + Bte^{3t} + t + 1$
2. $x(t) = 3 \cos 4t + \sin 4t$
3. 30.2 m
4. 3.93 s
5. $t \approx 6.1$ s
6. $a = \dfrac{g}{M + m} \left[M - m(\sin \theta + \mu_K \cos \theta) \right]$

CHAPTER 11

1. $F = m\omega \sqrt{\omega^2 r^2 + 4v^2}$

2. $\omega = \sqrt{\dfrac{\mu_S g}{r}}$

3. $\mathbf{C} = \left\langle 0, 0, \frac{5}{9} l \right\rangle$

4. $I = \frac{1}{2} m \left(R_1^2 + R_2^2 \right)$

5. $\mathcal{I} = \begin{bmatrix} \frac{1}{12} m(b^2 + c^2) & 0 & 0 \\ 0 & \frac{1}{12} m(a^2 + c^2) & 0 \\ 0 & 0 & \frac{1}{12} m(a^2 + b^2) \end{bmatrix}$

6. $a = \dfrac{g}{1 + I/mR^2} = \dfrac{g}{1 + M/2m}$

7. $a = \dfrac{g \sin \theta}{1 + I/mR^2} = \dfrac{5}{7} g \sin \theta$

8. $z = \dfrac{d}{2\mu_s}$

CHAPTER 12

1. 1.43 m/s
2. 0.0357 s

Bibliography

Beckmann, Petr, and Spizzichino, André, *The Scattering of Electromagnetic Waves from Rough Surfaces*, Macmillan, 1963.

Blinn, Jim, *Jim Blinn's Corner: A Trip Down the Graphics Pipeline*, Morgan-Kaufmann, 1996.

Blinn, Jim, *Jim Blinn's Corner: Dirty Pixels*, Morgan-Kaufmann, 1998.

Boyce, William E., and DiPrima, Richard C., *Elementary Differential Equations and Boundary Value Problems*, 4th edition, Wiley, 1986.

Cook, Robert L., and Torrance, Kenneth E., "A Reflectance Model for Computer Graphics," *ACM Transactions on Graphics*, Vol. 1, No. 1 (January 1982), pp. 7–24.

Dummit, David S., and Foote, Richard M., *Abstract Algebra*, Prentice-Hall, 1991.

Foley, James D., et al., *Computer Graphics: Principles and Practice*, 2nd edition, Addison-Wesley, 1990.

Gomez, Miguel, "Interactive Simulation of Water Surfaces," *Game Programming Gems*, Charles River Media, 2000.

Gonzalez, Rafael C., and Woods, Richard E., *Digital Image Processing*, Addison-Wesley, 1992.

Möller, Tomas, and Haines, Eric, *Real-Time Rendering*, AK Peters, 1999.

He, Xiao D., et al., "A Comprehensive Physical Model for Light Reflection," *SIGGRAPH '91, Computer Graphics*, Vol. 25, No. 4 (July 1991), pp. 175–186.

Johnson, Richard A., and Wichern, Dean W., *Applied Multivariate Statistical Analysis*, 4th edition, Prentice-Hall, 1998.

Kautz, Jan, et al., "Achieving Real-Time Realistic Reflections, Part 1," *Game Developer*, Vol. 8, No. 1 (January 2001), pp. 32–37.

Kautz, Jan, et al., "Achieving Real-Time Realistic Reflections, Part 2," *Game Developer*, Vol. 8, No. 2 (February 2001), pp. 38–44.

Lander, Jeff, "The Trials and Tribulations of Tribology," *Game Developer*, Vol. 6, No 8 (August 1999), pp. 19–24.

Lengyel, Eric, "Tweaking a Vertex's Projected Depth Value," *Game Programming Gems*, Charles River Media, 2000.

Lengyel, Eric, "A Fast Cylinder-Frustum Intersection Test," *Game Programming Gems*, Charles River Media, 2000.

Lengyel, Eric, "Applying Decals to Arbitrary Surfaces," *Game Programming Gems II*, Charles River Media, 2001.

Marion, Jerry B., and Thornton, Stephen T., *Classical Dynamics of Particles and Systems*, 3rd edition, Harcourt Brace Jovanovich, 1988.

O'Neil, Peter V., *Advanced Engineering Mathematics*, 3rd edition, PWS, 1991.

OpenGL Architecture Review Board, *OpenGL Programming Guide*, 3rd edition, Addison-Wesley, 1999.

OpenGL Architecture Review Board, *OpenGL Reference Manual*, 3rd edition, Addison-Wesley, 1999.

Press, William H., et al., *Numerical Recipes in C*, Cambridge, 1988.

Reitz, John R., Milford, Frederick J., and Christy, Robert W., *Foundations of Electromagnetic Theory*, 4th edition, Addison-Wesley, 1993.

Sears, Francis W., Zemansky, Mark W., and Young, Hugh D., *University Physics*, 7th edition, Addison-Wesley, 1987.

Sillion, François X., and Puech, Claude, *Radiosity and Global Illumination*, Morgan Kaufmann, 1994.

Schlick, Christophe, "An Inexpensive BRDF Model for Physically-based Rendering," *Proc. Eurographics '94, Computer Graphics Forum*, Vol. 13, No. 3, pp. 233–246.

Schwarze, Jochen, "Cubic and Quartic Roots," *Graphics Gems*, Academic Press, 1990.

Ward, Gregory J., "Measuring and Modeling Anisotropic Reflection," *SIGGRAPH '92, Computer Graphics*, Vol. 26, No. 2 (July 1992), pp. 265–272.

Wu, Xiaolin, "A Linear-Time Simple Bounding Volume Algorithm," *Graphics Gems III*, Academic Press, 1992.

Index